Inquiries in the Economics of Aging

A National Bureau
of Economic Research
Project Report

Inquiries in the Economics of Aging

Edited by David A. Wise

 The University of Chicago Press

Chicago and London

DAVID A. WISE is the John F. Stambaugh Professor of Political Economy at the John F. Kennedy School of Government, Harvard University, and director of the Health and Retirement Research Programs at the National Bureau of Economic Research.

The University of Chicago Press, Chicago 60637
The University of Chicago Press, Ltd., London
© 1998 by the National Bureau of Economic Research
All rights reserved. Published 1998
Printed in the United States of America
07 06 05 04 03 02 01 00 99 98   1 2 3 4 5
ISBN: 0-226-90303-6 (cloth)

Library of Congress Cataloging-in-Publication Data

Inquiries in the economics of aging / edited by David A. Wise.
      p.   cm. — (A National Bureau of Economic Research project report)
    "This volume consists of papers presented at a conference held at Carefree, Arizona, in May 1995"—CIP preface.
    Includes bibliographical references and index.
    ISBN 0-226-90303-6 (cloth : alk. paper)
    1. Aged—United States—Economic conditions—Congresses.
2. Insurance, Health—Economic aspects—United States—Congresses.   3. Retirement—Economic aspects—United States—Congresses.   4. Medical economics—United States—Congresses.
I. Wise, David A.   II. Series.
HQ1064.U5I543   1998
305.26—dc21   97-43207
                                                                CIP

∞ The paper used in this publication meets the minimum requirements of the American National Standard for Information Sciences—Permanence of Paper for Printed Library Materials, ANSI Z39.48-1992.

Relation of the Directors to the
Work and Publications of the
National Bureau of Economic Research

1. The object of the National Bureau of Economic Research is to ascertain and to present to the public important economic facts and their interpretation in a scientific and impartial manner. The Board of Directors is charged with the responsibility of ensuring that the work of the National Bureau is carried on in strict conformity with this object.

2. The President of the National Bureau shall submit to the Board of Directors, or to its Executive Committee, for their formal adoption all specific proposals for research to be instituted.

3. No research report shall be published by the National Bureau until the President has sent each member of the Board a notice that a manuscript is recommended for publication and that in the President's opinion it is suitable for publication in accordance with the principles of the National Bureau. Such notification will include an abstract or summary of the manuscript's content and a response form for use by those Directors who desire a copy of the manuscript for review. Each manuscript shall contain a summary drawing attention to the nature and treatment of the problem studied, the character of the data and their utilization in the report, and the main conclusions reached.

4. For each manuscript so submitted, a special committee of the Directors (including Directors Emeriti) shall be appointed by majority agreement of the President and Vice Presidents (or by the Executive Committee in case of inability to decide on the part of the President and Vice Presidents), consisting of three Directors selected as nearly as may be one from each general division of the Board. The names of the special manuscript committee shall be stated to each Director when notice of the proposed publication is submitted to him. It shall be the duty of each member of the special manuscript committee to read the manuscript. If each member of the manuscript committee signifies his approval within thirty days of the transmittal of the manuscript, the report may be published. If at the end of that period any member of the manuscript committee withholds his approval, the President shall then notify each member of the Board, requesting approval or disapproval of publication, and thirty days additional shall be granted for this purpose. The manuscript shall then not be published unless at least a majority of the entire Board who shall have voted on the proposal within the time fixed for the receipt of votes shall have approved.

5. No manuscript may be published, though approved by each member of the special manuscript committee, until forty-five days have elapsed from the transmittal of the report in manuscript form. The interval is allowed for the receipt of any memorandum of dissent or reservation, together with a brief statement of his reasons, that any member may wish to express; and such memorandum of dissent or reservation shall be published with the manuscript if he so desires. Publication does not, however, imply that each member of the Board has read the manuscript, or that either members of the Board in general or the special committee have passed on its validity in every detail.

6. Publications of the National Bureau issued for informational purposes concerning the work of the Bureau and its staff, or issued to inform the public of activities of Bureau staff, and volumes issued as a result of various conferences involving the National Bureau shall contain a specific disclaimer noting that such publication has not passed through the normal review procedures required in this resolution. The Executive Committee of the Board is charged with review of all such publications from time to time to ensure that they do not take on the character of formal research reports of the National Bureau, requiring formal Board approval.

7. Unless otherwise determined by the Board or exempted by the terms of paragraph 6, a copy of this resolution shall be printed in each National Bureau publication.

(Resolution adopted October 25, 1926, as revised through September 30, 1974)

Contents

Preface

This volume consists of papers presented at a conference held at Carefree, Arizona, in May 1995. It is part of the National Bureau of Economic Research's ongoing project on the economics of aging. The majority of the work reported here was sponsored by the U.S. Department of Health and Human Services, through National Institute on Aging grants P01-AG05842, R37-AG08146, and T32-AG00186 to the National Bureau of Economic Research.

Any opinions expressed in this volume are those of the respective authors and do not necessarily reflect the views of the National Bureau of Economic Research or the sponsoring organization.

Introduction

David A. Wise

This is the sixth in a series of volumes on the economics of aging. The previous ones were *The Economics of Aging, Issues in the Economics of Aging, Topics in the Economics of Aging, Studies in the Economics of Aging,* and *Advances in the Economics of Aging.* The papers in this volume cover aspects of health insurance and the increase in the cost of health care, retirement and caring for the elderly, and several methodological and data issues that will help to pave the way for future analysis. The papers are summarized in this introduction, which draws heavily on the authors' own summaries.

Health Insurance and the Cost of Health Care

Medical Saving Accounts

In "Insurance or Self-Insurance? Variation, Persistence, and Individual Health Accounts," Matthew Eichner, Mark McClellan, and I consider the feasibility of medical saving accounts as a means of helping to efficiently control health care costs. We conclude that medical saving accounts do offer a feasible way to provide medical insurance that helps to assure that the cost of care is matched by a corresponding benefit to the patient.

Economists have for some time emphasized the desirable incentive properties of catastrophic health insurance. Under such a system individuals would pay for their own health care unless the expenses were very large. Thus the temptation to spend too much, the "moral hazard," that is created by typical insurance provisions would be reduced or eliminated. A practical argument

David A. Wise is the John F. Stambaugh Professor of Political Economy at the John F. Kennedy School of Government, Harvard University, and director of the Health and Retirement Research Programs at the National Bureau of Economic Research.

against catastrophic insurance, however, is that a very large fraction of families have almost no liquid savings and would find it hard to make even small out-of-pocket payments, especially if they were not anticipated. Perhaps in recognition of this fact, employees have shown a willingness to pay very high premiums to avoid uncertainty about health expenditures, and many firms have experienced very low participation rates in "major medical" plans with substantial deductibles even though these plans are typically offered at generously low premiums.

The attention of American health reformers in recent years has turned to managed care plans, which place little reliance on "demand" incentives, instead using "supply side" and contractual restrictions to limit spending under insurance plans with low deductibles and copayments. Apparently, such plans have had some success in limiting health expenditures, although at the cost of increased regulation of doctor-patient transactions. But, ex post, insured patients bear only a small fraction of the cost of their care, suggesting that incentives for cost control are far from optimal. We begin with this paper a research agenda that emphasizes—and maybe reconsiders—price incentives in health insurance reform.

We explore the feasibility of catastrophic health insurance established in conjunction with individual health accounts (IHAs). Such an arrangement holds the potential for both reducing health care cost and encouraging saving. Under this plan, the employer establishes both a high-deductible health insurance plan and an IHA. Annual contributions to the IHA are equal to a substantial fraction of the deductible. Employee health care costs below the deductible are then paid out of the IHA; costs above the deductible are paid by the insurance plan. Assets remaining in the account when the employee retires, or becomes Medicare eligible, are then available for other purposes. The motivation for the parallel saving and insurance plans, of course, is that each employee is spending his or her "own" money for medical care, except in the event of serious illness. The plan thus combines the desirable features of catastrophic coverage for reducing medical expenditures with a mechanism that creates a reserve from which individual expenses can be paid.

But even if the IHA component provides the necessary liquidity, it may still be thought to be inequitable. To the extent that individuals experience different health shocks over many years, the plan could lead to large differences in IHA accumulations. A person who is never sick will accumulate large IHA balances, while someone who is always sick will accumulate nothing. If individual health expenditures over a working lifetime vary little, all persons will have the same IHA balance at retirement. On the other hand, if average individual expenditures vary widely over the working life, the plan may look like a savings plan to the healthy and self-insurance to the chronically ill.

Because individual health shocks clearly vary, the feasibility of an IHA plan depends on whether the gains (improved incentives for efficient health care spending and increased savings) outweigh the costs (more variation in individual health care costs than under more generous insurance plans). Indeed, we believe that in practice feasibility may depend largely on what the variation in IHA balances would "look like." Thus, as a crucial first step, we address that issue in this paper. Within the context of an illustrative IHA plan, we develop preliminary empirical evidence on the distribution of medical expenditures—and hence savings—under an IHA plan. Our analysis is based on longitudinal health insurance claims data from a large firm. In this analysis, we assume no behavioral response whatever to the increased cost sharing under an IHA plan.

We emphasize the balance in the IHA account at retirement. Although such a plan would produce a range of balances across employees, approximately 80 percent would retain over 50 percent of their contributions. Only about 5 percent would retain less than 20 percent of their contributions. The outcomes suggest to us that such a plan is feasible. And we believe that such a plan could be structured to increase retirement savings.

Medical Technology and Cost Increases

In "What Is Technological Change?" David Cutler and Mark McClellan examine the sources of health care expenditure growth, emphasizing the important effect of the diffusion of medical technology. The rising cost of health care has been among the most vexing problems facing the public sector in the past three decades. Spending on health care accounts for nearly 20 percent of federal revenues, and a similar share of state and local revenues. With real per capita health costs increasing by 4 to 5 percent annually, understanding the determinants of health care cost growth has become a substantial public concern.

Efforts to limit cost growth in the public sector have typically focused on price mechanisms. By lowering rates for the services it pays for, the federal government has hoped to limit overall reimbursement for medical care. And yet health costs continue to rise. Real per enrollee Medicare costs increased by over 6 percent annually between 1991 and 1993.

Cutler and McClellan explore the causes of this cost growth in detail. They begin with a discussion of the growth of inpatient Medicare costs. They show that the price that Medicare pays for admissions has been falling over time but the technological intensity of the treatment has been increasing. Since more intensive technologies are reimbursed at a higher rate than less intensive technologies, the growth of technology is at least partly responsible for the growth of Medicare costs.

To gain further insights into these trends, they turn to a detailed analysis of expenditure growth for one particular condition—acute myocardial infarctions (AMIs), or heart attacks, in elderly Medicare beneficiaries. The technologies used in treating AMI have progressed dramatically in the past decade. In the early 1980s, treatment for heart attacks consisted principally of medical management of the patient, primarily involving monitoring techniques, pharmacologic interventions, and counseling. During the 1980s, several new intensive technologies were implemented widely. These technologies, the authors show, including cardiac catheterization, coronary artery bypass surgery, and coronary angioplasty, have had major consequences for patient treatment. The authors then quantify the effects of the technologies on Medicare expenditures. In 1984, about 11 percent of people with a heart attack received one or more of these intensive treatments. Over the next seven years, the use of these treatments nearly quadrupled. As a result, even though the price of AMIs was constant or even falling, spending on heart attacks rose by 4 percent annually.

The authors then begin to develop evidence on the nature of this technological change by comparing the growth of technology across metropolitan statistical areas (MSAs). They consider a common contention—that new and cheaper technologies will substitute for older and more expensive technologies and thus lower costs. The most recent innovation for AMI treatment, angioplasty, is substantially cheaper than bypass surgery; thus substitution of angioplasty for bypass surgery could potentially reduce cost growth. Looking across MSAs, however, they find no evidence that areas with more rapid growth of angioplasty have had less rapid growth of bypass surgery. Thus they conclude that angioplasty has added significantly to the cost of AMI treatment by extending intensive interventions to a larger segment of AMI patients. Looking across MSAs, they find that some MSAs are technology "leaders" and others are "followers." Areas in which bypass surgery was more prevalent in 1984 are the first to adopt angioplasty, and they use this procedure more often.

Finally, the authors begin to explore the sources of intensity growth within geographic areas by considering the contribution of technology acquisition by hospitals to intensity growth. They find that technology diffusion to new facilities accounts for much intensity growth, but that more frequent use of intensive technologies within hospitals is also important, especially for the continued growth of relatively "established" technologies such as bypass surgery.

Retirement and Care of the Elderly

Is Retirement Saving Used for Retirement?

Personal retirement saving and employer-provided pension plans that may provide a lump sum to the employee at retirement or on earlier departure from the firm are becoming an increasingly important form of retirement saving. An important concern is whether these lump-sum distributions are in fact saved for retirement or used for other purposes. In "Lump-Sum Distributions from Retirement Saving Plans: Receipt and Utilization," James Poterba, Steven Venti, and I address this question, concluding that the vast majority of the funds, but a smaller proportion of individual accounts, do remain in retirement saving accounts.

The degree to which alternative pension systems preserve retirement benefits when individuals change jobs has long been a consideration in evaluating various retirement saving arrangements. Related preservation issues have also been raised with respect to targeted retirement saving accounts, such as individual retirement accounts (IRAs) and 401(k) plans, which permit contributors to withdraw funds, subject to a tax penalty, before they reach retirement age. As the incidence of targeted retirement saving plans increases, the number of taxpayers with the potential to trigger such withdrawals will also increase. Although a number of previous studies, including our own, have examined the determinants of participation and contribution behavior in retirement saving plans, withdrawal behavior has received much less attention.

The incidence and disposition of withdrawals from pension plans or other saving plans, known as lump-sum distributions, is a key determinant of the financial status of elderly households. Consider a 35-year-old who has accumulated $10,000 in a defined contribution (DC) pension plan, and who changes jobs. If these funds remain in a DC pension account and earn a 5 percent annual real return, the balance in this plan will be $44,817 when the beneficiary reaches age 65. If these funds are withdrawn and consumed when the pension plan participant changes jobs, however, they will not contribute to his financial well-being in retirement. Because a high fraction of lump-sum distributions occur when individuals change jobs early in their employment careers, withdrawing such assets forgoes the opportunity for many years of compound accumulation at pretax rates of return.

We consider the incidence and disposition of lump-sum distributions from pension plans and targeted retirement saving accounts and present exploratory empirical evidence on recipient characteristics that are correlated with the decision to rollover such distributions and preserve their associated retirement benefits. Although we are particularly interested in withdrawals from IRAs and 401(k) plans, we are not aware of any data source that provides detailed information on these withdrawals as distinct from distributions from employer-provided DB and DC pension plans. At least historically, payouts from pension plans are likely to account for the substantial majority of distributions. We therefore explore the general pattern of receipt and utilization of all distributions.

Using information from both the Current Population Survey and the Health and Retirement Survey, we demonstrate that lump-sum distributions are common and that most small distributions are not rolled over into qualified retirement saving accounts. Most large distributions are rolled over, however, and the fraction of distribution *dollars* that are reinvested in saving vehicles is substantially greater than the fraction of *distributions* that are reinvested. At least 80 percent of the dollar amount of distributions is either rolled over into an IRA or other pension plan, used to buy an annuity, or saved in another form. We also document a number of clear patterns with respect to the allocation of lump-sum distributions. More educated workers, older workers, and higher income workers are more likely to roll these distributions into some type of retirement saving account.

Medical Insurance and Retirement

Saving for retirement and the preservation of such saving speak to the preparation for retirement. The determinants of retirement have been emphasized extensively in prior volumes in this series. The effects of the provisions of employer-provided pension plans and the provisions of the social security system have received particular attention. Brigitte Madrian and Nancy Dean Beaulieu consider another potentially important influence on when people choose to retire. In "Does Medicare Eligibility Affect Retirement?" they consider whether the availability of Medicare insurance influences the timing of retirement. Based on the evidence that they develop, they conclude that it does.

Concern over the lack of portability associated with employer-provided health insurance has precipitated a recent flurry of research activity on the effects of health insurance on labor market outcomes. Several estimates suggest that the costs associated with changing doctors and losing coverage for preexisting conditions are sufficient to deter some individuals from changing jobs. These costs may be particularly important for older individuals contemplating retirement because a departure from the labor force may involve not only a change in doctors or lack of coverage for preexisting conditions but a complete loss of access to employer-provided group health insurance.

Although all individuals are eligible for government-provided group health insurance—Medicare—on reaching age 65, most individuals say that they would like to retire before age 65. In contrast with social security, however, there is no early retirement age before 65 when individuals qualify for Medicare. For some, this is not an issue because their employers provide postretirement health insurance benefits. The majority of workers, however, are not entitled to such benefits because their employers do not offer them. It is these workers whom we would expect to be most concerned about how early retirement will affect their health insurance coverage.

Understanding the role of health insurance in retirement decisions is important because the government is currently trying to encourage later retirement by increasing the social security normal retirement age to 67 in the future. There has been some talk about increasing the age of Medicare eligibility correspondingly. Madrian and Beaulieu emphasize, however, that health care reform that makes health insurance more portable from work to retirement may undermine this goal if the potential loss or change in health insurance coverage that currently exists is a significant deterrent to retirement.

Much of the emerging literature on health insurance and retirement has examined the impact of employer-provided retiree health insurance on retirement, concluding that such health insurance constitutes a significant inducement for early retirement. In contrast, there is little compelling evidence on the effect of Medicare. Madrian and Beaulieu consider the role of Medicare in the retirement decision and present evidence on whether it, too, affects retirement choice.

Although they are reluctant to draw strong conclusions about the effect of Medicare eligibility on retirement behavior, the authors conclude that the results presented in the paper suggest that Medicare may indeed influence the retirement decisions of men. They find the following: (1) 55–69-year-old men with Medicare-eligible spouses have a higher retirement hazard than men without Medicare-eligible spouses. (2) The retirement hazard exhibits a pattern with respect to spouse's age that is consistent with what would be expected if Medicare were an important consideration in the retirement decision. It is inconsistent with a story that other factors more generally related to spouse's age, such as a spouse's health status, are strong determinants of retirement as the retirement hazard appears to be roughly constant after the spouse reaches age 65 rather than generally increasing. (3) The pattern of effects is approximately the same when the sample is confined to men whose wives have never worked. This latter group of men cannot be affected by any financial considerations inducing their wives to retire. Furthermore, having a nonworking spouse cannot differentially impact the retirement hazard with respect to spouse's age of this group because their wives have never worked. The most plausible explanation, the authors conclude, for the pattern of retirement effects exhibited by this latter group is the Medicare eligibility of their wives. Because the effects are similar for the whole population of men regardless of spouse's work history, it is likely that Medicare is also an important determinant of retirement for all men, Madrian and Beaulieu believe.

Who Cares for the Elderly?

In her paper, "Caring for the Elderly: The Role of Adult Children," Kathleen McGarry considers the care received by the elderly from their children. She finds that only about 2 percent of children provide cash assistance to their parents and 10 percent provide other forms of help. Nonetheless, the parents who are most in "need" are most likely to receive help.

Much of the rising cost of health care for the elderly results from long-term care. In 1989, 77 percent of Medicaid funding directed toward those aged 65 or over was spent on nursing homes or home health care. Various strategies have been proposed to combat these growing expenditures. McGarry points to Governor Pataki of New York State, who has proposed drastic cuts in spending for home health care and housekeeping services, in an effort to balance the state's budget. On the other hand, President Clinton has proposed expanded home services as a substitute for more expensive nursing homes. To evaluate the potential impacts of such policies, McGarry argues, we need a clear understanding of the use and provision of home health care. Who are the preferred caregivers? How much substitution is there between formal and informal care? Will increasing the availability and affordability of home health care decrease more expensive nursing home admissions and therefore costs, or will the substitution away from unpaid care toward formal paid care be large enough to offset any savings?

McGarry uses the new survey of Asset and Health Dynamics among the Oldest Old to document the current use of home health care by the population aged 70 or over. She expands on the past work on this subject by exploring the role played by financial compensation from parents to children as a method of encouraging children to provide care, and by controlling more completely for factors such as income and wealth that may affect access to services.

She provides a descriptive analysis of the caregiving environment faced by disabled and impaired elderly. She finds that the strongest predictor of receiving care is need. Approximately two-thirds of those with a limitation receive assistance. Those who are not receiving care are on average better off in several dimensions, including having greater financial resources and better health. In many ways the type of caregiving relationship depends on the recipient's needs. Children, including non-coresident children, provide assistance with housekeeping tasks, while coresident individuals (spouses, children, and others) help with personal care needs.

On the other hand, McGarry finds that little assistance is provided by children. Only 10 percent of children provide time help to their parents (8.5 percent of non-coresident children). For some children, the provision of cash assistance would be a logical substitute. However, fewer than 2 percent of children are reported to have made cash transfers to their impaired parents. Perhaps more surprising, cash transfers are positively correlated with the provision of time assistance. Thus it is not the case that children who are unable to spend time helping a parent compensate with financial assistance. McGarry warns that the results should be interpreted with a degree of caution.

Measurement, Methodological, and Data Issues

Measuring Poverty

Several papers in this volume consider how we measure the economic status of the elderly and other methodological and data issues. Some of these concerns arise simply out of continuing interest in "how to do it right" or simply "how to do it at all." But other issues arise because of opportunities presented by new data, in particular the Health and Retirement Survey (HRS) and the survey of Asset and Health Dynamics among the Oldest Old (AHEAD), which will be widely used to study a host of aging issues in the future.

The paper by Angus Deaton and Christina Paxson, "Measuring Poverty among the Elderly," is in the first category. In the United States in 1992, there were four million elderly adults who were officially classified as poor. There were 31 million elderly in the United States in 1992, so the poverty rate was just under 13 percent. Children were much more likely to be poor than the elderly; 22 percent, or 15 million children, were poor. Deaton and Paxson address the questions of where such numbers come from and what, "if anything," they mean. The authors emphasize that the data used to make the official calculations do not tell us anything about individual poverty. Instead they provide information on the income of *families,* information that is used to construct a set of poverty counts about individuals. The transformation from families to individuals makes many assumptions, about the allocation of resources within the household, about the differential needs of children, adults, and the elderly, and about the extent of economies of scale. Given the data, the effect of these assumptions on the poverty count depends on living arrangements, on how people combine to form families, on whether people are married or cohabit, and on whether the elderly live by themselves or with other younger adults.

Deaton and Paxson examine how living arrangements affect poverty measurement in the United States. Conclusions about the living standards of the elderly are less determined by the data than by assumptions about who gets what and how poverty lines vary with household composition. Deaton and Paxson demonstrate the fact by calculating the sensitivity of poverty counts to key assumptions in their construction, they examine the basis for the assumptions, and they explore whether the empirical evidence has anything useful to contribute.

There are two problems in passing from family resources to individual welfare, one of which is the main topic of their paper. The first issue, about which they say little, is the intrahousehold allocation of resources. The measurement of individual poverty requires a rule for assigning welfare levels to individuals, based on the consumption or income level of the family or household in which they live. Any rule inevitably contains implicit assumptions about how resources are shared between different household members, for example, by age or sex.

The second problem is the one to which they give most attention. Even if resources are distributed equitably across household members, the size and age structure of households affects the welfare levels of their members. The same level of income or income per capita does not give the same standard of living to a large family as to a small one, or to an all-adult household compared with one with children. Larger households may be able to take advantage of "scale economies" when they share the consumption of public goods in the household, so that members of large households are likely to be better off than those of small households, even controlling for per capita income or total expenditure. Likewise, if children cost less than adults, then households with more children will require lower incomes to achieve a specified standard of living, given total household size. These issues are likely to be of particular importance when comparing poverty rates across age groups and are also likely to play out differently in countries with different living arrangements for elderly individuals. In the United States, where the elderly typically live in small households with few children, the treatment of child costs is unlikely to have large effects on the numbers of old people in poverty, although it can potentially have large effects on the poverty of the old relative to the young. Even when old people live alone, so that we can measure their resources from a household survey, we cannot classify them as poor or nonpoor without a standard of comparison, a standard that cannot be derived without assessing the needs of other nonelderly members of the population. The treatment of scale economies is likely to be an important issue for both absolute and relative poverty rates of the elderly.

Deaton and Paxson first examine the sensitivity of poverty measures in the United States to assumptions about child costs and scale economies. They then estimate the size of scale economies and child costs in the United States, for which they have suitable consumption data. They begin by describing how official poverty measures are derived, and they present official poverty counts and rates for members of different age groups. They show that poverty measures for different age groups are quite sensitive to the treatment of scale economies and costs of children.

Based on their more formal analysis, they summarize: "But it is hard to escape the conclusion that expenditure patterns respond to family size in ways that are a good deal more complex than the simple story of public and private goods that we have considered in this paper. Constructing better models of this process remains a challenge for the future."

Measuring the Quality of Health Care

For some time, the Health Care Financing Administration (HCFA) has published "standardized" mortality scores for each hospital in the country as an indicator of the quality of care. Similarly, patient mortality has been widely used in studies of the determinants of quality of care in hospitals. "The Covariance Structure of Mortality Rates in Hospitals" by Douglas Staiger raises serious questions about the meaningfulness of these numbers.

Staiger emphasizes that, despite the widespread acceptance of patient mortality as a proxy for quality of care, little is known about the statistical properties of this variable. A number of questions are of particular interest. First, how much useful information is there in such inherently noisy measures of quality; for example, how large is the signal-to-noise ratio? A related question is how persistent are these measures of quality of care: Are hospitals with unexpectedly high mortality rates this year likely to have unexpectedly high mortality rates next year, in five years, in ten years? Is the presumption of high persistence, commonly assumed by the public, consistent with the data? A third question is whether there is a correlation in patient mortality for patients with distinct diagnoses admitted to the same hospital? If so, then combining information from different types of patients may prove to be a useful way of summarizing common hospital-level components of quality of care. A final question of interest is what has happened to the cross-sectional distribution of patient mortality over time: for example, has there been convergence or divergence across hospitals? Have there been any noticeable changes in the variation of these measures in recent years as reimbursement and competitive pressures have grown?

Staiger uses annual data from 1974–87 for 492 large hospitals to investigate these questions. He analyzes data on standardized mortality rates for Medicare admissions in both specific diagnoses and in aggregate. In addition to presenting simple descriptive evidence on the distribution of the mortality measures, he estimates covariance structures using general method of moment methods, which provide a simple and powerful description of the basic features of the data.

Staiger concludes that the empirical results presented in his paper have a number of implications. Perhaps the key one is this: "For those using these mortality variables as proxies for quality of care, the statistical properties of mortality should raise some concern. The amount of noise in these measures is on the order of 80 to 90 percent of the total variance." In thinking more generally about the process that determines quality of care in a hospital, the model may give some insight. An obvious interpretation of the "three factor" model used in the analysis is one in which the hospital effect represents general infrastructure such as the nursing staff, physical plant, or skill of the medical staff. These characteristics might be expected to be fairly permanent and in fact may represent what one often thinks of when thinking of a top-notch hospital. In contrast, the diagnosis-specific component could be thought of as technological innovations specific to that diagnosis. Casual observation suggests that AMI is a diagnosis that has had substantial technological innovation over the past 20 years, and this is consistent with the fact that the variance of the diagnosis-specific factor is much larger in AMI than in congestive heart failure, for example. On the other hand, such innovations tend to diffuse to other hospitals fairly rapidly, and so it is not surprising that this diagnosis-specific component does not persist much beyond five years.

Of course, there are alternative interpretations of the results. For example, the hospital component may reflect permanent differences in the population that each hospital serves, which are not captured by the adjustment for expected mortality. Distinguishing the quality-of-care interpretation from the case-mix interpretation is an important topic of future research, Staiger says.

Finally, the results suggest that there have been important changes in the distribution of patient mortality across hospitals between the mid-1970s and the 1980s. The reasons for this shift, and the corresponding change in the autocovariance structure of mortality, are unknown. It remains to be seen whether a simple extension of the models considered here can explain this anomaly. One possible explanation is that important technology shocks always begin with flagship hospitals and then diffuse through the remainder of the population. Thus mortality in "innovative" years might be much more correlated than in average years.

Measuring Wealth and Using Subjective Probabilities

One of the innovations in the new HRS and AHEAD surveys is the use of "bracketing" to obtain information about the financial resources of the elderly.

If a respondent does not give an answer when asked, for example, how much money is in the bank, then the interviewer asks whether it is less than some amount (like $10,000) or between two amounts (like $10,000 and $50,000). In "Household Wealth of the Elderly under Alternative Imputation Procedures," Hilary Hoynes, Michael Hurd, and Harish Chand conclude that the use of brackets, together with the use of other individual information, can substantially improve measurement of household wealth.

At retirement the economic resources of the elderly can include housing equity, nonhousing wealth, social security benefits, and pension rights. Housing and social security are the most important resources because a substantial fraction reach retirement with little saving and no claim to a pension. In many surveys of assets the rate of missing data in individual asset items is high, about 30 to 40 percent among those with the asset. This raises the issues of the reliability of wealth measures because respondents who refuse or are unable to give a value to an asset item may not be representative of the population.

Hoynes, Hurd, and Chand use the AHEAD survey to examine the distribution of wealth among the elderly. Because of the data collection methods in the survey, they are able to reduce the rate of missing data on wealth and, they hope, obtain better estimates of the distribution of wealth than are available with other data sources. They devote considerable effort to the measurement of each of the components of wealth. Their methods preserve the relationships among measures of economic status to a greater extent than previous methods, and this, they believe, should increase both the mean and the skewness of the wealth distribution. To illustrate the effects of their methods, they compare estimates of the distribution of wealth using their preferred imputation method with estimates based on other commonly used methods.

They conclude that the most important AHEAD innovation is the extensive use of bracketing: the brackets reduce substantially the rate of missing data and, most important for studying individual behavior, provide individual-level information that cannot be obtained from imputation based solely on personal characteristics. In addition, the bracketing changes averages, which is important for assessing the economic status of the elderly.

The use of other personal information also helped impute some asset levels. For example, the covariates reduced housing wealth considerably among the "incompletely bracketed" respondents. While the authors believe the use of covariates is a considerable improvement, they conclude that the use of brackets with small samples needs further study.

Another innovation in the new HRS and AHEAD surveys is collection of information on individual expectations about future events. Respondents are asked how likely it is that they will work past age 62, for example; how likely it is they will live past age 80; and so forth. The responses to such questions have become known as subjective probabilities. In "Subjective Survival Curves and Life Cycle Behavior," Michael Hurd, Daniel McFadden, and Li Gan consider the use of individual subjective data on survival in economic models. Although these data accord well with external data on survival, the authors conclude that the concentration of survey responses at "focal" points—such as 0.5—must be addressed if the data are to be generally used in models of economic behavior.

Hurd et al. point out that many economic models are based on forward-looking behavior. Although it is often said that "expectations" about future events are important in these models, more precisely it is the probability distributions of future events that enter the models. For example, consumption and saving decisions of an individual are thought to depend on what he or she thinks about future interest rates, the likelihood of dying, and the risk of substantial future medical expenditures. According to economic theories, decision makers have probability distributions about these and other events, and they use them to make decisions about saving. This implies that data on these distributions should be used in estimation. The authors note, however, that in few cases are data available that may plausibly be assumed to approximate those contemplated in the models. The life cycle model of consumption in which mortality risk helps determine saving is the leading example.

The authors recognize that individual survival probabilities can be obtained by using individual attributes to adjust population life tables. But, they say, individuals are likely to have subjective probability distributions that partly are related to observable variables but partly are not. It is these subjective probability distributions that should enter life cycle models of saving, so any models that rely on fitted probability distributions have intrinsic limitations.

AHEAD has eight measures of subjective probabilities. The authors find that these measures have informational content but that they cannot be used without modification as right-hand variables in a model of decision making because of "cognition" and observation error. They propose and estimate a model of cognition error and then apply the model to life tables and to data from AHEAD to produce usable subjective probabilities of survival.

They find that stated probabilities are distorted by focal points. The evidence from the model is that there is in addition reporting error in nonfocal responses but that this error is small relative to variation in individual expectations. They conclude that nonfocal responses can be used with relatively minor adjustments to predict personal survival curves. More substantial adjustments are required to predict survival curves for focal respondents, however. Their preliminary analysis of the relationship between survival probabilities and saving behavior suggests that there is a weak correlation but that there remains considerable unexplained variation in saving rates. Because medical expenditures or other factors may influence current saving rates, they cannot draw any conclusions about the direction of causality between survival probabilities and economic decisions regarding wealth and savings.

Specific Disease and Survival

Jayanta Bhattacharya, Alan Garber, and Thomas MaCurdy also address questions of survival, but from a very different perspective. In their paper, "Cause-Specific Mortality among Medicare Enrollees," they explore the use of

Medicare insurance claims data to estimate survival curves. They believe that their methods can be used, for example, to provide survival probabilities, and thus future Medicare expenditures, for the care of persons with specific diagnoses.

To motivate their analysis, the authors note that attempts to forecast health expenditures, to determine costs of specific illnesses, and to assess the long-term impact of programs designed to prevent or relieve specific diseases all require accurate estimates of mortality rates. Many such efforts build on information about the cause and timing of death for people who have certain diseases. However, the empirical basis for making accurate projections of cause-specific mortality, particularly for well-defined demographic and clinical subgroups, is often weak.

The standard life table framework offers a simple and powerful method for drawing inferences about the distribution of survival. Yet seldom have the data proved capable of supporting detailed studies of mortality by cause for well-defined populations. Standard U.S. life tables, based on birth records and death certificate data, with cause-of-death data, are published every several years by the National Center for Health Statistics. Life tables compiled by age, race, and sex are published annually. Although these sources offer useful information about mortality trends by demographic group, they provide little information about the survival distribution pertinent to people with specific health conditions and risk profiles. Thus it is difficult to obtain, for example, a life table applicable to 70-year-old men who are discharged from a hospital with a diagnosis of myocardial infarction. Small clinical studies and registries often provide information of this kind, but they usually are limited either by the selection criteria used to define the study population or by small sample sizes. They are not sufficiently comprehensive to cover a wide range of conditions, or to analyze a nationally representative sample.

Bhattacharya et al. describe the first steps toward developing such life tables. They lay out an approach to estimating survival patterns among the elderly that is based on longitudinal analysis of data from Medicare eligibility and claims files. These files offer a nationally representative sample of the elderly. Information about the cause of death, derived from hospital discharge files, allows them to link additional information about the terminal hospitalization and provides the opportunity to obtain confirmatory data that are not routinely available from death certificate information. They develop a flexible functional form model to relate annual mortality rates to a set of individual characteristics.

The longitudinal analysis they describe, which focuses on cause of death, can be a building block for studies that address a number of additional issues. For example, it can be extended to estimate future Medicare expenditures for the care of individuals who carry specific diagnoses. It can provide information about the expected pattern of expenditures for persons with a given set of characteristics, including not only age and gender, but also race, comorbidities, and prior hospital utilization. Similarly, such analysis can be used to identify populations who should be targeted for either preventive interventions or the identification and treatment of diseases. Finally, it can inform efforts to determine whether otherwise identical patients who receive different treatments have different outcomes.

I   Health Insurance and the Cost of Health Care

1 Insurance or Self-Insurance? Variation, Persistence, and Individual Health Accounts

Matthew J. Eichner, Mark B. McClellan, and
David A. Wise

Economists have for some time emphasized the desirable incentive properties of catastrophic health insurance. Under such a system individuals would pay for their own health care unless the expenses were very large. Thus the temptation to spend too much, the "moral hazard," that is created by typical insurance provisions would be reduced or eliminated. Indeed, Arrow (1963) demonstrated that in the presence of moral hazard and risk aversion a catastrophic plan is optimal. A practical argument against catastrophic insurance, however, is that a very large fraction of families have almost no liquid savings and would find it hard to make even small out-of-pocket payments, especially if they were not anticipated. Perhaps in recognition of this fact, employees have shown a willingness to pay very high premiums to avoid uncertainty about health expenditures, and many firms have experienced very low participation rates in "major risk" plans with substantial deductibles even though these plans are typically offered at generously low premiums.

The attention of American health reformers in recent years has turned to managed care plans, which place little reliance on "demand" incentives, instead using "supply side" and contractual restrictions to limit spending under insurance plans with low deductibles and copayments. Apparently, such plans have had some success in limiting health expenditures, although at the cost of increased regulation of doctor-patient transactions. But, ex post, insured pa-

Matthew J. Eichner is assistant professor of finance and economics at Columbia University Graduate School of Business and a faculty research fellow of the National Bureau of Economic Research. Mark B. McClellan is professor of economics and medicine at Stanford University and a faculty research fellow of the National Bureau of Economic Research. David A. Wise is the John F. Stambaugh Professor of Political Economy at the John F. Kennedy School of Government, Harvard University, and director of the Health and Retirement Research Programs at the National Bureau of Economic Research.

Research support from the National Institutes of Health through a grant to the National Bureau of Economic Research is gratefully acknowledged.

tients bear only a small fraction of the cost of their care, suggesting that incentives for cost control are far from optimal. We begin with this paper a research agenda that emphasizes—and maybe reconsiders—price incentives in health insurance reform.

We explore the feasibility of catastrophic health insurance established in conjunction with individual health accounts (IHAs). Such an arrangement holds the potential for both reducing health care cost and encouraging saving. Under this plan, the employer establishes both a high-deductible health insurance plan and an IHA. Annual contributions to the IHA are equal to a substantial fraction of the deductible. Employee health care costs below the deductible are then paid out of the IHA; costs above the deductible are paid by the insurance plan. Assets remaining in the account when the employee retires, or becomes Medicare eligible, are then available for other purposes. The motivation for the parallel saving and insurance plans, of course, is that each employee is spending his or her "own" money for medical care, except in the event of serious illness. The plan thus combines the desirable features of catastrophic coverage for reducing medical expenditures, as advocated by Feldstein (1971) and by Feldstein and Gruber (1994), with a mechanism that creates a reserve from which individual expenses can be paid.

But even if the IHA component provides the necessary liquidity, it may still be thought to be inequitable. To the extent that individuals experience different health shocks over many years, the plan could lead to large differences in IHA accumulations. A person who is never sick will accumulate large IHA balances, while someone who is always sick will accumulate nothing. If individual health expenditures over a working lifetime vary little, all persons will have the same IHA balance at retirement. On the other hand, if average individual expenditures vary widely over the working life, the plan may look like a savings plan to the healthy and self-insurance to the chronically ill. Though mitigating measures could be appended to a basic IHA plan to limit such inequality, unequal accumulation is an unavoidable consequence of individual financial risk. Equal accumulations under an IHA plan can only be guaranteed if all individuals have the same health shock experience over their lifetimes. Of course, equal premiums under a comprehensive health plan with first-dollar coverage also assure equal individual cost.

Because individual health shocks clearly vary, the feasibility of an IHA plan depends on whether the gains (improved incentives for efficient health care spending and increased savings) outweigh the costs (more variation in individual health care costs than under more generous insurance plans). Indeed, we believe that in practice feasibility may depend largely on what the variation in IHA balances would "look like." Thus, as a crucial first step, we address that issue in this paper. Within the context of an illustrative IHA plan, we develop preliminary empirical evidence on the distribution of medical expenditures—and hence savings—under an IHA plan. Our analysis is based on longitudinal health insurance claims data from a large firm. In this analysis, we assume no behavioral response whatever to the increased cost sharing under an IHA plan. Feldstein and Gruber (1994) suggest that the response could be substantial. To the extent that individuals respond to price incentives, expenditure will be more equal—perhaps substantially more equal—than our results suggest. We hope to provide an upper bound on expenditure variation, as measured by variation in IHA accumulation.

We begin with examples that illustrate the enormous variation in health care costs in a single year and the persistence of individual expenditures from one year to the next. The illustrations are similar to those in McClellan and Wise (1994). That paper emphasized persistence in individual health care costs and demonstrated that persons with large expenditures in one year are likely to have large average expenditures, whether calculated over one or several years. In addition, we emphasize here that, although not insignificant, the relationship between expenditures two years apart is substantially weaker than the relationship between expenditures one year apart. And thus, while persistence is important, the descriptive data also suggest that high expenditure levels typically do not last for many years.

Next we explain the statistical model that underlies our conclusions on the distribution of health care expenditures. The goal is to approximate the distribution of medical expenditures over a working lifetime in a large firm. We have data on employee expenditures over a three-year period. We estimate a model that captures the pattern of expenditures among employees and then use the model to simulate the lifetime distribution of expenditures. We give particular attention to two issues: One is the extent of persistence, the expected expenditure in one year conditional on expenditure in prior years. The second is the "unexplained" residual variance, or "shock," in expenditure conditional on expenditure in prior years. An important aspect of the data is that this unexplained variance is very large and is not approximated well by any analytic distribution. Thus our simulation procedure depends heavily on nonparametric analysis based on the empirical distribution of conditional expenditures.

We next explain the results of simulations based on the model. We find that many employees will have no large medical expenditures over an entire working life. Others will have one or more episodes that generate large expenditures in one year and possibly in at least a few subsequent years as well. The concentration of expenditures that is observed in one year, and even when three years are combined, declines consistently as expenditures are cumulated over more years. Nonetheless, even over a working lifetime there is a noticeable concentration of expenditures. We illustrate the implications of the concentration by considering the distribution of balances at retirement in an IHA account with a $2,000 annual contribution. Although the vast majority of participants retire with substantial IHA balances, some incur substantial out-of-pocket costs and thus retire with only small balances. About 80 percent of employees are left with at least 50 percent of total IHA contributions, but about 5 percent have less than 20 percent.

We conclude with a discussion of the implications and limitations of this preliminary analysis. We comment on issues that are not addressed and on future research plans.

1.1 The Data and Summary Description

1.1.1 Medical Claims Data

The data are medical claims of employees in a large Fortune 500 manufacturing firm. The analysis is based on all fee-for-service insurance claims over the three-year period 1989–91. Over this period approximately 300,000 employees and their dependents were covered through these insurance plans.

The firm has two fee-for-service plans, one for hourly and another for salaried employees. The hourly plan, with benefits negotiated in union contracts, provides "first-dollar" coverage for virtually all health care. Because of this virtually unlimited coverage, hourly employees have no financial incentives to join managed care or HMO plans, though specific provider relationships and location considerations may provide some nonfinancial incentives. The salaried plan has an annual deductible of $200 per individual and $250 per family, a 20 percent coinsurance rate for all expenses, and an out-of-pocket annual limit (including the deductible) of $500 per family. Routine physical examinations are not covered. Both plans incorporate limited case management for certain high-cost medical conditions and concurrent review of hospital stays. The hourly plan includes preadmission certification requirements for certain elective admissions; patients who elect admission despite precertification denial are responsible for 20 percent copayments up to $750 per individual and $1,500 per family. Both plans also require second opinions for 16 elective surgical procedures, though the procedures are covered regardless of the second opinion finding. Both plans have very generous hospital stay limits: 365 days per stay, renewable after 60 days out of the hospital. Mental health and substance abuse inpatient care has a stricter day limit of 45 days, also renewable after 60 days out of the hospital. (During the time period covered by the data, a managed care program was implemented for mental health and substance abuse services.)

1.1.2 Summary Data

Many studies have documented that medical expenditures in a particular year are concentrated among a small proportion of the insured. Less evidence, and hence less attention, has been directed to the persistence of individual expenditures over longer time periods and to the relationship between persistence and concentration of expenditures. Together, both have important implications for insurance in general and in particular for the feasibility, incidence, and other consequences of insurance market reforms. Before presenting more formal analysis, we present descriptive evidence on these issues using longitudinal individual claims data for the period 1989–91. We consider first a tabular description of the relationship between expenditures in three successive years. We then consider the concentration of expenditures and present more detailed descriptions of persistence, considering expenditures in consecutive years conditional on the decile (or quintile) ranking of expenditures in the first year.

Medical Claims in Successive Years

The distributions of expenditures in 1990 and in 1991 conditional on 1989 expenditures are shown in table 1.1. Consider, for example, persons aged 18–35 in the first panel of the table. Conditional on no expenditure in 1989, 4 percent of persons have expenditures above $5,000 in 1990. In contrast, over 20 percent of persons with expenditures above $5,000 in 1989 have expenditures above $5,000 in 1990. Persistence appears to increase with age. Almost 30 percent of persons aged 46–55 who had expenditures greater than $5,000 in 1989 also had expenditures greater than $5,000 in 1990. In contrast, only 5 percent of the persons in this age group with no expenditures in 1989 had expenditures above $5,000 in 1990. If there were no persistence across years, only 8 percent of the individuals with expenditures greater than $5,000 would have such high expenditures again in 1990.

Comparison of the first panel of table 1.1 and the second—which shows data for 1991 conditional on spending in 1989—reveals that persistence diminishes with time. For example, in the 18–35 age group, about 15 percent of those with expenditures above $5,000 in 1989 had expenditures above $5,000 in 1991, compared to almost 21 percent in 1990. For the persons aged 46–55, about 22 percent of those with expenditures above $5,000 in 1989 had expenditures exceeding $5,000 in 1991, compared to almost 29 percent in 1990.

Individual Concentration of Expenditures

The relationship between persistence and concentration is shown in figure 1.1. The figure shows that in 1989 about 80 percent of cost was incurred by 10 percent of enrollees, roughly comparable to concentration results from other studies. Fifty percent of employees incurred virtually no cost. Figure 1.1 also shows the concentration of annual expenditures *averaged* over the two-year period 1989–90 and over the three-year period 1989–91. If there were no persistence in cost from one year to the next, costs averaged over several years would be much less concentrated among a few enrollees than costs in a single year. The curves show that, although concentration declines as the time period increases, even over three years a small proportion of employees incur an enormous fraction of health care costs. Averaged over three years, 10 percent of enrollees account for a full 65 percent of expenditures. If there were no persistence from year to year, then averaged over many years the cost accounted for by the highest cost decile would approach 10 percent. The more formal analy-

Table 1.1

Table 1.1 **Percentage Distribution of 1990 and 1991 Expenditures, by 1989 Expenditure Interval and by Age**

Age	1989 Expenditure ($)	1990 Expenditure ($)				
		0	0–300	300–1,000	1,000–5,000	Above 5,000
0–17	0	43.9	37.25	11.42	5.57	1.86
	0–300	45.4	34.84	12.56	5.75	1.44
	300–1,000	29	32.32	22.97	12.19	3.52
	1,000–5,000	28.1	25.69	20.92	19.05	6.25
	Above 5,000	23.28	19.32	17.43	20.76	19.21
18–35	0	40.94	33.97	12.92	8.25	3.92
	0–300	51.62	26.57	11.36	7.27	3.19
	300–1,000	35.55	25.5	18.76	13.69	6.51
	1,000–5,000	32.9	20.93	17.12	19	10.05
	Above 5,000	29.17	17.36	14.76	17.92	20.79
36–45	0	40.27	33.06	13.6	8.65	4.41
	0–300	36.57	33.03	16.11	10.12	4.18
	300–1,000	23.93	26.83	24.07	18.25	6.92
	1,000–5,000	18.88	19.97	21.19	27.93	12.04
	Above 5,000	18.63	16.82	16.67	22.81	25.07
46–55	0	37.65	32.14	14.52	10.15	5.53
	0–300	30.99	34.29	17.9	11.61	5.21
	300–1,000	17.84	26.35	28.2	19.47	8.13
	1,000–5,000	15.59	19.55	22.41	28.76	13.7
	Above 5,000	14.41	15.73	16.88	24.38	28.6
56–65	0	31.14	34.73	15.64	10.89	7.6
	0–300	35.87	31.89	16.52	10.14	5.58
	300–1,000	22.62	24.54	26.68	17.36	8.8
	1,000–5,000	19.17	18.87	21.66	26.07	14.23
	Above 5,000	21.5	13.82	15.67	22.42	26.6
0–17	0	28.29	46.98	14.87	7.49	2.37
	0–300	51.94	29.34	11.47	5.67	1.58
	300–1,000	38.92	28.29	19.03	10.31	3.45
	1,000–5,000	39.44	23.35	17.52	14.47	5.22
	Above 5,000	38.65	18.18	17.43	14.11	11.64
18–35	0	28.57	39.13	15.95	10.81	5.53
	0–300	63.58	19.21	8.98	5.54	2.69
	300–1,000	52.13	18.86	14	10.26	4.75
	1,000–5,000	48.7	16.2	13.49	14.87	6.73
	Above 5,000	46.32	13.9	11.17	13.69	14.92
36–45	0	24.43	40.28	17.38	11.98	5.91
	0–300	40.43	29.4	15.88	9.83	4.46
	300–1,000	31.02	24.29	21.79	15.94	6.96
	1,000–5,000	26.95	18.88	20.37	23.77	10.03
	Above 5,000	27.19	16.51	15.15	20.3	20.86
46–55	0	23.23	37.97	17.87	13.13	7.79
	0–300	32.73	31.41	17.85	11.89	6.13

Table 1.1   (continued)

Age	1989 Expenditure ($)	1990 Expenditure ($)				
		0	0–300	300–1,000	1,000–5,000	Above 5,000
	300–1,000	21.86	24.75	26.06	18.54	8.79
	1,000–5,000	20.33	19.27	20.69	26.75	12.95
	Above 5,000	22.66	15.85	16.05	23.6	21.83
56–65	0	29.58	33.78	16.54	11.92	8.18
	0–300	44.32	25.3	14.75	9.7	5.93
	300–1,000	34.87	19.25	21.41	15.85	8.62
	1,000–5,000	31.96	15.95	18.28	21.31	12.5
	Above 5,000	38.09	13	12.46	18.33	18.13

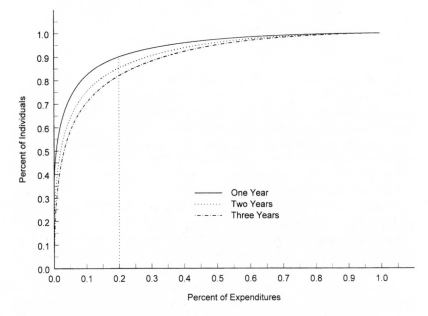

Fig. 1.1   **Concentration of expenditures over one, two, and three years**

sis presented below shows that concentration declines continuously as more and more years of expenditures are cumulated but is still substantial even averaged over a working lifetime.

Expenditure Decile and Subsequent Expenditures

Table 1.1 shows persistence in expenditures for selected age groups. Figure 1.2 presents a more detailed picture of persistence for all ages combined. Enrollees are divided into deciles based on 1989 claims. The figure shows expen-

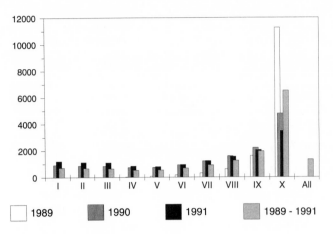

Fig. 1.2   Mean annual cost by 1989 decile

ditures in 1989 by decile and then, also by 1989 decile, average annual expenditures one year later in 1990 and two years later in 1991. For comparison, the figure also shows average expenditures for all enrollees over these three years, which was $1,314. Persons in the tenth decile in 1989 in that year spent over eight times as much as the average. They spent close to five times the average in 1990 and almost three times the average in 1991. Averaged over all three years, those in the highest decile in 1989 spent about five times the average.

An alternative description is shown in figures 1.3A, 1.3B, and 1.3C. Figure 1.3A shows the distribution of costs by quintile over the 1989–91 period for each 1989 quintile (determined by 1989 expenditures). The figure shows, for example, that almost 60 percent of persons who were in the highest quintile in 1989 were also in the highest quintile averaged over three years. Another 35 percent were in the second highest quintile averaged over three years. By contrast fewer than 10 percent of persons in the lowest 1989 quintile were in the highest quintile over three years, and only about 10 percent were in the second highest quintile. Figure 1.3B shows the distribution of costs in 1990, and figure 1.3C shows the distribution in 1991, conditional on the 1989 quintile. Over 40 percent of persons in the highest quintile in 1989 are in the highest quintile in 1990, and about 35 percent are in the highest quintile in 1991.

These descriptive data show that, on average, persons with high expenses in one year also tend to have much higher than average expenses in the next year and also higher than average, but lower, expenses in the following year. These data are used in more formal estimation to allow extrapolation of this persistence pattern over subsequent years. The formal analysis also shows that the importance of the persistence revealed in mean expenditures appears to be dominated by the enormous variation in expenditure shocks, conditional on any past expenditure pattern.

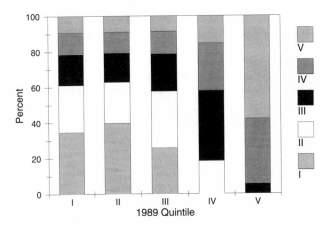

Fig. 1.3A   1989–91 Quintile by 1989 quintile

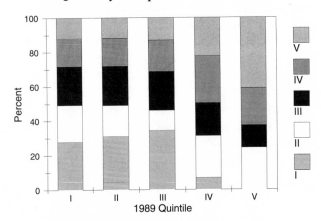

Fig. 1.3B   1990 Quintile by 1989 quintile

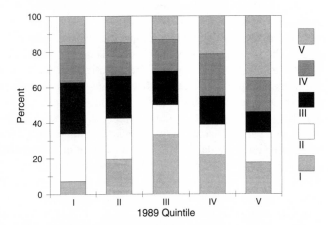

Fig. 1.3C   1991 Quintile by 1989 quintile

1.2   A "Model" of Persistence and Expenditure Shocks

Our goal is a formal description of medical expenditures that will allow us to simulate the pattern of expenditures over the working life. We begin with a description of the model specification and then explain the simulation procedure. A critical feature of the model is the extent to which it captures actual expenditure patterns, and thus we give considerable attention to the model fit.

1.2.1   Specification

The descriptive specification must capture two critical features of health care expenditures: (1) the enormous variation across individuals in the same year and (2) the persistence of expenditures from one year to the next. In this version of the analysis we describe annual expenditures. We assume that medical expenditures in year t, M_t, can be predicted by three factors: (1) demographic characteristics, denoted by D, which include age, sex, and employment status (hourly or salaried); (2) past expenditures M_{lag}, which in this version include expenditures in years $t - 1$ and $t - 2$; and (3) random shocks, ε:

$$(1) \qquad M_t = \alpha + \beta D + \gamma M_{\text{lag}} + \varepsilon.$$

The critical components are the random shocks and persistence (measured by γ). Because a large fraction of employees have no expenditures in a given year, it is useful to consider explicitly the expected value of M_t, given by

$$(2) \quad E(M_t) = \Pr[M_t \leq 0] \times 0 + \Pr[M_t > 0] \times E(M_t \mid M_t > 0).$$

We estimate the two components—$\Pr[M_t > 0]$ and $E(M_t \mid M_t > 0)$—separately. The first is estimated using a linear probability specification, and the second using a log linear regression.

The model estimates, together with exact specifications, are shown in appendix table 1A.1. The specification used in the analysis is presented in the bottom panel of the table. The basic structure of the specification, however, is more easily seen in the simpler specification that is shown in the top panel. This specification shows three variables (D1, D2, D12) that identify persons with no expenditures in $t - 1$, no expenditures in $t - 2$, and no expenditures in either prior period. Variables containing expenditure amounts for persons who had claims in prior years are defined using similar notation. For example, M1 gives expenditure amounts for persons who had claims in period $t - 1$ (for whom D1 = 0) and is zero for persons who did not file a claim in period $t - 1$. For persons with claims in both $t - 1$ and $t - 2$ (the "base" group), there are two expenditure variables, M*1 and M*2, for $t - 1$ and $t - 2$, respectively. The estimated coefficients are difficult to interpret individually. (E.g., the coefficient associated with D1 in the simplified expenditure equation [-0.7485]

indicates that the expenditure in period t for persons with zero expenditures in both $t - 1$ and $t - 2$ is about 75 percent lower than the expenditures—*evaluated at $M*1 = M*2 = 0$, the "intercept"*—of persons with positive expenditures in both prior periods.) Thus we give scant attention to individual parameter estimates; instead we emphasize below the degree to which the specification reproduces actual expenditure patterns. The more flexible specification relaxes the simplified version in two ways: the lagged expenditure variables are piecewise linear and the lagged expenditure variables are interacted with age—distinguishing persons who are younger from those who are older than 45.

Possibly the most important component of the estimates is the large residual variance. Consider a given set of right-hand variables and the associated mean expenditure. The estimated standard error of the estimate (1.644) suggests that to capture, say, 95 percent of expenditures one would have to cover the range from 0.04 to 27 times the mean.

1.2.2 Prediction and Simulation Method

The key to prediction is the distribution of random shocks. We want the distribution that is used in prediction to "match" as closely as possible the actual distribution, which is extremely skewed. Here, we use the distribution conditional on the demographic variables D and lagged expenditures. In particular, given D and 25 cells in the five-by-five matrix of $t - 1$ and $t - 2$ expenditure intervals (used in table 1.1), we randomly choose from the distribution of residuals from the two components of equation (2), using a six-year window centered at the age of the individual whose expenditures are being predicted. Given D and the expenditure history captured by M_{lag}, we follow this exact procedure: First, choose a residual from the first component of equation (2) conditional on the demographic characteristics and expenditure history (as captured by the individual's position in the five-by-five matrix discussed above). If the first component of equation (2) evaluated at the independent variables and the chosen residual is greater than 0.5, the individual is assumed to have positive expenditures. Second, and only if the individual is assumed to have positive expenditures, choose a residual from the second component of equation (2) again conditional on demographics and expenditure history. Using this selected shock, we predict the magnitude of expenditure for those assumed to have positive expenditure.

The goal here is not to obtain "behavioral" estimates of marginal effects of predictor variables. Instead, we seek a prediction procedure that captures both the dynamic and cross-sectional features of health care expenditure over a lifetime. Below, we evaluate how well we have succeeded in attaining this goal.

This initial analysis has at least one potentially important limitation. It assumes that, given expenditures in $t - 1$ and $t - 2$, expenditures in prior years add no additional information about expenditures in t. Prior expenditures may, however, contribute additional information and could yield better predictions of persistence.

1.2.3   The Fit

There are at least four ways to check the extent to which the model captures the actual distribution of medical expenditures. All are based on a comparison between simulation results and the actual data. Some of the comparisons emphasize the dynamic properties of our simulation process—the degree to which the simulated expenditures capture the distribution of expenses over time. Others emphasize the extent to which the short-run model predictions capture the persistence observed in the three-year data panel. We consider the mean of expenditures by age, actual versus predicted expenditure distributions in year t given expenditures in $t - 1$ and in $t - 2$, actual versus predicted persistence over a three-year period, and the distribution of lifetime predictions at particular ages versus actual distributions at those ages.

Actual versus Predicted Means by Age

Figure 1.4 shows actual and predicted average expenditures by age for hourly and salaried males and females. The actual averages are based on the full sample of 230,497. The predicted averages are determined as follows: Begin with a sample of 1,000 employees aged 25. Then apply equations (1) and (2) repeatedly, producing a stream of expenditures for each person through age 60. The predicted averages for a given age are the averages of the predicted

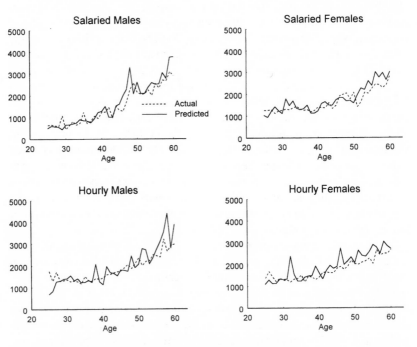

Fig. 1.4   Actual vs. predicted annual expenditures (dollars)

values at that age. Because the predicted values are based on a rather small number of persons there is more variation in the predicted than the actual averages, but the overall match seems quite close. (One might assume that any simple model—like a Tobit—would yield such a match. But because of the very skewed distributions of health expenditures this is not the case. Indeed, simple Tobit estimates yield means that are at least twice as large as the actual means.)

Actual versus Predicted Third-Year Expenditure Distributions

Figures 1.5A through 1.5D show the actual versus predicted distributions of third-year (1991) expenditures at selected ages—30, 40, 50, and 60—for hourly and salaried men and women. The predicted distribution is based on the demographic variables and expenditures for the first two years (1989 and 1990). Overall, the predicted and actual distributions are very similar.

Actual versus Predicted Persistence

Table 1.2 shows mean actual and predicted expenditures, conditional on the expenditure interval in each of the preceding two years. To illustrate, consider persons aged 36–45: for employees who had no claims in periods $t - 1$ and $t - 2$, the actual mean expenditure in period t was $1,295, compared to a predicted mean of $1,337. Overall, the predicted values capture quite well the pattern in the actual data with one exception. For individuals with spending above $5,000 in both $t - 1$ and $t - 2$, the prediction of $11,949 substantially exceeds the actual value of $9,934. Because of the very skewed distribution of shocks, random draws of very high shocks in the simulation can have a substantial effect on predicted means.

Distributions of Lifetime Predictions at Selected Ages versus
Actual Distributions

Our simulations are designed to predict the expenditures of employees over a working lifetime. The comparison above suggested that the distribution of the model predictions of third-year expenditures were very close to the actual distribution of third-year expenditures. Now we consider a comparison that is intended to test the long-run implications of the model. We start with the expenditures of a sample of persons aged 25 in 1991. Then we simulate their expenditures through age 60. We want to know in particular that the distribution of predicted expenditures approximates the actual distribution at older ages. Figures 1.6A and 1.6B show predicted versus actual distributions at ages 45 and 55. Two comparisons are made: The first compares the predicted distribution at age 45 with the distribution of the actual expenditures of persons 45 years old in our sample. The second comparison shows the distribution of predicted and actual cumulated expenditures over three years, ages 45 through 47. Overall, the distributions of predicted expenditures are very close to actual distributions. Given the small (1,000) sample used for the simulations, simula-

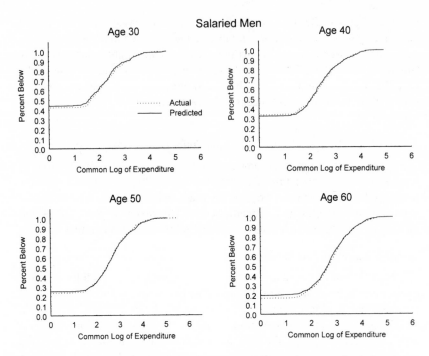

Fig. 1.5A   Actual vs. predicted third-year expenditures by age: salaried men

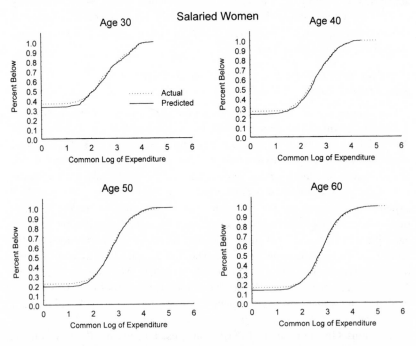

Fig. 1.5B   Actual vs. predicted third-year expenditures by age: salaried women

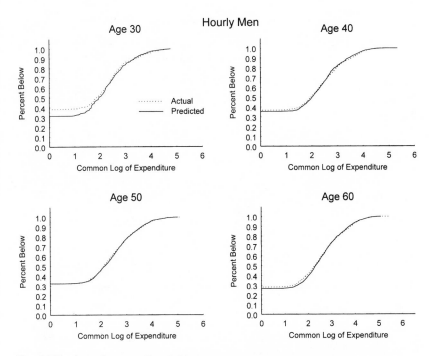

Fig. 1.5C   Actual vs. predicted third-year expenditures by age: hourly men

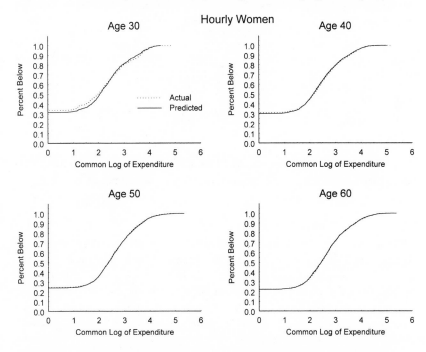

Fig. 1.5D   Actual vs. predicted third-year expenditures by age: hourly women

Table 1.2   Mean 1991 Expenditures Conditional on 1989 and 1990
                 Expenditures   (dollars)

1989 Expenditure ($)	1990 Expenditure ($)				
	0	0–300	300–1,000	1,000–5,000	Above 5,000
			Enrollees Aged 36–45		
			Actual Mean for 1991		
0	1,295	742	1,162	1,677	4,383
0–300	435	761	1,130	1,732	3,584
300–1,000	607	825	1,452	2,334	4,390
1,000–5,000	697	1,154	1,719	2,449	4,178
Above 5,000	844	1,811	2,175	4,003	9,934
			Predicted Mean for 1991		
0	1,337	727	1,206	1,828	4,153
0–300	459	780	1,199	1,797	3,751
300–1,000	639	776	1,419	2,507	5,903
1,000–5,000	1,206	1,386	1,847	2,543	4,659
Above 5,000	1,014	1,727	2,281	3,991	11,949
			Enrollees Aged 46–55		
			Actual Mean for 1991		
0	1,718	1,042	1,471	2,132	4,854
0–300	725	1,038	1,490	2,066	4,238
300–1,000	819	1,589	1,882	2,398	5,267
1,000–5,000	950	1,564	2,223	3,413	6,377
Above 5,000	1,593	2,069	2,965	4,327	10,380
			Predicted Mean for 1991		
0	1,739	991	1,477	1,998	5,824
0–300	691	1,094	1,554	2,364	4,163
300–1,000	695	1,674	1,729	2,440	4,809
1,000–5,000	1,086	1,524	2,076	3,459	7,031
Above 5,000	3,253	1,642	3,343	4,545	13,012

tions based on different samples yield somewhat different comparisons. But our experience has been that there is no appreciable difference in the overall results.

Other Validation Comparisons

Finally, we considered two additional comparisons to confirm that the persistence implications of the model were consistent with the data. Recall that the model assumes that, given expenditures in $t - 1$ and $t - 2$, expenditures in prior years add no information about expenditures in year t. But although it is likely that there is also some information contained in the pattern of expenditures in previous years, the model lag structure does imply that expenditure shocks will "last" for several years.

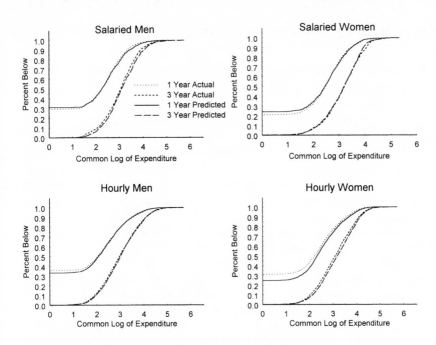

Fig. 1.6A   Actual vs. predicted life cycle distribution at age 45 by gender and employment status

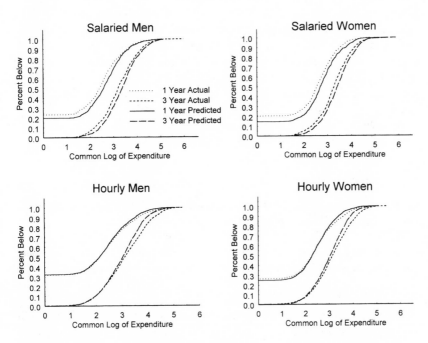

Fig. 1.6B   Actual vs. predicted life cycle distribution at age 55 by gender and employment status

First, we considered all persons with high expenditures—over $10,000 and over $15,000—at ages 35 and 45 in 1989. We then used the model to simulate their expenditures in the 10 subsequent years. We compared the predictions in the subsequent two years with the actual data. For the first two years, for which we have matching actual data, the actual and simulated means are very close. The lag structure in the model is of course a way to extrapolate the decline in expenditures to future years, and the simulations imply that after four or five years the expenditures of persons with large shocks approach the overall sample mean. The simulated and actual "decay" patterns are shown in appendix figure 1A.1.

Second, we considered the future expenditures of persons with specific 1989 diagnoses that are typically associated with high expenditures. In particular, we were concerned that the expenditure decay in these cases be consistent with the implications of the model. We considered these 1989 diagnosis: acute myocardial infarction (AMI), cancer, mental health disorder (with inpatient care), and pregnancy. Only 45 percent of 1989 AMI patients had expenditures greater than $1,000 one year later in 1990; only 34 percent had expenditures greater than $1,000 two years later in 1991. (Over 14 percent had zero expenditures in 1990, and 25 percent in 1991.) Less than 25 percent of cancer patients had expenditures over $1,000 in 1990, and only 20 percent in 1991. There was more persistence in the expenditures of inpatient mental health patients: 54 percent had expenditures over $1,000 in 1990, and 42 percent in 1991. Pregnancy is one of the most important contributors to firm health care costs, but with minimal persistence. Only 17 percent of women with pregnancy-related diagnosis in 1989 had expenditures over $1,000 in 1990, and only 13 percent in 1991. We take these results as evidence that our simulated decay rates are not unreasonable. In particular, we find no reason to suspect that they are too rapid.

We conclude that simulated expenditure patterns match closely actual expenditure patterns revealed in the three years of our data.

1.3   Simulation Results

We have simulated the lifetime expenditures of 1,000 employees who begin work at age 25 and retire at age 60. We realize that few, if any, persons would work for the same firm for that length of time, but it is the expenditure pattern that we want to capture, assuming that employees continued to face an insurance scheme like the one at this firm.

1.3.1   Distribution of Lifetime Expenditures

The distribution of cumulative expenditures at selected ages is shown in figure 1.7A. Figure 1.7B shows the concentration version of the data. Over a working lifetime, expenditures of salaried males vary from less than $10,000 (about 10 percent of employees) to over $100,000 (about 10 percent of employ-

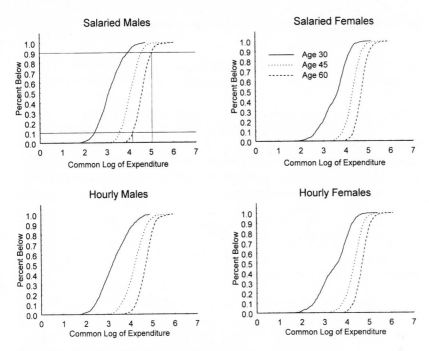

Fig. 1.7A   Simulated distribution of expenditures at various ages

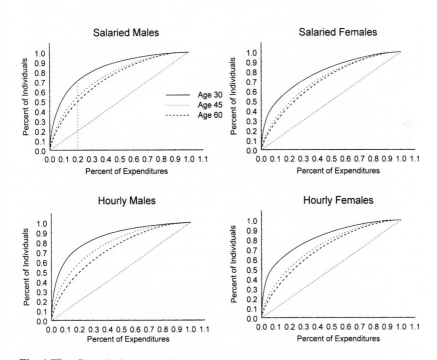

Fig. 1.7B   Cumulative expenditure concentration at various ages

ees). The median is about $32,000, as shown in figure 1.7A. The distributions for the other gender and employee status groups are similar to those for salaried males.

Figure 1.7A shows that the distribution of expenditures is much less concentrated over a lifetime than over five years (at age 30). Figure 1.1 (above) shows that in a single year about 80 percent of expenditures are accounted for by about 10 percent of employees. For salaried males, figure 1.7B shows that after five years (at age 30) about 29 percent of employees account for 80 percent of expenditures. Over a lifetime about 48 percent of employees account for 80 percent of expenditures.

1.3.2   IHA Balances

Given the distribution of expenditures described above, how might an IHA plan work? We consider this plan:

- The employer puts $2,000 in each employee's IHA at the beginning of each year.

- The health insurance plan has a $4,000 annual deductible, with expenses below the deductible paid by the employee (out of the IHA) and 100 percent of expenditures above the deductible covered by the health insurance plan. If the IHA balance goes to zero, all expenses are paid by the insurance plan.

The distribution of IHA balances at selected ages is shown in figure 1.8. Consider salaried males: After five years (at age 30), about 50 percent of men have balances close to $10,000. Only about 10 percent have balances less than about $6,000. After a lifetime, there is more variation in the IHA balances, but most employees are left with a substantial accumulation. About 90 percent of the employees have a balance at age 60 that exceeds $25,000, while 75 percent have more than $40,000 and 50 percent have more than $50,000. The distributions are similar for salaried females and for hourly employees.

Another way to understand the implications of the plan is to consider the proportion of IHA contributions that remain at selected ages. The distribution of these proportions is shown in figure 1.9. Two features of the distribution stand out: the fraction declines with age, but even at retirement the fraction remaining is large for almost all employees. At retirement, only about 20 percent of employees have less than 50 percent of their contributions, about 10 percent have less than 35 percent, and about 5 percent have less than 20 percent. And 50 percent still hold more than 70 percent of their IHA contributions.

The average balance remaining in the IHA is shown by age in figure 1.10. The fraction can be compared to the 45 degree line that represents the accumulation path if there are no withdrawals to cover health care costs. The fraction remaining is higher for salaried than for hourly employees and highest for salaried males. The average balance of salaried males is about $46,000 at age 60.

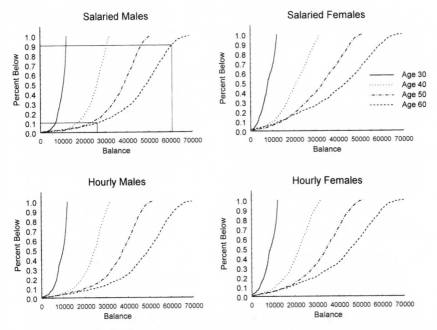

Fig. 1.8   IHA balances (dollars) at selected ages

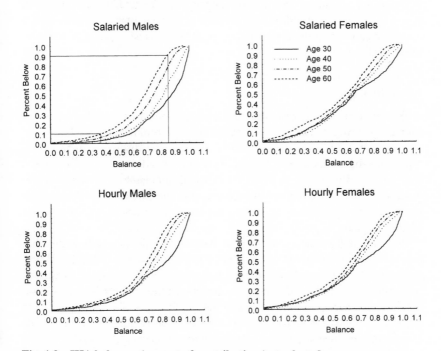

Fig. 1.9   IHA balances (percent of contributions) at selected ages

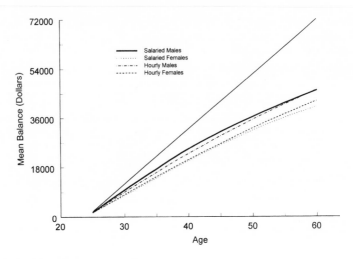

Fig. 1.10   Mean IHA balances by age

The higher average for salaried than for hourly employees may be attributed in large part to differences in plan provisions. The hourly plan provides first-dollar coverage, while the salaried plan includes copayments and a deductible. We have not accounted here for any behavioral effects. If the difference in expenditures of hourly and salaried employees is due to plan provisions, it may be an indication that the behavioral response to a catastrophic plan could be substantial as well.

1.4   Discussion

A health insurance system featuring IHAs combined with a catastrophic insurance plan would insure employees against high health care costs but would also subject a large fraction of expenditures to the discipline imparted by "spending your own money." A potential drawback of this scheme is increased risk, measured by variation in IHA balance accumulation. The variation depends critically on the lifetime distribution of health care costs. With emphasis on this issue, our goal was to present preliminary evidence on the feasibility of an IHA plan.

We developed a nonparametric method to describe the longitudinal distribution of health care expenditures in a large firm. Comparisons with actual firm data suggest that the model captures well the important features of the expenditure distribution. Using this model to simulate the lifetime distribution of individual health care costs, we evaluated the implications of variation in health care expenditures for variation in IHA balances at retirement. Although the plan would produce a range of balances across employees, approximately 80 percent of employees would retain more than 50 percent of their IHA contributions. Only about 5 percent of employees would retain less than 20 percent of their contributions. These outcomes do not appear to us to be so extreme as to make the plan a nonstarter.

To say more we need to incorporate additional components into the analysis. While we believe that such a plan would reduce medical expenses substantially, we must quantify the behavioral response that would occur as employees spend more of their own money. Rough calculations suggest that the proportion of payments subject to this restraint would increase from virtually zero to as much as 45 percent (depending on whether the payment that pushes the total over the $4,000 deductible is counted). And we believe that such a plan could be structured to increase retirement saving. The benefits of reduced health care costs and increased saving must be considered against the risk associated with increased variance in lifetime medical expenditures. Traditional insurance plans that offer near total insurance, and erect a large moral hazard along the way, dampen this variability in lifetime expenditures. By considering risk aversion and time preferences, we can address these trade-offs more formally in the context of utility analysis.

An IHA plan could have important implications for the composition and, possibly, the level of employee compensation. The overall annual cost of the firm's current health plan is around $1,400 per participant. With no behavioral effects, the IHA plan we consider would reduce this premium to around $700 per participant. Employee health care costs would increase by about $700. Assuming no reduction in other nonwage benefits, the IHA contribution of $2,000 would result in a net increase in total employee benefits of approximately $1,300. Evidence on 401(k) plans suggests that offsetting effects on other employee benefits are unclear. Many 401(k) plans were established with no apparent reductions in other components of employee compensation, at least in the short run.

The actual additional cost to be divided between the firm and its employees may be substantially lessened not only by any behavioral effect but also by the favorable tax treatment accorded to 401(k) and other retirement programs, as well as health insurance premiums. For example, if contributions to an IHA were also treated in this manner and perhaps combined with a retirement savings program, copayments and deductibles now made by employees with after-tax earnings might be replaced by payments made with pretax earnings from an IHA account.

We also need to explore variations in the structure of IHA plans to understand the implications of alternative IHA contributions, savings accumulations, and out-of-pocket expenditures. Our analysis reveals that small changes in the structure of the plan can substantially alter the "way the numbers look." For example, if the IHA contribution is made at the end of the year—and thus is not available to fund expenditures in the current year—virtually no one would be left with IHA accumulations less than 35–40 percent of their contributions (although this would generate a somewhat higher insurance premium). The results would also look quite different if the IHA contribution were $1,000 instead of $2,000.

We intend to consider all these issues more thoroughly in future work. We also plan to reestimate the parameters of our model with longer panels of expenditure data when they become available, and to consider other kinds of health plan reforms from the perspective of lifetime expenditures.

Appendix

Table 1A.1   **Model Parameter Estimates**

Variable	Linear Probability		Log Linear if Amount > 0	
	Estimate	t-Statistic	Estimate	t-Statistic
Simplified Specification				
Constant	0.831471	130.294065	5.968484	177.958314
Age	−0.001120	−9.105254	0.007943	12.126717
Sex	0.044624	5.543992	0.207343	4.951444
(Age)(Sex)	−0.000237	−1.441283	−0.003874	−4.481654
Hourly	−0.023953	−12.092770	−0.027556	−2.862969
D1	−0.449010	−184.611500	−0.542924	−33.122375
D2	−0.183226	−73.009823	−0.302466	−23.604705
D12	0.203681	69.794990	−0.748530	−60.388999
M1	0.000004	14.447127	0.000043	30.102726
M2	−0.000003	−13.460566	0.000041	9.894052
M*1	0.000001	10.385432	0.000040	60.611868
M*2	−0.000000	−2.210547	0.000028	37.152903
Piecewise Linear with Age Interaction				
Constant	0.767076	76.081033	5.218912	102.262185
Age	−0.005531	−31.751904	0.001529	1.688721
Sex	0.038068	4.781396	0.199626	4.886164
(Age)(Sex)	−0.000180	−1.105580	−0.004235	−5.019273
Hourly	−0.017851	−9.112001	−0.001713	−0.182322
D1	−0.267524	−28.154423	0.078253	1.357532
D2	−0.072295	−7.645898	0.138964	2.882726
D12	0.421501	54.552813	0.200218	5.465471
M1	0.000407	11.373989	0.001937	10.145843
$M1_{300}$	−0.000308	−6.716501	−0.001345	−5.583627
$M1_{1000}$	−0.000097	−7.018825	−0.000560	−8.153725
M2	0.000223	5.931243	0.001604	6.105962
$M2_{300}$	−0.000256	−5.280451	−0.001434	−4.221094
$M2_{1000}$	0.000030	1.989208	−0.000157	−1.449693
M*1	0.000529	19.042785	0.001386	10.339624
$M*1_{300}$	−0.000441	−12.932473	−0.000490	−3.015251
$M*1_{1000}$	−0.000088	−9.944736	−0.000868	−21.430002
M*2	0.000183	6.669677	0.000811	6.275513
$M*2_{300}$	−0.000171	−5.061111	−0.000228	−1.444769

Table 1A.1 (continued)

Variable	Linear Probability		Log Linear if Amount > 0	
	Estimate	t-Statistic	Estimate	t-Statistic
	Piecewise Linear with Age Interaction			
$M*2_{1000}$	−0.000013	−1.448336	−0.000562	−13.744969
Age45	0.131443	14.109861	0.071001	1.571068
(D1)(Age45)	−0.016230	−1.306935	0.132904	1.749148
(D2)(Age45)	−0.035120	−2.738827	0.091063	1.360564
(D12)(Age45)	−0.043627	−4.236622	0.099796	2.078911
(M1)(Age45)	0.000055	1.075926	−0.000170	−0.622411
$(M1_{300})$(Age45)	−0.000063	−0.963313	0.000211	0.616798
$(M1_{1000})$(Age45)	0.000006	0.310614	−0.000046	−0.479565
(M2)(Age45)	−0.000079	−1.587965	−0.000168	−0.477427
$(M2_{300})$(Age45)	0.000066	1.027559	0.000211	0.463816
$(M2_{1000})$(Age45)	0.000014	0.709447	−0.000034	−0.239341
(M*1)(Age45)	0.000047	1.335356	0.000065	0.381546
$(M*1_{300})$(Age45)	−0.000070	−1.623723	−0.000028	−0.136822
$(M*1_{1000})$(Age45)	0.000022	2.014475	−0.000041	−0.809818
(M*2)(Age45)	−0.000006	−0.168130	0.000305	1.868320
$(M*2_{300})$(Age45)	−0.000014	−0.317268	−0.000340	−1.710830
$(M*2_{1000})$(Age45)	0.000019	1.673649	0.000025	0.494918

Variable Definitions:

Age	Age in 1989
Sex	1 if female; 0 otherwise
(Age)(Sex)	Age interacted with Sex
Hourly	1 if hourly worker; 0 otherwise
D1	1 if no expenditures in period $t - 1$; 0 otherwise
D2	1 if no expenditures in period $t - 2$; 0 otherwise
D12	1 if no expenditures in periods $t - 1$ and $t - 2$; 0 otherwise
M1	Expenditure in $t - 1$ if no expenditure in $t - 2$
$M1_{300}$	Expenditure in $t - 1$ minus 300 if no expenditure in $t - 2$ and expenditure in $t - 1$ above 300
$M1_{1000}$	Expenditure in $t - 1$ minus 1,000 if no expenditure in $t - 2$ and expenditure in $t - 1$ above 1,000
M2	Expenditure in $t - 2$ if no expenditure in $t - 1$
$M2_{300}$	Expenditure in $t - 2$ minus 300 if no expenditure in $t - 1$ and expenditure in $t - 2$ above 300
$M2_{1000}$	Expenditure in $t - 2$ minus 1,000 if no expenditure in $t - 1$ and expenditure in $t - 2$ above 1000
M*1	Expenditure in $t - 1$ if expenditure in both $t - 1$ and $t - 2$
$M*1_{300}$	Expenditure in $t - 1$ minus 300 if expenditure in both $t - 1$ and $t - 2$ and expenditure in $t - 1$ above 300
$M*1_{1000}$	Expenditure in $t - 1$ minus 1,000 if expenditure in both $t - 1$ and $t - 2$ and expenditure in $t - 1$ above 1,000
M*2	Expenditure in $t - 2$ if expenditure in both $t - 1$ and $t - 2$
$M*2_{300}$	Expenditure in $t - 2$ minus 300 if expenditure in both $t - 1$ and $t - 2$ and expenditure in $t - 2$ above 300
$M*2_{1000}$	Expenditure in $t - 2$ minus 1,000 if expenditure in both $t - 1$ and $t - 2$ and expenditure in $t - 2$ above 1,000

(*continued*)

Table 1A.1   (continued)

Age45	1 if age in 1989 above 45; 0 otherwise
(D1)(Age45)	D1 interacted with Age45
(D2)(Age45)	D2 interacted with Age45
(D12)(Age45)	D12 interacted with Age45
(M1)(Age45)	M1 interacted with Age45
(M1$_{300}$)(Age45)	M1$_{300}$ interacted with Age45
(M1$_{1000}$)(Age45)	M1$_{1000}$ interacted with Age45
(M2)(Age45)	M2 interacted with Age45
(M2$_{300}$)(Age45)	M2$_{300}$ interacted with Age45
(M2$_{1000}$)(Age45)	M2$_{1000}$ interacted with Age45
(M*1)(Age45)	M*1 interacted with Age45
(M*1$_{300}$)(Age45)	M*1$_{300}$ interacted with Age45
(M*1$_{1000}$)(Age45)	M*1$_{1000}$ interacted with Age45
(M*2)(Age45)	M*2 interacted with Age45
(M*2$_{300}$)(Age45)	M*2$_{300}$ interacted with Age45
(M*2$_{1000}$)(Age45)	M*2$_{1000}$ interacted with Age45

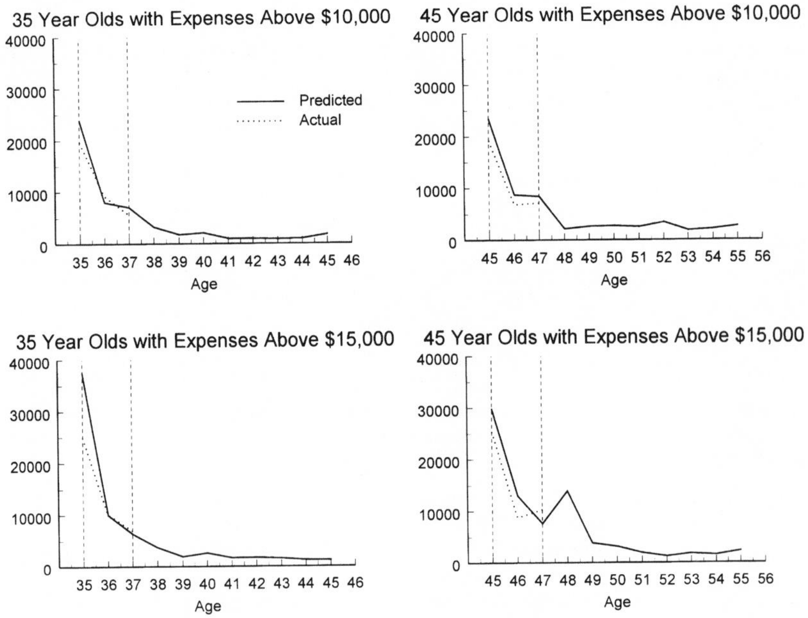

Fig. 1A.1   **Decay pattern after large shocks: salaried men**

References

Arrow, Kenneth J. 1963. Uncertainty and the welfare economics of medical care. *American Economic Review* 53:941–73.

Feldstein, Martin. 1971. A new approach to national health insurance. *Public Interest* 23:93–105.

Feldstein, Martin, and Jonathan Gruber. 1994. A major risk approach to health insurance reform. NBER Working Paper no. 4852. Cambridge, Mass.: National Bureau of Economic Research.
McClellan, Mark B., and David A. Wise. 1994. Where the money goes: Medical expenditures in a large corporation. Paper prepared for the JCER-NBER Conference on Health Care, December.

Comment   Jonathan Gruber

I really enjoyed this paper, and I think that it helps us to focus on an important debate within the health economics community. Many economists and health policy analysts are in agreement that increasing price incentives and consumer shopping will increase efficiency in health care markets. But there is considerable divergence over the point at which those price incentives should be introduced.

Traditionally, economists such as Arrow and Feldstein emphasized incentives at the *point of service,* such as through high copayment rates and deductibles. The effectiveness of this mechanism was demonstrated by the RAND Health Insurance Experiment, which found that individuals did use significantly less medical care if they faced a significant price on the margin.

More recently, however, the emphasis has shifted to price incentives at the *point of health insurance plan choice.* Rather than demand-side copayments, the Clinton plan emphasized having employees pay a larger share of their insurance premiums, to get them to shift to managed care plans, which use supply-side controls. The effectiveness of this mechanism is more questionable, however. While strictly defined HMOs do appear to have lower costs, even controlling for selection, there is little evidence that other forms of managed care have been particularly successful in lowering costs. And no form of managed care has managed to restrain cost growth, either at the level of a particular managed care institution or if one compares medical cost growth across states with more or less managed care in place.

Thus, it seems sensible to shift the focus back to demand-side cost sharing, at least to some extent. The natural way to do this is with large copayments and deductibles, but these are often viewed as politically unpalatable. An alternative, which has the same incentive properties but simply redistributes resources, is to have "individual health accounts" (IHAs). Under this plan, individuals get an account with some funds in it. They then face 100 percent of their medical costs up to some level, say $2,000. Any spending up to this level comes out of their accounts, and they get to keep the rest. Under the particular variant described by the authors, they keep it in a pensionlike savings account

Jonathan Gruber is professor of economics at the Massachusetts Institute of Technology and a faculty research fellow of the National Bureau of Economic Research.

that they get at retirement, which has the virtue of subsidizing retirement savings.

An important criticism of this plan, however, is that serial dependence in health expenditures could lead to substantial inequities in plan accumulation. That is, if individuals who are high spenders are lifetime high spenders, then they will use up their money every year and have little in their accounts at retirement. Although it is only mentioned briefly by the authors, this has potentially nasty distributional implications. Those individuals who are lifetime high spenders may be exactly the persons about whose retirement resources we are most worried, for example, because they were unable to advance in their jobs due to health problems, or because their spouses had to stay home to help with the health problems. Furthermore, these are the persons who will continue to face high expenditures when retired, given the high deductibles and copayments under the Medicare program.

So the critical question to ask in evaluating the magnitude of this redistribution is: is there such a thing as lifetime sick or healthy? Strikingly, however, we know virtually nothing about the intertemporal correlation of medical spending for an individual. I know of only one article on this subject, by Dan Feenberg and Jon Skinner, using data on catastrophic spending from tax returns, but this is very specialized data on only a limited set of spending events.

Into this critical gap jump the Eichner et al. team. The goal of their careful empirical work is exactly to measure this illusive parameter: the intertemporal correlation in medical spending. The authors do so using a unique database on medical spending at a large firm. They have information on spending for 300,000 workers over a three-year period. And they use these data to demonstrate two facts about the distribution of medical spending. First, medical spending is very concentrated at a point in time. Second, the *intertemporal* concentration is much lower than the point-in-time concentration. The raw data show that, of those who spend more than $5,000 on medical care in one year, only 20 percent spend that much two years later. And only 35 percent of those in the highest quintile of spending in one year are in that quintile two years later.

The authors then present a formal statistical model to project the persistence of expenditures. This is a two-part model, with one equation for predicting whether there is spending and one equation modeling the level of spending conditional on having expenditure. The dependent variable is the level of spending in the third year. The explanatory variables include a limited set of demographic characteristics and detailed controls for spending over the previous two years.

Their model predicts only moderate persistence over a period as long as five years, and little persistence over a lifetime. This is illustrated most graphically in appendix figure 1A.1, which shows that spending is predicted to revert rather quickly to the mean for high spenders. Overall, the authors find that, over a lifetime, 48 percent of workers account for 80 percent of expenditures, rather than the 10 percent in a single cross section. So this suggests that there will not be a problem with substantial inequities in the ultimate distribution of IHA balances.

I find this to be quite an important and provocative conclusion, and what I would like to do is offer a couple of observations or criticisms on the methods. First, the obvious limitation of the empirical work is that the authors have only three years of data to work with in projecting lifetime concentrations. The authors are aware of this limitation and ultimately hope to remedy it by adding more data. However, this may not be as important a limitation as one would initially think. Examining their appendix figures and results, one notes that most of the decay in spending happens after only one year, so that having more years of data may not be very important.

In fact, this suggests an additional specification check of their model. The authors could fit the model based on the second year of data, rather than the last year, and model spending as a function of a one-year lag only. They could then do an out-of-sample projection on the third year to see how well the model fits. This would be more convincing than the tests that they do now, since it is both truly out of sample and can be compared to actual outcomes. Another way to say this is: if a second year of lag does not add much to the fit of the model, then further years may not matter either.

On the other hand, more years could make an important difference if medical spending follows a sort of "S-s" pattern, rather than a smooth intertemporal decline. That is, individuals may have chronic illnesses that flare up, requiring expensive care every fourth year but not much in between. I do not have much insight into whether spending is more likely to be continuously high or to flare up, but presumably the team could usefully draw on Dr. McClellan's insights here as to how much of a problem this is likely to be in reality.

Second, there are a couple of specification issues with their model. One picky point is that, even though they only have a limited set of demographic variables, they do not use them as fully as possible. Given their sample size, there would be no problem including much more detailed age-by-sex categories in the model, rather than just a linear age * sex interaction. A more important point, which is recognized by the authors, is that they build in no correlation between the error terms of the 1/0 spend/don't spend equation and the level-of-spending equation. These errors are clearly correlated in an important way, and accounting for this could improve the fit of the model even further. I appreciate the difficulty of modeling this error correlation with such bizarrely distributed data, but the new innovations in nonparametric modeling of error distributions could perhaps be usefully applied here.

Third, the analysis does not incorporate any behavioral response to the IHA plan. If demand for medical care is elastic at the point of service, overall spending will fall under an IHA plan. But, at the same time, the lifetime concentration of medical expenditures may increase, if the chronically high spenders are less elastic in their responses than are low spenders. So introducing behavioral responses could exacerbate the ultimate inequities in IHA balances at retirement. This is clearly an important priority for future work with these data.

Finally, in terms of where this work goes next, I think that the authors should spend some time thinking about three critical design questions involved in an IHA-type plan. First, should this be a savings account or should individuals just get the money back at the end of the year? There are obvious advantages to structuring IHAs as savings vehicles. But one cost of doing so is that individuals may not perceive the funds left in the IHA to be as valuable as if they got the money back. This is important because the elasticity of response to this incentive may be a function of the value that individuals place on the money that they get to keep in their accounts.

This is a major concern with current cafeteria plans such as that at MIT. These plans allow individuals to put away a certain amount of money that can be used on a pretax basis for out-of-pocket medical spending during the year. But whatever is left over at the end of the year is lost to the individual. As a result, individuals with money left at the end of the year have a "wheel of fortune" mentality, either purchasing unnecessary care or substituting forward care that would have been delivered in some future year. Presumably, such a severe response would not arise with an IHA where you got the money back. But it might arise with an IHA where the money is saved, if individuals do not value those savings, which may be true for younger employees. More generally, the behavioral response to the incentives embodied in an IHA might be larger if the cash is received back directly rather than saved. So there is a trade-off here between the cost of limiting the incentive effects on medical spending and the gains from inducing increased saving by employees.

Second, should IHAs use deductibles or copayments? An alternative to individuals' paying all of their costs up to $2,000 would be to have them pay 50 percent of their costs up to $4,000. This would make individuals somewhat less sensitive to medical spending but do so over a much larger range. In my work with Martin Feldstein on behavioral responses to catastrophic health care plans, we found that the reduction in deadweight loss is larger for a copayment plan than for a deductible plan with the same maximum out-of-pocket exposure. This is because the initial increases in cost sharing have the greatest marginal reduction in deadweight loss, so spreading a moderate cost-sharing increase over a greater sensitive range is more efficient. Furthermore, we also found that the increase in risk bearing was much greater for the deductible plan. This follows obviously from the point that the total out-of-pocket exposure is the same under both plans, but individuals will spend more out of pocket on average with the deductible plan. Thus, our calculations suggest that a copayment plan dominates a deductible plan if the goal is to reduce deadweight loss while minimizing the increase in risk bearing. In future work, the authors should consider the distributional implications of copayment plans instead of deductible plans, along with building in an elasticity-of-spending response.

Finally, what other government interventions might be necessary in an IHA world? It is worth noting that there is little use of very high deductible plans in practice. There are two obvious reasons for this. One is the tax subsidy to employer-provided insurance, which distorts individual preferences toward more generous insurance plans. The other is the possibility of supplemental insurance purchase, which could undo the spending incentives put into place by a catastrophic-type plan. If an IHA is to be an effective means of controlling spending, some type of restriction on the use of such supplemental plans may have to be put in place.

To conclude, let me highlight my belief that this line of research has the potential to help guide the policy agenda on IHAs. And I urge the authors to continue to update and improve their vast array of data in order to confirm and extend their interesting results.

2   What Is Technological Change?

David M. Cutler and Mark B. McClellan

The rising cost of health care has been among the most vexing problems facing the public sector in the past three decades. Spending on health care accounts for nearly 20 percent of federal revenues and a similar share of state and local revenues. With real per capita health costs increasing by 4 to 5 percent annually, understanding the determinants of health care cost growth has become a substantial public concern.

Efforts to limit cost growth in the public sector have typically focused on price mechanisms. By lowering rates for the services it pays for, the federal government has hoped to limit overall reimbursement for medical care. And yet health costs continue to rise. Real per enrollee Medicare costs increased by over 6 percent annually between 1991 and 1993.

In this paper we explore the causes of this cost growth in detail. We begin with a discussion of the growth of inpatient Medicare costs. We show that the price that Medicare pays for admissions has been falling over time but the technological intensity of the treatment has been increasing. Since more intensive technologies are reimbursed at a higher rate than less intensive technologies, the growth of technology is at least partly responsible for the growth of Medicare costs.

To gain further insights into these trends, we then turn to a detailed analysis of expenditure growth for one particular condition—acute myocardial infarctions (AMIs), or heart attacks, in elderly Medicare beneficiaries. Section 2.2

David M. Cutler is professor of economics at Harvard University and a research associate of the National Bureau of Economic Research. Mark B. McClellan is assistant professor of economics and medicine at Stanford University and a faculty research fellow of the National Bureau of Economic Research.

The authors are grateful to Jeff Geppert, Helen Levy, and Elaine Rabin for exceptional research assistance, to Jon Gruber for helpful comments, and to the National Institute on Aging for research support.

reviews the technical details of AMI treatment and reimbursement. The technologies used in treating AMI have progressed dramatically in the past decade. In the early 1980s, treatment for heart attacks consisted principally of medical management of the patient, primarily involving monitoring techniques, pharmacologic interventions, and counseling. During the 1980s, several new intensive technologies were implemented widely. These technologies, including cardiac catheterization, coronary artery bypass surgery, and coronary angioplasty, have had major consequences for patient treatment. In section 2.3, we quantify their effects on Medicare expenditures. In 1984, about 11 percent of people with a heart attack received one or more of these intensive treatments. Over the next seven years, the use of these treatments nearly quadrupled. As a result, even though the price of particular treatments for AMIs was constant or even falling, spending on heart attacks rose by 4 percent annually.

In section 2.4, we begin to develop evidence on the nature of this technological change by comparing the growth of technology across metropolitan statistical areas (MSAs). We consider a common contention—that new and cheaper technologies will substitute for older and more expensive technologies and thus lower costs. The most recent innovation for AMI treatment, angioplasty, is substantially cheaper than bypass surgery; thus, substitution of angioplasty for bypass surgery could potentially reduce cost growth. Looking across MSAs, however, we find no evidence that areas with more rapid growth of angioplasty have had less rapid growth of bypass surgery. We thus conclude that angioplasty has added significantly to the cost of AMI treatment by extending intensive interventions to a larger segment of AMI patients. We then look across MSAs to see whether some MSAs are technology "leaders" and others are "followers." We find evidence that this is the case. Areas in which bypass surgery was more prevalent in 1984 are the first to adopt angioplasty, and they use this procedure more often.

In section 2.5, we begin to explore the sources of intensity growth within geographic areas by considering the contribution of technology acquisition by hospitals to intensity growth. We find that technology diffusion to new facilities accounts for much intensity growth but that more frequent use of intensive technologies within hospitals is also important, especially for the continued growth of relatively "established" technologies such as bypass surgery.

We conclude our exploration of technological change in the management of AMI in the elderly with a review of some of the questions raised by our preliminary studies, suggesting a potential agenda for further research on the determinants of technological change in health care.

2.1 The Sources of Medicare Cost Increases

Figure 2.1 shows the growth of Medicare hospital payments per beneficiary from 1968 through 1993. The figure is concerning from the perspective of federal expenditures. From 1965 to the early 1980s, Medicare paid hospitals

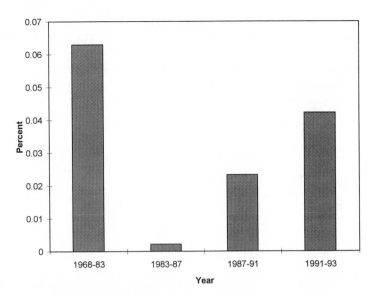

Fig. 2.1   Growth in real spending per beneficiary, Medicare inpatient services
Source: Prospective Payment Assessment Commission (1994).

on a retrospective, cost-plus basis. Generally, hospitals reported the costs of treating each patient and were reimbursed that amount.[1] Real payments per beneficiary grew rapidly during this period, at an annual rate of over 6 percent. By the early 1980s, it was apparent that a new payment system was needed. As a result, in fiscal year 1984 the federal government began paying for Medicare admissions on a more prospective basis, termed the Prospective Payment System (PPS).[2]

Under PPS, all admissions are grouped into one of roughly 470 diagnosis-related groups (DRGs)—a collection of related diagnoses, for example, "circulatory disorders with acute myocardial infarction and cardiovascular complications." DRGs are assigned a relative weight, reflecting the cost of treating patients in that DRG compared to the national average cost of a hospital admission. Circulatory disorders with AMI and cardiovascular complications, for example, has a relative weight in 1995 of 1.60. Reimbursement is the product of the DRG weight and the hospital's update factor:

(1) $\text{Reimbursement/patient}_{i,h} = \text{Weight}_i \cdot \text{Update}_h$.

1. The system was more complicated than this; for example, hospital payments for specific services were subject to "reasonable cost" regulation, and reimbursement for capital costs was also regulated. But hospitals had relatively few incentives to limit costs.
2. See Cutler (1995b) for a more detailed description of the implementation of prospective payment.

The update factor is on the order of $4,000 per DRG unit for a typical hospital.[3] Thus, a typical hospital would receive about $6,400 for the circulatory disorder patient noted above. Hospitals receive approximately the same payment for all patients in a given DRG, regardless of what services they perform.

It was hoped that prospective payment would solve the budget problem. Total reimbursement is given by

$$(2) \qquad \text{Reimbursement}_h = \sum_{\text{patients}} \text{Weight}_i \cdot \text{Update}_h.$$

By controlling the update factor, the government can, in principle, control the growth of total spending.[4] As figure 2.1 shows, however, this has not been the case. While real cost growth was low for several years after the implementation of PPS, in recent years cost growth has again accelerated.

Table 2.1 presents evidence on why Medicare payments have increased. The first column shows the growth of reimbursement per discharge.[5] Reimbursement growth was very rapid in 1984 and then slowed substantially in the next several years. In the late 1980s and early 1990s, cost growth accelerated.

The rapid increase in payments has *not* been because of increases in the update factor. As the second column of table 2.1 shows, the real update factor has been zero or negative almost every year since prospective payment was implemented. The reason for cost increases, in contrast, has been that the average patient has been in increasingly higher weighted DRGs over time. The average DRG weight of Medicare admissions (the first term in eq. [2]) is known as the "case-mix index" and is displayed in the third column of table 2.1. The case-mix index has grown at 2 to 3 percent annually since the middle of the 1980s.

There are two principal reasons for the increase in case-mix index over time. The first is termed "upcoding"—the incentive for hospitals to place patients into higher weighted DRGs and thus receive greater reimbursement. Several studies suggested that upcoding of patients was a substantial part of the dramatic increase in DRG weights associated with the implementation of prospective payment.[6]

---

3. There are additional payments for teaching hospitals, hospitals that care for the poor, capital costs, and patients that are large outliers in terms of resources, but the text describes the most important part of reimbursement.

4. Note that this refers only to inpatient spending. Any substitution in the site of care—e.g., moving rehabilitation services out of the hospital, shifting psychiatric patients to separate facilities, or increasing use of outpatient surgeries—will show up as lower inpatient costs but increases in other spending.

5. The difference between this column and fig. 2.1 is the share of beneficiaries who are hospitalized in a given year. In the first several years after PPS was adopted, the admission rate fell by 3 percent annually. Since then, the reduction in admissions has been less dramatic.

6. E.g., Carter and Ginsberg (1985) and Carter, Newhouse, and Relles (1990) estimated that over one-third of the case-mix index increase in the first few years of PPS was due to the "creep" of patients whose treatment did not change into more complex DRGs, principally from DRGs without complicating conditions to DRGs with a specified set of complicating conditions. Indeed, the sense that much of the growth of costs was due to DRG upcoding was one reason for the extremely low increase in the update factor in the 1986–88 period.

Table 2.1   **Sources of Medicare Inpatient Hospital Cost Increases**

Year	Reimbursement/ Discharge (%)	Update (%)	Case-Mix Index (%)
1984	14.2	0.3	–
1985	6.8	0.8	5.6
1986	0.7	−2.1	2.9
1987	2.1	−2.0	2.6
1988	2.0	−2.4	3.5
1989	2.2	−1.1	2.7
1990	1.8	0.3[a]	2.2
1991	1.9	−0.4	2.7
1992	2.1	0.2	1.9

Source: Prospective Payment Assessment Commission (1995).
Note: Costs and update are in real terms relative to the GDP deflator.
[a]Reflects 1.22 percent across-the-board reduction in DRG weights.

The second reason for increases in the case-mix index, and the one we focus on most heavily, is technological change. While reimbursement within a DRG does not depend on an individual patient's costs, DRGs do distinguish between patients who receive surgery and those who do not. Surgical DRGs generally have higher weights than medical DRGs for similar patients. As a result, when more patients receive intensive surgical treatments, the case-mix index will increase, as will Medicare payments. This is particularly important because technological change has been an integral feature of the U.S. health system for the past 50 years (Newhouse 1992).

We illustrate how technological change may affect growth of Medicare payments using treatment for AMIs (heart attacks) in the elderly.

2.2 AMI Treatments and Reimbursement: Technical Background

Acute myocardial infarction (AMI) exemplifies technological change in health care. AMI is a common condition in the elderly (about 230,000 new cases per year), the cost involved is substantial (over $10,000 per case in one-year hospital costs alone), and treatment involves a variety of intensive technologies with important cost implications. In addition, patients diagnosed with an AMI will always be hospitalized, so there are no consequential issues of changes in the site of care.

We divide AMI treatments into four groups of treatment intensity. Figure 2.2 shows a schematic diagram of AMI treatments, and table 2.2 shows the intensity groups and principal DRGs with which they are associated. The least invasive treatment for an AMI patient is medical management (the lower part of fig. 2.2). This typically involves drug therapy, monitoring, and (in the longer run) counseling and treatment for reducing risk factors such as high cholesterol levels and smoking. Medical management of AMI leads to one of three DRG classifications, based on the patient's health characteristics: circulatory disor-

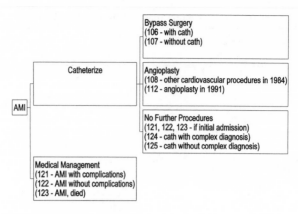

Fig. 2.2   Treatment of heart attacks

Table 2.2   Reimbursement for Patients with AMI, 1984 and 1991

| Treatment | DRG | Weight | | Change (% |
		1985	1991	
Medical management	121 Circulatory disorders with AMI and cardiovascular complications	1.8454	1.6210	−12
	122 Circulatory disorders with AMI without cardiovascular complications	1.3509	1.1667	−14
	123 Circulatory disorders with AMI, expired	1.1242	1.3920	24
Catheterization	124 Circulatory disorders (no AMI) with catheterization and complex diagnosis	2.1969	1.1973	−46
	125 Circulatory disorders (no AMI) with catheterization without complex diagnosis	1.6284	0.7387	−55
Bypass surgery	106 Coronary bypass with catheterization	5.2077	5.4470	−5
	107 Coronary bypass without catheterization	3.9476	4.9616	26
Angioplasty	108 Cardiothoracic procedures except valve and bypass, with pump	4.3301		
	112 Percutaneous cardiovascular procedures		2.0163	−53

Source: Prospective Payment Assessment Commission (1985, 1991).

ders with AMI and cardiovascular complications (DRG 121); circulatory disorders with AMI without cardiovascular complications (DRG 122); and circulatory disorders with AMI, expired (DRG 123). As table 2.2 shows, the weight of DRG 121 declined from 1.85 to 1.62, and the weight of DRG 122 declined from 1.35 to 1.17—roughly 12 to 14 percent. The weight of DRG 123 increased during this period, from 1.12 to 1.39.

An alternative to "medical" management of an AMI is to use one or more invasive cardiac procedures (the upper branch of fig. 2.2). Invasive treatment begins with a *cardiac catheterization,* a diagnostic procedure that involves inserting a catheter into the entrance of the blood vessels supplying the heart and injecting dye. This procedure documents areas of no flow or limited flow, which may be involved in the current or possible subsequent AMIs. Performing a cardiac catheterization requires a specialized cardiac catheterization laboratory, with dedicated equipment and a specially trained staff of cardiologists and cardiac nurses.

Reimbursement for patients who undergo a catheterization is somewhat complicated. If a patient receives a catheterization during initial AMI admission, reimbursement is in one of the AMI DRGs noted above (121, 122, or 123). If a patient is readmitted specifically for a catheterization, the readmission is reimbursed in DRG 124 or 125—circulatory disorders (no AMI) with catheterization with/without complex diagnosis. As table 2.2 shows, the weights for both of these DRGs declined substantially between 1984 and 1991—by about 50 percent.

If the catheterization procedure detects important blockages in the arteries supplying the heart, more intensive *revascularization* procedures may be used to treat the blockages. The first, older technology is coronary artery bypass graft (CABG) surgery. CABG is a highly intensive, open-heart surgical procedure that involves grafting arteries or leg veins to bypass occluded or near-occluded regions of the heart's blood flow. A more recent innovation in coronary revascularization, which is less intensive than CABG, is percutaneous transluminal coronary angioplasty (PTCA). In this procedure, a balloon-tipped catheter is inserted into the blocked artery and inflated, with the goal of restoring blood flow through the artery without having to undertake open-heart surgery.[7]

Patients who receive bypass surgery are placed in DRG 106 or 107, which are defined exclusively for patients who undergo CABG (the DRGs differ in whether catheterization was or was not performed on the same admission). DRG 106 had weights of 5.21 in 1984 and 5.45 in 1991, far above either medical management or catheterization without further surgical procedures.

Reimbursement for angioplasty (PTCA) has a more complex regulatory history, reflecting its relatively recent development. In 1984, angioplasty was a

---

7. Sometimes, PTCA procedures are performed in association with stent placement (i.e., the insertion of a mesh tube into reopened artery to help prevent the artery from closing off again).

virtually new procedure. Patients who underwent angioplasty were placed in DRG 108—cardiothoracic procedures except valve and bypass, with pump—which included a variety of other invasive cardiac procedures, most of which were more intensive than angioplasty. The DRG weight, 4.33 in 1985, was high relative to average resource requirements for performing angioplasty. As angioplasty became more common, Medicare officials realized it was substantially overreimbursed. In fiscal year 1986, angioplasty was moved into DRG 112, with a much lower weight of 2.02 in 1991. Even with this lower weight, however, angioplasty is still reimbursed considerably more than medical management of AMI or catheterization without additional surgery. Thus, increases in the rate of angioplasty over time will lead to increases in Medicare spending, provided they result from use of angioplasty in patients who would have been treated medically rather than with CABG.

2.3 AMI Treatments and Reimbursement, 1984–91

To examine the effects of these technological changes on Medicare costs, we assembled a data set consisting of essentially all elderly Medicare beneficiaries admitted with an AMI between 1984 and 1991. The data set was created in several steps.[8]

We began with all hospital claims for every Medicare beneficiary who had an AMI in this time period. We excluded nonelderly patients, patients treated in HMOs, patients who did not have continuous Medicare enrollment following their AMIs (unreliable claims data), patients who were treated for their AMIs outside acute care U.S. hospitals, and patients whose lengths of stay (less than five days, discharged to home alive) made it very unlikely that they had "true" AMIs. We used reported procedure codes to identify use of cardiac procedures and secondary diagnoses at the time of initial AMI admission to identify complicating conditions preceding the AMI. We used unique patient identifiers to link all hospital admissions for each patient over time, enabling us to identify the most intensive cardiac treatment received by each patient in the 90-day episode of care after the AMI. On average there were about 230,000 new AMI patients admitted each year; this cohort size declined slightly during the time period of the study. Table 2.3 shows the number of patients by year.

Our data also contain information on the DRG assignment for each admission and on the total DRG payments (including any outlier payments and hospital-specific adjustments) for each admission. We use this information to determine the total hospital payments for each patient in the year after AMI and to determine the total weight of the DRG payments (without outlier and hospital-specific adjustments). For this section, we concentrate on reimburse-

---

8. These data were assembled as part of a larger project on the costs and benefits of intensive medical treatment in the elderly. See McClellan and Newhouse (1994) and McClellan, McNeil, and Newhouse (1994) for more detail.

Table 2.3   **Number of Observations**

Year	Number
1984	233,295
1985	233,898
1985	223,589
1987	227,925
1988	223,199
1989	218,269
1990	221,167
1991	227,182

Source: Authors' calculations.

ment information for patients treated in 1984 and 1991. We analyze payments for hospital stays only; spending for physician services and outpatient services are not included. Measuring these costs involves linking together a much more extensive set of patient records, which we have not yet attempted.

Table 2.4 documents how DRG weights translate into reimbursement for AMI patients and how reimbursement for the different intensity groups has changed over time. AMI patients tend to receive intensive cardiac procedures soon after the AMI occurs. Nonetheless, treatment for even an acute health shock such as AMI involves a series of decisions over time involving not only procedure use but also decisions about transfers and readmissions after the patient initially presents with AMI. Because DRG payments are admission based, the weights of AMI-related DRGs as well as number and DRG weights of subsequent admissions affect cumulative payments.

To determine the contribution of these effects to the growth in AMI reimbursement, we grouped all admissions during the year after AMI into DRG categories corresponding to our AMI treatment intensity categories, plus a residual category consisting of all other admissions. The change in reimbursement for each AMI treatment intensity group depends on the change in the frequency of admissions and the change in DRG weight for each type of admission.

The first row of table 2.4 shows that patients who receive only medical management averaged around 1.1 admissions in a medical management AMI DRG in both 1984 and 1991, just over half of their total admissions in the year dating from their AMI. The average cumulative DRG weight of the admissions for patients with medical management increased slightly, from 2.61 to 2.87, between 1984 and 1991. This increase was due entirely to a somewhat higher number and intensity of non-AMI admissions for these AMI patients.

The second row of table 2.4 shows the corresponding admission pattern for patients treated with catheterization but no revascularization procedures after AMI. The medical management AMI DRGs were also the most important determinant of payments in this treatment intensity group. DRGs related to cathe-

Table 2.4   Average Admissions and DRG Weights for Patients with AMI

Treatment	1984 AMI Patients						1991 AMI Patients						Change, 1984–91					
	All Admits	Admits in Specific Types of DRGs					All Admits	Admits in Specific Types of DRGs					All Admits	Admits in Specific Types of DRGs				
		Med	Cath	CABG	PTCA	Other		Med	Cath	CABG	PTCA	Other		Med	Cath	CABG	PTCA	Other
1. Medical management																		
Admits	1.94	1.12	0.02	0.01	0.00	0.80	2.05	1.08	0.02	0.01	0.01	0.94	0.11	−0.04	0.00	0.00	0.01	0.14
Weight	2.61	1.62	0.03	0.05	0.01	0.90	2.87	1.56	0.02	0.06	0.02	1.20	0.26	−0.06	−0.01	0.01	0.01	0.30
2. Catheterization																		
Admits	2.55	1.31	0.34	0.04	0.02	0.83	2.43	1.23	0.16	0.03	0.05	0.95	−0.12	−0.08	−0.18	−0.01	0.03	0.12
Weight	3.88	1.96	0.62	0.18	0.08	1.05	3.63	1.74	0.17	0.15	0.10	1.47	−0.25	−0.22	−0.45	−0.03	0.03	0.42
3. Bypass surgery (CABG)																		
Admits	2.83	0.91	0.10	0.97	0.01	0.85	2.66	0.68	0.06	0.90	0.04	0.98	−0.17	−0.23	−0.04	−0.07	0.03	0.13
Weight	7.03	1.36	0.18	4.36	0.04	1.10	7.93	0.96	0.06	4.75	0.08	2.09	0.90	−0.40	−0.12	0.39	0.04	0.99
4. Angioplasty (PTCA)																		
Admits	2.48	0.65	0.16	0.03	1.07	0.57	2.61	0.59	0.11	0.04	1.09	0.78	0.13	−0.06	−0.06	0.01	0.02	0.21
Weight	6.62	0.95	0.29	0.15	4.63	0.60	4.52	0.81	0.11	0.23	2.20	1.17	−2.10	−0.14	−0.18	0.07	−2.43	0.57

Note: The weight is the average cumulative DRG weight for patients receiving that treatment.

terization accounted for a weight of 0.62 in 1984 but fell to 0.17 by 1991. In part, this fall was the result of a trend toward performing catheterization earlier after AMI. In 1984, almost one-third of patients treated with catheterization only were initially admitted in a medical management AMI DRG and subsequently readmitted in a catheterization DRG. By 1991, about one-seventh of patients followed this admission pattern; the remainder were treated with catheterization on their initial admission and thus only were admitted in the medical management AMI DRGs. Coupling this trend in admissions with the reduction in DRG weights for both medical management and catheterization outside of an AMI, the result was a substantial reduction in payment for patients receiving only catheterization; this reduction was only partially offset by more intensive admissions in other categories.[9]

The last two rows of table 2.4 describe treatment and reimbursement patterns for patients receiving catheterization and revascularization. The cumulative DRG weight for patients receiving bypass increased, as a result of an increase in the average DRG weight for admissions in CABG DRGs and an increase in the intensity of admissions in the "other" DRG category (principally more use of other intensive surgical procedures). The net result of these changes was 10 percent growth in the average DRG weight for AMI patients receiving bypass, with a corresponding increase in payments for these patients. In contrast, the DRG weight for AMI patients receiving angioplasty declined by over 40 percent, from 6.62 in 1984 (a level near that of bypass surgery) to 4.52 in 1991. This reduction was entirely attributable to the reduced weight of the DRG associated with angioplasty.

Table 2.5 summarizes how these DRG weights translate into Medicare payments per AMI patient in 1984 and 1991. As the first row shows, average spending on AMIs was $11,175 in 1984 and $14,722 in 1991 (both in $1991), implying an annual growth rate of 4.1 percent. By comparison, average spending per Medicare beneficiary was $2,581 in 1984 and $3,226 in 1991, an annual growth rate of 3.2 percent.

This growth in treatment costs is substantial. With about 230,000 admissions annually, total reimbursement for heart attacks alone rose from $2.6 billion in 1984 to $3.4 billion in 1991, an increase of $0.8 billion. This is nearly 10 percent of the increase in all Medicare inpatient spending over this period. Indeed, Medicare spending on heart attacks alone was a third of the total amount that Medicaid spent on poor children in 1991.

The substantial increase in AMI reimbursement occurred despite falling or flat DRG weights for all categories of intensive treatment, suggesting that shifts in the probabilities of treatment in each intensity category were the key factors in the growth of AMI expense in the past decade. To demonstrate this hypothesis, we decompose spending growth into prices and quantities of procedures.

---

9. In addition, as we discuss below, many more hospitals are performing catheterizations; fewer patients must be transferred (and hence readmitted) to undergo the procedure.

Table 2.5   Growth in Spending for AMIs, 1984–91

Measure	Year		Annual Percentage Change
	1984	1991	
Average reimbursement ($)	11,175	14,772	4.1
Average reimbursement by treatment ($)			
None	9,829	10,783	1.3
Catheterization	15,380	13,716	−1.6
PTCA	25,841	17,040	−5.9
CABG	28,135	32,117	1.9
Price index ($)	14,981	14,772	−0.2
Share of patients by treatment[a] (%)			
None	88.7	59.4	−4.2
Catheterization	5.5	15.5	1.4
PTCA	0.9	12.0	1.6
CABG	4.9	13.0	1.2
Resource index ($)	12,047	14,772	2.9

Note: Costs for 1984 are in 1991 dollars, adjusted using the GDP deflator.
[a]Growth is average percentage point change each year.

We begin with the identity that spending per AMI is the product of the price of each type of procedure, $P_{i,t}$, and the share of patients that receive that procedure, $q_{i,t}$:

(3)
$$\text{Spend/AMI}_t = \sum_{i=1}^{T} P_{i,t} \cdot q_{i,t}.$$

In our case, there are four possible treatments ($T = 4$).

The middle block of table 2.5 shows average reimbursement for patients with each treatment, and the bottom block shows the share of patients receiving each treatment, in 1984 and 1991. The real price of treatment for patients whose AMI was medically managed rose by only 1.3 percent annually. As table 2.4 indicated, the real price of treatment *fell* substantially for patients who received invasive cardiac procedures. Reimbursement for patients who received catheterization only fell by 1.6 percent annually, reflecting the reduction in DRG weights and increased occurrence of catheterizations during the first admission. Reimbursement for PTCA fell by 5.9 percent annually. Reimbursement for CABG rose, but by only 1.9 percent annually.

We form a "price index" for AMI using equation (3). Holding quantities constant, the price index is given by

$$\text{Price index}_t = \sum_{i=1}^{T} P_{i,t} \cdot q_{i,\bar{t}},$$

where $\tilde{t}$ is quantity in some base year. Using 1991 quantities as weights suggests a price decline of 0.2 percent annually.[10] This decline reflects the real reductions in the update factor, the regulatory changes in DRG relative weights, and the changes in admission patterns for AMI patients we have described.

In contrast to the price reductions, there was a dramatic increase in the utilization of high-tech procedures. As figure 2.3 and the bottom panel of table 2.5 show, catheterization rates, bypass surgery rates, and angioplasty rates rose consistently throughout our study period. The share of patients receiving a catheterization rose from 11 percent to 41 percent, an increase of nearly 300 percent. The share of patients receiving bypass surgery nearly tripled, and the share of patients receiving angioplasty rose 10-fold. Indeed, as figure 2.3 shows, the increase in quantity of care was essentially continuous over this period.

Analogous to the price index, we can form an index of real resource intensity from equation (3) by holding prices constant and evaluating the change in quantities:

$$\text{Resource index}_t = \sum_{i=1}^{T} P_{i,\tilde{t}} \cdot q_{i,t}.$$

Using reimbursement levels in 1991 as the index prices, average resource intensity rose by 2.9 percent annually. Figure 2.4 shows resource use annually. Real resource use increased by 2 to 3 percent essentially each year.

Changes in $q_{i,t}$ and thus in the resource index reflect two factors. First, the treatment of "similar" patients over time may change. Second, the mix of patients may change; AMI patients in 1991 might be more suitable candidates for intensive procedures than AMI patients in 1984. Younger patients, for example, are more likely to receive intensive treatments than older patients. An increasing share of younger patients over time would naturally translate into an increasing procedure rate. It is important to determine the extent to which our finding of increasing resource utilization is the result of changes in the composition of patients, versus changes in procedure use for a given set of patients.

To address this issue, we classify patients along four dimensions: age (65–69, 70–74, 75–79, 80–89, and 90+), sex, race, and severity of illness. To characterize treatment of patients with poorer health status, we identified AMI patients with one or more of the following comorbid conditions noted at the time of AMI: renal disease, cerebrovascular disease, chronic pulmonary disease, diabetes, and cancer.

Table 2.6 shows information on the distribution of patients across these dem-

---

10. Using 1984 quantities as weights yields a price increase of 1 percent annually. The difference is that the large price decrease for angioplasty is essentially uncounted when initial-year quantity weights are used.

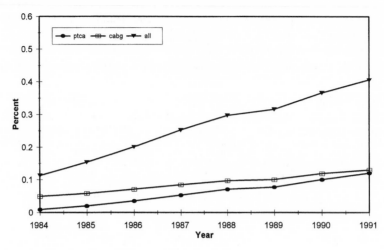

Fig. 2.3   Growth of surgical treatment for AMI

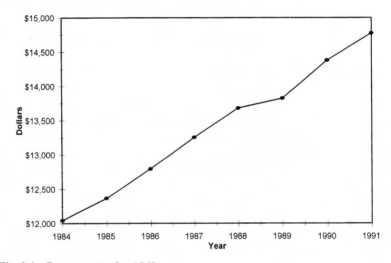

Fig. 2.4   Resource use for AMI

ographic groups. On average, the AMI population was older in 1991 than in 1984, and more likely to have a severe comorbidity reported. There was no substantial change in the sex or racial mix of the population. As the next columns show, older patients and more severely ill patients are less likely to receive intensive treatment (in this case any surgical procedure) than younger patients and patients who are less severely ill. Thus, the changes in the demographic mix of the population suggest procedure use would *fall* over time, not rise. Indeed, as the last column of the table shows, the use of intensive cardiac procedures increased in prevalence in all of the particular demographic groups we consider.

Table 2.6   Changes in the Demographic Mix of the AMI Population, 1984–91

Measure	Demographic Composition (%)			Percentage with Surgical Procedure (%)		
	1984	1991	Change (%)	1984	1991	Change (%)
Age						
65–69	23	22	−1	23	64	41
70–74	26	23	−3	15	55	40
75–79	22	22	0	7	40	33
80–89	25	28	3	2	17	15
90+	4	5	1	0	2	2
Sex						
Male	51	51	0	14	47	33
Female	49	49	0	8	34	26
Race						
Nonblack	95	94	−1	11	41	30
Black	5	6	1	7	32	25
Severity						
Not severe	74	63	−11	12	43	31
Severe	26	37	11	9	36	27

Source: Authors' calculations based on microdata for 1984 and 1991.

We can quantify this observation using the resource index noted above. Denoting by $q_{d,t}$ the share of patients in demographic group d at time t, we can rewrite the quantity index as

$$\text{Resource index}_t = \sum_{i=1}^{T}\sum_{d=1}^{D} P_{i,\bar{\imath}} \cdot q_{d,t} \cdot q_{i,d,t} .$$

We can then decompose the growth of the quantity index into three parts: the change in procedure utilization within demographic groups ($\Delta q_{i,d}$), the change in the share of the population in different demographic groups (Δq_d), and the covariance between the change in the share of patients and the change in procedure utilization

$$\Delta \text{Resource index} = \sum_{i=1}^{T}\sum_{d=1}^{D} P_{i,\bar{\imath}} \cdot \left(q_{d,0} \cdot \Delta q_{i,d} + \Delta q_d \cdot q_{i,d,0} + \Delta q_d \cdot \Delta q_{i,d} \right) .$$

The decomposition into these three terms yields the following:

Decomposition of Resource Intensity Growth

Share Due To	Amount ($)	Percentage
Total	2,711	
Intensity	3,012	111
Demographics	−114	−4
Covariance	−188	−7

Demographic change has a small negative effect on growth in resource use for AMI treatment. All of the growth in expenditures is due to increased intensity of treatment within demographic groups.

In summary: The experience of AMI in the elderly illustrates extremely well the difficulties involved in Medicare cost containment. Since the mid-1980s, reimbursement *given the level of technology* has fallen by about 0.2 percent annually. Payments for catheterization and angioplasty fell in real terms, and reimbursement for medical management and bypass surgery increased but only by a small amount. The dramatic increase in technology utilization, however, more than made up for this price reduction. The share of patients who received invasive cardiac procedures tripled, and the resource intensity of the average AMI case rose by almost 3 percent annually. Essentially all of this change was the result of increased procedure utilization for a given type of patient—within age, sex, race, and illness severity groups—rather than a shift in the distribution of patients. The result was a net increase in spending per patient of 4 percent annually.

The experience of AMI demonstrates that simply reducing hospital fees will not lead to long-run cost containment if the volume of intensive procedures continues to grow. Rather, changes in the use of technology are the key to reducing health spending.[11]

In the remainder of this paper, we present further evidence on the nature of technological change in AMI treatment. First, we examine the diffusion of intensive technologies for AMI treatment across metropolitan areas. By comparing growth rates of angioplasty and bypass, we address whether there is any evidence that the adoption of "cheaper" intensive treatments such as angioplasty leads to less expenditure growth than might otherwise have been observed, and whether there is any evidence that technology diffusion differs systematically across areas. Second, we examine the effect of technology adoption by hospitals on treatment decisions for their AMI patients. This evidence is preliminary, but it suggests that more careful analysis of the determinants of technology diffusion may lead to a better understanding of how health care cost containment can be achieved.

2.4   The Nature of Technological Change: Comparisons across Metropolitan Areas

In the previous section, we showed that *on net* technological change led to increased health costs. Some have argued, however, that the introduction of technologies such as angioplasty—a less expensive and less morbid approach to revascularization—*reduces* health cost growth. If the growth of angioplasty substituted for the growth of bypass surgery, the introduction of this technol-

---

11. See Cutler (1995a) for more discussion on the implications of this distinction for Medicare policy.

ogy would lead to lower health expenditures than if these patients had received bypass surgery. Conversely, to the extent that angioplasty patients would not have undergone bypass surgery, the adoption of angioplasty has added to expenditures.

The natural question, then, is whether the use of angioplasty substitutes for or complements the use of bypass surgery. To examine this issue, we use data on the change in the share of patients receiving each treatment in different metropolitan statistical areas (MSAs).[12] If angioplasty and bypass surgery are substitutes, then MSAs in which angioplasty grew most rapidly will have relatively slower growth in bypass surgery. If the two are complements, then growth of the two procedures will be positively correlated across MSAs.

Figure 2.5 shows the growth in the rate of bypass surgery and angioplasty in different MSAs between 1984 and 1991, using data from 247 MSAs. The data are weighted by the number of patients in 1984. The figure does not suggest a strong correlation either positively or negatively. Some MSAs (such as Sioux Falls, S.D., and Lubbock, Tex.) have very rapid growth of angioplasty and less rapid growth of bypass surgery, and others (such as Little Rock, Ark., and Savannah, Ga.) have rapid growth of bypass surgery but not of angioplasty. On net, however, there appears to be little relation between the growth of the two procedures. Indeed, the correlation is only $-.03$. There is therefore no evidence that the growth of angioplasty has led to a reduction in bypass surgery, and thus a cost savings.

In addition, we can use area-level comparisons to examine two alternative views of technology diffusion. One is that some areas are technological "leaders" and others are "followers." The leading areas of innovation—for example, areas with major medical facilities and major metropolitan areas—adopt technologies first, then "follower" areas catch up. In this scenario, to understand why technological change is so rapid we would need to understand the incentives of the leaders—why they choose to innovate, in what directions they choose to innovate—and of followers—why they choose to imitate, and whom they choose to imitate.

An alternative view is that areas "specialize" differently. This hypothesis suggests that different areas will innovate in different ways, either as a result of an active effort to set themselves apart or as a result of different "random walks" in technology adoption. For example, cardiologists in some areas may concentrate on developing innovations in bypass surgery, or may happen to have a good series of experiences with patient outcomes, while cardiologists in other areas may have better experiences with medical management or angi-

---

12. The comparisons in this paper are based on simple population means; they are not "adjusted" for demographic differences across MSAs. We plan to estimate more general models in future work, but we have no reason to expect that these adjustments will have any substantial effect on our results. Like previous investigators, we find little variation in the demographic composition of AMI patients across MSAs. Moreover, in the previous section we demonstrated that technological growth has been a general phenomenon, not confined to any particular demographic groups.

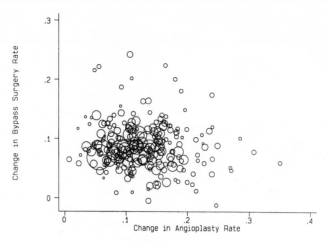

Fig. 2.5   Growth of bypass and angioplasty, 1984–91

oplasty. If this scenario is correct, we need to understand the incentives or historical accidents driving different areas to specialize in different treatments, and how one treatment comes to dominate another. Differentiating between these two views is clearly essential to our understanding of the dynamics of technological change.

As a first pass at these alternative hypotheses, table 2.7 shows the correlation of technological utilization in different areas in 1984 and 1991. Consider in particular the correlation between bypass surgery and angioplasty. If some areas are technological leaders, the rates of these two procedures will be positively correlated. If areas specialize in new technologies, however, the procedure rates will be negatively correlated. As table 2.7 shows, rates of bypass surgery and angioplasty are strongly positively correlated in both 1984 (.437) and 1991 (.359). The implication is that the same areas are more advanced in the use of both technologies.

Indeed, using the dynamic aspect of the data, we can address this question in more detail. Since angioplasty was essentially new in 1984, we can examine which areas applied this technology most rapidly over the 1984–91 period. We divide MSAs into three groups: (1) those that were most technologically advanced (defined as bypass surgery rates of at least 5 percent—roughly the mean level in 1984); (2) those that were "medium technology" areas (defined as catheterization rates of at least 5 percent but bypass surgery rates below 5 percent); and (3) those that were least technologically advanced (the remaining areas).

Figure 2.6 shows the growth of angioplasty rates for these three areas. While all three areas had increases in the rate of angioplasty over time, the figure shows a clear positive relation between initial rates of technology utilization and subsequent growth of angioplasty. In 1984, angioplasty rates were essen-

Table 2.7   **Correlation of Technologies across Areas**

Technology	Catheterization	PTCA	CABG
1984			
Catheterization	1.000		
PTCA	.502	1.000	
CABG	.621	.437	1.000
1991			
Catheterization	1.000		
PTCA	.471	1.000	
CABG	.369	.359	1.000

Note: The correlations are for 247 MSAs and are weighted by the number of AMIs in that MSA and year.

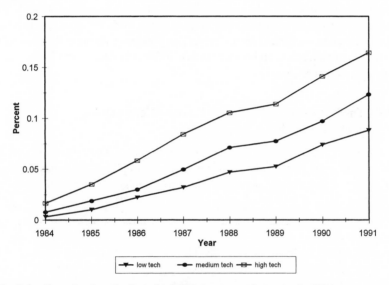

Fig. 2.6   Growth of angioplasty by MSA treatment intensity in 1984

tially equal (and close to zero) in all areas. By 1988, high-technology areas had angioplasty rates that were close to 4 percentage points above medium-technology areas and about 6 percentage points greater than low-technology areas. The data strongly suggest that a model of leaders and followers is more appropriate than one of specialization of technology.

What makes certain areas technology leaders, and what determines how closely other areas follow? Examining this issue in detail is beyond our scope here, but we do consider one simple explanation. It is commonly asserted that major teaching centers are the leaders in technological innovation and that other areas simply follow the teaching centers.

To examine this hypothesis, we first developed a definition of "major teaching areas": the 14 U.S. cities with at least 1,000 medical residents in 1990.

These areas are common to most lists of innovative practice in medicine: Atlanta, Baltimore, Boston, Chicago, Cleveland, Dallas, Detroit, Los Angeles, Nassau–Suffolk County, New York, Philadelphia, Pittsburgh, St. Louis, and Washington, D.C. We then divided our MSA sample into three groups based on distance to a teaching center: (1) within 20 miles of a major teaching center (about 20 percent of the patients); (2) between 20 and 250 miles (about 50 percent of the patients); and (3) over 250 miles (about 30 percent of the patients).

Figure 2.7 shows the growth of angioplasty in each of these three areas. The most striking conclusion is that technological change does *not* appear to be most rapid in areas with the most teaching hospitals. Indeed, major teaching centers are, if anything, less likely to perform angioplasty than are areas farther away. Clearly, other factors mediate the extent of technology diffusion. We intend to explore these factors more fully in future work. Previous research has shown that one important factor is technology adoption decisions by particular hospitals in each MSA, and we turn to evidence on the role of hospital technology adoption decisions now.

2.5   The Nature of Technological Change: Comparisons across Hospitals

Hospitals cannot provide high-tech care if they do not have the capability to do so. Performance of cardiac catheterization, angioplasty, and bypass surgery at a hospital each requires substantial investment in specialized equipment and

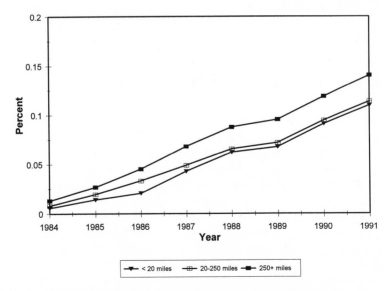

Fig. 2.7   Growth of angioplasty by proximity to major teaching center

staffing by medical and nursing personnel with the technical expertise to perform the procedure. Thus, any examination of technological change must involve hospital-level analysis of the utilization of different types of care. While estimating the determinants of hospital-level investment decisions is beyond our scope here, an important first step in this analysis is to determine the contribution of technology diffusion between and within hospitals to intensity growth in AMI treatment. If increased procedure use largely reflects a one-time shift in the propensity of the hospital's physicians to treat patients with intensive procedures, then the analysis of technological change should concentrate on these adoption decisions. On the other hand, if most technology diffusion is within-hospital, then analyses should concentrate on how practices change within a hospital given the availability of intensive resources.

In previous work, McClellan (1993) and McClellan and Newhouse (1994) examined the differential use of intensive procedures in AMI treatment across hospitals. Those papers documented that having and adopting the capacity to perform intensive procedures was associated with much higher rates of procedure use. These hospital-level differences in procedure use were not explained by observed or unobserved differences in patient mix across the hospitals. In this section, we quantify the contribution of new technology adoption by hospitals and of within-hospital diffusion (given the hospital's technological capabilities) to the growth in AMI treatment intensity.

Examining technological change at the hospital level requires a method for assigning patients to specific hospitals. There is more than one admitting hospital, however, when a patient is transferred or readmitted. To focus on the episode of care, we classify patients by the hospital they were initially admitted to. With this classification, many patients will receive intensive surgery even if they were initially admitted to a nonintensive hospital. Understanding the propensity of these transfers and readmissions, however, is an important component of analyzing technological change.

Figure 2.8 shows cardiac catheterization rates for patients grouped by the year of adoption of the capacity to perform catheterization at the hospital to which they were initially admitted. The figure shows that in 1984, patients admitted to hospitals that were already performing catheterization were more than twice as likely to receive the procedure as those admitted to noncatheterization hospitals. The gap in procedure use between catheterization and noncatheterization hospitals increased steadily in absolute terms during the subsequent eight years, from 10 to 22 percentage points. This divergence in practice patterns between catheterization and noncatheterization hospitals over time suggests that within-hospital differences in technology diffusion are correlated with the hospital's technological capabilities.

However, figure 2.8 also confirms that hospital technology adoption decisions have a fundamental impact on how AMI patients are treated by the hospital. Within two years after adoption, catheterization rates consistently increase from the baseline level of noncatheterization hospitals to within several per-

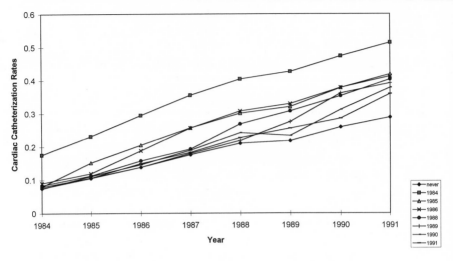

Fig. 2.8   Catheterization rate by year of technology acquisition

centage points of the current catheterization rate at the hospitals adopting before 1984. Moreover, even after several years of reequilibration, subsequent trends in catheterization rates remain higher than the preadoption trend. Thus, adoption not only had a one-time effect on the use of intensive procedures; it also affected subsequent technological change in the treatment of AMI at the hospital.

Figures 2.9 and 2.10 show analogous trends in bypass surgery and angioplasty rates for patients grouped on the basis of the capabilities of the hospital to which they were initially admitted. The same kinds of effects—substantial one-time step-ups in procedure use and differential long-term growth rates in procedure use—are also evident here. Indeed, within two years of acquiring bypass surgery technology, essentially all hospitals performing this surgery do so at the same rate. For angioplasty, technological utilization is correlated with initial year of acquisition, even several years out.

In table 2.8, we quantify the contribution of these different types of hospital-level technological change to intensity growth. In 1984, 35 percent of patients were admitted to hospitals that performed catheterization; the share of patients admitted to these hospitals increased by 3 percentage points during the panel. These hospitals had relatively rapid growth in catheterization use—averaging almost 5 percentage points per year—and thus accounted for a disproportionate share of total growth (45 percent). In contrast, the share of patients treated at hospitals that did not have the capacity to perform catheterization by 1991 declined by 5 percentage points, and catheterization rates increased by an average annual rate of only 3 percentage points; consequently, this group of hospitals accounted for only one-fourth of the growth in catheterization use. Finally, the share of patients treated by hospitals adopting catheterization between

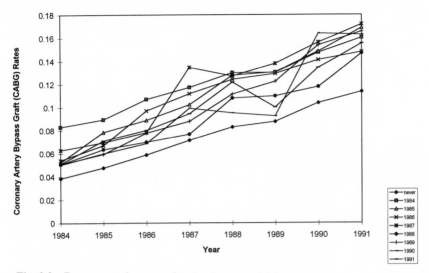

Fig. 2.9   Bypass rate by year of technology acquisition

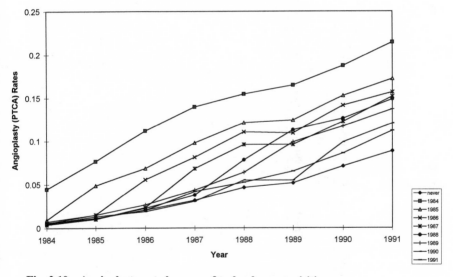

Fig. 2.10   Angioplasty rate by year of technology acquisition

1984 and 1991 increased slightly, and catheterization rates increased by as much as at the hospitals performing catheterization in 1984. (The higher growth rates compared to hospitals with catheterization in the few years after adoption appear to be approximately balanced by the lower growth rates in the years before adoption, so that the cumulative change in rates is comparable.) These hospitals consequently accounted for slightly more of the growth in procedure use than their share of patients would suggest. The bottom two panels of

Table 2.8   Sources of Technology Utilization by Hospital Type in 1984

Technology Status	Share of Patients (%)			Technology Utilization (%)			Share of Total Change[a] (%)
	1984	1991	Change (%)	1984	1991	Change (%)	
Catheterization							
Acquired by 1984	35	38	3	17.6	51.4	33.8	45
Acquired between 1984 and 1991	24	26	2	8.1	40.0	31.9	29
None by 1991	41	36	−5	7.8	29.6	21.8	26
Bypass surgery							
Acquired by 1984	19	22	3	8.3	16.0	7.7	23
Acquired between 1984 and 1991	12	13	1	5.4	16.1	10.7	19
None by 1991	69	65	−4	3.9	11.4	7.5	59
Angioplasty							
Acquired by 1984	10	12	2	4.5	21.5	17.0	19
Acquired between 1984 and 1991	24	26	2	0.6	15.2	14.6	34
None by 1991	67	63	−4	0.5	9.0	8.5	48

[a]Share of the total growth of the procedure that occurred in hospitals based on their technology status.

table 2.8, which show comparable statistics for bypass surgery and angioplasty, demonstrate qualitatively similar effects.

Figures 2.8 through 2.10 and table 2.8 demonstrate that both kinds of technological change at hospitals—one-time changes in treatment decisions resulting from changes in technology availability and long-term changes in trends in treatment intensity associated with technology availability—contribute substantially to technological change.

One might suspect that as technologies become more widespread across hospitals, within-hospital technological change would become relatively more important for further growth. Indeed, if we had analyzed a shorter panel of AMI patients, then the share of growth associated with changes in technological capabilities at hospitals would have been smaller, because a smaller share of patients would have been treated by the smaller number of adopting hospitals.

Figures 2.11 and 2.12 address the dynamics of new adoption of catheterization and angioplasty versus expansion to additional patients by hospitals. The figures decompose growth in the rates of procedure utilization into the shares due to hospitals that adopted the procedure within the preceding year ("New" section, top), to hospitals that adopted the procedure in earlier years ("Old" section, middle), and to hospitals that had not yet adopted the procedure ("Never" section, bottom). Figure 2.11 documents that, even by 1985, catheterization was a relatively mature technology in that increasing intensity was mostly due to increased use in hospitals that already had adopted catheteriza-

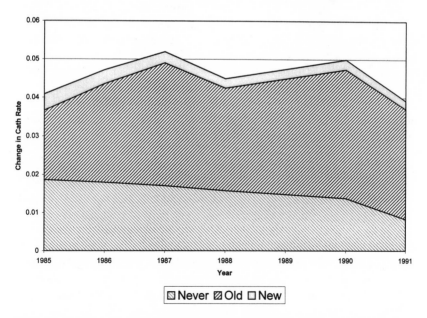

Fig. 2.11   Share of change in catheterization rate by new technology acquisition

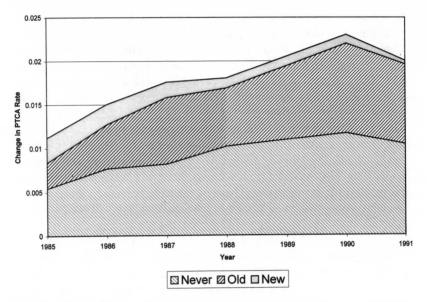

Fig. 2.12   Share of change in angioplasty rate by new technology acquisition

tion. As catheterization continued to diffuse, the share of catheterization growth attributable to additional hospital adoptions declined, from close to 20 percent of the growth in 1985 to around 10 percent of the growth by 1991.

In contrast, adoption of angioplasty during the initial years was much more among hospitals just acquiring the procedure. In 1985, the share of utilization growth due to new adopters was almost exactly the same as the share due to hospitals that already had the procedure. By 1991, however, much more of the growth was within hospitals that had already acquired the procedure, rather than among new hospitals. Clearly, understanding the nature of technology diffusion requires a model both of the initial adoption decision and of the increase in technology utilization within hospitals over time.

2.6   Conclusion

In this paper, we have reviewed the sources of Medicare expenditure growth for heart attacks in elderly Medicare beneficiaries. We found that *all* expenditure growth was attributable to growth in the use of intensive cardiac procedures. Two of these technologies, cardiac catheterization and bypass surgery, were relatively established in 1984. A third technology, angioplasty, was essentially new in 1984. All three of these technologies expanded rapidly over the period 1984–91, however, resulting in cost growth of 4 percent annually.

Given the critical importance of these technologies for Medicare cost growth, we then turned to some preliminary explorations of the nature of changes in their use. Analysis across MSAs documented that angioplasty did *not* appear to be a cost-saving technology in the sense that its diffusion led to reductions in more intensive types of surgery. The analysis across MSAs also showed that certain areas appeared to be "leaders" and others "followers" in terms of trends in technology use, though more aggressive use of intensive technologies was not associated with being a medical center. We then turned to preliminary analyses at the hospital level, which showed not only that technology adoption had a dramatic effect on treatment decisions for AMI patients at the hospital at a point in time but also that adoption led to a fundamental shift in the growth rate of technology use at the hospital.

We have documented that both area- and hospital-level factors have substantial effects on technological change in the treatment of AMIs. What remains is to analyze how these factors are related, and thus to develop a more comprehensive model of how technological change is mediated. Does earlier technology adoption by hospitals in an area, or more rapid changes in treatment patterns at hospitals that have adopted intensive technologies, contribute to more rapid growth in the "leading" areas? What area characteristics are associated with relatively rapid growth? How do these factors affect hospital technology adoption decisions? While such analyses have been conducted in other industries (see the review in Griliches 1988), they have rarely been addressed in this context. Answering such questions, however, appears crucial for understanding growth in health spending.

References

Carter, Grace, and Paul B. Ginsberg. 1985. The Medicare case mix index increase: Medical practice changes, aging, and DRG creep. Rand R-3292, Santa Monica, Calif.: RAND, June.

Carter, Grace, Joseph P. Newhouse, and Daniel A. Relles. 1990. How much change in the DRG index is DRG creep? *Journal of Health Economics* 9 (4): 411–28.

Cutler, David M. 1995a. Cutting costs and improving health: Making reform work. *Health Affairs* 15 (Spring): 161–72.

———. 1995b. The incidence of adverse medical outcomes under prospective payment. *Econometrica* 63 (1): 29–50.

Griliches, Zvi. 1988. *Technology, education, and productivity.* New York: Blackwell.

McClellan, Mark. 1993. The effect of hospital characteristics on medical treatment intensity: Acute myocardial infarction in the elderly. Ph.D. diss., Massachusetts Institute of Technology, Cambridge.

McClellan, Mark, Barbara J. McNeil, and Joseph P. Newhouse. 1994. Does more intensive treatment of acute myocardial infarction in the elderly reduce mortality? *Journal of the American Medical Association* 272: 859–66.

McClellan, Mark, and Joseph P. Newhouse. 1994. The costs and benefits of medical technology. Cambridge, Mass.: Harvard University. Mimeograph.

Newhouse, Joseph P. 1992. Medical care costs: How much welfare loss? *Journal of Economic Perspectives* 6 (Summer): 1–26.

Prospective Payment Assessment Commission. 1994–95. *Annual report to Congress.* Washington, D.C.: Prospective Payment Assessment Commission.
———. 1985 and 1991. *Medicare and the American Health Care System.* Washington, D.C.: Prospective Payment Assessment Commission.

Comment   Jonathan Gruber

Cutler and McClellan's paper focuses on what is, in my view, the most important topic in health economics today: the diffusion of new medical technologies. The rapid rise in medical costs over the past 40 years, as medical spending has tripled as a share of GNP, is a natural source of concern to both academics and policymakers. Careful efforts to account for this cost increase by factors such as the aging of the population, increased incomes, or increased insurance coverage has left the majority of the increase unexplained. And this residual is generally attributed to "technological advance" in medicine.

This attribution, however, raises two critical questions. First, can we find *direct evidence* that technological advance is the culprit? As with any such exercise, labeling a residual by default is never very satisfying. So rather than calling the residual "technology," we need to document that it is in fact new technologies that are driving medical costs upward. While, on one level, this is just an accounting exercise, it is also the crucial first step toward thinking about whether we want a policy response to rising costs, and how to design that policy response.

Second, what drives technological adoption and diffusion in the health care sector? While analysts such as Burt Weisbrod have written "big think" pieces conjecturing about the source of technological advance, there is strikingly little hard evidence on the critical factors driving diffusion.

This ambitious paper tries to tackle both of these questions. Ultimately, I think that the authors do a good job on the first, but they only scratch the surface of the second.

They begin by noting that price regulation in Medicare has not been able to slow cost growth in that program. Despite aggressive reimbursement reforms under Medicare's Prospective Payment System (PPS), costs are rising just as fast now as they were in the years before price regulation. As McClellan (1993) showed, the main reason why costs keep rising for Medicare is that there has been a huge rise in surgical admissions, and surgical diagnosis-related groups (DRGs) are reimbursed more highly than nonsurgical DRGs.

This paper illustrates that point in more detail, within the context of a specific illness, acute myocardial infarction (AMI). I think that the most interesting results in the paper are in table 2.5, which decomposes the 4.1 percent

Jonathan Gruber is professor of economics at the Massachusetts Institute of Technology and a faculty research fellow of the National Bureau of Economic Research.

annual increase in reimbursement for AMI into price and treatment changes. The authors find that, if AMI had been treated in a constant way over time, average reimbursement would have actually *fallen*. This is because Medicare, perhaps in reaction to increasing AMI costs, lowered the reimbursement rate for some of the "high-tech" means of treating AMIs. As a result, the large rise in costs was driven solely by a shift in the treatment of AMIs toward more expensive interventions. Thus, this provides some of the first solid evidence for technological change as a source of medical cost increase.

I have two reactions to these interesting findings. First, on a picky note, there is potentially a price index problem here. The authors use the 1991 prices and distribution of treatments to calculate their price and quantity indexes. Given the dramatic shift in treatment styles from 1984 to 1991, I would be interested to see how sensitive their answers are to the base year chosen. But my guess is that the result would be relatively robust.

Second, and more important, this finding immediately raises the second question posed above: what was the *source* of this rapid technological change? Was it driven by innovations in medical treatment techniques that were *exogenous* to changes in Medicare pricing policy? Or was it an *endogenous* response to the reimbursement schedule set up by Medicare, which reimbursed intensive interventions much more highly? Health economists like to draw an analogy between trying to regulate medical costs and squeezing a pillow—if you try to do it by squeezing one end, you just get a larger response on the other side. In this case, the side that is being squeezed is treatment-specific prices, and the side where you may see the responses is changes in treatment technology.

So the key question is: would we have seen this dramatic change in the treatment of AMI in the *absence* of PPS, or was it *caused* by the pricing structure put in place by Medicare, as the "pillow" hypothesis would suggest? If technological advance was exogenous to Medicare policy, then this is an interesting descriptive exercise on why Medicare could not control costs, but it has little policy weight. But if it was an endogenous response, then it suggests that this type of pillow effect is critical, and that it must be incorporated in analyzing the net effects on the program of changing relative prices.

I bring this up because I think that the authors could do a lot more here. In particular, during their sample period we see dramatic changes in the relative reimbursements of these different treatments for AMI. For example, they report that in 1990 the reimbursement rate for angioplasty was *halved*. Did use of angioplasty respond? Did we see a slowing of the rapid move toward this new type of technology? More generally, the authors have a critical opportunity here to move beyond simply describing the technological change to ask what role reimbursement policy played.

The authors do spend some time trying to model the use of new technologies, using variation in technology use across metropolitan statistical areas (MSAs). The most interesting question that they ask is whether the increased use of angioplasty actually saved Medicare money, since it is cheaper than alternative treatments such as bypass surgery. This is important because it is popularly perceived that new medical technologies can be money saving, much like technology in other areas such as computers. But health economists are largely skeptical of this claim.

In fact, however, we have little existing evidence to support the skepticism of health economists. Cutler and McClellan attempt to provide such evidence by asking whether MSAs that saw increased use of relatively low cost angioplasty also saw decreased use of high-cost bypass surgery. They find that, in fact, there is no correlation across MSAs in the change in these two types of treatments—that is, places that starting using more angioplasty used no less bypass surgery.

This is a striking finding, but I think that it is not fully convincing. This is sort of like the tests of the physician-induced demand hypothesis, which posits that physicians will respond to negative income shocks by doing more procedures on their patients. Most tests of this view have generally proceeded by asking whether places with more surgeons have more surgery, and they have found that this is the case. But if there is some omitted area change that is correlated with taste for surgery, then this omission biases these tests toward finding a positive correlation between surgeon density and surgery rates. Similarly, in Cutler and McClellan's data, if there is some omitted MSA-specific change that leads individuals to demand more intensive interventions, then it will bias the authors toward finding a positive correlation between angioplasty changes and bypass changes. This could mask a true substitution pattern between the two types of treatment.

At a minimum, the authors need to control for demographic changes across areas. Another test might be to look at what was happening to bypass use right before angioplasty grew. That is, the authors could look at the difference in growth rates of bypass before and after the widespread availability of angioplasty. Were the MSAs that adopted angioplasty the ones in which bypass was growing most rapidly anyway?

In the final table, the authors try another accounting exercise, which is to decompose the total change in technology utilization into utilization in hospitals that had the technology in 1984, those that acquired it between 1984 and 1991, and those that did not have it by 1991. The authors highlight the fact that, for catheterization, over half of the change was in hospitals that had the technology in 1984. The more striking finding, to my mind, is the rapid growth in catheterization at hospitals that did not have a catheterization lab by 1991. In fact, for revascularization, the majority of the growth occurs at hospitals that cannot do revascularization!

The key to understanding these potentially confusing findings is the role of *transfers* and *readmits*. That is, the hospital to which the authors refer is the hospital to which the person is admitted. If the patient is then transferred or discharged and readmitted within the 90-day window to some hospital that has catheterization or revascularization capability, the patient can get the intensive treatment.

I think that the huge role of transfers and readmits here is interesting and should not be overlooked, and it suggests two further directions for the analysis. First, the authors could examine transfer and readmit patterns. For example, what is the maximum distance that most patients are transferred, or the farthest hospital to which they are readmitted? This could have important implications for the finding that being near a teaching hospital is not associated with higher use of expensive technology. This finding could simply result from the fact that even individuals far from a teaching hospital are transferred there for care.

Second, they could look at within-MSA technology adoption decisions. That is, the authors could turn to a *within-area* model of "leaders" and "followers," versus "specialization." Is there a "medical arms race," whereby one hospital's adoption of a technology triggers its adoption at nearby hospitals? Or do these technologies have more of a public goods feature, where some hospitals specialize in their use, and other hospitals transfer patients to the hospitals that have the technology? Once again, testing this runs into the same types of omitted-variables bias problems encountered by the earlier results on technology substitution. But if the authors can deal with these problems this might be a fruitful direction to pursue in answering the second question, about what drives technological advance in the medical care marketplace.

Reference

McClellan, Mark. 1993. The effect of hospital characteristics on medical treatment intensity: Acute myocardial infarction in the elderly. Ph.D. diss., Massachusetts Institute of Technology, Cambridge.

II   Retirement and Care of the Elderly

3 Lump-Sum Distributions from Retirement Saving Plans: Receipt and Utilization

James M. Poterba, Steven F. Venti, and David A. Wise

The degree to which alternative pension systems preserve retirement benefits when individuals change jobs has long been a consideration in evaluating various retirement saving arrangements. Related preservation issues have also been raised with respect to targeted retirement saving accounts, such as individual retirement accounts (IRAs) and 401(k) plans, which permit contributors to withdraw funds, subject to a tax penalty, before they reach retirement age. As the incidence of targeted retirement saving plans increases, the number of taxpayers with the potential to trigger such withdrawals will also increase. Although a number of previous studies, including our own (1994a, 1995), have examined the determinants of participation and contribution behavior in retirement saving plans, withdrawal behavior has received much less attention.

The incidence and disposition of withdrawals from pension plans or other saving plans, known as lump-sum distributions, is a key determinant of the financial status of elderly households. Consider a 35-year-old who has accumulated $10,000 in a defined contribution pension plan, and who changes jobs. If these funds remain in a defined contribution pension account and earn a 5 percent annual real return, the balance in this plan will be $44,817 when the beneficiary reaches age 65. If these funds are withdrawn and consumed when

James M. Poterba is the Mitsui Professor of Economics at the Massachusetts Institute of Technology and director of the Public Economics Research Program at the National Bureau of Economic Research. Steven F. Venti is professor of economics at Dartmouth College and a research associate of the National Bureau of Economic Research. David A. Wise is the John F. Stambaugh Professor of Political Economy at the John F. Kennedy School of Government, Harvard University, and director of the Health and Retirement Research Programs at the National Bureau of Economic Research.

The authors are grateful to the National Institute on Aging, the National Science Foundation, and the James Phillips Fund for research support; to Marianne Bitler, Matthew Eichner, and Jonah Gelbach for excellent research assistance; and to John Shoven and Paul Yakoboski for helpful discussions.

the pension plan participant changes jobs, however, they will not contribute to his financial well-being in retirement. Because a high fraction of lump-sum distributions occur when individuals change jobs early in their employment careers, withdrawing such assets forgoes the opportunity for many years of compound accumulation at pretax rates of return.

This paper considers the incidence and disposition of lump-sum distributions from pension plans and targeted retirement saving accounts, and it presents exploratory empirical evidence on recipient characteristics that are correlated with the decision to roll over such distributions and preserve their associated retirement benefits. Although we are particularly interested in withdrawals from IRAs and 401(k) plans, we are not aware of any data source that provides detailed information on these withdrawals as distinct from distributions from defined benefit and defined contribution pension plans. At least historically, payouts from pension plans are likely to account for the substantial majority of distributions. We therefore explore the general pattern of receipt and utilization of all distributions.

The paper is divided into five sections. Section 3.1 presents descriptive information on the nature and tax treatment of lump-sum distributions. Section 3.2 summarizes previous work on the incidence and utilization of these distributions, noting an apparent disparity between estimates of the number of these distributions based on IRS information return filings and estimates based on self-reports in sample surveys. Section 3.3 describes the two data sets that we use to analyze the incidence and utilization of lump-sum distributions: the April 1993 Employee Benefits Supplement (EBS) to the Current Population Survey (CPS) and the first wave of the Health and Retirement Survey (HRS). This is followed by a summary of the patterns of lump-sum distribution receipt in these two surveys.

Section 3.4 presents evidence on the utilization of lump-sum distributions and the factors that are related to decisions to save these distributions. We find that the probability that a distribution is saved or rolled over into a targeted retirement saving account such as an IRA rises with the size of the distribution, the age of the recipient, and the income and education of the recipient. These patterns suggest that individuals who are likely to have accumulated more assets by retirement are less likely to consume premature lump-sum distributions. The paper closes with a brief section suggesting a number of directions for future work.

3.1   Background Information: What Are Lump-Sum Distributions?

Lump-sum distributions can arise in conjunction with defined contribution (DC) or defined benefit (DB) pension plans, 401(k) or 403(b) retirement saving plans, or IRAs. Such distributions are defined as *premature* if they are received before the retirement plan participant reaches age 59½ or dies. Distributions may be voluntary—for example, when an individual elects to withdraw funds from a 401(k) plan without any change in employment status—or involuntary. Involuntary distributions are usually triggered by changes in employment status, and they result when an employer elects to "cash out" a former employee's assets in a pension plan.

Defined contribution plans, which maintain separate accounts for each individual participant, typically make lump-sum distributions when participants retire or terminate their employment before retirement. The rapid growth of DC pension plans since the passage of the Employee Retirement Income Security Act (ERISA) has increased the actual and potential importance of lump-sum distributions. Lump-sum distributions can also arise when vested employees terminate employment at firms that offer DB pension plans. ERISA permitted an employer who sponsors a DB plan to "cash out" a terminated employee, without the employee's consent, if accrued benefits were less than $1,750. This limit was raised to $3,500 by the Retirement Income Act of 1984.

Lump-sum distributions are included in taxable income in the year when they are received, although the tax burden on such distributions may be reduced in some cases. Prior to 1986, taxpayers receiving these distributions could elect a 10-year forward averaging option on their distributions, in essence distributing their distribution across 10 tax years. This provision was repealed in 1986, when the Tax Reform Act (TRA86) replaced it with a five-year forward averaging option for taxpayers over the age of 59½. Each taxpayer may elect such forward averaging once in his lifetime.

A number of tax code provisions that have been enacted in the past decade encourage individuals who receive lump-sum distributions before the age of 59½ to preserve these distributions for prospective retirement income. TRA86 imposes a 10 percent excise tax on preretirement distributions to taxpayers younger than age 59½.[1] In addition, 1992 legislation imposed a 20 percent *withholding tax* on distributions received before age 59½ if these distributions are not rolled over into a tax-qualified investment vehicle. This withholding tax does not affect the total tax liability of lump-sum distribution recipients, but it does affect the *timing* of taxes. It implies that those who do not elect a fiduciary-to-fiduciary transfer do not receive the full amount of their distribution, but rather receive 80 percent of the amount of the distribution. There is some evidence that the share of lump-sum distributions that are rolled over into qualified retirement saving plans has increased over time. This is probably due in part to the enactment of these tax incentives.

Lump-sum distributions are an important factor in the evolution of total asset balances in targeted retirement saving accounts. Because many such distributions are rolled into IRAs, we consider these accounts. In tax year 1990, taxable income from IRA distributions equaled $17.5 billion, greater than the

---

1. The penalty tax is waived if the recipient converts the distribution to an annuity-like stream of payments, if the recipient is disabled, or if the distribution is triggered by the death of the plan participant.

$15.6 billion of "ordinary" contributions made by 9.3 million taxpayers contributing to these accounts.[2] Yakoboski's (1994) tabulation of IRS Form 1099-R and Form 5498 filings shows that in 1990, 8.2 million recipients received $107.2 billion in lump-sum payouts. Of these recipients, 3.1 million rolled over their distributions into IRAs, with a total rollover of $71.4 billion.[3] This is a lower bound for the extent of rollovers, since it does not include rollovers into 401(k) plans or other qualified DC plans because such rollovers do not trigger Form 5498 filings.

To place the various flows into and out of IRAs and related accounts in perspective, it is helpful to consider the flows during calendar year 1990. At the beginning of the year, the balance in IRAs and Keogh plan accounts was $501.7 billion. Ordinary IRA contributions totaled $15.6 billion during 1990, and withdrawals amounted to $17.5 billion. Rollovers were $71.4 billion, or nearly the change during the year in the value of assets held in these accounts.

A direct way to estimate the flow of distributions that are not rolled over relies on taxes collected on premature distributions from IRAs and other qualified retirement plans. Line 52 of Form 1040 indicates the amount of this tax, which was $1.196 billion in 1990. Since the tax rate on withdrawals is 10 percent, this revenue flow grosses up to approximately $12 billion in distributions. This value is an upper estimate for the flow of premature distributions, since the tax shown on line 52 can be triggered by any of four events: a premature withdrawal from an IRA or qualified DC pension plan, an excess contribution to an IRA, excess accumulation in a qualified retirement plan, or an excess distribution (in excess of $150,000 in one year) from a qualified retirement plan.

Table 3.1 presents more detailed information on the nature of lump-sum distributions as reported in Yakoboski's (1994) tabulation of IRS Form 1099-R data. The distributions are divided into two broad groups, which can be distinguished on tax forms: those from IRA or SEP-IRA accounts and those from other accounts. Payouts from DB and DC pension plans and 401(k) plans would appear in the "other" category. The table shows that in 1990, more than half of all distributions were premature, that is, to recipients who had not yet reached age 59½. Premature distributions accounted for only 32 percent of all distributions, however. Distributions triggered by the death of a pension plan

2. Tabulations from Form 1040 show 5.2 million contributions, contributing $9.9 billion, to IRAs in 1990. This is substantially lower than the $15.6 billion estimate of contributions for two reasons. First, nondeductible IRA contributions are not indicated on Form 1040. Second, contributions to SEP-IRAs (Simplified Employee Pensions) are not aggregated with IRA contributions on Form 1040, but they are combined on Form 5498, which is the basis for the $15.6 billion estimate. SEP-IRAs are pension plan arrangements that allow an employer to make contributions to his or her own IRA (if self-employed) as well as to each employee's IRA. These plans allow small businesses to avoid becoming involved in more complex retirement arrangements. The individual sets up an IRA, and then the employer contributes to this account up to a maximum of 15 percent of compensation or $30,000.

3. The flow of rollovers increased over the time period for which the IRS data are available, from $39.3 billion in 1987 to $45.9 billion (1988), $63.0 billion (1989), and $71.4 billion (1990).

Table 3.1   **Total Lump-Sum Distributions from Pension Plans and Targeted Retirement Saving Accounts, 1990**

Type	Distributions from Accounts Other Than IRAs or SEP-IRAs	Distributions from IRAs or SEP-IRAs
	Number of Distributions (million)	
Total	8.20 (100)	2.60 (100)
Normal	1.72 (21)	0.96 (37)
Premature	4.76 (58)	1.24 (53)
Premature but exempt from penalty tax	0.25 (3)	0.05 (2)
Death	0.33 (4)	0.18 (7)
Section 1035 exchange	0.58 (7)	0.0
Other or uncoded	0.58 (7)	0.03 (1)
	Amount of Distributions (billion $)	
Total	107.2 (100)	18.6 (100)
Normal	35.4 (33)	7.8 (42)
Premature	34.3 (32)	7.6 (41)
Premature but exempt from penalty tax	5.4 (5)	0.6 (3)
Death	6.4 (6)	2.4 (13)
Section 1035 exchange	7.5 (7)	0.0
Other or uncoded	18.2 (17)	0.2 (1)

Sources: Yakoboski (1994), based on tabulations of IRS Form 1099-R data for 1990, and authors' calculations.

Note: Numbers in parentheses are percentages of total.

participant account for 6 percent of the value of all distributions. Normal distributions, such as payouts to individuals over age 59½ who are retiring from a firm with a DC pension plan, account for 21 percent of all distributions but 33 percent of all distributed dollars.

We have not presented detailed tabulations on the characteristics of lump-sum distribution recipients; these are available in Employee Benefit Research Institute (EBRI 1994) and elsewhere. Several points are nevertheless worth noting. In the 1993 CPS, 11 percent of the respondents who received a lump-sum distribution reported that this distribution was less than $500, another 20 percent that it was between $500 and $1,000, and a further 20 percent that it was between $1,000 and $2,500. More than 60 percent of all distributions were for less than $5,000.

Previous tabulations also show that most lump-sum distribution recipients are relatively young. EBRI (1994) reports that 39 percent of recipients reported that their most recent distribution was received before they turned 30, with another 36 percent of respondents receiving distributions between the ages of 31 and 40. Thus most distributions are small and are received relatively early in life, in part reflecting the greater degree of job mobility during this part of the life cycle.

3.2   Previous Research on Lump-Sum Distributions

A number of previous studies have analyzed the potential for lump-sum distributions as well as the utilization of these distributions by those who receive them. Most of these studies have relied on data from the CPS supplements on employee benefits, which were conducted in 1979, 1983, 1988, and 1993. We are not aware of any previous work that has analyzed the HRS data on lump-sum distributions.

One of the first studies of lump-sum distributions was by Atkins (1986), who presented information from the 1983 CPS EBS. He related the probability of saving a lump-sum distribution to individual characteristics. He concluded that most distributions were spent, not saved, and that the groups with substantial saving probabilities were older, were better educated, and received larger distributions. Our findings based on the 1993 CPS supplement confirm many of these patterns.

The growth in lump-sum distributions during the 1980s drew increased attention to these payouts. Andrews (1991), Chang (1993), EBRI (1989), Fernandez (1992), and Piacentini (1990) all analyze the 1988 CPS EBS data on the receipt and utilization of lump-sum distributions. Fernandez (1992) and Piacentini (1990) present largely descriptive information. Fernandez (1992) summarizes the data available in the 1988 survey and presents some comparisons between the 1983 and 1988 EBS. She finds that 8.5 million workers reported having received at least one lump-sum distribution from a previous employer's pension plan. She also finds a substantial increase in the fraction of lump-sum distributions that are rolled over into qualified retirement saving vehicles such as IRAs between the 1983 and 1988 CPS.[4]

Andrews (1991) and Chang (1993) also analyze the 1988 EBS, but their studies develop formal econometric models for recipient behavior. Andrews (1991) analyzes the determinants of rollover behavior; her work in some ways resembles our analysis of the 1993 EBS data. She models both the probability that a given respondent will report having received a lump-sum distribution and the factors that affect the allocation of that distribution. Her definitions of "saving" are substantially broader than those in our study since she considers distributions that are used to buy a house or pay a mortgage, used to start a business, or used to pay other debts as "saving." Her results nevertheless suggest a number of interesting patterns, including a higher probability of saving distributions by households that have made contributions to an IRA, and by those who receive interest or dividend income. She does not find substantial effects of education on the probability of saving a distribution, a result that is

4. EBRI's (1989) analysis of the 1988 data is broader than Fernandez's (1992) focus on lump-sum payouts. It includes summary tabulations for other variables that are included in the supplemental survey. Piacentini (1990) includes a broader discussion of current public policies that affect the preservation of retirement benefits.

contrary to our findings below and to Atkins's (1986) findings with the 1983 EBS.

Chang's (1993) study concentrates on the effect of the 10 percent excise tax on premature distributions, enacted in 1986, on the utilization of lump-sum distributions. She compares the use of distributions by those who received distributions before and after 1986 and concludes that the excise tax reduced the probability of consuming a distribution by approximately 6 percentage points.

The most recent CPS supplementary survey on employee benefits, the April 1993 survey, has already been the basis for several studies of lump-sum distributions. EBRI (1994) presents detailed summary information on many variables from the 1993 EBS including those related to lump-sum distributions. This study is an extremely valuable source of background information, but it is largely confined to studying rollover behavior along single dimensions of individual characteristics, such as income or age. Gelbach (1995), another study that is closely related to our analysis of saving decisions, uses the 1993 EBS to estimate a multinomial logit model for whether households roll over their distributions into an IRA, save them in other ways, or spend them. His results suggest that older recipients, and those who receive larger distributions, are substantially more likely to save these distributions than are younger recipients of small distributions.

As this brief summary demonstrates, we are hardly the first group of researchers to explore household behavior with respect to lump-sum distributions. Our analysis differs from that in most previous studies in our use of a new database, the HRS, and in our consideration of several potential definitions of saving, including a strict definition (rolled over into an IRA) and a more general definition encompassing other nonconsumption uses of a lump-sum distribution.

3.3   Data Sources and Summary Statistics

Our analysis relies on two sources of information on lump-sum distributions and their utilization: the May 1993 CPS EBS and the HRS. We begin with brief descriptions of these surveys and then summarize the information on lump-sum distributions contained in each.

3.3.1   CPS-Based Evidence on Lump-Sum Distributions

The CPS EBS questionnaire was administered to a representative subsample of over 27,000 CPS participants in April 1993. It contains detailed information on pension plan coverage, on access to employer-provided health insurance, as well as on a respondent's experience with lump-sum distributions.[5] The rele-

---

5. EBRI (1994) presents a detailed set of tabulations for many of the questions included in the May 1993 EBS.

vant questions on these distributions began with the question "Have you ever received a lump-sum payment from a pension plan or retirement plan on a previous job?" Those who responded affirmatively to this question were then asked about the year in which they received the lump-sum payment, the approximate amount of this payment, and how they spent or invested the distribution. The last question offered a variety of options, such as "rolled over into an IRA" and "put into a savings account," and respondents were permitted to select more than one response without indicating the fraction of the distribution that was allocated to each use. The CPS top-codes responses to the value of the lump-sum distribution at $100,000.

Two features of the CPS data deserve note. First, if a respondent had received more than one lump-sum distribution, he was directed to confine his answers to the *most recent* distribution. This implies that the historical aggregate flow of lump-sum distributions recorded in the CPS will understate actual distributions, with greater overstatement at earlier dates.[6] This feature of the CPS data should be contrasted with the HRS, which collects information on multiple distributions. Second, the question is restricted to distributions received from a *former employer.* This means that, for example, an individual who had received a lump-sum distribution from his current employer's 401(k) plan, perhaps by withdrawing his employee contributions to this plan, would *not* be identified as a recipient of a lump-sum distribution.

In the 1993 CPS EBS, 2,736 respondents indicated that they had received a lump-sum distribution. Of this group, 31 did not respond to the question on how the distribution was used. This left a sample of 2,705 respondents for our study. Using the sample weights in the CPS, this group corresponds to 11.7 million individuals in the U.S. population.

Table 3.2 presents summary information on the probability of ever having received a lump-sum distribution by age group in the 1993 CPS.[7] The table, which is stratified by age of respondent in 1993, mixes the effect of aging within a given cohort and differential experience of different cohorts. It shows that the probability of ever having received a distribution rises as one considers older workers up to roughly age 40, but the probability is relatively stable thereafter. Table 3.2 presents separate tabulations for men and women and shows that the rates of distribution receipt do not differ substantially between young men and women, although older women are less likely to have received such distributions than their male counterparts. This presumably reflects their lower probability of having been covered by employer-provided pensions.

In addition to information on who receives lump-sum distributions, the EBS

---

6. Approximately 31 percent of the lump-sum distributions described by EBS participants were received after 1985, 25 percent after 1990. One-sixth were received before 1980.

7. In both table 3.2 and table 3.4, we identify the universe of individuals who could have received lump-sum distributions by conditioning on a nonmissing response to the CPS question about the size of the firm that the individual currently or previously worked for. This restriction eliminates an additional 108 respondents with lump-sum distributions from our analysis.

Table 3.2   **Age-Specific Incidence of Lump-Sum Distribution Receipt, May 1993 CPS (percent)**

Age Group	Men	Women	All
16–20	0.2	0.0	0.1
	(1.1)	(1.1)	(0.8)
21–30	4.9	5.7	5.2
	(0.5)	(0.5)	(0.4)
31–40	11.8	13.0	12.4
	(0.5)	(0.5)	(0.3)
41–50	12.7	14.0	13.3
	(0.5)	(0.6)	(0.4)
51–55	12.7	9.7	11.3
	(0.9)	(1.0)	(0.7)
56–60	11.7	10.0	11.0
	(1.1)	(1.2)	(0.8)
61–64	12.3	9.8	11.2
	(1.5)	(1.7)	(1.1)
65+	14.1	6.9	11.0
	(1.5)	(1.8)	(1.1)
Total	9.9	10.0	9.9
	(0.3)	(0.3)	(0.2)

Source: Authors' tabulations from April 1988 and May 1993 Employee Benefit Supplements to the Current Population Survey.

Notes: Each entry shows the probability that an individual in a given demographic category reported ever having received a lump-sum distribution from a pension plan. Numbers in parentheses are standard errors for the estimated probabilities.

also contains data on the disposition of such distributions. Respondents are allowed to indicate more than one use of their lump sums, although only one-sixth of the respondents actually indicated more than one use. Table 3.3 presents summary results on the uses to which these distributions were put. The table focuses on two age groups, all ages and the subgroup that corresponds to the HRS participants. It also presents two tabulations for each age group, one reporting the fraction of distribution recipients in each category, the other the fraction of distribution dollars by category.

The table shows that a relatively small fraction of lump-sum distribution recipients roll their distributions into an IRA or the retirement plan administered by their new employer. If we consider "saving" a lump sum to include IRA or employer plan rollovers or investment in an IRA, an annuity, or a savings account, then the overall probability that a lump-sum distribution will be saved is 33.2 percent.[8] The table illustrates, however, that this probability is much higher if distributions are weighted by their values. In this case, the prob-

8. Saving could in fact be defined much more broadly to include reductions in debt, purchases of consumer durables, and similar transactions that do not reduce household net worth as current consumption would. The probability of such expanded saving measures can also be computed from the data in table 3.2.

Table 3.3   CPS Respondents Reporting *Any* Part of Lump-Sum Distribution Used for Various Purposes (percent)

Use of Lump-Sum Distribution	All Ages		Ages 52–61	
	Unweighted	Value Weighted	Unweighted	Value Weighted
Rolled over into IRA or new employer plan	14.2	31.1	18.0	31.0
Invested in				
IRA	7.4	15.8	11.1	14.5
Insurance annuity or other retirement program	2.0	4.6	2.7	5.8
Savings account	9.6	7.0	12.1	8.4
Other financial instrument	5.9	11.6	9.9	17.5
"Other ways"	2.2	1.7	2.1	1.2
Used to purchase or start a business	3.6	6.4	5.9	8.0
Bought house/paid mortgage	9.2	8.7	7.4	6.8
Paid other loans or debt	19.0	10.7	14.1	6.6
Bought consumer durables	7.3	4.8	5.5	3.1
Paid medical or dental bills	1.9	1.5	1.5	1.7
Paid educational expenses	3.0	2.5	1.5	1.6
Used for everyday expenses	21.7	11.0	18.3	9.9
Other spending	6.5	4.8	6.2	7.2
Other uses	4.1	3.3	4.0	2.3

Source: Authors' tabulations using May 1993 Employee Benefit Supplement to the Current Population Survey.

ability of preserving a lump-sum distribution is 58.6 percent. Table 3.3 also shows that recipients use lump-sum distributions for a wide range of purposes, with repayment of debts or bills as the largest single item after saving. Comparing the various columns in table 3.3 suggests relatively small differences in the disposition of lump-sum distributions between those currently approaching retirement and younger workers. In part, this reflects the fact that older workers who are reporting on lump-sum distributions may have received these distributions much earlier in their working careers.

3.3.2   HRS-Based Evidence on Lump-Sum Distributions

The HRS is a new panel survey designed to collect information on households as they approach retirement. Its sampling frame is the population between the ages of 51 and 61 in 1992, with some oversampling of Florida residents and those who live in heavily black or Hispanic areas. The full HRS sample includes just over 12,000 respondents, so it is substantially smaller than the CPS. For the relevant age range, however, the CPS and HRS are likely to yield results of similar precision. Our analysis relies on the first wave of the HRS, which was collected in 1992.

The HRS includes a detailed battery of questions on pension coverage at current and previous employers. If the respondent is currently employed and indicates that he worked at a previous employer for more than five years, he is asked if he was included in a pension or retirement plan, or tax-deferred saving plan, at that job. If he is retired, he is asked about the pension plan at his last employer. In both cases, the respondent is then asked whether the retirement plan was a DB or DC plan, and what happened when he left that employer. One of the potential responses at this stage is "cash settlement," and another is "rolled over into an IRA." Those who received a cash settlement are subsequently asked the amount of the settlement, and whether they spent this settlement, saved and invested it, paid off debts, or rolled the settlement into an IRA. One difficulty with the HRS data is that respondents who rolled payouts from previous employer plans into their new employer plans, or who used the proceeds to purchase insurance annuities, were *not* asked about the amounts of these distributions. Thus HRS-based tabulations that use information on distribution amounts are limited to a subsample of all distribution recipients.

Table 3.4 presents summary information on lump-sum distribution recipients in the HRS. Because of the limited age variation within the HRS, the data are not stratified by age, as in table 3.2, but by the current labor income of the respondent. For comparison, table 3.4 presents similar stratification from the entire sample of CPS respondents, and from the subset of CPS respondents whose ages in 1993 conform to those of the HRS respondents. The HRS data show a rising probability of ever having received a lump-sum distribution as the respondent's current income rises.

The same pattern is observed in the CPS data, but with two notable differences. First, the *rate* of lump-sum distribution receipt in the HRS sample is nearly 4 percentage points higher than that in the all-age CPS sample. Nearly half of this disparity is apparently due to the age criterion used to select the HRS sample, but the last column in table 3.4 shows that even the HRS-aged subsample of the CPS displays a lower incidence of lump-sum distribution receipt than the HRS respondents. Second, there is a substantial difference in the probability of lump-sum distribution receipt between low-income respondents in the HRS and in the CPS. Those with labor income below $5,000 account for a much larger share of the lump-sum distributions, and a much larger share of the dollar value of these payouts, in the HRS than in the CPS. The source of these disparities warrants further analysis.

The HRS also collects some information on how lump-sum distributions were used, although respondents have fewer options than the CPS EBS provides. Table 3.5 summarizes the responses to these questions. The results confirm the substantial differences between recipient-weighted and distribution-weighted statistics on the utilization of lump sums. While 33 percent of those

Table 3.4   **Lump-Sum Distribution Receipt by Labor Income Category**

Income Category ($)	HRS	1993 CPS, All Ages	1993 CPS, Ages 52–61
Probability of Ever Having Received a Lump-Sum Distribution (%)			
Below 5,000	11.4	3.7	23.2
5,000–10,000	11.5	5.4	10.4
10,000–20,000	12.9	8.0	8.5
20,000–30,000	14.0	11.4	13.0
30,000–50,000	15.1	12.9	13.8
50,000–75,000	16.1	16.9	14.4
75,000+	20.6	16.8	12.5
All income groups	13.9	10.0	12.1
Percentage of Lump-Sum Distributions Reported by Each Income Group			
Below 5,000	27.4	0.1	0.3
5,000–10,000	5.6	3.6	0.2
10,000–20,000	5.7	22.8	0.9
20,000–30,000	15.1	37.5	16.8
30,000–50,000	12.1	22.5	65.4
50,000–75,000	14.5	8.5	2.2
75,000+	19.7	5.1	14.2
All income groups	100	100	100

Source: Authors' tabulations from 1992 Health and Retirement Survey and March 1993 Current Population Employee Benefit Supplement. The number of respondents in the HRS sample is 12,654, of whom 1,624 reported receipt of a lump-sum distribution. The CPS tabulations in the lower panel are not weighted by sampling probabilities, and they exclude individuals who do not report information on their last or current employer (firm size). This selection rule excludes some low-income households that are no longer working and probably accounts for the difference between the HRS results and the CPS results for the HRS age sample.

Table 3.5   **HRS Evidence on Use of Lump-Sum Distributions**

Use of Lump-Sum Distribution	Percentage of Those Receiving Distributions	Percentage of Distributions
Rolled into IRA or transfer to other retirement assets	33.2	66.8
Purchase of annuity	2.6	5.9
Cash		
Spent	23.6	7.6
Saved or invested	12.1	7.6
Paid bills	7.8	5.2
Other	15.3	6.7
Other	5.4	1.5

Source: Authors' tabulations from 1992 Health and Retirement Survey.

who received lump-sum distributions reported rolling them into IRAs or transferring them to the retirement plan of a new employer, their distributions accounted for 67 percent of all distributions reported in the HRS.[9]

3.4 Rollovers, Savings, and Lump-Sum Distributions

The decision to roll over a lump-sum distribution into an IRA, to transfer the assets to the retirement plan of a new employer, or to otherwise invest them is of central importance for analyzing the preservation of accumulated retirement assets.[10] In this section, we analyze the factors that appear to influence such rollover or reinvestment decisions. We begin with a set of summary tables focusing on the age of the recipient and the size of the distribution and then report estimates of linear probability models for the decision to channel lump-sum distributions to IRAs or to other types of financial asset saving.

Throughout our analysis we consider two possible definitions of financial asset saving for a lump-sum distribution. The first is rolling over the distribution to an IRA or a new employer's plan, and the second is rollover as well as investment in an IRA or other retirement plan, or investment in a saving account.[11] A distribution that is saved through a saving account or other "traditional" saving plan will not accumulate as rapidly as a distribution that is transferred to a qualified retirement saving account, because taxes on asset income will slow asset growth. Neither of these definitions corresponds to the set of uses of lump-sum distributions that do not diminish household net worth, as consumption spending would. That set would include paying down debts, purchasing durables, and a variety of other behaviors that were shown in several earlier tables.

To motivate our analysis, table 3.6 presents probabilities of rollover into an IRA or new employer pension plan, stratified by the size of the distribution and the age of the recipient at the time when the distribution was received. For the distribution to be considered as a "rollover," the respondent had to indicate that this was at least one of the uses to which he or she put the distribution. We have done a similar analysis of the restricted sample of respondents who indicated that they devoted *all* of their distribution to a single use, with broadly similar findings. The table includes some empty cells corresponding to cases for which there were no individuals in the relevant age/income category in our sample of distribution recipients.

9. The HRS does not indicate when a distribution was received; the CPS EBS does. This means that the HRS and CPS tabulations for amounts of distributions are not quite comparable: the CPS tabulations consider all distributions measured in 1993 dollars, while the HRS tabulations weight distributions by the reported nominal values.

10. The decision of whether to "take" a lump-sum distribution, by those who are eligible for such distributions, is also a critical determinant of the preservation of retirement saving assets. We discuss this further in the conclusion.

11. The distinction between "rolled over into an IRA" and "invested in an IRA" is presumably the absence of a fiduciary-to-fiduciary transfer in the second case.

Table 3.6   **Probability That Lump-Sum Distribution Is Rolled Over to an IRA or to a New Employer's Plan, by Age of Receipt and Amount of Distribution**

Distribution Value (1993 $)	Age When Received						
	<25	25–34	35–44	45–54	55–64	65+	All Ages
0–500	.024	.048	.089	.000	.000		.046
	(.040)	(.037)	(.055)	(.112)	(.606)		(.024)
501–1,000	.093	.073	.086	.000	.000	.000	.078
	(.058)	(.034)	(.069)	(.111)	(.473)	(.301)	(.027)
1,001–2,500	.035	.135	.164	.129	.689	.000	.129
	(.044)	(.025)	(.034)	(.060)	(.202)	(.270)	(.018)
2,501–5,000	.009	.160	.211	.189	.350		.158
	(.057)	(.025)	(.045)	(.063)	(.113)		(.019)
5,001–10,000	.007	.250	.300	.431	.201	.000	.259
	(.072)	(.029)	(.034)	(.066)	(.093)	(.193)	(.020)
10,001–15,000	.156	.117	.349	.415	.759	.000	.265
	(.188)	(.039)	(.046)	(.069)	(.137)	(.477)	(.027)
15,001–25,000	.417	.248	.337	.410	.376		.319
	(.285)	(.042)	(.049)	(.063)	(.099)		(.028)
25,000–50,000	.000	.386	.459	.693	.317	.000	.483
	(.280)	(.077)	(.053)	(.060)	(.090)	(.252)	(.033)
50,000+	.000	.586	.792	.664	.592		.686
	(.463)	(.115)	(.058)	(.065)	(.077)		(.036)
Total	.044	.161	.279	.387	.420	.000	.215
	(.022)	(.012)	(.015)	(.022)	(.038)	(.097)	(.008)

Source: Authors' tabulations from 1993 Current Population Survey, Employee Benefit Supplement. Affirmative answers to questions on whether the lump-sum distribution was rolled over into an IRA or into a new employer's plan, or invested in an IRA, were used to define the positive value for the indicator variable.

Note: Numbers in parentheses are standard errors for the reported probabilities.

The results in table 3.6 suggest a definite pattern: the probability of rollover is much lower in the upper left-hand corner of the table than in the lower right-hand corner. For those who receive distributions of more than $25,000, the probability of rollover exceeds .50, while for those who receive distributions of less than $1,000, the probability is less than .10. There are similar substantial age differences in rollover rates, rising from less than 20 percent for those under the age of 35 to nearly 45 percent for those aged 55–64.

Table 3.7 presents similar estimates of the probability that a distribution will be channeled to particular financial investments, by size and age of recipient. This probability is substantially greater (.39 on average) than the probability that it will be rolled over (.22). The pattern across ages and sizes of distributions is nevertheless similar to that in table 3.6. Older recipients, and those who receive larger distributions, are more likely to use their distributions to invest in an IRA, roll over to an IRA or qualified plan, or invest in a saving account. These findings underscore our discussion in the last section of the importance of distinguishing between the allocation of distributions and the

Table 3.7   **Probability That Lump-Sum Distribution Is Reinvested, by Age of Receipt and Amount of Distribution**

Distribution Value (1993 $)	Age When Received						
	<25	25–34	35–44	45–54	55–64	65+	All Ages
0–500	.114	.149	.166	.148	.000		.139
	(.047)	(.044)	(.065)	(.080)	(.717)		(.028)
501–1,000	.172	.182	.200	.082	.000	1.000	.194
	(.068)	(.041)	(.082)	(.131)	(.560)	(.356)	(.031)
1,001–2,500	.210	.293	.389	.236	1.000	.000	.305
	(.052)	(.030)	(.040)	(.072)	(.239)	(.320)	(.021)
2,501–5,000	.174	.313	.422	.414	.496		.329
	(.068)	(.030)	(.053)	(.074)	(.133)		(.023)
5,001–10,000	.235	.390	.486	.506	.485	.087	.420
	(.085)	(.034)	(.041)	(.078)	(.110)	(.229)	(.023)
10,001–15,000	.413	.378	.558	.626	1.000	1.000	.502
	(.223)	(.047)	(.054)	(.081)	(.162)	(.565)	(.032)
15,001–25,000	.417	.541	.676	.651	.810		.627
	(.338)	(.050)	(.058)	(.075)	(.118)		(.033)
25,000–50,000	.000	.675	.584	.822	.724	.000	.671
	(.331)	(.091)	(.062)	(.071)	(.107)	(.300)	(.039)
50,000+	.000	.789	.908	.930	.865		.888
	(.549)	(.137)	(.069)	(.078)	(.091)		(.043)
Total	.186	.322	.480	.569	.728	.385	.393
	(.026)	(.014)	(.018)	(.026)	(.045)	(.115)	(.009)

Source: Authors' tabulations from 1993 Current Population Survey, Employee Benefit Supplement. Distributions were defined as saved if the respondent indicated that they were rolled over into an existing IRA or new employer's retirement plan, invested in an IRA or other retirement plan, or invested in a saving account.

Note: Numbers in parentheses are standard errors for the reported probabilities.

allocation of *distributed dollars.* Large distributions are more likely to be rolled over or reinvested than smaller payouts.

To provide further information on the behavior of recipients of lump-sum distributions, table 3.8 reports estimates of a linear probability model for rollover behavior.[12] We report several different specifications. The first relates the probability of rollover to a set of categorical variables for age and size of distribution. The second specification augments the first with indicator variables for different levels of educational attainment, and the third adds current income to the specification as well. In each set of variables, the "lowest" category (age < 25, distribution size < $1,000, less than a high school education, and income less than $10,000) is the excluded group.

The estimates confirm the patterns we observed in tables 3.6 and 3.7, but

12. We have estimated models similar to those in table 3.8 using standard discrete choice models (logit and probit), with results very similar to those from the linear probability models. We report the latter because of the easy interpretation of the coefficient estimates.

Table 3.8   Linear Probability Models for Decision to Roll Over Lump-Sum Distribution

Variable	(1)	(2)	(3)
Constant	−.008	−.078	−.103
	(.026)	(.047)	(.057)
Age when received distribution			
25–34	.067	.055	.054
	(.027)	(.027)	(.028)
35–44	.158	.155	.155
	(.030)	(.029)	(.031)
45–54	.196	.209	.214
	(.035)	(.035)	(.038)
55–64	.245	.268	.356
	(.049)	(.049)	(.055)
65+	−.122	−.108	−.058
	(.150)	(.148)	(.149)
Size of distribution ($)			
1,000–5,000	.073	.065	.064
	(.023)	(.023)	(.024)
5,001–10,000	.165	.149	.150
	(.028)	(.028)	(.030)
10,000+	.252	.236	.214
	(.026)	(.026)	(.028)
Education indicators			
High school		.014	−.010
		(.043)	(.047)
Some college		.069	.052
		(.043)	(.047)
College degree		.175	.143
		(.043)	(.048)
College+		.106	.045
		(.045)	(.051)
Income indicators ($)			
10,000–20,000			.037
			(.033)
20,001–30,000			.044
			(.034)
30,001–50,000			.076
			(.034)
50,000+			.137
			(.040)
Adjusted R^2	.101	.122	.134

Source: Authors' estimates using data from the May 1993 Employee Benefit Supplement to the Current Population Survey.

Note: Numbers in parentheses are standard errors.

they provide more information on the interaction between various effects. The indicator variables for age at time of receipt increase monotonically between ages 25 and 64, but there is a sharp decline in the probability of rollover for households over the age of 65. There is also a clear increase in the probability of rollover as the size of the distribution rises. The probability that a distribution worth more than $25,000 will be rolled over is 25 percentage points higher than the analogous probability for a distribution worth less than $1,000 and 18 percentage points higher than the probability for a distribution worth between $1,000 and $5,000. The pattern of coefficients for the age and size of distribution categories is affected relatively little by controlling for household earned income. The most notable effect is an increase in the point estimate for the probability of rolling over a distribution if the recipient is between the ages of 55 and 64.

The equations in columns (2) and (3) include education, and then education and income, indicator variables. Educational attainment does have an important predictive effect on the likelihood of rollover. The probability that those with a college degree will roll over a lump-sum distribution is 15 percentage points higher than the probability for those with high school education. This differential is *not* just the result of differences in income: it is evident in equations with and without controls for earned income. There is some indication, although it is not statistically significant at standard confidence levels, that those with postcollege education are less likely to roll over lump-sum distributions than are those with only college degrees. The estimates in column (3) of table 3.8 add labor income to the set of control variables. The probability that a lump-sum distribution is rolled over rises with the income of the recipient, with a particularly large effect for incomes over $50,000.

Table 3.9 presents results analogous to those in table 3.8, except the dependent variable is the probability that a lump-sum distribution is rolled over, reinvested in an IRA, or invested in a saving account. The general patterns in table 3.8 are confirmed in table 3.9, with one exception. The coefficient on the indicator variable for age 65+ in table 3.8 is negative, implying that this age group is *less likely* to roll over a distribution than any other age group. This is not the case in table 3.9. The coefficient estimates suggest that the age 65+ group is more likely to channel a lump-sum distribution to the various financial investments we consider than any other age group except the age 55–64 group. The patterns of coefficients in education and income, and the effects of including these variables on the other estimated coefficients, are similar in tables 3.8 and 3.9.

The low rate of rollover activity among those aged 65+ is difficult to explain. For a person aged 59½ or above, an IRA functions like an ordinary investment vehicle with the additional benefit of tax deferral. It is therefore puzzling that households in this age group do not take advantage of this opportunity to reduce their taxes.

Table 3.9   **Linear Probability Models for Decision to Reinvest Lump-Sum Distribution**

Variable	(1)	(2)	(3)
Constant	.087	−.068	−.069
	(.030)	(.054)	(.067)
Age when received distribution			
25–34	.081	.071	.069
	(.031)	(.031)	(.033)
35–44	.178	.177	.181
	(.034)	(.034)	(.036)
45–54	.214	.230	.232
	(.041)	(.041)	(.045)
55–64	.353	.379	.442
	(.057)	(.057)	(.065)
65+	.311	.321	.443
	(.173)	(.172)	(.185)
Size of distribution ($)			
1,000–5,000	.115	.109	.120
	(.027)	(.026)	(.028)
5,001–10,000	.185	.169	.185
	(.032)	(.032)	(.035)
10,000+	.363	.352	.342
	(.030)	(.030)	(.033)
Education indicators			
High school		.114	.105
		(.050)	(.054)
Some college		.158	.155
		(.049)	(.055)
College degree		.254	.228
		(.050)	(.057)
College+		.166	.105
		(.053)	(.060)
Income indicators ($)			
10,000–20,000			−.012
			(.040)
20,001–30,000			−.006
			(.040)
30,001–50,000			.039
			(.040)
50,000+			.101
			(.047)
Adjusted R^2	.129	.143	.151

Source: Authors' estimates using data from the May 1993 Employee Benefit Supplement to the Current Population Survey.

Note: Numbers in parentheses are standard errors.

As a check on the robustness of the CPS results, we also estimated similar equations for the allocation of lump-sum distributions using the HRS. The results are shown in table 3.10. Because the HRS age sample is limited, we do not include indicator variables for different age groups. We do include variables for the size of the distribution, the education of the respondent, and the respondent's current income. The results support the broad patterns of the CPS data, but the differential effects across subgroups are more muted than in the CPS. Increases in the size of the distribution raise the probability that it will be reinvested, as do increases in the respondent's education level up to a college degree. The same *decline* in the probability of reinvesting a distribution between those with college and postcollege education is observed in the CPS and HRS data. There is also a small increase in the probability of reinvesting the distribution as the respondent's income rises, but the effect is only one-fourth as large as that in the CPS.

Table 3.10   **Linear Probability Models for Decision to Reinvest Lump-Sum Distribution**

Variable	Allowing Multiple Distributions per Household	Largest Distribution per Household
Constant	−.012	−.015
	(.011)	(.013)
Size of distribution ($)		
1,000–5,000	.239	.242
	(.015)	(.018)
5,001–10,000	.298	.290
	(.020)	(.024)
10,000+	.317	.313
	(.012)	(.014)
Education indicators		
High school	.033	.031
	(.013)	(.015)
Some college	.043	.045
	(.015)	(.018)
College degree	.084	.097
	(.017)	(.021)
College+	.017	.028
	(.018)	(.022)
Income indicators ($)		
30,000–50,000	−.005	−.002
	(.012)	(.015)
50,000+	.022	.023
	(.013)	(.015)
Adjusted R^2	.183	.174

Source: Authors' estimates using data from the 1992 Health and Retirement Survey.
Note: Numbers in parentheses are standard errors.

Table 3.10 presents two equations estimated using the HRS data, exploiting the more detailed information on the history of lump-sum distribution receipt. The first uses the distribution as the unit of observation, so a given household might appear more than once in the analysis if it received more than one payout. The second column limits the analysis to the largest distribution per household. There are no substantial differences between the two sets of results.

3.5   Conclusion and Future Directions

This paper summarizes existing evidence on the receipt and utilization of lump-sum distributions from qualified retirement saving plans. Using information from both the CPS and the HRS, we demonstrate that lump-sum distributions are common, and that most such distributions are not rolled over into qualified retirement saving accounts. Most *large* distributions are rolled over, however, and the fraction of distribution *dollars* that are reinvested in saving vehicles is substantially greater than the fraction of *distributions* that are reinvested. We document a number of clear patterns with respect to the allocation of lump-sum distributions. More educated workers, older workers, and higher income workers are more likely to roll these distributions into some type of retirement saving account.

Our analysis does not address whether individuals who are *eligible* for lump-sum distributions take such distributions. There is at least some evidence that a substantial group of individuals who separate from their employers do not exercise their right to collect a lump sum, but rather become inactive participants in their employer's qualified pension plan. In 1991, for example, Form 5500 filings show that 6.0 percent of 401(k) participants, 14.5 percent of DB plan participants, and 6.4 percent of DC plan participants were "separated participants with vested rights to benefits." Because choosing not to receive lump-sum distributions is an important means of saving such potential distributions, this margin of individual behavior demands further analysis in the future.

This work represents the first step in a research program that complements our earlier work on eligibility for, and contribution behavior to, 401(k) plans, IRAs, and related saving vehicles. To evaluate the prospective impact of targeted retirement saving plans on the financial status of households that will reach retirement age early in the next century, it is essential to model three decisions: the decision to contribute to these accounts, the decision to roll over funds from other accounts into these accounts, and the decision to withdraw funds from these accounts. A detailed age-specific profile with respect to each of these behaviors is needed as an input to any simulation algorithm for evaluating future financial status, and for comparison with data such as those in our (1994b) paper on actual financial status.

Our preliminary findings, when compared with information tabulated from tax return filings and reported in Yakoboski (1994), suggest the need for further data on the incidence and utilization of lump-sum distributions. IRS tabulations suggest that a very substantial fraction of cash inflows to IRAs is now from rollovers rather than ordinary contributions. These data also suggest that the aggregate flow of premature withdrawals from IRAs and other qualified retirement plans is relatively small, no greater than $12 billion in 1990. This flow should be compared with 1990 contributions to qualified retirement plans, IRAs, and Keogh accounts of nearly $115 billion, and total assets in these accounts of $2.25 trillion.

Our results have also stopped short of a behavioral model of household decisions with respect to lump-sum distributions. In part this reflects the difficulty of modeling a decision that is in part embedded in a more complex choice problem, as many involuntary distributions are associated with job changes. We have not yet been able to focus on voluntary distributions from retirement saving plans, although that is one of our key interests in this area. We plan to address these questions in future work.

References

Andrews, E. S. 1991. Retirement savings and lump sum distributions. *Benefits Quarterly* 2:47–58.

Atkins, G. L. 1986. *Spend it or save it? Pension lump sum distributions and tax reform.* Washington, D.C.: Employee Benefit Research Institute.

Chang, A. 1993. Tax policy, lump sum pension distributions, and household saving. New York: Federal Reserve Bank of New York. Mimeograph.

Employee Benefit Research Institute (EBRI). 1989. Pension coverage and benefit entitlement: New findings from 1988. EBRI Issue Brief no. 94. Washington, D.C.: Employee Benefit Research Institute.

———. 1994. Employment-based retirement income benefits: Analysis of the April 1993 Current Population Survey. EBRI Issue Brief no. 153. Washington, D.C.: Employee Benefit Research Institute.

Fernandez, P. A. 1992. Preretirement lump sum distributions. In *Trends in pensions 1992,* ed. J. Turner and D. Beller. Washington, D.C.: U.S. Department of Labor.

Gelbach, J. 1995. The disposition of lump sum payments from pension plans: A logit analysis. Cambridge: Massachusetts Institute of Technology, Department of Economics. Mimeograph.

Piacentini, J. S. 1990. Preservation of pension benefits. EBRI Issue Brief no. 98. Washington, D.C.: Employee Benefit Research Institute.

Poterba, J. M., S. F. Venti, and D. A. Wise. 1994a. 401(k) plans and tax-deferred saving. In *Studies in the economics of aging,* ed. D. Wise, 105–38. Chicago: University of Chicago Press.

———. 1994b. Targeted retirement saving and the net worth of elderly Americans. *American Economic Review Papers and Proceedings* 84:180–85.

———. 1995. Do 401(k) contributions crowd out other personal saving? *Journal of Public Economics* 58:1–32.

Yakoboski, P. 1994. Retirement program lump-sum distributions: Hundreds of billions in hidden pension income. EBRI Issue Brief no. 146. Washington, D.C.: Employee Benefit Research Institute, February.

Comment   John B. Shoven

This is a difficult paper for a discussant. Certainly it concerns an important topic, the incidence of lump-sum distributions from pension saving plans and the use of the money after the distributions. It also offers value-added on the topic by examining two relatively new data sources, the Employee Benefits Supplement to the 1993 Current Population Survey (CPS) and the first wave (1992) of the Health and Retirement Survey (HRS). Only a few other papers have looked at the 1993 CPS supplement data with this issue in mind, and this is the first paper to use the HRS data for this topic. The difficulty in taking issue with the paper is that it is so straightforward and sensible that it leaves the discussant with little to complain about.

Nonetheless, there are a couple of matters worth mentioning. First, the authors give some statistics in the initial section of the paper that should convince any skeptics that this is an important topic. In 1990, 8.2 million people received lump-sum distributions totaling over $107 billion. In the same year, more than $71 billion was rolled over into individual retirement accounts (IRAs), an amount that exceeds the "normal" contributions to IRAs. The point here is not to criticize the authors, but rather to reinforce their argument—by any measure, the sums involved in lump-sum distributions are massive, and the use of those funds will have a significant impact on the retirement resources of many Americans.

A second matter worth discussing is the definition of when a lump-sum distribution is saved or when the retirement accumulation is preserved. The authors offer two alternative definitions of saving. The first is what they call the "strict" definition, and with it the lump-sum distribution is saved or preserved only if it is rolled over directly into an IRA, invested in a new IRA, or rolled into a new pension plan. The second definition, the broader one, classifies a lump-sum distribution as having been saved if the money is used for any of the "strict definition" purposes or if it is added to a savings account. Clearly, even this modest expansion of the definition of saving of lump-sum distributions makes a difference in the picture the paper paints. Under the strict definition the overall percentage of distributions saved is only 21.6, whereas with the slightly broader definition the figure is 38.0 percent. The issue I want to raise, however, is, why is the broader definition so narrow? In particular, why is there not just as much preservation of saving if the recipient of a lump-sum distribution uses the money to pay off debts rather than deposit the proceeds in a savings account? I do not see the distinction. The real issue should be whether the net wealth of the household drops with the distribution. Ignoring tax issues for the moment, it is clear that debt repayment and asset purchase both can

John B. Shoven is the Charles R. Schwab Professor of Economics and dean of the School of Humanities and Sciences, Stanford University, and a research associate of the National Bureau of Economic Research.

offset the loss of the pension asset that occurs with the disbursement. If one looks at the categories in table 3.3 of the paper, such categories as "used to purchase or start a business," "bought house/paid mortgage," and "paid other loans or debt" are clearly wealth preserving. There are even additional categories, such as "paid educational expenses," where an argument could be made that this is a form of saving or investment. The important point is that, when the authors claim to present two definitions of the preservation of lump-sum saving, both of their definitions are quite narrow and they certainly do not span the entire range of reasonable definitions.

It is not so clear what can be done about the third and final point that I will make about the paper, but it sure would be nice to know something about the precipitating event that caused the lump-sum distribution. There seem to be three broad classes of such events: (1) a job loss or plan termination (i.e., an involuntary or automatic distribution), (2) an income or expenditure shock to the family (a spouse's job loss, a large and unanticipated medical expense, etc.), and (3) planned large expenses such as those associated with the college education of children. In the case of job separation, in many cases whether a lump-sum distribution is made is out of the control of the pension participant. In the case of an income and expenditure shock, an interesting question is whether households tap this money only as a last resort. Do they liquidate other financial assets first, do they exhaust the borrowing available against their home equity, and the like? Given the tax-sheltered aspect of 401(k) plans (other plans may not have the option of hardship withdrawals and not all 401(k) plans do), it probably makes sense to treat it as a last resort source of funds, but the empirical question is whether that is how people behave. If it is last resort money, it still may not make sense to withdraw it since it may be possible to declare bankruptcy and still preserve this wealth.

The question about large planned expenses is whether people use their pension assets strategically to finance such bills as college expenses. The 10 percent early withdrawal penalty can be offset by the tax deferral advantage over a period of six or seven years. In fact, 401(k) or IRA accumulations may be an ideal way to save for college costs because pension assets are usually not taken into account when colleges assess a family's ability to pay and therefore allocate financial aid. There are, of course, several other large expenses, such as the down payment for a house, that could be planned for through pension fund accumulations. As with hardship withdrawals, however, only a minority of plans (typically supplemental plans) allow for voluntary withdrawals.

In order to address the issue of the nature of the precipitating event for the withdrawal and the possible strategic use of these assets for nonretirement accumulations, the authors would need a different data set. Just such a data set has been acquired by Jason Scott, a current Stanford graduate student. The Principal Financial Group gave him the contribution histories of several thousand 401(k) participants as well as demographic and employment data for these individuals. Scott does find some evidence that the probability of withdrawals rises after a holding period of six or seven years, indicating that some of the strategic use of the accounts is indeed occurring.

I would like to end this comment on a positive note. This is a very important topic that has a great deal to do with the economic resources that current pension plan participants will enjoy in retirement. This paper advances our knowledge of this topic considerably, but there is clearly a real need for further research in this area.

4   Does Medicare Eligibility Affect Retirement?

Brigitte C. Madrian and Nancy Dean Beaulieu

4.1   Introduction

Concern over the lack of portability associated with employer-provided health insurance has precipitated a recent flurry of research activity on the effects of health insurance on labor market outcomes. Several estimates suggest that the costs associated with changing doctors and losing coverage for preexisting conditions are sufficient to deter individuals from changing jobs. These costs may be particularly important for older individuals contemplating retirement because a departure from the labor force may involve not only a change in doctors or lack of coverage for preexisting conditions but a complete loss of access to employer-provided group health insurance.

Although all individuals are eligible for government-provided group health insurance—Medicare—upon reaching age 65, most individuals state a desire to retire before age 65 (Employee Benefit Research Institute 1990). In contrast with social security, however, there is no early retirement age before 65 when individuals qualify for Medicare. For some, this is not an issue because their employers provide postretirement health insurance benefits. The majority of workers, however, are not entitled to such benefits because their employers do not offer them. It is these workers whom we would expect to be most concerned about how early retirement will affect their health insurance coverage.

Understanding the role of health insurance in retirement decisions is important because the government is currently trying to encourage later retirement by increasing the social security normal retirement age to 67 over the next

Brigitte C. Madrian is assistant professor of economics at the University of Chicago and a faculty research fellow of the National Bureau of Economic Research. Nancy Dean Beaulieu is a Ph.D. candidate in health policy at Harvard University.

The authors thank Jonathan Gruber, David Cutler, conference participants, and especially James Stock for helpful comments. Brigitte Madrian acknowledges support from an NBER Health and Aging Fellowship and the Harvard University Milton Fund.

several years. There has been some talk about increasing the age of Medicare eligibility correspondingly. Health care reform that makes health insurance more portable from work to retirement may undermine this goal, however, if the potential loss or change in health insurance coverage that currently exists is a significant deterrent to retirement.

While determining the effect of health insurance on retirement is important in its own right, properly accounting for the role of health insurance may also matter in accurately assessing the effects of other factors that have been more extensively studied. For example, previous research by others has concluded that the financial incentives associated with pensions and social security explain a significant fraction of observed retirement behavior; however, these two factors consistently underestimate the retirement that occurs at age 65. One explanation for this "excess" retirement is that individuals wait to retire until they are eligible for Medicare. Separating the effect of social security on retirement at age 65 from that of Medicare is difficult, however, since eligibility for Medicare coincides with the social security normal retirement age of 65. Correctly modeling the role of Medicare may therefore be important in assessing the effects of social security on retirement.

Much of the emerging literature on health insurance and retirement has examined the impact of employer-provided retiree health insurance on retirement, concluding that such health insurance constitutes a significant inducement for early retirement. In contrast, there is little compelling evidence on the effect of Medicare. This paper considers the role of Medicare in the retirement decision and aims to present evidence on whether it, too, impacts this decision.

4.2   The Relationship between Health Insurance and Retirement

4.2.1   Evidence on the Relationship between Health Insurance and Retirement

Table 4.1 summarizes the recent research that considers the relationship between health insurance and retirement. These studies have used several different data sets and a variety of statistical approaches to estimate how health insurance affects retirement. Five of the nine studies listed consider the effect of retiree health insurance on retirement (Madrian 1994; Headen, Clark, and Ghent 1995; Karoly and Rogowski 1994; Gustman and Steinmeier 1994a; Hurd and McGarry 1996). Because such insurance enables individuals to leave the labor force while maintaining the same health insurance coverage available while working, it eliminates the cost associated with giving up one's employer-provided health insurance on retirement. All other things equal, individuals with access to retiree health insurance should thus be expected to retire earlier than individuals without access to such coverage. Indeed, using data from the Current Population Survey (CPS), the National Medical Expenditure Survey (NMES), the Survey of Income and Program Participation (SIPP), the Retire-

Table 4.1   **Estimates of the Effect of Health Insurance (HI) on Retirement**

Study	Data and Sample	Estimation	Results
Rust and Phelan (1997)	Data: RHS Sample: Men 58–63 in 1969 with data through 1979 and no private pension	Structural model of age at retirement *HI variable: 0/1 employer nonretiree HI, 0/1 other HI*	Employer nonretiree HI increases probability of working until 65; Medicare explains spike in retirement hazard at 65 not explained by social security
Gruber and Madrian (1996)	Data: CPS Merged Outgoing Rotation Group 1980–90 Sample: All men 55–64	Probit for being currently retired *HI variable: continuation coverage*	One year of continuation coverage increases probability of being retired by 20 percent
Hurd and McGarry (1996)	Data: HRS Wave I Sample: Men 51–61 and women 46–61, work more than 35 hours/week	Nonlinear regressions for probability of retiring before 62 or 65 *HI variables: 0/1 employer HI and 0/1 retiree HI*	Employer HI increases expected probability of working past 62 or 65; retiree HI decreases these probabilities
Gruber and Madrian (1995)	Data: CPS March 1980–90; SIPP 1984–87 panels Sample: Men 55–64, initial workers	CPS: Probit for retiring during the past year SIPP: Retirement hazard *HI variable: continuation coverage*	One year of continuation coverage increases retirement hazard by 30 percent
Headen, Clark, and Ghent (1995)	Data: CPS August 1988 Sample: All men 55–64 and all women 55–64	Ordered probit for length of time retired *HI variable: 0/1 retiree HI*	Retiree HI increases probability of being retired by 6 percentage points
Madrian (1994)	Data: NMES (1987); SIPP 1984–86 panels Sample: Men 55–84, retired	Truncated regression for age at retirement; probit for retiring before 65 *HI variable: 0/1 retiree HI*	Retiree HI decreases age at retirement by one year; increases probability of retiring before 65 by 7.5 percentage points
Karoly and Rogowski (1994)	Data: SIPP 1984, 1986, and 1988 panels Sample: Men 55–62, initial civilian nongovernmental workers	Probit for retiring during SIPP panel *HI variable: imputed 0/1 retiree HI*	Retiree HI increases retirement hazard by 50 percent
Gustman and Steinmeier (1994a)	Data: RHS Sample: Men 58–63 in 1969 with data through 1979	Structural model of age at retirement *HI variable: imputed value of retiree HI*	Retiree HI delays retirement until age of eligibility, then accelerates it; overall, decreases

(continued)

Table 4.1   (continued)

Study	Data and Sample	Estimation	Results
			retirement age by 3.9 months
Lumsdaine, Stock, and Wise (1994a)	Data: Proprietary firm administrative data Sample: Men and women, initial workers	Structural model of age at retirement *HI variable: imputed value of Medicare*	Value of Medicare has little effect on age at retirement

ment History Survey (RHS), and the Health and Retirement Survey (HRS), all five of these studies estimate that retiree health insurance does encourage early retirement.

Two of the studies assess whether continuation of coverage mandates, which allow individuals to maintain their employer-provided health insurance for a limited period of time after retirement, have a similar impact on retirement (Gruber and Madrian 1995, 1996). Using data from the SIPP and the CPS, this research concludes that such mandates also encourage early retirement.

Only two studies focus on the role of Medicare in the retirement decision: Rust and Phelan (1997) and Lumsdaine, Stock, and Wise (1994a). Using data from the RHS on men without pensions, Rust and Phelan find that individuals with employer-provided health insurance that does not continue past retirement are much less likely to retire than those who have other forms of health insurance (including retiree health insurance) or no health insurance; this effect, however, is smaller after age 65, when these individuals become eligible for Medicare, than before. Overall, they conclude that Medicare explains almost all of the excess spike in the retirement hazard at age 65 after the financial incentives associated with social security have been accounted for.

Using administrative data from a single large employer, Lumsdaine et al. reach the opposite conclusion—that Medicare has little effect on retirement. This result is surprising given the consistent results from the previously mentioned studies suggesting that other forms of health insurance are important factors in deciding when to retire. It is difficult, however, to extend the conclusions in Lumsdaine et al. to the population as a whole because the firm that employed all of the individuals in their data set provided postretirement health insurance benefits. With the opportunity to continue their employer-provided health insurance after retirement, it is not surprising that Medicare would not affect the retirement decisions of these particular individuals.

4.2.2   The Role of Medicare in the Retirement Decision

What role should Medicare play in the retirement decision? The answer depends on a variety of factors. While Medicare has several features that distinguish it from the health insurance policies typically provided by employers or in the private market, there are three characteristics that are important in assessing its effect on retirement. The first is eligibility. All individuals, whether retired or not, are eligible for Medicare on reaching age 65. As mentioned earlier, although the age of Medicare eligibility corresponds to the social security normal retirement age, there is no corresponding early accessibility to Medicare if individuals choose to start receiving their social security benefits early, between the ages of 62 and 65 (although some individuals younger than 65 may also receive Medicare coverage if they are eligible for disability benefits).

A second feature distinguishing Medicare from many other insurance plans is that there are no exclusions for preexisting conditions; all medical conditions are covered from the first day of eligibility onward, whether or not individuals have previously sought treatment for these conditions. A third characteristic of Medicare that differentiates it from other forms of health insurance is that coverage is available *only to individuals*. There is no provision allowing for coverage of spouses, children, or other dependents of individuals who are themselves eligible for Medicare coverage.

The interaction between these characteristics of the Medicare program and the availability of employer-provided health insurance for active employees as well as retirees implies that Medicare will have different effects on the retirement decisions of individuals depending on their own health insurance and family situations. For individuals working in jobs that do not provide health insurance, there is no health insurance loss from early retirement. While these individuals may welcome Medicare coverage, it should not affect their retirement decisions; they will receive Medicare on turning 65 regardless of when they retire from their jobs.

Similarly, individuals who work for employers that do provide health insurance for their active employees and who have the option of maintaining this health insurance when they retire should not have their retirement decisions affected by Medicare. Their health insurance situation will be the same whether or not they are retired, both before age 65, when they have access to employer-provided health insurance, and after, when they have access to both Medicare and employer-provided health insurance.

The individuals who should possibly have their retirement decisions affected by Medicare are those who have employer-provided health insurance while employed but who do not have access to employer-provided retiree health insurance on retirement. For these individuals, retiring before age 65 may involve a loss or change in health insurance coverage. To the extent that losing one's employer-provided health insurance is costly, these individuals have an incentive to postpone retirement until age 65. If, however, these individuals have dependents, then retirement, even at age 65, will involve a loss of health insurance coverage for some members of the family. Such individuals

Table 4.2   Health Insurance Coverage of Non–Medicare-Eligible
                   Women (percent)

	Husband's Age	
Health Insurance	Below 65	65 or Above
Private	83.5	80.0
Employer		
provided	74.5	52.1
Other group	1.2	5.8
Nongroup	6.0	22.4
Medicare	0.7	4.3
Medicaid	2.0	1.7
CHAMPUS	10.5	11.5
No health insurance	12.0	14.5

Source: Authors' calculations using data from the 1987 National Medical Expenditure Survey.

may thus find it in their interest to further postpone retirement until their family members can be covered by other forms of health insurance.

Table 4.2 illustrates the differences in the sources of health insurance coverage for women not yet categorically eligible for Medicare stratified on the basis of whether their husbands are younger or older than age 65. Although non–Medicare-eligible wives of Medicare-eligible husbands are only slightly more likely to be uninsured than wives of non–Medicare-eligible husbands (14.5 percent vs. 12.0 percent), the sources of their health insurance coverage are very different. They are much *less* likely to be covered by employer-provided group health insurance (52.1 percent vs. 74.5 percent) and much *more* likely to be covered by private nongroup health insurance (22.4 percent vs. 6.0 percent). These numbers suggest that a significant fraction of women lose access to employer-provided group health insurance when their husbands retire. Many are able to substitute nongroup health insurance coverage. However, this may be quite costly (especially if individuals have preexisting conditions), and there are likely many women who would find themselves without health insurance except for the fact that their husbands continue to work after age 65 in order to maintain coverage for their wives.

4.2.3   Identifying the Effect of Medicare on Retirement

The discussion above suggests that one possible identification strategy that could be used to estimate the effect of Medicare on retirement is to compare the retirement behavior of three groups of individuals: (1) those whose employers do not provide health insurance, (2) those whose employers provide health insurance to both active employees and retirees, and (3) those whose employers provide health insurance to active employees but not to retirees. If maintaining health insurance coverage is valuable, then, all other things equal, those in the third group should be least likely to retire before age 65. If Medicare provides coverage that is as valued as employer-provided health insurance, then after age 65 there should be no difference in the likelihood of being retired for these three groups.[1]

There are two problems with empirically implementing this identification strategy. The first is that there are no currently available longitudinal data sets that allow us to observe the type of health insurance available to individuals before they retire and to subsequently track their retirement behavior.[2] While the new HRS will make this type of analysis possible, it will not be feasible until more waves of the data have been released.

The second problem is that all other things are not equal for individuals in the three groups described above. In particular, firms that provide health insurance also tend to provide pensions, and pensions tend to have provisions that encourage retirement at particular ages. Thus, using individuals whose employers provide retiree health insurance as a "control" in assessing the retirement behavior of individuals whose employers provide health insurance but not retiree health insurance will not be valid unless it is possible to adequately account for the differential pension incentives that individuals in these two groups face. Once again, the HRS will allow for this type of analysis when sufficient waves of the data are available, but currently the only data sets with detailed pension information either come from a single firm (as used in several papers by Lumsdaine, Stock, and Wise) or do not also include adequate information on health insurance (as is the case with the Survey of Consumer Finances data used by Samwick, 1993).

Rust and Phelan circumvent this latter problem by restricting their sample to individuals who report having no pension. The earlier discussion on how Medicare should affect retirement suggests another possible identification strategy, however. Because Medicare is provided only to individuals and not to their dependents, there will still be a health insurance cost associated with retiring at age 65 if an individual has dependents who are covered by his or her employer-provided health insurance. Thus, we can determine whether Medicare has an effect on retirement by comparing the retirement behavior of individuals with and without dependents who obtain health insurance from that individual's employment.

Because the majority of individuals who provide health insurance to other

---

1. In fact, Medicare is much less generous than the typical employer-provided health insurance policy. Thus, there may still be some value in maintaining one's employer-provided health insurance even after becoming eligible for Medicare.

2. The RHS does include some information on health insurance coverage. Rust and Phelan (1994) and Gustman and Steinmeier (1994a) have used these data to infer what type of health insurance coverage was available to individuals before they retired. Gustman and Steinmeier, however, have substantially lower health insurance coverage rates than found in data sets typically cited as sources of health insurance coverage such as the NMES or the SIPP. In contrast, Rust and Phelan have coverage rates than are substantially higher for their subset of the population than is found in these other sources. Thus, the health insurance data in the RHS appear to be somewhat unreliable.

family members are men, this paper focuses on the retirement behavior of men. Although some older men nearing the age of retirement still have dependent children at home, most do not. The majority, however, are married. The identification strategy used in this paper will be to compare the retirement behavior of men who have spouses older than age 65 and are thus already eligible for Medicare with the retirement behavior of men whose spouses are not yet eligible for Medicare.

Consider a simple specification for the retirement hazard of an individual covered by employer-provided health insurance that does not continue into retirement:

$$\Pr(\text{Retire}_t | \text{Not retired}_{t-1}) = \alpha \text{ (Demographic characteristics)}$$

(1)
$$+ \beta \text{ (Own financial incentives)}$$

$$+ \gamma \text{ (Spouse's financial incentives)} + \varepsilon$$

The function $\alpha(\cdot)$ may contain such factors as age, health status, marital status, education, and other things that would affect the value of leisure. The function $\beta(\cdot)$ includes financial variables that directly affect one's retirement:

$$(2) \quad \beta_1 \cdot \left(\begin{array}{c} \text{Social} \\ \text{security} \end{array} \right) + \beta_2 \cdot \left(\begin{array}{c} \text{Private} \\ \text{pension} \end{array} \right) + \beta_3 \cdot \left(\begin{array}{c} \text{Medicare} \\ \text{eligibility} \end{array} \right) + \beta_4 \cdot \left(\begin{array}{c} \text{Other} \\ \text{wealth} \end{array} \right).$$

$\beta(\cdot)$ could also include other factors such as an individual's earning capacity. Recent research suggests that both the level of pension and social security wealth and expected future accruals affect retirement. The function $\gamma(\cdot)$ would include a similar vector of variables for the individual's spouse that may also impact the individual's retirement decision: the social security and pension incentives that encourage one spouse to retire at a particular age may also provide liquidity that enables the other spouse to retire as well; similarly, whether a spouse is eligible for Medicare will affect the amount of wealth that can be used to finance nonhealth consumption during retirement in the same way that an individual's own Medicare eligibility does.

Because Medicare eligibility coincides with the social security normal retirement age for most individuals, and with the normal retirement age of many private pension plans, it is difficult to separately identify β_1, β_2, and β_3 in equation (2) above. Similarly, if a spouse has worked and also qualifies for a pension or social security in her own right, it will be difficult to separately identify γ_1, γ_2, and γ_3. There is, however, a nontrivial fraction of older women who have never participated in the labor force. For men married to these women, there are no financial benefits associated with a wife's retirement that would also encourage their own retirement. If a woman has never worked, she can only claim social security benefits based on her husband's earnings, and she can only do so *after* her husband begins to claim benefits himself. In this case, $\gamma_1 = \gamma_2 = 0$ and the effect of a spouse's Medicare eligibility, γ_3, can be identified.

If men value health insurance coverage of themselves and their wives equally, then $\gamma_3 = \beta_3$ and the effect of own Medicare eligibility is identified as well. If men value their own health insurance coverage more than that of their wives, then γ_3 will provide a lower bound on the effect of own Medicare eligibility on retirement.

Note that this identification strategy is essentially based on the spouse's age since, with the exception of those with disabilities, eligibility for Medicare occurs at age 65. Thus, all other things equal, retirement rates should be higher among men with wives who are age 65 or older than among men with wives who are younger than 65.

4.3 Data

We use data from the 5 percent public use samples of the 1980 and 1990 censuses. The primary advantage of census data is that they afford a large sample size. This is particularly important given the identification strategy outlined above based on whether a spouse is eligible for Medicare. Figure 4.1 shows the distribution of the differences between husband's age and wife's age in the census. Over half of the men in figure 4.1 have spouses who are the same age or between one and four years younger than themselves. Because the distribu-

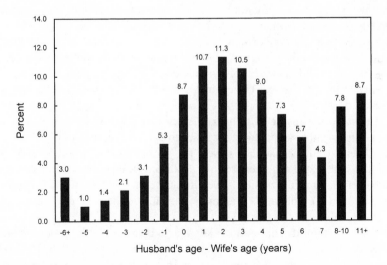

Fig. 4.1 Distribution of spousal age differences: men aged 55–69
Source: Authors' calculations using the 5 percent public use samples from the 1980 and 1990 censuses.

tion of spouse's age relative to own age is so compressed, a big data set like the census allows us to exploit a broader range of variation in spouse's age. The disadvantage of the census is that it includes no information on health insurance coverage. It is therefore impossible to compare the retirement probabilities of those with and without health insurance in order to see whether, as predicted, the effect of Medicare on retirement is confined to those who actually did have employer-provided health insurance before retirement. This, however, should bias us *against* finding an effect of Medicare on retirement since we will essentially be estimating the average of no effect among those without employer-provided health insurance or with retiree health insurance and whatever effect may exist for those with employer-provided health insurance.

The census also does not contain information on pension benefits or expected social security benefits. Rather than impute the values of these variables for individuals, we exclude them from the estimation and assume that spouse's age is uncorrelated with these factors which, by exclusion, become a part of the error term, ε. To us, this does not seem like an unreasonable assumption. We find it unlikely that men who married in their 20s and 30s chose a spouse of a specified age based on their tastes for retirement. It is more likely the case that divorce and later remarriage could be correlated with tastes for retirement or other unobserved factors such as pension benefits. For example, men with extremely generous pension benefits may be more likely to attract "trophy" spouses. We will assume, however, that these effects are small.

Spouse's age may, however, be correlated with who is in the sample. In particular, retirement-aged men who had at one time married women much older than themselves will be more likely to be widowers because their spouses are already deceased. These men will thus be excluded from the sample (divorce will cause a similar type of sample selection problem). This exclusion will be on the basis of spouse's age. As long as the assumption that spouse's age is exogenous is valid, however, this will merely result in a thinning of the sample for men with older wives. The estimates will be less precise, but they will not be biased.

The sample is restricted to married men with a spouse in the data set. We further restrict the sample to men whose wives are no more than 15 years older or 20 years younger than themselves. The restriction is imposed because, beyond this range, the cell sizes are quite small and we do not want the estimation to be driven by a few outliers. Overall, our census sample includes approximately 800,000 individuals. Summary statistics on these individuals are presented in table 4.3.

The definition of retiring in the last year is being currently out of the labor force but having worked one or more weeks in the previous calendar year. In the census, "the last year" represents a 16-month window since the census is conducted in April and the work question is asked about the previous calendar year. Using this definition, 14.4 percent of our sample retired in the last "year."

Table 4.3   **Summary Statistics**

Statistic	Value
Sample size	799,069
Race	
White	91.6%
Nonwhite	8.4
Education	
Less than high school	34.1
High school graduate	29.5
Some college	16.5
College graduate	19.9
Retired in last year (if worked last year)	14.4
Age	60.4
Age of wife	57.1
Spouse never worked	7.5

Source: Authors' tabulations using data from the 5 percent public use samples of the 1980 and 1990 censuses. Sample is all married men aged 55–69 who worked at least one week in the previous calendar year and whose spouses are not more than 15 years older or 20 years younger than themselves.

4.4   Estimating the Effect of Medicare on the Probability of Being Retired

4.4.1   Basic Results

We begin in table 4.4 by simply tabulating the retirement hazards for men whose wives are not Medicare eligible (wife's age < 65) and for those whose wives are Medicare eligible (wife's age ≥ 65). The smallest cell size is 654 for individuals who are age 55 and have a wife older than age 65. These estimates, therefore, are fairly reliable. As would be expected, the retirement hazard is small for men still in their 50s and increases quite substantially at ages 62 and 65. The typical spikes in the retirement hazard at ages 62 and 65 are not as pronounced in the census data because the definition of retirement is one that occurred within the past 16 months and the age in the table is current age rather than age at the start of this 16-month period. Thus, the retirement hazard of individuals initially aged 61 will be spread out over 62- and 63-year-olds in the table.

The retirement hazards in table 4.4 are, as we would predict, higher at all ages for those whose wives are eligible for Medicare. The absolute percentage point differential between these two hazards (the last column) appears roughly constant at about 3 or 4 percentage points. Although these results are suggestive that Medicare eligibility does encourage retirement, one could expect similar results for other reasons. For example, if women face greater financial incentives to retire at older ages and these financial rewards also make it easier for their husbands to retire, then conditional on own age, men with older wives

Table 4.4   **Retirement Hazard by Age and Wife's Medicare Eligibility**

| | Wife's Age | | |
| | Below 65 | 65 or Older | Difference |
Age	(1)	(2)	(1) − (2)
55	0.0468	0.0780	0.0312
56	0.0515	0.0958	0.0443
57	0.0563	0.0880	0.0317
58	0.0625	0.0903	0.0278
59	0.0700	0.0995	0.0295
60	0.0936	0.1390	0.0454
61	0.1075	0.1359	0.0284
62	0.2170	0.2859	0.0689
63	0.2254	0.2737	0.0483
64	0.2139	0.2423	0.0284
65	0.3154	0.3484	0.0330
66	0.3131	0.3425	0.0294
67	0.2915	0.3249	0.0334
68	0.2892	0.3334	0.0442
69	0.3025	0.3419	0.0394

Source: Authors' tabulations using data from the 5 percent public use samples of the 1980 and 1990 censuses. Sample is all married men aged 55–69 who worked at least one week in the previous calendar year and whose spouses are not more than 15 years older or 20 years younger than themselves.

will be more likely to retire. Alternatively, men may value their own leisure time more if their wives are retired, and this too will make husbands more likely to retire if their wives are older and more likely to be retired (for a discussion of joint retirement issues, see Hurd 1990; Gustman and Steinmeier 1994b; Blau 1994, 1995). Or, to the extent that continued work competes with the amount of time that men can spend with their wives before the health problems incumbent with age set in, men with older wives will be more likely to retire than men with younger wives. By stratifying the sample on the basis of whether wife's age is greater or less than 65, one would find a pattern of results similar to those in table 4.4 even if it were not Medicare eligibility per se but one of these other reasons that also implied that having an older spouse leads to earlier retirement.

One way to gauge the importance of these alternative explanations is to look at the pattern of retirement rates associated with spouse's age. Consider the following general specification for a retirement hazard that incorporates all three of the above explanations:

$$(3) \quad \Pr(\text{Retire}_t | \text{Not retired}_{t-1}) = \alpha \left(\frac{\text{PDV}}{\text{assets}} \right) + \beta \left(\begin{array}{c} \text{Spouse not} \\ \text{working} \end{array} \right) + \gamma \left(\begin{array}{c} \text{Age of} \\ \text{spouse} \end{array} \right) + \varepsilon.$$

A spouse's ineligibility for Medicare will operate through the $\alpha(\cdot)$ function above, affecting the retirement hazard by decreasing the present discounted value (PDV) of assets that can be used to finance nonhealth consumption. If the discount rate is positive and the relationship between assets and retirement is linear, then, conditional on own age, the effect of spouse's age on the retirement hazard will be as pictured in figure 4.2A. Before the spouse reaches age 65, the retirement hazard should decline as the spouse is younger and has successively more years before becoming eligible for Medicare. The rate of de-

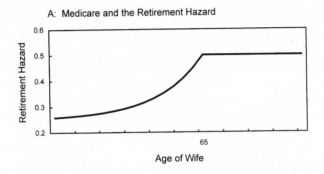

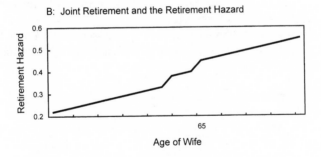

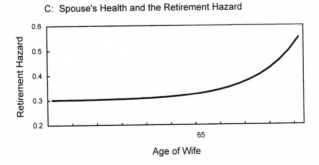

Fig. 4.2 **Factors affecting the retirement hazard**

cline should slow, however, as expected medical and/or insurance expenditures in the future are discounted. After the spouse is 65, however, there is no further health insurance cost in terms of leaving the spouse without employer-provided health insurance; thus, the hazard rate should not change with spouse's age after the spouse reaches age 65.

Joint retirement considerations will affect the retirement hazard through the $\beta(\cdot)$ function in equation (3). If they are the primary force behind the retirement hazard's increasing with spouse's age, we should see a steady increase in retirement probabilities as the spouse gets older and is herself more likely to retire. We might expect to see especially large increases as the spouse reaches ages 62 and 65 and faces the incentives associated with social security that increase the retirement hazard at these ages (see fig. 4.2B). To the extent that most women have already retired by age 65, the joint retirement hypothesis would not be inconsistent with a constant hazard after the spouse has reached age 65; if there are continued incentives for women to retire after age 65, however, and enough women are still working at this age, then the joint retirement explanation should be associated with increasing retirement hazards with respect to spouse's age even after the spouse is age 65.

Finally, the $\gamma(\cdot)$ function in equation (3) characterizes the effect of spouse's health on retirement. If it is spouse's health that is driving the results in table 4.4, then the retirement hazard should be increasing at an *increasing* rate in spouse's age, as shown in figure 4.2C, as health becomes progressively worse (and mortality more likely) with age.

To examine which of these alternatives appear to be borne out in the data, figure 4.3 graphs the retirement hazards of men at various ages against the

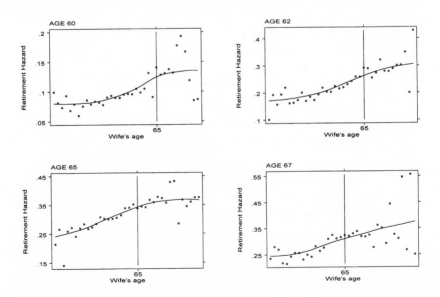

Fig. 4.3   Retirement hazard by wife's age

differences between their ages and their spouses' ages (the ages shown in fig. 4.3 are 60, 62, 65, and 67).[3] The circles in the graph give the actual retirement rates calculated from the 1980 and 1990 censuses for each age difference. The vertical line gives the age at which the wife becomes eligible for Medicare; thus, this line shifts to the right as the age considered in the graph increases. The line drawn through the circles in the graph is a nonparametric weighted smoothed mean (with bandwidth = 0.7). This smoothing was done to decrease the noise in the retirement rates in the tails of the age difference distribution.

The graphs for ages 60, 62, and 65 show a pattern not inconsistent with that in figure 4.2A: roughly constant for spouses older than 65 and decreasing at a decreasing rate with spouse's age less than 65. None of the graphs gives any suggestion of the retirement pattern in figure 4.2C that would prevail if spousal health concerns were a predominant consideration in retirement decisions. None of the graphs is completely inconsistent with the joint retirement hypothesis.

We can parameterize the patterns shown in figure 4.3 with the following regression:

$$\Pr(\text{Retire} \mid \text{Not retired}_{t-1}) = \beta_1 \cdot \underline{\text{Age}} + \beta_2 \cdot \underline{\text{Age}}$$
$$* \left[\ln(65 - \text{Wife's Age}) \mid \text{Wife} < 65 \right]$$
$$+ \beta_3 \cdot \underline{\text{Age}} * (\text{Wife} \geq 65) + \beta_4 \cdot \underline{\text{Age}}$$
$$* (\text{Wife's Age} - 65).$$

(4)

In this regression, $\underline{\text{Age}}$ is a vector of age dummies and the coefficient vector β_1 will give a baseline retirement hazard for each age. The second term, $[\ln(65 - \text{Wife's Age}) \mid \text{Wife} < 65]$, equals zero if wife's age is 65 or older and equals the log of $(65 - \text{Wife's Age})$ if wife's age is less than 65. This term is meant to capture the decreasing retirement hazard with respect to wife's age for wives younger than 65 shown in figure 4.2A. The third term is a dummy variable for whether or not wife's age is 65 or older. Finally, the fourth term is the preceding dummy variable interacted with the difference between wife's age and age 65 for Medicare-eligible women. The coefficient β_4 will thus measure whether there is any slope in the retirement hazard with respect to wife's age for men with wives older than 65. Note that the last three terms in equation (4) are all interacted with the vector of age dummies so that each variable will be associated with a vector of coefficients for each age between 55 and 69.

Table 4.5 presents the coefficients from estimating equation (4) using ordinary least squares. The regression coefficients tell a story similar to that of figure 4.3. The vector of constant terms, β_1, increases with age and exhibits the familiar spikes at both age 62 and age 65. The β_2 coefficients are all nega-

---

3. Note that these are not mutually exclusive arguments for why men with older wives are more likely to be retired. Indeed, there are men who probably make retirement decisions for all of the reasons suggested.

Table 4.5   Effect of Spouse's Age and Medicare Eligibility on Retirement

		Independent Variable		
Age	Constant (β_1)	ln(65 − Wife's Age) if Wife < 65 (β_2)	Wife ≥ 65 (β_3)	Wife's Age − 65 if Wife ≥ 65 (β_4)
55	.0704	−.0094	.0074	.0002
	(.0080)	(.0031)	(.0205)	(.0083)
56	.0775	−.0107	.0074	.0058
	(.0075)	(.0030)	(.0190)	(.0067)
57	.0740	−.0075	.0074	.0032
	(.0069)	(.0029)	(.0157)	(.0049)
58	.0871	−.0110	−.0108	.0063
	(.0063)	(.0027)	(.0142)	(.0041)
59	.0947	−.0115	.0017	.0013
	(.0056)	(.0026)	(.0123)	(.0033)
60	.1210	−.0135	.0161	.0007
	(.0052)	(.0025)	(.0108)	(.0026)
61	.1431	−.0187	−.0164	.0038
	(.0048)	(.0024)	(.0086)	(.0023)
62	.2747	−.0326	.0075	.0016
	(.0042)	(.0023)	(.0082)	(.0020)
63	.2705	−.0278	−.0101	.0057
	(.0040)	(.0029)	(.0074)	(.0017)
64	.2453	−.0211	−.0042	.0006
	(.0038)	(.0023)	(.0065)	(.0016)
65	.3619	−.0337	−.0221	.0044
	(.0039)	(.0024)	(.0059)	(.0014)
66	.3551	−.0321	−.0150	.0012
	(.0044)	(.0028)	(.0061)	(.0013)
67	.3302	−.0305	−.0090	.0016
	(.0050)	(.0033)	(.0065)	(.0013)
68	.3356	−.0372	−.0156	.0052
	(.0060)	(.0038)	(.0071)	(.0012)
69	.3382	−.0287	.0010	.0009
	(.0066)	(.0044)	(.0079)	(.0011)

Source: Authors' calculations using data from the 5 percent public use samples of the 1980 and 1990 censuses. Sample is all married men aged 55–69 who worked at least one week in the previous calendar year and whose spouses are not more than 15 years older or 20 years younger than themselves. The sample size is 799,069, and the R^2 = 0.219.

tive and significant (with t-statistics ranging from 2.6 to 14.4) and increase in magnitude with own age from roughly −.010 for ages less than 60 to −.030 for ages greater than 65. These coefficients confirm the hypothesis that at all ages men with wives not yet eligible for Medicare are less likely to retire the younger are their spouses. We might also expect the magnitude of the coefficients to increase with age as spouse's lack of Medicare eligibility should have a greater absolute effect on the retirement hazard for men who themselves have a greater likelihood of retiring. The β_3 and β_4 coefficients in table 4.5 show no strong patterns, change in sign, and are generally insignificant (only 6 of the 30 coefficients have t-statistics exceeding 2 in magnitude). These results suggest that the retirement hazard is roughly constant with respect to wife's age once the wife is 65 or older and eligible for Medicare.

4.4.2   Alternative Explanations

Although the lack of a slope in the retirement hazard with respect to spouse's age greater than 65 is consistent with Medicare eligibility's playing an important role in retirement decisions, it is not, as mentioned earlier, completely inconsistent with a joint retirement story. This explanation for the patterns in the retirement hazard, however, relies on the premise that the wife is or at one time was working. If the effects presented in table 4.5 derive only from the financial rewards associated with the wife's collection of social security and/or pension benefits before age 65 or other joint retirement considerations, they should be confined to those men who have wives who have a history of labor force participation and there should be no effect among men whose wives have never worked. That is, in the specification of the retirement hazard in equation (4), the function $\beta(\cdot)$ will have no differential impact by spouse's age.

Because the census collects data on work history, this comparison is possible. Fortunately, a large enough fraction of the cohorts of men aged 55–69 in 1980 and 1990 had wives who reported never having worked (about 8 percent), so the comparison is feasible as well. Table 4.6 gives the retirement hazards shown in table 4.4 for the subsample of men whose wives never worked. As before, the hazards for those with spouses older than 65 tend to be greater than the hazards for those with spouses younger than 65. The wife older than 65 hazard and the differential (last column) is somewhat more noisy for those whose spouses have never worked because this stratification breaks even the census into somewhat small cell sizes for those at young ages who have Medicare-eligible spouses. For the older ages, however, the results suggest that even among those who have never worked, having a Medicare-eligible spouse increases the retirement hazard. The differential is on average smaller for those whose spouses have never worked than for those whose spouses have worked, suggesting that some of the effects in table 4.4 can perhaps be attributed to joint retirement or other considerations associated with having a spouse older than oneself.

Table 4.7 presents the regression coefficients of table 4.5 for the subsample of men whose wives never worked. The baseline retirement rate, β_1, is slightly higher for this subsample of men than for the full sample. The effect of having a spouse not yet eligible for Medicare (β_2) is, as in table 4.5, always negative, although at younger ages the coefficients are not significant. This is due in part to a significantly smaller sample, and to the fact that the coefficient estimates bounce around a little more. The overall pattern of coefficients, however, is very similar to that in table 4.5—increasing and becoming more significant

Table 4.6   **Retirement Hazard by Age and Wife's Medicare Eligibility if Spouse Never Worked**

| | Wife's Age | | |
| | Below 65 | 65 or Older | Difference |
Age	(1)	(2)	(1) − (2)
55	0.0656	0.0517	−0.0139
56	0.0713	0.1045	0.0332
57	0.0784	0.0722	−0.0062
58	0.0772	0.0598	−0.0174
59	0.0861	0.0943	0.0082
60	0.1092	0.1759	0.0667
61	0.1295	0.1368	0.0073
62	0.2582	0.2914	0.0332
63	0.2582	0.3152	0.0570
64	0.2447	0.2764	0.0317
65	0.3579	0.3931	0.0352
66	0.3708	0.3721	0.0013
67	0.3135	0.3530	0.0395
68	0.3269	0.3515	0.0246
69	0.3505	0.3778	0.0273

Source: Authors' calculations using data from the 5 percent public use samples of the 1980 and 1990 censuses and the 1980–94 March Current Population Survey. Sample is all married men aged 55–69 who worked at least one week in the previous calendar year and whose spouses are not more than 15 years older or 20 years younger than themselves.

with age. Similarly, the vectors of β_3 and β_4 coefficients are also similar to those in table 4.5: they jump around in magnitude, they change sign, and they are generally insignificant. Restricting the sample to men whose wives have never worked thus yields results very similar to those obtained from the full sample of men.

4.5   Conclusions

While we hesitate to draw strong conclusions about the effect of Medicare eligibility on retirement behavior because the census data used in the analysis are less than ideal, we think that the results presented in the paper are suggestive that Medicare may indeed influence the retirement decisions of men. Our main findings are as follows: (1) 55–69-year-old men with Medicare-eligible spouses have a higher retirement hazard than men without Medicare-eligible spouses. (2) The retirement hazard exhibits a pattern with respect to spouse's age that is consistent with what would be expected if Medicare were an important consideration in the retirement decision. It is inconsistent with a story that other factors more generally related to spouse's age, such as a spouse's health status, are strong determinants of retirement as the retirement hazard appears to be roughly constant after the spouse reaches age 65 rather than generally

Table 4.7   Effect of Spouse's Age and Medicare Eligibility on Retirement if Spouse Never Worked

		Independent Variable		
Age	Constant (β_1)	ln(65 − Wife's Age) if Wife < 65 (β_2)	Wife ≥ 65 (β_3)	Wife's Age − 65 if Wife ≥ 65 (β_4)
55	.0815	−0.0063	−.0130	−.0114
	(.0351)	(.0138)	(.0781)	(.0338)
56	.0970	−.0105	.0620	−.0253
	(.0338)	(.0137)	(.0770)	(.0242)
57	.0839	−.0023	−.0238	.0053
	(.0309)	(.0129)	(.0648)	(.0187)
58	.1169	−.0177	−.0642	.0028
	(.0274)	(.0120)	(.0581)	(.0146)
59	.1078	−.0101	−.0361	.0080
	(.0248)	(.0113)	(.0516)	(.0121)
60	.1199	−.0053	.0219	.0141
	(.0215)	(.0103)	(.0422)	(.0107)
61	.1502	−.0110	−.0251	.0045
	(.0189)	(.0096)	(.0362)	(.0083)
62	.3236	−.0377	−.0219	−.0040
	(.0167)	(.0091)	(.0309)	(.0069)
63	.2899	−.0200	−.0112	.0149
	(.0161)	(.0094)	(.0278)	(.0061)
64	.2790	−.0238	.0080	−.0050
	(.0144)	(.0089)	(.0244)	(.0058)
65	.3856	−.0208	−.0161	.0115
	(.0144)	(.0094)	(.0213)	(.0047)
66	.3943	−.0195	−.0266	.0022
	(.0151)	(.0104)	(.0210)	(.0045)
67	.3655	−.0441	−.0418	.0130
	(.0180)	(.0137)	(.0229)	(.0042)
68	.3490	−.0200	−.0059	.0032
	(.0195)	(.0143)	(.0239)	(.0037)
69	.3976	−.0434	−.0294	.0031
	(.0232)	(.0173)	(.0271)	(.0034)

Source: Authors' calculations using data from the 5 percent public use samples of the 1980 and 1990 censuses. Sample is all married men aged 55–69 who worked at least one week in the previous calendar year and whose spouses are not more than 15 years older or 20 years younger than themselves. The sample size equals 59,731 and $R^2 = 0.263$.

increasing. (3) The pattern of effects is approximately the same when the sample is confined to men whose wives have never worked. This latter group of men cannot be affected by any financial considerations inducing their wives to retire. Furthermore, having a nonworking spouse cannot differentially impact the retirement hazard with respect to spouse's age of this group because their wives have never worked. The most plausible explanation for the pattern of retirement effects exhibited by this latter group is the Medicare eligibility of their wives. Because the effects are similar for the whole population of men regardless of spouse's work history, it is likely that Medicare is also an important determinant of retirement for all men.

References

Blau, David M. 1994. Labor force dynamics of older married couples. Chapel Hill: University of North Carolina. Mimeograph.
———. 1995. Social security and the labor supply of older married couples. Chapel Hill: University of North Carolina. Mimeograph.
Employee Benefit Research Institute. 1990. *Employee benefit notes.* Washington, D.C.: Employee Benefit Research Institute, November.
Gruber, Jonathan, and Brigitte C. Madrian. 1995. Health insurance availability and the retirement decision. *American Economic Review* 85:938–48.
———. 1996. Health insurance and early retirement: Evidence from the availability of continuation coverage. In *Advances in the economics of aging,* ed. David A. Wise. Chicago: University of Chicago Press.
Gustman, Alan L., and Thomas L. Steinmeier. 1994a. Employer provided health insurance and retirement behavior. *Industrial and Labor Relations Review* 48:124–40.
———. 1994b. Retirement in a family context: A structural model for husbands and wives. NBER Working Paper no. 4629. Cambridge, Mass.: National Bureau of Economic Research.
Headen, Alvin E., Robert L. Clark, and Linda Shumaker Ghent. 1995. Retiree health insurance and the retirement timing of older workers. Raleigh: North Carolina State University. Mimeograph.
Hurd, Michael D. 1990. The joint retirement decision of husbands and wives. In *Issues in the economics of aging,* ed. David A. Wise. Chicago: University of Chicago Press.
Hurd, Michael D., and Kathleen McGarry. 1996. Prospective retirement: Effects of job characteristics, pensions, and health insurance. Mimeograph.
Karoly, Lynn A. and Jeanette A. Rogowski. 1994. The effect of access to post-retirement health insurance on the decision to retire early. *Industrial and Labor Relations Review* 48:103–23.
Lumsdaine, Robin L., James H. Stock, and David A. Wise. 1994a. Pension plan provisions and retirement: Men and women, Medicare, and models. In *Studies in the economics of aging,* ed. David A. Wise. Chicago: University of Chicago Press.
———. 1994b. Retirement incentives: The interaction between employer-provided pensions, social security, and retiree health benefits. NBER Working Paper no. 4613. Cambridge, Mass.: National Bureau of Economic Research.
Madrian, Brigitte C. 1994. The effect of health insurance on retirement. *Brookings Papers on Economic Activity* 1:181–252.
Rust, John, and Christopher Phelan. 1997. How social security and Medicare affect retirement behavior in a world of incomplete markets. *Econometrics* 65:781–832.
Samwick, Andrew A. 1993. Retirement incentives in the 1983 Pension Provider Survey. Hanover, N.H.: Dartmouth College. Mimeograph.

Comment   James H. Stock

This paper addresses a question at the intersection of two important areas of economic and policy research, the economic effects of health insurance and the retirement behavior of older workers. Because health care use increases with age, it makes sense that the particulars of a worker's health care situation will have a substantial impact on his or her retirement decisions. Moreover, to the extent that Medicare eligibility affects the timing of retirement, policy proposals that would change the age of Medicare eligibility could have significant effects on the ages of retirement. Quantifying these interactions is of evident importance both to those interested the economics of aging and to Medicare policy analysts.

Before proceeding to the particulars of Madrian and Beaulieu's empirical analysis, it is useful to lay out the central economic issues of the effect of Medicare on retirement. As discussed by Madrian and Beaulieu, there is now a well-developed literature on the retirement behavior of individuals. It is well established that economic incentives have significant and, importantly, predictable effects on retirement rates. For example, defined benefit plans typically induce spikes in retirement hazards at ages of eligibility and at ages in which the present value of benefits increase sharply. Because Medicare can be thought of as another retirement benefit, in light of this literature it would be quite surprising were Medicare eligibility *not* to have an effect on retirement. Rather, the relevant economic and policy question is whether Medicare is valued by potential retirees at more than its marginal cost to the government, or at more than its private replacement cost were retirees instead to purchase health insurance on the private market. This is not implausible if individuals are risk averse about changing medical coverage or if they are unable to obtain suitable coverage because of exclusions on preexisting conditions. If a dollar of government spending on Medicare is valued more on the margin than a dollar of government spending on social security, then it would be welfare improving to reduce social security expenditures and increase Medicare expenditures.

Results already in the literature can be used to obtain a rough estimate of the effect of Medicare on retirement rates at age 65. Consider a couple with employer-provided health insurance, and suppose that private insurance for the couple costs $6,500 in 1995 dollars. If the couple values Medicare at this private replacement cost, then the availability of Medicare corresponds to an accrual of retirement benefits of $6,500 when the couple becomes eligible for Medicare. Although the estimates of the effects of a $6,500 accrual on retirement differ depending on the couple's other benefits and on the model used, a typical estimate can be obtained from the retirement models in table 4 of

James H. Stock is professor of political economy at the John F. Kennedy School of Government, Harvard University, a research associate of the National Bureau of Economic Research, a fellow of the Econometric Society, and chair of the board of editors of the *Review of Economics and Statistics*.

Lumsdaine, Stock, and Wise (1993), which predicts an increase in the retirement hazard by between 3 and 6 percentage points. This corresponds to approximately one-fifth to one-third of the jump in retirement hazards observed at age 65, depending on the data set. One question thus is whether Medicare eligibility in fact produces an increase in retirement rates greater than those predicted by current structural models of retirement. If so, this would be evidence either that the models are misspecified or that individuals value Medicare at more than its private replacement cost.

With these general remarks in mind, now turn to the particulars of Madrian and Beaulieu's paper. In contrast to the parametric, structural model approaches pursued by most papers on retirement, Madrian and Beaulieu take a more nonparametric approach. The thought experiment is to find two otherwise identical couples, one who will bear costs of medical insurance and one who will be eligible for some Medicare coverage. To implement this strategy empirically, one would like to have data on pensions, wages, and social security benefits, by individual. However, these variables are not observed in Madrian and Beaulieu's data set, so additional assumptions are needed to identify the effect of Medicare.

To examine the identification strategy more precisely, it is useful to refer to the authors' initial equation linking the retirement hazard to demographic characteristics, the man's financial incentives, his spouse's financial incentives, and other determinants (the error term). As Madrian and Beaulieu point out, if the spouse has never worked, then the spouse's financial incentives will be restricted to Medicare, which is strictly linked to her age. Present value calculations suggest a particular functional form for the effect on the man's retirement of this benefit as a function of spouse's age. If, furthermore, the difference between husband's age and spouse's age is uncorrelated with any of the man's (unmeasured) financial incentives, then estimation of hazard functions involving this spouse's age effect should reveal the effect of Medicare.

This is a clever idea, and surely some of what it measures is related to the effect of Medicare. One unmeasurable effect is, however, the benefits a couple would get from joint retirement, both financial (possibly some cost reductions, or from moving) and, arguably more important, nonfinancial. It stands to reason that, all else equal, the older the spouse the more likely the husband is to choose retirement, simply so the couple can enjoy their retirement together. Presumably this effect is also nonlinear in both of their ages, although the precise form of the nonlinearity is presumably hard to determine.

It is useful to contemplate a hypothetical data structure that would permit controlling for this joint retirement effect. One would be if some spouses were randomly assigned to be Medicare eligible, while some spouses were randomly denied eligibility; this random assignment would need to be done far enough in advance for the couple to incorporate it into their retirement planning. Thinking of this approach makes it clear that Medicare eligibility has two effects: the direct subsidy at a certain age, but also the disincentive effect on savings, so that in a world without Medicare individuals would have different preretirement asset profiles. Both these effects will impact the decision to retire.

In summary, Madrian and Beaulieu's idea of quantifying the effect of Medicare eligibility using nonparametric comparisons is appealing, and the evidence they present is consistent with the view that Medicare provides a significant incentive for retirement. Some of the challenges to achieving identification arise from data limitations in the census, and these will be reduced with new data sets with greater information about retirement decisions that will soon become available. However, some of these difficulties are inherent in the nonfinancial issues surrounding joint retirement.

The set of issues surrounding health insurance and retirement are of central importance for analyzing the impact of current policy proposals such as postponing the date of Medicare eligibility and cutting back Medicare and/or social security funding. Related is whether individuals value the marginal Medicare expenditure at more than it costs the government to provide, in which case a dollar taken out of social security would arguably be more acceptable to the elderly than a dollar taken out of Medicare, all else equal. I look forward to seeing further work by Madrian and Beaulieu and others addressing these important problems.

Reference

Lumsdaine, R. L., J. H. Stock, and D. A. Wise. 1993. Why are retirement rates so high at age 65? Cambridge, Mass.: Harvard University, Kennedy School of Government. Manuscript.

5 Caring for the Elderly: The Role of Adult Children

Kathleen McGarry

5.1 Introduction

The soaring cost of medical care for the elderly has imposed a sizable burden on society. In 1992 average health care expenditures for those aged 65 or over were $9,125, compared to $2,349 for those under age 65 (American Federation of Aging Research and Alliance for Aging Research 1995). For the elderly, much of the cost results from long-term care. In 1989, 77 percent of Medicaid funding directed toward those aged 65 or over was spent on nursing homes or home health care.

Policymakers have devised various strategies to combat these growing expenditures. Governor Pataki of New York State has proposed drastic cuts in spending for home health care and housekeeping services, in an effort to balance the state's budget. President Clinton has taken the opposite approach, proposing expanded home services as a substitute for more expensive nursing homes (Lewin-VHI, Inc. 1993). To evaluate the potential impacts of such policies, we need a clear understanding of the use and provision of home health care.[1] Who are the preferred caregivers? How much substitution is there between formal and informal care? Will increasing the availability and affordability of home health care decrease more expensive nursing home admissions and therefore costs, or will the substitution away from unpaid care toward formal paid care be large enough to offset any savings?

Kathleen McGarry is assistant professor of economics at the University of California, Los Angeles, and a faculty research fellow of the National Bureau of Economic Research.

The author thanks Michael Hurd, Hilary Sigman, and James P. Smith for helpful comments. Financial support from the Brookdale Foundation and from a National Institute on Aging fellowship through grant T32-AG00186 to the NBER is gratefully acknowledged.

1. Throughout the paper I will use the terms "home health care" and "home care" interchangeably. In a strict sense home health care refers to medically related services while home care refers to housekeeping services.

Underlying these issues is the larger question of what drives transfers between family members. Much has been written about the magnitude of financial transfers made between generations (Gale and Scholz 1994; Kotlikoff and Summers 1981; McGarry and Schoeni 1997). Are the resources we observe flowing between parents and children given for altruistic reasons or are they made as part of an exchange? By considering the possibility that home care is provided in exchange for financial compensation, I will begin to address this issue.

This paper takes advantage of the new survey of the Asset and Health Dynamics among the Oldest Old (AHEAD) to document the current use of home health care by the population aged 70 or over. It expands on past work in this subject by exploring the role played by financial compensation from parents to children as a method of encouraging children to provide care, and by controlling more completely for factors such as income and wealth that may affect access to services.

In section 5.2 I describe the data in more detail, in particular pointing out the advantages of AHEAD in addressing these issues. Section 5.3 presents some descriptive statistics for the sample and for the measures of impairment I use in the remainder of the paper. Sections 5.4 and 5.5 analyze the receipt and provision of care in a multivariate framework. A final section concludes and offers directions for future research.

5.2 Data

AHEAD is a longitudinal survey of individuals born in 1923 or earlier and their spouses or partners. Baseline interviews were completed in the fall of 1993 when respondents were approximately 70 years old or older. The second wave of interviews is scheduled to be administered in the fall of 1995. Thus, at the time of this writing, only cross-sectional information is available.

AHEAD is unique in providing a large nationally representative sample of older Americans.[2] The survey contains detailed questions on income, assets, health, as well as a good deal of information on each of the respondent's children. The breadth of the survey allows for improvements over past studies of the provision of home health care. A respondent's financial resources can be carefully controlled for along with the presence or absence of health insurance. Thus it will be possible to examine how the choice of paid or unpaid care varies with the ability to pay. Similarly detailed health indicators allow for precise measurement of impairment. As described below, the survey collects information on limitations with respect to specific activities of daily living (ADLs) and instrumental activities of daily living (IADLs), as well as on the

---

2. Individuals in heavily black and Hispanic areas and residents of Florida were oversampled. Population comparisons therefore require weighting. With the exception of the regressions that control for race, the results reported in this paper are based on weighted observations.

existence of specific diseases, overall health measures, and service use. The information available on the number of children the respondent has, the child's geographic distance from the respondent, his employment status, family income or earnings, and the number of own children (grandchildren to the respondent) will help explain the choice of informal home care arrangements and the distribution of responsibility across siblings.

The entire sample consists of 8,224 individuals.[3] From this original sample I exclude 132 respondents for whom the interview is incomplete, bringing the sample size down to 8,092.[4] Many of these elderly have health problems: 35 percent report themselves to be in fair or poor health, 22 percent have been hospitalized in the past year, and 89 percent have been to the doctor in the past year, with the average number of office visits just over five.

Respondents are asked whether they are limited with respect to certain ADLs or IADLs, and whether they receive assistance with these tasks. In general, ADLs are personal care items while IADLs relate to housekeeping tasks. The six ADLs are walking across a room, dressing, bathing, eating, getting in or out of bed, and toileting. The five IADLs are preparing meals, grocery shopping, using the phone, taking medication, and managing money. The ADL questions are of the form

Does anyone ever help you bathe or shower?

Do you get that help most of the time, some of the time, or only occasionally?

Do you have any difficulty bathing (even when someone helps you/without help)?

Who most often helps you bathe?

Similar questions are asked with respect to the other ADLs. Individuals are coded as having an ADL limitation if they state that they get help, they use equipment (for walking and getting in or out of bed), they have difficulty with the task, or they do not do the activity for health reasons; 28.9 percent of respondents were limited with respect to at least one ADL.

The IADL questions are similar:

Are you able to prepare hot meals without help?

Is that because of a health problem?

Without help do you have any difficulty preparing meals?

Who most often helps you?

Who else most often helps you?

Again respondents are coded as having difficulty with an IADL if they needed help or did not do the task because of a health problem; 29.3 percent of the

---

3. These results are based on the "post-alpha" release of AHEAD.
4. Although 783 of the respondents are below the age of 70, I include these individuals in the study in order to keep the sample sizes as large as possible.

sample have difficulty with at least one IADL. Forty percent have at least one ADL or IADL constraint. The proportion of individuals with various ADL and IADL limitations is shown in table 5.1. The most common ADL difficulty is in walking. Twenty-three percent of the entire sample have difficulty walking across the room without help or the use of equipment. Thirteen percent have difficulty dressing, and 12 percent have difficulty bathing. With respect IADLs, almost 18 percent have difficulty handling their finances, and nearly that proportion have problems with grocery shopping. I also report the proportion with various limitations conditional on having at least one ADL or IADL limitation (the "impaired sample"). Of those experiencing difficulty with at least one task, 58 percent have difficulty walking across the room, and 44 percent have difficulty with grocery shopping.

The means for variables used in the analysis are shown in table 5.2 for the full sample, and separately by whether the respondent has a limitation. The latter two groups differ in the expected ways. The impaired sample is older (with a mean age of 79 vs. 75 among the nonimpaired), more likely to be nonwhite (20 percent vs. 13 percent), less likely to be male, and in generally worse health. Fifty-six percent of the impaired sample report themselves to be in fair or poor health, compared to just 21 percent of the nonimpaired sample.

Those who require assistance are less well off in terms of both income and wealth. Their mean income is $19,073, compared to $26,299 for the healthier sample, and mean wealth is $136,379, compared to $214,787. Those who have limitations also have a greater number of children living within 10 miles, although the total number of children does not differ significantly. The impaired sample is less likely to be married and more likely to live with an individual who is not a spouse, probably because of their need for care. Surprisingly, 82 percent of the "healthy" sample have private health insurance (typically as a

Table 5.1   **Percentage of Sample with Various ADL and IADL Limitations**

Task	Percentage of Entire Sample	Percentage of Impaired Sample
ADLs		
Walking	23.1	57.9
Dressing	12.6	31.7
Bathing	11.8	29.7
Eating	5.1	12.8
In/out bed	9.3	23.2
Toileting	4.5	11.2
Any ADL	28.9	72.4
IADLs		
Preparing meals	9.1	22.9
Grocery shopping	17.5	43.9
Using telephone	5.1	12.7
Taking medication	4.8	11.9
Managing money	17.6	44.2
Any IADL	29.3	73.6

Table 5.2   **Comparison of Means**

Variable	All Respondents $n = 8{,}092$[a] Mean	S.E.	Need Assistance $n = 3{,}261$[a] Mean	S.E.	Do Not Need Assistance $n = 4{,}831$[a] Mean	S.E.
Demographic characteristics						
Age	76.67	0.070	79.08	0.117	75.07	0.079
Nonwhite	0.157	0.004	0.201	0.006	0.129	0.004
Male	0.368	0.005	0.343	0.008	0.384	0.006
Highest grade completed	10.93	0.038	9.84	0.065	11.65	0.044
Health measures						
Health excellent/very good	0.344	0.005	0.174	0.006	0.456	0.007
Health good	0.305	0.005	0.266	0.007	0.331	0.006
Health fair/poor	0.351	0.005	0.560	0.008	0.212	0.005
Number of ADL limitations	0.663	0.014	1.664	0.027	–	–
Number of IADL limitations	0.561	0.011	1.408	0.022	–	–
Number of nights in hospital	2.429	0.132	4.490	0.315	1.070	0.057
Prob. of living 10 yrs[b]	0.428	0.004	0.351	0.007	0.465	0.005
Prob. of entering nursing home (5 yrs)[b]	0.140	0.002	0.178	0.005	0.121	0.003
Access/affordability						
Wealth	183,536	3,846	136,379	5,741	214,787	5,106
Income	23,419	284	19,073	372	26,299	399
Medicare coverage	0.951	0.002	0.958	0.003	0.946	0.003
Medicaid coverage	0.091	0.003	0.151	0.006	0.051	0.003
Private insurance coverage	0.770	0.004	0.688	0.007	0.824	0.005
Number of children	2.72	0.022	2.75	0.036	2.70	0.027
Number of kids in 10 miles	0.869	0.012	0.929	0.020	0.830	0.015
Married	0.537	0.005	0.467	0.008	0.583	0.007
Live with others (incl. children)	0.203	0.004	0.264	0.007	0.162	0.005
Family linkages						
Prob. of leaving inheritance[b]	0.550	0.005	0.463	0.008	0.594	0.006
Child(ren) in will 0/1	0.530	0.005	0.465	0.008	0.573	0.007
Child(ren) on deed to home 0/1	0.099	0.003	0.114	0.005	0.089	0.004
Value of home	74,452	1,292	57,540	1,518	85,659	1,893
Child(ren) beneficiaries of life insurance 0/1	0.178	0.004	0.180	0.006	0.177	0.005
Face value of life insurance	757.6	101.8	523.8	55.8	912.6	166.3

(*continued*)

Table 5.2   (continued)

Variable	All Respondents $n = 8,092^a$		Need Assistance $n = 3,261^a$		Do Not Need Assistance $n = 4,831^a$	
	Mean	S.E.	Mean	S.E.	Mean	S.E.
Number of kids gave						
$5,000+ (past 10 yrs)	0.359	0.009	0.266	0.012	0.420	0.013
Trust for child(ren) 0/1	0.091	0.003	0.076	0.004	0.101	0.004
Value of trust	22,808	1,618	13,019	1,407	29,323	2,538
Number of kids gave						
transfer (last year)	0.378	0.009	0.289	0.012	0.436	0.012
Total value of transfers						
(last year)	1,304	101	1,028	92.5	1,486	157

Note: S.E. = standard error.

[a]Number of observations for some variables differs due to missing values.

[b]Means calculated over nonmissing observations.

supplement to Medicare), compared to 69 percent of the impaired sample. This difference could indicate that access to health insurance has a protective effect, or perhaps that the decision to purchase insurance is influenced by affordability rather than by adverse selection (Hurd and McGarry 1997).[5]

The degree of impairment differs along income and wealth lines, perhaps indicating a lifetime history of illness that may have hindered labor market performance. As shown in table 5.3, 44 percent of those in the lowest income quartile had at least one ADL limitation, and the mean number of ADL limitations was 1.11 for this group. In the highest income quartile, 18 percent of the population had at least one ADL limitation, and the mean number of such limitations was 0.38. The results are similar for the number of IADL limitations, and for a stratification by wealth rather than income. The respondents in the lowest quartiles are more than twice as likely to face difficulties with daily tasks as respondents in the highest quartiles.

5.3   Characteristics of the Impaired Population

The analyses in the remainder of the paper are restricted to the sample of 3,261 individuals with one or more ADL or IADL limitation.

---

5. The sample of impaired elderly appears similar to other data sets. See, e.g., Ettner (1994), Soldo, Wolf, and Agree (1990), and Stone, Cafferata, and Sangl (1987), all of whom use the National Long-Term Care Survey (NLTCS), and Mutchler and Bullers (1994), who use the 1984 Survey of Income and Program Participation (SIPP). In contrast to the NLTCS, AHEAD collects data on all children and household members, thus providing information on *potential* caregivers. AHEAD also provides a substantially larger sample of needy respondents, more detailed information on potential caregivers, and more extensive health information than does SIPP.

Table 5.3   **ADL and IADL Limitations by Income and Wealth Quartiles**

	Quartile			
Limitation	Lowest	2nd	3rd	4th
By Income				
ADLs				
Percentage with any	43.99	32.66	22.76	18.10
Mean number	1.11	0.73	0.51	0.38
IADLs				
Percentage with any	44.63	31.78	23.05	19.85
Mean number	0.93	0.61	0.42	0.33
By Wealth				
ADLs				
Percentage with any	44.67	31.89	23.31	18.33
Mean number	1.15	0.71	0.46	0.40
IADLs				
Percentage with any	44.67	31.26	23.14	20.00
Mean number	1.01	0.56	0.40	0.32
Number of observations[a]	1,988	2,054	2,026	2,024

[a]Quartiles do not each contain 25 percent due to lumping of observations.

Table 5.4   **Distribution of ADL and IADL Limitations (percent of sample)**

Number of ADL Limitations	Number of IADL Limitations						
	0	1	2	3	4	5	Total
0	–	21.69	4.01	0.97	0.56	0.38	27.59
1	18.37	9.27	2.73	1.47	0.49	0.33	32.67
2	5.46	4.90	2.48	1.06	0.73	0.50	15.12
3	1.73	2.85	2.32	1.26	0.67	0.43	9.25
4	0.57	1.61	1.32	1.14	0.59	0.84	6.06
5	0.26	0.57	1.09	0.94	0.64	0.87	4.36
6	0.02	0.24	0.42	0.63	0.94	2.69	4.94
Total	26.41	41.12	14.38	7.46	4.61	6.03	100

Note: Calculations based on a sample of 3,261 observations with at least one ADL or IADL limitation. Numbers may not sum to 100 percent due to rounding.

5.3.1   Limitations

Many respondents suffer from multiple problems. The distribution for the total number of ADL and IADL limitations for this impaired sample is shown in table 5.4. The Clinton health care proposal classified individuals as disabled if they suffered three or more ADL limitations (Lewin-VHI, Inc. 1993). One-quarter of the individuals in my subsample (or 10 percent of the entire survey population) would be so classified. Eighteen percent have difficulty with three or more IADLs. Fully 5 percent of this restricted sample have difficulty with all ADLs, and 6 percent have difficulty with all IADLs. Close to 3 percent of the sample have difficulty with all given activities.

As one would expect, the existence of various ADL and IADL limitations is positively correlated (table 5.5). The largest correlation is between the IADLs of using a phone and managing money at 0.56. Among the ADLs, the largest correlation is between dressing and bathing at 0.48. The correlations typically range from 0.25 to 0.45, and all but the correlation between getting in or out of bed and managing money are significant at the 1 percent level. The latter is significant at the 1.4 percent level.

Difficulties with the various tasks are not equally restrictive. Needing a cane to cross the room is less of a burden than being unable to bathe without help. Similarly, difficulty managing money may be less limiting than difficulty preparing meals or using a telephone. As is apparent from table 5.5, the correlations between walking or managing money and the other variables are less strong than some of the other correlations. For example, the correlations between having difficulty dressing and difficulty with the other ADLs are all larger than those between walking and the same ADLs.

5.3.2   Caregivers

When looking at who provides the care, the results from AHEAD should be interpreted with some caution. With respect to ADL limitations, respondents are asked who "*most often*" helps them walk, dress, and so forth, so that only the primary caregiver is obtained for each task. If, for example, two children share the caregiving chores, information is only obtained on the one who helps most often with each particular task. While the questions are asked with respect to each ADL, it is generally the case that the same person helps "most often" with each task with which the respondent needs assistance. This result

Table 5.5   **Correlations between Limitations**

| Task | ADLs | | | | | | IADLs | | | | |
	Walk	Dress	Bath	Eat	Bed	Toilet	Meals	Shop	Phone	Med	Money
Walking	1.00	0.24	0.28	0.20	0.32	0.22	0.18	0.20	0.07	0.10	−0.16
Dressing		1.00	0.48	0.37	0.41	0.40	0.35	0.29	0.22	0.30	0.05
Bathing			1.00	0.38	0.41	0.38	0.29	0.38	0.25	0.33	0.11
Eating				1.00	0.32	0.39	0.22	0.29	0.37	0.41	0.21
Bed					1.00	0.43	0.30	0.27	0.21	0.24	0.04
Toileting						1.00	0.05	0.25	0.26	0.31	0.12
Meals							1.00	0.48	0.42	0.45	0.24
Shopping								1.00	0.27	0.32	0.16
Phone									1.00	0.56	0.26
Medicine										1.00	0.33
Money											1.00

Notes: Calculations based on 3,261 observations with at least one ADL or IADL limitation. Correlations are all significant at the 1 percent level except Money*Bed, which is significant at the 1.4 percent level.

is to be expected. It would be difficult to imagine a case in which one individual helped the respondent get out of bed and a second individual stood by to help with dressing or toileting. In fact, of those who receive help with at least one ADL, 84 percent report help from just one caregiver. The questions are also problematic in that information on a helper is only obtained if the respondent receives help "most of the time," and not if she receives help either "some of the time" or "only occasionally." In the analyses that follow, approximately 5 percent of the sample receive care, but the source of the care is not obtained. The sequence of questions for IADL limitations is similar, but up to two helpers are obtained for each limitation.

Hours of care provided by each caregiver are also obtained from the respondent. The total amount of time can be derived from two questions in the AHEAD survey, although the calculation requires some assumptions. For each individual who is listed as providing assistance with an ADL or IADL limitation, respondents are asked

How often in the last month did HELPER n help you? (Every day, several times a week, about once a week, less than once a week, or not at all)

Those who responded every day, several times a week, or about once a week were asked to report a number of hours per day. Total number of hours per week (or per month) can therefore be calculated. I use the straightforward imputation supplied by the AHEAD staff. For those who helped every day, the reported number of hours per day was multiplied by seven. Those who helped "several times a week" were assumed to help 3.5 days, and the number of hours was multiplied by 3.5. "About once a week" was assumed to mean exactly once a week. Those who helped less than once a week, and for whom there is therefore no information on hours, were assumed to provide exactly one hour of care per week. Finally, those who did not help in the past month were assigned zero hours of care. I did not impute a value if the respondent could not give an answer to either the question about number of days or the question about number of hours of help.[6]

Fortunately, the majority of those in need do receive care. Of the 3,261 respondents with at least one ADL or IADL limitation, 61 percent (weighted) received assistance from a caregiver of some sort. Table 5.6 shows the breakdown of helpers by the relationship of the caregiver. Twenty-seven percent of caregivers are spouses, and approximately 32 percent are children (20.5 percent are non-coresident children and 11.3 coresident). Grandchildren and children-in-law together make up 6.5 percent of all caregivers. Other relatives account for 5.3 percent, and live-in help, either paid or unpaid, represents 8 percent of the caregivers. Other individuals make up 12.5 percent of caregiv-

6. See Wolf, Freedman, and Soldo (1995) for a similar imputation that assigns values to these missing data points.

Table 5.6   Distribution of Helper Relationships by Marital Status of Recipient (percent of helpers)

Relationship	Marital Status of Recipient		
	All	Married	Single
Spouse	27.0	67.2	–
Child, non-coresident	20.5	12.2	25.9
Child, coresident	11.3	3.9	16.2
Child-in-law, non-coresident	2.4	0.9	3.4
Child-in-law, coresident	1.6	0.4	2.4
Grandchild	2.5	0.6	3.8
Other relative	5.3	3.4	6.6
Live-in helper, paid	1.0	0.0	1.6
Live-in helper, not paid	7.0	1.5	10.6
Other person, paid	6.0	3.0	7.9
Other person, not paid	6.5	2.3	9.2
Organization, paid	6.3	3.0	8.5
Organization, not paid	2.5	1.1	3.5
Total[a]	100.0	100.0	100.0
Number of observations	2,721	1,088	1,633

[a]Columns may not sum to 100 percent due to rounding.

ers, divided evenly between paid and unpaid persons. Organizations constitute the remaining 9 percent, the majority of whom are paid for their services.

This distribution varies by several factors. Respondents who are not married (table 5.6) obviously do not receive care from a spouse. For these individuals, children shoulder much of the burden, comprising 42 percent of the caregivers for those who are unmarried, compared to only 16 percent for the married sample. The number of coresident children or children-in-law providing care increases dramatically among those who are unmarried, as does the proportion of live-in helpers. The "other person" category and the proportion of organizations are also substantially more important among unmarried individuals.

The choice of caregiver also varies by the type of limitation. In table 5.7, the distribution of caregivers who help with ADL limitations is shown separately from the distribution of those who help with IADL limitations. An individual can provide help with each type of task and can therefore be included in each column. Those helping with ADLs are far more likely to be paid helpers than are those helping with IADLs. Almost 30 percent of ADL helpers are paid, compared with just 11 percent of IADL helpers. Spouses are equally likely to perform both types of help, as are coresident children, while non-coresident children are represented more heavily among IADL caregivers than among ADL providers. As one would expect given the types of activities involved, it is apparently difficult or costly for non-coresident individuals to assist with ADLs.

Table 5.7   **Distribution of Helper Relationships by Type of Help Provided (percent of helpers)**

	Type of Help[a]		
Relationship	All	ADL	IADL
Spouse	27.0	29.5	28.5
Child, non-coresident	20.5	7.4	20.4
Child, coresident	11.3	13.7	12.4
Child-in-law, non-coresident	2.4	1.2	2.4
Child-in-law, coresident	1.6	2.1	1.8
Grandchild	2.5	0.5	2.6
Other relative	5.3	2.8	4.8
Live-in helper, paid	1.0	2.6	1.1
Live-in helper, not paid	7.0	8.5	7.8
Other person, paid	6.0	12.7	5.2
Other person, not paid	6.5	2.2	6.4
Organization, paid	6.3	13.6	4.4
Organization, not paid	2.5	3.3	2.1
Total[b]	100.0	100.0	100.0
Number of observations	2,721	753	2,346

[a]A helper may be in both columns.

[b]Columns may not sum to 100 percent due to rounding.

Table 5.8 shows that the number of hours provided varies substantially with the type of caregiver. Spouses work almost "full time" at 35 hours per week (among those with positive hours). Help from children differs greatly by whether the child coresides with the parent. Non-coresident children provide an average of 8.5 hours per week, and coresident children, 38.4 hours. The largest average number of hours is provided by paid live-in helpers, who apparently supply help almost around the clock, averaging 114 hours in a week.

As demonstrated in table 5.9, the individual providing the care is substantially more likely to be female than male, regardless of the relationship between the caregiver and the recipient. This difference is well documented in other studies. For example, Coward and Dwyer (1990) find that daughters are three times more likely to provide care to parents than are sons. My differences are less dramatic, but still striking. An even larger sex difference exists among children-in-law who provide care. Here daughters-in-law often provide care for their husbands' parents whereas sons-in-law scarcely ever care for their spouses' parents. Over 80 percent of the children-in-law who provide care are female (for additional evidence and discussion, see Stoller, Forster, and Duniho 1992).

The results in table 5.9 are consistent with the widely held belief that daughters are more likely to provide care than are sons. In my sample, the probability that a daughter of an impaired parent provides care is 0.14 compared with 0.06 for a son (not shown). Even among those children providing care, daughters

Table 5.8   Mean Number of Hours of Help by Relationship of Helper

Relationship	Mean Hours	Standard Error
Spouse	34.9	1.71
Child, non-coresident	8.5	0.58
Child, coresident	38.4	2.71
Child-in-law, non-coresident	6.0	0.79
Child-in-law, coresident	22.4	4.67
Grandchild	6.1	0.97
Other relative	12.8	1.80
Live-in helper, paid	114.2	12.23
Live-in helper, not paid	35.6	3.22
Other person, paid	31.3	2.75
Other person, not paid	7.5	1.37
Organization, paid	16.5	1.84
Organization, not paid	6.6	0.84

Table 5.9   Percentage of Helpers Who Are Female by Relationship of Helper

Relationship	Percentage Female	Relationship	Percentage Female
Spouse	64.5	Other relative	73.1
Child, non-coresident	70.6	Live-in helper, paid	94.9
Child, coresident	67.9	Live-in helper, not paid	69.5
Child-in-law, non-coresident	81.4	Other person, paid	68.4
Child-in-law, coresident	80.7	Other person, not paid	63.3
Grandchild	76.1		

provide a greater number of hours than do sons, 16.5 hours per week versus 11.8 hours.

Because men earn more than women in the labor market, it may be more efficient for sons to work additional hours and provide *financial* assistance rather than their time to an elderly parent. However, differences in the provision of financial assistance by the sex of the child are small. Only 1.09 percent of daughters in the sample made a cash transfer to their impaired parents in the last year (as reported by the parents), compared with 1.07 percent of sons. The amounts given by daughters, however, are somewhat lower than those by sons. Over positive values the mean amount of the transfer was $2,119 for daughters and $3,345 for sons. However, because only 74 daughters and 71 sons gave transfers, it is impossible to draw any significant conclusions from these numbers. In the following section I explore gender differences in caregiving in a multivariate context.

While almost two-thirds of the sample who need assistance do receive help, a substantial portion of those with one or more ADL or IADL limitations receive no help.[7] One would hope that those who do not receive assistance are less severely impaired than their counterparts who do receive care. Table 5.10 demonstrates the difference in the means for these two groups: those with ADL or IADL limitations who receive care and those with limitations who do not.

In fact, it does appear that those not receiving care are less impaired. They are younger and more schooled, both characteristics that are positively correlated with health. They have significantly fewer ADL and IADL limitations, are less likely to report their health status as fair or poor, and on average spent fewer nights in a hospital. Those who are not helped have greater income and more wealth. They are also significantly more likely to be married.

5.3.3   Motivation for the Provision of Care

Why do children provide care to a parent? One broad model holds that transfers between family members are exchange based (for a discussion of the theories of transfers, see Cox 1987; Altonji, Hayashi, and Kotlikoff 1994). Thus children are perhaps providing assistance to their parents in exchange for financial help or the promise of an inheritance (Bernheim, Shleifer, and Summers 1985). However, the simple correlations provide little support for this theory. The higher the probability with which an individual expects to leave an inheritance, the lower the probability of that individual's receiving help from children. The correlation is -0.21 and is significantly different from zero at the 1 percent level. Similarly, the correlation between wealth (or the potential size of the estate) and the probability of receiving care from children is also negative, -0.12, and significantly different from zero at the 1 percent level. The transfer of cash ($5,000 or more) in the past 10 years to children is also negatively related to the probability of help from a child, and the relationship is significantly different from zero. There is no significant relationship between these variables and the probability of receiving paid help.

Wealthier parents, even those with at least one ADL or IADL limitation, are likely to be in better health and therefore need less care than do poorer parents. Thus the simple correlations confound a number of factors. Below I control for many of these components of the decision simultaneously.

5.4   Care Provided to Elderly Individuals

Which needy elderly receive help and which must manage on their own depends on a number of factors that must be controlled for simultaneously. Certainly, the availability of kin to provide care, and the existence of financial resources to purchase care, will influence whether care is received as well as the type of care. Similarly, the severity of the limitation will influence care. In this section I examine the relationship between numerous observable characteristics of the respondent and her family and whether care is received, whether

7. In table 5.10, 2,149 out of the 3,261 respondents, or 66 percent, receive care. If these numbers are scaled by sample weights, the fraction receiving care falls slightly, to 61 percent.

Table 5.10   **Comparison of Means**

Variable	Impaired Respondents $n = 3,261^a$		Helped $n = 2,149^a$		Not Helped $n = 1,112^a$	
	Mean	S.E.	Mean	S.E.	Mean	S.E.
Demographic characteristics						
Age	79.08	0.11	80.25	0.15	76.85	0.18
Nonwhite	0.201	0.006	0.226	0.008	0.153	0.010
Male	0.343	0.008	0.349	0.009	0.331	0.013
Highest grade completed	9.84	0.065	9.36	0.082	10.75	0.098
Health measures						
Health excellent/very good	0.174	0.006	0.133	0.007	0.250	0.012
Health good	0.266	0.007	0.237	0.008	0.320	0.013
Health fair/poor	0.560	0.008	0.628	0.009	0.430	0.014
Number of ADL limitations	1.664	0.027	2.070	0.036	0.891	0.023
Number of IADL limitations	1.408	0.022	1.909	0.028	0.660	0.013
Number of nights in hospital	4.49	0.315	5.64	0.468	2.31	0.180
Prob. of living 10 yrs[b]	0.351	0.007	0.327	0.010	0.383	0.011
Prob. of entering nursing home (5 yrs)[b]	0.178	0.005	0.177	0.007	0.180	0.008
Access/affordability						
Wealth	136,379	5,741	119,032	7,994	169,362	6,601
Income	19,073	372	17,252	435	22,537	686
Own home	0.7493	0.0044	0.6589	0.0076	0.8091	0.0052
Medicaid coverage	0.151	0.006	0.186	0.008	0.085	0.008
Private insurance coverage	0.688	0.007	0.640	0.009	0.778	0.011
Number of children	2.75	0.036	2.82	0.046	2.62	0.056
Number of kids in 10 miles	0.929	0.020	0.994	0.025	0.805	0.030
Married	0.467	0.008	0.446	0.010	0.507	0.014
Live with others (incl. children)	0.264	0.007	0.315	0.009	0.166	0.010
Family linkages						
Prob. of leaving inheritance[b]	0.463	0.008	0.412	0.011	0.445	0.012
Child(ren) in will 0/1	0.465	0.008	0.431	0.010	0.530	0.014
Child(ren) on deed to home 0/1	0.114	0.005	0.122	0.006	0.101	0.008
Value of home	57,540	1,518	49,773	1,892	72,309	2,490
Child(ren) beneficiaries of life insurance 0/1	0.180	0.006	0.177	0.007	0.186	0.011
Face value of life insurance	523.8	55.8	549.0	77.4	475.7	66.4
Number of kids gave $5,000+ (past 10 yrs)	0.266	0.012	0.230	0.014	0.335	0.024
Trust for child(ren) 0/1	0.076	0.004	0.063	0.005	0.100	0.008
Value of trust	13,019	1,407	9,739	1,514	19,346	2,918
Number of kids gave transfer (last year)	0.289	0.012	0.260	0.015	0.345	0.021
Total value of transfers (last year)	1,028	92.5	871	100	1,327	189.5

Note: S.E. = standard error.

[a]Number of observations for some variables differs due to missing values.

[b]Means calculated over nonmissing observations.

care is purchased, and whether care is received from a non-coresident child. Section 5.5 looks at the decision from the caregivers' point of view and examines which children are likely to provide care.

Other researchers have limited their samples to unmarried individuals under the assumption that married people are cared for almost exclusively by a spouse. As shown in table 5.5, this assumption is not entirely consistent with the data. Certainly, a spouse is the most likely caregiver, but married individuals also receive help from children, as well as paid care.[8] Furthermore, because almost half (47 percent) of the sample is married, eliminating these individuals excludes a large part of the sample. I therefore include all individuals in the regressions, regardless of marital status. I control for the difference in the set of potential caregivers by including variables for marital status and the number of children. I also allow marital status to be interacted with sex to allow for differential effects for male and female respondents.[9]

5.4.1 Receipt of Care

I look first at the question of who among those with a limitation receives care. The comparison of means showed that healthier individuals were less likely to receive assistance. Here I estimate a probit model that controls for a number of factors.[10] Included in the equation as right-hand–side variables are several controls for health: the respondent's self-assessed health status (excellent or very good, good [omitted], fair or poor), her age, number of ADL limitations, number of IADL limitations, number of nights spent in a hospital in the past year, the respondent's self-reported probability of living approximately 10 more years, and the reported probability of entering a nursing home in the next five years.[11]

I control for the availability of informal care by including the respondent's marital status, number of children, and number of daughters (because daughters appear to be more likely to provide care). I also include the number of children who live within 10 miles of the parent, and whether there are individuals other than a spouse present in the home. A spouse is likely to be a primary

---

8. It is likely that care from children is underestimated because the survey design tends to capture only the primary caregiver.

9. Estimating the model separately by marital status resulted in small changes in several coefficients. These changes do not alter the conclusions or provide any insight into the decision process. I therefore present the regression estimates based on the entire sample.

10. Results for a linear probability model are similar and are reported in an earlier version of the paper.

11. AHEAD queries respondents about an array of diseases. The various illnesses are quite prevalent: 55 percent of the sample have high blood pressure, 35 percent have had a heart attack or have a heart condition, and 20 percent have had a stroke. If dummy variables indicating the presence of each of the noted conditions (high blood pressure, diabetes, cancer, lung disease, heart disease, stroke, broken hip, and surgical replacement of any joint) are included in the regressions, they are jointly significant at the 5 percent level, but not at the 1 percent level. The coefficients on the remaining variables are not altered by the inclusion of disease measures. Surprisingly, even the indicators of excellent or poor health are largely unchanged. To simplify the discussion I do not include the disease controls here.

source of care, yet husbands may provide a different level of care than do wives. I therefore include an interaction of sex and marital status, allowing married women to have a different probability of receiving care than married men. Similarly, I interact marital status with race to allow for differential effects.

To proxy the affordability of paid care, I include income and wealth (in quartiles), the existence of a private insurance policy,[12] and whether the respondent was eligible for Medicaid.

To examine the importance of exchange, I include numerous measures that could serve as avenues of exchange: The number of children to whom the respondent gave $5,000 or more in the past 10 years, the number of children receiving cash assistance in the past year, and whether a child's name is on the deed to the parent's home. I also include the total amount of cash transferred to all children during the past year, and the value of the home if the parent has put a child's name on the deed. If parents are holding resources until their death in order to motivate attentive behavior in children, they may do so through wills, life insurance, and trusts. I include variables for whether the respondent names a child in her will, whether she has established a trust, the value of the trust, whether a child is listed as a beneficiary on a life insurance policy, and the face value of those policies. The larger the possible inheritance, the more the children ought to want to please their parents, if bequests are made strategically. Similarly, I include a variable indicating whether the parent owns a home.[13]

Finally, demographic characteristics are included: age, race, sex, and schooling level of the respondent.

The estimated coefficients are reported in table 5.11 along with the derivatives evaluated at the means of the right-hand–side variables. Significance levels are indicated by superscripts on the coefficient estimates. The results provide strong evidence that assistance is determined in large part by need. Older respondents, those with a greater number of ADL or IADL difficulties, and those with more nights in a hospital are all significantly more likely to get help, with significance determined at the 5 percent level. Those in excellent health are significantly less likely to receive assistance. The effects, in most cases, are large. Each additional IADL difficulty increases the probability of assistance by almost 20 percentage points. The effect of ADL limitations is smaller; each increases the probability by only 6.4 percent. The difference between the effect of ADL limitations and IADL limitations on the probability of receiving help is perhaps due to the difficulty of providing help with personal care relative to housekeeping chores.

---

12. Ninety-six percent of the sample had Medicare coverage, so for the majority of respondents this insurance is a supplement to Medicare.

13. While these variables are certainly plausible means of exchange, they likely also measure the degree of closeness of the family. Future work taking advantage of the multiple observations within a family will attempt to disentangle the two explanations.

Table 5.11   **Probit Estimates for the Probability of Receiving Care and Type of Care**

Variable	Probability of Receiving Care		Probability of Paying for Care		Probability of Care from Children	
	Coeff.	Deriv.[a]	Coeff.	Deriv.[a]	Coeff.	Deriv.[a]
Demographic characteristics						
Age	0.0023**	0.0036	0.0131*	0.0020	0.0147*	0.0038
Nonwhite	−0.1163	−0.0186	−0.1363	−0.0211	−0.3348**	−0.0864
Male	−0.1258	−0.0202	0.0452	0.0069	−0.3738**	−0.0965
Highest grade	0.0045	0.0007	0.0052	0.0008	−0.0219*	−0.0057
Highest grade missing	−0.1521	−0.0244	0.2943	0.0452	−0.0416	−0.0107
Health measures						
Health excellent/very good	−0.1858*	−0.0298	0.1474	0.0226	−0.0757	−0.0195
Health good (omitted)						
Health fair/poor	0.0726	0.0116	0.0994	0.0153	0.1679	0.0433
Number of ADLs	0.4014**	0.0643	0.1912**	0.0294	0.0004	0.001
Number of IADLs	1.2369**	0.1982	0.1896**	0.0291	0.1446**	0.0373
Number of nights in hospital	0.0093*	0.0015	0.0018	0.0003	−0.0004	−0.0001
Prob. of living 10 yrs	−0.0025	−0.0004	−0.1293	−0.0199	0.0167	0.0043
Prob. missing	0.1400	0.0224	0.1056	0.0162	−0.0437	−0.0113
Prob. of entering nursing home (5 yrs)	−0.3824**	−0.0613	0.1648	0.0253	0.1061	0.0274
Prob. missing	−0.2729**	−0.0437	−0.1153	−0.0177	−0.0582	−0.0150
Access/affordability						
Wealth						
1st wealth quartile (lowest)	0.1951	0.0313	−0.2500	−0.0384	0.2691	0.0695
2nd wealth quartile	0.2885**	0.0429	−0.1177	−0.0181	0.2295	0.0592
3rd wealth quartile	0.2504**	0.0401	−0.2084	−0.0320	0.1520	0.0392
4th wealth quartile (omitted)						
Income						
1st income quartile (lowest)	0.0555	0.0089	−0.1657	−0.0255	−0.1090	−0.0281
2nd income quartile	−0.0236	−0.0038	−0.1356	−0.0208	−0.0531	−0.0137
3rd income quartile	−0.0791	−0.0127	−0.0530	−0.0081	−0.0327	−0.0084
4th income quartile (omitted)						
Own home	−0.1917+	−0.0307	−0.3070*	−0.0472	0.1065	0.0275
Medicaid coverage	0.1247	0.0200	0.3203**	0.0492	0.0389	0.0100
Private insurance coverage	−0.0804	−0.0129	0.0101	0.0016	−0.0601	−0.0155
Number of children	0.0119	0.0019	0.0044	0.0007	0.0118	0.0030
Number of girls	−0.0335	−0.0054	−0.0657	−0.0101	0.0376	0.0097
Number of kids in 10 miles	0.0581+	0.0093	−0.6389	−0.0028	0.3354**	0.0866
Married	0.3996**	0.0640	−1.3455**	−0.2067	−1.2915**	−0.3334
Female*Married	−0.4681**	−0.0750	0.5996**	0.0921	0.1860	0.0480
Nonwhite*Married	0.1325	0.0212	0.4796*	0.0737	0.6718**	0.1734
Live with others	0.1493+	0.0239	−0.6389**	−0.0982	−1.0302**	−0.2659

(*continued*)

Table 5.11   (continued)

Variable	Probability of Receiving Care		Probability of Paying for Care		Probability of Care from Children	
	Coeff.	Deriv.[a]	Coeff.	Deriv.[a]	Coeff.	Deriv.[a]
Measures of exchange						
Prob. of leaving inheritance	−0.0380	−0.0061	0.3660**	0.0563	−0.1608	−0.0415
Prob. missing	0.0876	0.0140	0.2045	0.0314	0.2035	0.0525
Child(ren) in will 0/1	−0.0835	−0.0134	−0.0421	−0.0065	0.1248	0.0322
Child(ren) on deed to home 0/1	0.0287	0.0046	0.2992	0.0460	0.2147[+]	0.0554
Value of home ($100,000)	0.0343	0.0055	0.0081	−0.0012	−0.0705	−0.0182
Child(ren) beneficiaries of life insurance 0/1	−0.0875	−0.0140	−0.2592*	−0.0398	0.1511	0.0390
Face value of life insurance ($10,000)	0.0468	0.0075	−0.0412	−0.0063	0.138	0.0356
Number of kids gave $5,000+ (past 10 yrs)	0.0523	0.0084	−0.0805	−0.0124	−0.0013	−0.0003
Trust for child(ren) 0/1	0.1549	0.0248	0.0939	0.0144	−0.5686	−0.1468
Value of trust (million $)	−0.4737	−0.0759	−0.5251	−0.0807	1.257	0.3245
Number of kids gave transfer (last year)	−0.0029	−0.0005	0.0775	0.0119	−0.0058	−0.0015
Value of transfer ($10,000)	−0.0223	−0.0036	−0.3311[+]	−0.0509	−0.2262[+]	−0.0687
Proxy respondent	0.1676	0.0268	−0.2474[+]	0.0380	−0.1270	−0.0328
Intercept	−3.0003**	−0.4806	−2.1008**	−0.3228	−1.7697**	−0.4568
Mean of dependent variable	0.66		0.18		0.30	
Number of observations	3,115		1,893		1,750	

[a]Derivatives are evaluated at the means of the right-hand-side variables.
[+]Significant at the 10 percent level.
*Significant at the 5 percent level.
**Significant at the 1 percent level.

Respondents could report a high probability of entering a nursing home for two reasons. They might believe that their health is deteriorating quickly and they will require the intensive care provided by such a facility. Alternatively, they may have found it difficult to obtain acceptable home care. Thus the correlation between the probability of care and the probability of entering a nursing home could be either positive, if poor health is the motivation, or negative, if entrance into a nursing home is due to lack of available alternatives. In the regression the coefficient on potential nursing home admission is negative and significant at the 1 percent level, indicating that those who expect to enter a nursing home are currently less likely to be receiving care, everything else held constant.

Other measures of informal care also play important roles in whether care is received, although the effects are not as strong. Being married increases the probability of receiving care by 6.4 percentage points, though, as hypothesized, the effect for married women is significantly lower. Married women have a 7.5 percentage point lower probability of receiving care than do married men, so the net effect of marriage for women is almost zero. There is no significant difference in the effect of marital status between whites and nonwhites, though nonwhites are 2 percentage points (insignificant) less likely to get help.[14]

Those living with someone in addition to or other than a spouse are only 2 percentage points more likely to get care than those who do not have additional household members. Each additional child who lives within a 10-mile radius of the parent increases the probability of receiving care by only 0.9 percent. Surprisingly, additional children (either males or females) do not significantly affect the probability of receiving care.[15]

The proxies for the affordability of professional care do not have a significant impact on whether an individual *receives* care. Income, health insurance, and Medicaid coverage are all insignificant predictors of the receipt of care. The effect of wealth is nonlinear, with those in the middle quartiles being more likely to receive care than those in the highest quartile.

None of the variables that proxy avenues of exchange is a significant predictor of care received. The probability of leaving an inheritance, naming children in a will or as beneficiaries of life insurance policies, making cash transfers to children, either currently or in the past, establishing a trust fund, and the value of these transfers and future transfers are all insignificant predictors of assistance, and the magnitudes of the effects are small relative to the impact of health measures. Thus it appears that, regardless of family structure or wealth, those who most need care are most likely to receive it. Financial status has almost no effect on the probability, whereas health measures have strong predictive power.

5.4.2   Purchase of Care

I now explore the source of care. In the first comparison I look at the choice of paid versus unpaid care. Of those who receive assistance, 18 percent pay for at least some of the time. I again estimate a probit model for the 66 percent of the impaired sample who receive some sort of care. The results are reported in the second two columns of table 5.11. I am most interested in determining whether paid care is chosen if individuals can afford it or, conversely, whether those with resources are instead making transfers to children as a means of

---

14. Belgrave and Bradsher (1994) using the Longitudinal Study of Aging find that 85 percent of whites and only 76 percent of African Americans with an ADL limitation got help, though the percentages receiving help with IADL limitations were similar. Because I combine those with difficulties with ADLs and IADLs I obtain an "average" estimate.

15. The number of living brothers and sisters of the respondent did not significantly affect the probability of receiving care, and these variables were excluded from the estimation presented here.

encouraging children to provide care. If those with money choose to "pay" children rather than make formal caregiving arrangements, it would suggest that children are the preferred caregivers.

The measures of need are less strong predictors of the decision to purchase care than of whether care of any kind is received. Self-assessed health status is not a significant predictor of the purchase of help. Older individuals are more likely to pay for care, but the effect is small with an additional year worth 0.2 percentage points on a base of 18 percent. The number of ADL and IADL limitations, however, remain among the strongest predictors. Each additional limitation increases the probability of paid care by 2.94 percentage points for ADLs and 2.91 for IADLs. Table 5.7 showed that children provided help with IADL limitations while paid caregivers were used more frequently to assist with ADLs. In the probit estimates there is a small difference between the two types of limitations in the probability of receiving paid care, with ADL difficulties having a larger effect, although the difference is statistically insignificant.

The presence of another individual in the home, whether a spouse or other person, significantly decreases the probability of paid care. Married individuals have a 21 percentage point lower probability of paying for care. The importance of marital status is significantly attenuated for both females and for nonwhites. Respondents who live with an additional household member (other than a spouse) have a 10 percentage point lower probability of purchasing care. Based on an average probability of paying for care of 18 percent these represent large changes. As shown earlier, those with greater ADL needs were more likely to rely on live-in companions or paid care than to rely on children. Consistent with those results, the number of children, the number of daughters, and the number of children living within 10 miles all have little explanatory power in this equation.

The dummy variable indicating Medicaid coverage has a large positive effect on the probability of paying for services. Because Medicaid pays for home health care and housekeeping services, such coverage often makes home care costless to the recipient. The change in the probability of paid care associated with Medicaid coverage is 5 percentage points. Individuals in lower income quartiles also have a lower probability of paid care as expected, although the point estimates are not significantly different from zero.

As with the receipt of care, there is little evidence of exchange in the decision to pay for care. An exchange model would predict that paid care would be less likely and help from a child more likely in response to the existence of an inheritance—a possible payment for services from the child. However, those with a higher probability of leaving an inheritance have a 6 percentage point greater probability of paying for care. This relationship is probably the result of an association between the probability of leaving a bequest and financial well-being, and this in turn is associated with the decision to purchase formal care. When a child is the beneficiary of a life insurance policy, the likelihood of paid care decreases by 4 percentage points. Additional dollars transferred to the children also decrease the probability of paid care, although the effect is small. A transfer of an additional $10,000 decreases the probability of paid care by 5 percentage points. Whether a transfer is made, however, has no effect on the probability.

Thus, whereas the receipt of care is determined in large part by need, the use of paid assistance is driven by affordability, as measured by insurance status, and the availability of substitutes to paid care to assist with ADLs. A live-in caregiver can substitute for paid help, but non-coresident children, even those who live nearby, cannot.

5.4.3   Care from Children

If a respondent lives with either a spouse or child, the likelihood that this individual provides care is high. For non-coresident children, however, the decision is more interesting. Thus, in addition to the decision to purchase paid care, I explore the "choice" to receive help from non-coresident children. I estimate a probit model with the left-hand–side variable equal to one if the respondent receives any care from a non-coresident child and zero if she does not. The covariates are identical to the previous regressions. The estimates and derivatives are reported in the final two columns of table 5.11.

As is the case with the probability of paying for care, older respondents are more likely to get help from children. This result, in both cases, is likely due to the decreased availability of a spouse, siblings, and friends with old age. Again, self-reported health measures do not significantly affect the decision. Interestingly, consistent with table 5.7, help from children is strongly related to the number of IADL limitations—each limitation increases the probability by 4 percentage points on a base of 30—but is not at all affected by the number of ADL difficulties. Thus again there is evidence that children help with housekeeping tasks rather than with personal care.

Being married and living with other individuals have the largest effects on receiving help from a non-coresident child. A spouse decreases the probability by almost 33 percentage points, and the presence of others in the household decreases the probability by 27 percentage points. On a base of 30 percent these are large changes. In this case, there is not a significantly different effect of marital status for women. For nonwhites, however, the effect of marriage is attenuated by 17 percentage points. The coefficient on the linear term for race is large and negatively related to receiving help from a child, as is the dummy variable indicating that the respondent is male. Nonwhites are 9 percentage points less likely to get care from a child, while men are 10 percentage points less likely.

Neither the absolute number of children nor the number of daughters has a significant effect, but the presence of children within a 10-mile radius increases the probability of help from a child by 9 percentage points. The implication is that only nearby children are able to provide assistance.

Neither insurance nor income affect the probability of care.

The estimates give little evidence of an exchange motive. The probability of leaving an inheritance, the amount of bequeathable wealth, naming children in a will, and naming children as beneficiaries of a life insurance policy all have no effect on the probability of receiving help from non-coresident children. In fact, wealth operates in the opposite direction: poor parents are more likely to get help from children, although the effects are not significant. Naming a child on the deed to a home increases the probability of help, but cash transfers operate in the opposite direction. Each additional $10,000 given is associated with a 7 percentage point lower probability of receiving assistance. Other indicators of cash transfers are also negatively related to time assistance even after controlling for health.

5.4.4 Summary of Care Received

The results from the three regressions reported in table 5.11 describe a consistent story of the receipt of care. Whether an elderly individual gets care is a function of need. Those with more limitations are more likely to receive assistance, while income and wealth measures are unimportant. The choice of the type of care is also strongly dependent on need. Help with ADLs requires a live-in companion or professional assistance, while non-coresident children provide help with the housekeeping-type services captured in the measure of IADL limitations.

Assuming that difficulty with household chores precedes difficulty with personal care, these results suggest a possible progression of caregiving services as an individual's health worsens. In the absence of a spouse, an elderly woman may first rely on children to help with tasks such as shopping. As her condition deteriorates and she begins to experience difficulty with personal care needs, she may seek to live with a child or, alternatively, purchase professional care if she can afford to do so. In the panel, this type of progression can be observed, and it presents a logical method of verifying this hypothesis.

Surprisingly, despite the intriguing theoretical work that has been done on exchange motives for transfers, there appears to be little support for this hypothesis with respect to observed transfers both to and from the impaired elderly.

5.5 The Child's Perspective

If care is to come from children, a decision must be made about which child will provide the care. In this section I examine the caregiving decision from the point of view of the child, looking for patterns associated with which child provides the care.

As discussed in section 5.3, in simple comparisons, daughters appear to be more likely to provide care than are sons. However, there are a number of other factors involved. For example, the majority of the sample of elderly impaired individuals is female (66 percent), particularly those who are unmarried. Individuals may prefer to be cared for by a same-sex child, thus increasing the responsibilities of daughters. Or, alternatively, if parents must "buy help" by financially compensating a child in order to receive care, the price of a daughter's time may be less than that of a son's due to differences in market wage rates for men and women. In the following regression analysis I control for as many of these factors as possible. All information used in the analyses is reported by the respondent; the respondent's children were not interviewed.

For children who live with the respondent, AHEAD obtains earnings information that is included in the estimated equations. For the majority of children (those who do not coreside with the respondent), I do not have earnings data, but rather family income. I use this variable to proxy the value of the child's time. I also include the usual predictors of wages: age, sex, schooling, and part-time/full-time status. The opportunity cost of time is positively related to age, being male, schooling, and full-time status. Rather than predict wage rates using information from other data sets, I include these regressors directly and estimate a reduced-form equation. I also include a dummy variable for whether the child is over age 65.[16] Also important for the opportunity cost of the child's time is whether he has his own children.[17] I therefore include a dummy variable equal to one if the respondent's child has at least one child of his own. In addition to measures of family income, I include a measure of the child's income relative to that of the parent.[18]

To capture the possibility of exchange, I include variables similar to those in table 5.11: whether the child is a beneficiary of a life insurance policy, whether his name is on the deed to the parent's house, whether he is named in the respondent's will, and the probability with which the respondent expects to leave an inheritance. I also include the value of the respondent's bequeathable wealth (in quartiles), representing the value of the potential inheritance (as well as the respondent's ability to pay for professional care), the value of the life insurance policy, and the equity in the home for which the child's name is on the deed. Finally, I include variables indicating whether the child received a cash transfer of $500 or more in the past year, or of $5,000 or more in the past 10 years. If transfers were made in the past year, I include the amount of these transfers.[19]

To allow for the possibility that a well-off child may substitute cash assistance for time help (McGarry and Schoeni 1995), I include a dummy variable for whether the child made a transfer to the parent in the past year, and a variable indicating the amount.

16. Similar variables for the child's spouse (spouse's age, schooling, and work status) were not significantly different from zero and are not included in the results presented here.

17. While children make different demands on a parent at different ages, the survey does not obtain the ages of these grandchildren.

18. This variable is based on a question in AHEAD that asked respondents whether their children were better off, the same, or worse off financially than they themselves were. It is not obtained by comparing reported measures of family income.

19. The actual amount transferred over the previous 10 years is not obtained.

If there are social norms about who is responsible for caring for parents, then birth order and the number of brothers and sisters a given child has may affect the probability that he provides care. I include separate dummy variables indicating the oldest and the youngest child and allow these variables to differ by the sex of the child. I also control for the number of sisters a particular child has interacted with the child's sex, whether someone is an only child, and, finally, the total number of children in the family.

Included also are characteristics of the respondent. Her age, race, sex, whether the child and the respondent are of the same sex, the respondent's income and wealth, marital status,[20] and insurance status (Medicaid and/or private insurance).

The means of these variables are presented in table 5.12 for the entire sample of 9,056 children, and separately by whether the child provides care.[21] From the comparison of means we see that those who provide assistance are less likely to be married or to be male. They are older on average and less likely to work, both of which likely indicate the availability of time. The largest differences are with respect to living arrangements. Children who provide care are much more likely to live with their parents or to live within 10 miles of their parents. Children who provide help are also less well off financially than their siblings. In addition to providing time help, these caregiving children are more likely to have provided cash assistance to their parents, despite the fact that their average incomes are lower.

The decision of a child to provide care ought to be influenced by the amount of care provided by his siblings. However, Wolf et al. (1995) do not find a significant effect of siblings' hours on one's own supply of time help. Future work will explore this relationship in the AHEAD data.

In the multivariate analysis (table 5.13) the variables that proxy the opportunity cost of the child's time do not have an effect on the probability of providing assistance. The magnitude of the child's earnings if he lives at home, or his family income if he does not, are not significantly different from zero, nor is the child's sex (exclusive of family composition), his schooling, his work status, or whether he has children of his own.

The measures of exchange offer some explanatory power, although the results are far from conclusive. Being the beneficiary of a life insurance policy

20. If a child has two living parents, he may be faced with the situation of providing care to both. Certainly, there are returns to scale. It does not seem possible to help one's mother with grocery shopping and not provide the same care to a father. I therefore experimented with including indicators of whether the child helps the second parent and the number of hours spent helping the second parent. Adding these variables improved the fit of the regression but did not alter the estimated values of other coefficients. Because fewer than 1 percent of children belong to a family in which both parents need care, I exclude these variables from the final analysis. However, because the limitations of the second parent may also prevent that parent from assisting his spouse, I do include the number of ADL or IADL limitations experienced by the second parent.

21. Children-in-law were deleted from the sample. Four percent of caregivers are children-in-law. The regression results are substantially unchanged if all children-in-law (those who provide care and those who do not) are included in the sample, and appropriate control variables are added.

Table 5.12   Comparison of Means for Children of Respondents

Variable	All $n = 9,056$[a] Mean	S.E.	Help $n = 921$[a] Mean	S.E.	Do Not Help $n = 8,135$[a] Mean	S.E.
Opportunity cost						
Age	48.38	0.09	52.45	0.30	47.91	0.10
Male	0.488	0.005	0.312	0.014	0.508	0.005
Schooling	12.26	0.037	12.03	0.103	12.28	0.039
Married	0.687	0.004	0.581	0.015	0.699	0.005
Children 0/1						
(grandchildren)	0.831	0.004	0.823	0.011	0.832	0.004
Employed[b]	0.727	0.004	0.578	0.015	0.745	0.004
Employed part time	0.085	0.003	0.097	0.009	0.084	0.003
Earnings[b] (coresident						
only)	25,541	873	27,916	1,436	23,685	1,084
Income measures[b] (non-coresident)						
Less than $20,000	0.144	0.003	0.180	0.014	0.141	0.004
$20,000–$30,000	0.115	0.003	0.132	0.012	0.113	0.003
$30,000–$50,000	0.204	0.004	0.190	0.014	0.205	0.004
More than $50,000	0.183	0.004	0.127	0.012	0.188	0.004
Less than $30,000	0.025	0.002	0.038	0.007	0.025	0.002
More than $30,000	0.050	0.002	0.038	0.007	0.051	0.002
Less than $50,000	0.044	0.002	0.045	0.008	0.044	0.002
Income unknown	0.235	0.004	0.252	0.016	0.234	0.004
Better off than parents	0.539	0.005	0.588	0.018	0.535	0.005
Same as parents	0.210	0.004	0.251	0.016	0.207	0.004
Worse off than parents	0.167	0.004	0.100	0.011	0.172	0.004
Relative income missing	0.084	0.003	0.061	0.009	0.086	0.003
Measures of exchange						
Child in will 0/1	0.272	0.004	0.132	0.010	0.288	0.005
Child on deed to home 0/1	0.060	0.002	0.128	0.010	0.052	0.002
Child beneficiary of life						
insurance 0/1	0.118	0.003	0.255	0.013	0.103	0.003
Face value of life						
insurance	319.0	25.3	622.3	141.9	284.6	23.1
Child got $5,000+ in past						
10 yrs 0/1	0.096	0.003	0.075	0.008	0.098	0.003
Transfer last year	0.104	0.003	0.088	0.008	0.106	0.003
Value of transfer	376.4	25.1	186.8	40.8	397.9	27.6
Gave parents financial						
assistance	0.016	0.001	0.039	0.006	0.014	0.001
Amount of assistance	44.15	5.64	121.83	24.17	35.35	5.65
Accessibility/availability						
Lives within 10 miles of						
parents	0.416	0.005	0.808	0.012	0.371	0.005
Lives with parents	0.079	0.003	0.344	0.014	0.049	0.002
Child owns home	0.678	0.004	0.518	0.015	0.697	0.005

Note: S.E. = standard error.

[a]Number of observations for some variables differs due to missing values.

[b]Statistics calculated over valid observations (coresident or non-coresident child).

Table 5.13   **Probit Estimates of Probability of Providing Care**

Variable	Probability of Providing Care	
	Coefficient	Derivative[a]
Opportunity cost		
Age	0.0086*	0.0008
Age > 65	−0.1279	−0.0122
Male	0.0033	0.0203
Schooling	0.0014	0.0003
Married	−0.0497	−0.0047
Married*Female	0.1386	0.0132
Children 0/1 (grandchildren)	−0.0330	−0.0031
Employed	−0.1173	−0.0112
Employed*Female	0.0653	0.0062
Employed part time	0.1136	0.0108
Employment missing	−0.2731	−0.0261
Earnings (coresident only; $10,000)	0.0266	0.0025
Income measures (non-coresident)		
Less than $20,000	0.1394	0.0133
$20,000–$30,000	0.1084	0.0103
$30,000–$50,000	0.1014	0.0097
More than $50,000 (omitted)		
Less than $30,000	0.1287	0.0123
More than $30,000	0.1966	0.0188
Less than $50,000	−0.0870	−0.0083
Income unknown	0.1545	0.0147
Better off than parents	−0.0699	−0.0067
Same as parents (omitted)		
Worse off than parents	−0.1612+	−0.0154
Relative income missing	−0.1399	−0.0133
Measures of exchange		
Child in will 0/1	−0.0072	−0.0007
Child on deed to home 0/1	0.3888**	0.0371
Value of home ($100,000)	−0.0577	0.0055
Child beneficiary on life insurance 0/1	0.3014**	0.0288
Face value of life insurance ($10,000)	0.0409	0.0039
Child got $5,000+ in past 10 yrs 0/1	0.1765	0.0168
Transfer last year	0.0532	0.0051
Value of transfer ($10,000)	−0.2492	−0.0238
Gave parents financial assistance	0.2082	0.0199
Amount of assistance ($10,000)	0.497	0.0474
Prob. of inheritance	−0.0319	−0.0030
Prob. missing	0.0473	0.0045
Living arrangements		
Lives within 10 miles of parents	0.8052**	0.0768
Lives with parents	0.7448**	0.0711
Child owns home	0.0940	0.0090

Table 5.13　　　(continued)

Variable	Probability of Providing Care	
	Coefficient	Derivative[a]
Family composition		
Number of sisters*Male	−0.5831**	−0.0556
Number of sisters*Female	0.0585	0.0056
Oldest*Male	0.2773**	0.0265
Oldest*Female	−0.0399	−0.0038
Youngest*Male	0.2569*	0.0245
Youngest*Female	0.1593*	0.0152
Only child	0.1614	0.0154
Parent's characteristics		
Number of children	−0.0344**	−0.0033
Wealth		
1st wealth quartile (lowest)	0.2288[+]	0.0218
2nd wealth quartile	0.2491*	0.0238
3rd wealth quartile	0.1085	0.0104
4th wealth quartile (omitted)		
Income		
1st income quartile (lowest)	0.1968	0.0188
2nd income quartile	0.2502	0.0239
3rd income quartile	0.1395	0.0133
4th income quartile (omitted)		
Own home	−0.0002	−0.0000
Medicaid coverage	0.0710	0.0068
Private insurance coverage	−0.0350	−0.0033
Age	0.0093[+]	0.0009
Nonwhite	0.0008	0.0001
Sex	−0.1052	−0.0100
Parent and child same sex	0.0029	0.0003
Married	−0.5635**	−0.0538
Female*Married	0.2475*	0.0236
Number of ADLs	0.0074	0.0007
Number of IADLs	0.2053**	0.0196
Number of spouse's ADLs	−0.1646[+]	−0.0157
Proxy respondent	−0.1214	−0.0116
Intercept	−3.4795**	−0.3320
Mean of dependent variable	0.085	
Number of observations	7,907	

[a]Derivatives are evaluated at the means of the right-hand-side variables.

[+]Significant at the 10 percent level.

*Significant at the 5 percent level.

**Significant at the 1 percent level.

and being listed on the deed to a home increase the probability of helping by 3 and 4 percentage points, respectively. Other factors that could be associated with exchange are all insignificant predictors of assistance. Past transfers are positively related to help, whereas the value of current transfers is negatively related. Wealth operates in the opposite direction from that predicted by the strategic bequest motive. A child is 2 to 2.5 percentage points more likely to provide assistance if his parent is in the lowest two wealth quartiles than if she is in the highest quartile.

As expected, a child is less likely to provide care to a married respondent, since the spouse in this case is likely the primary caregiver.

There is no evidence that children substitute between providing time and cash assistance. In fact, the more financial assistance the child gives, the more likely he is to give time assistance as well. Giving any cash assistance increases the probability of providing time assistance by 2 percentage points. Each additional $1,000 of cash transferred to a parent further increases the probability of a transfer of time by 0.5 percentage points.

Despite the lack of significance of many of these economic variables, the gender composition of the family and the number of siblings has a strong effect. Sons begin with a 2 percentage point (insignificant) greater probability of helping a parent. For each sister, a son's probability of helping is reduced by 5.6 percentage points. Female siblings, however, increase a daughter's probability of helping, although the effect is small relative to that for sons and not significantly different from zero. Additional siblings of any sex lower the probability of helping by a small but significant amount, as there is likely some substitution between children. Oldest children of either sex are no more likely to provide assistance than are middle children, but the youngest child is more likely than children elsewhere in the family to provide care, regardless of sex. If the child is the youngest and male the magnitude of the effect is 2.5 percentage points, compared to 1.5 if the youngest child is female. Children who are the same sex as the needy parent are more likely to provide care, although the effect is small. This difference too works in the direction of more care being provided by daughters than sons because approximately 66 percent of the impaired elderly are female.

Because of the number of family composition variables, I present some comparisons for sample families in table 5.14. I compare the marginal probabilities of helping for siblings in families with three children. The calculations make use of the following variables: male, number of sisters interacted with the child's sex, oldest interacted with sex, and youngest interacted with sex. All other variables are assumed constant. Using these coefficients it is possible to compare the marginal probability of a child's helping in different families. For example, compare two particular families, one in which the order of the children is girl, boy, girl (GBG) and the other which is the reverse, boy, girl, boy (BGB). The probability of the middle son's helping in the first family (GBG) is 10 percentage points lower than the probability of the middle daughter's

Table 5.14   **Marginal Probability of Providing Help to Parent by Gender of Siblings**

Family Composition	First Child	Second Child	Third Child
GGG	0.0055	0.0085	0.0384
GGB	0.0013	0.0042	−0.0857
GBG	0.0013	−0.1086	0.0342
GBB	−0.0029	−0.0571	−0.0342
BGG	−0.0921	0.0042	0.0342
BGB	−0.0406	0.0	−0.0342
BBG	−0.0406	−0.0571	0.0299
BBB	0.0109	−0.0056	0.0173

Notes: G = girl, B = boy. Calculations are based on the estimated coefficients: 0.0203*(Male) − 0.0556*(Male*Num sisters) + 0.0056*(Female*Num sisters) + 0.0256*(Oldest*Male) − 0.0038*(Oldest*Female) + 0.0245*(Youngest*Male) + 0.0152*(Youngest*Female). Other variables are held constant.

helping in the second family. If the family is GGB the probability that the youngest child provides care is just over 11 percentage points lower than if the family is BBG. Different family structures yield similar results. The differences are large given that the mean probability of providing help is 8.5 percent.

Despite allowing for differences in the opportunity cost of time, the preference of respondents for same-sex helpers, and the possibility that cash transfers by children substitute for time transfers, males continue to provide significantly less assistance to infirmed parents. The lack of care from sons is strongly related to whether they have sisters. Male-only children are no less likely to provide care than are female-only children. I interpret this result to mean that, while parents will not go uncared for in the absence of daughters, if there are daughters in the family, they will bear the burden of caring for parents. Thus it is daughters, rather than elderly parents, who should be concerned about this result.

5.6   Conclusion

This paper has provided a descriptive analysis of the caregiving environment faced by the disabled and impaired elderly. The results are encouraging in that the strongest predictor of receiving care is need. Approximately two-thirds of those with limitations receive assistance. Those who are not receiving care are on average better off in several dimensions, including having greater financial resources and better health. In many ways the type of caregiving relationship depends on the recipient's needs. Children, including non-coresident children, provide assistance with housekeeping tasks, while coresident individuals (spouses, children, and others) help with personal care needs.

An important caveat, however, is that the information reported by the respondent is largely subjective. Needing assistance with a task is likely related to the availability of help. If no help is available, an individual may manage to complete the task, while if help is readily available (e.g., from a spouse), a small amount of difficulty may deter the respondent from attempting the activity on her own.

One discouraging finding of this study is the paucity of assistance provided by children. Only 10 percent of children provide time help to their parents (8.5 percent of non-coresident children). For children who do not live near a parent or whose hours are taken up with work and other responsibilities, the provision of cash assistance would be a logical substitute. However, fewer than 2 percent of children are reported to have made cash transfers to their impaired parents. Even more surprising, cash transfers are *positively* correlated with the provision of time assistance. Thus it is not the case that children who are unable to spend time helping a parent compensate with financial assistance.

These results too should be interpreted with a degree of caution. Because of the structure of the survey, only the primary caregiver is likely to be named. Thus, if children are secondary caregivers (perhaps second to a spouse), they may be omitted. Additionally, financial assistance from children is reported by the parent. Although it is unlikely that the parent would intentionally misrepresent such assistance, she may forget or may not fully value gifts in kind. It is also possible that a parent is uninformed about financial assistance from a child, for example, if a child pays bills without the parent's knowledge. Evidence of underreporting of transfers can be found by examining data from the Health and Retirement Survey (HRS). The HRS is based on a sample of individuals born between 1931 and 1941. HRS respondents are therefore approximately the same age as many of the children of AHEAD respondents. Approximately 9 percent of HRS respondents reportedly gave $500 or more to a parent or parent-in-law in the past year (McGarry and Schoeni 1997), while AHEAD respondents reported that just over 1 percent of their children gave them financial assistance. While the results from the two surveys would not be expected to compare perfectly, the large differences between the two samples are suspicious, and perhaps due to failing memories or different valuation of noncash gifts.

A number of issues have been raised that need to be addressed in future work. The different patterns observed with respect to who provides help with ADLs and IADLs suggest that disaggregated measures of need should be examined. A more difficult problem is raised by the number of simultaneous decisions being made. If a great deal of care is required by an elderly parent, shared living arrangements may be the most efficient alternative other than a nursing home. The child with whom the parent lives will likely assume a large responsibility, not only for the physical care of the parent but also for her financial well-being. This decision needs to be investigated. Similarly, the number of hours supplied to a parent by one sibling ought to affect the hours provided by the others. No attempt is made in this paper to model simultaneously the decisions of all the respondent's offspring. This task too remains for future work.

References

Altonji, Joseph G., Fumio Hayashi, and Laurence Kotlikoff. 1994. Parental altruism and inter vivos transfers: Theory and evidence. Evanston, Ill.: Northwestern University, February. Mimeograph.

American Federation of Aging Research and Alliance for Aging Research. 1995. Putting aging on hold: Delaying the diseases of old age. New York: American Federation of Aging Research.

Belgrave, Linda Liska, and Julia E. Bradsher. 1994. Health as a factor in institutionalization disparities between African Americans and whites. *Research on Aging* 16 (2): 115–41.

Bernheim, Douglas B., Andrei Shleifer, and Lawrence H. Summers. 1985. The strategic bequest motive. *Journal of Political Economy* 93 (6): 1045–76.

Coward, Raymond T., and Jeffrey Dwyer. 1990. The association of gender, sibling network composition, and patterns of parent care by adult children. *Research on Aging* 12 (2): 158–81.

Cox, Donald. 1987. Motives for private income transfers. *Journal of Political Economy* 95 (3): 509–46.

Ettner, Susan. 1994. The effect of the Medicaid home health care benefit on long-term care choices of the elderly. *Economic Inquiry* 32 (1): 103–27.

Gale, William, and John Karl Scholz. 1994. Intergenerational transfers and the accumulation of wealth. *Journal of Economic Perspectives* 8 (4): 145–60.

Hurd, Michael D., and Kathleen McGarry. 1997. Medical insurance and the use of health care services by the elderly. *Journal of Health Economics* 16 (2): 129–54.

Kotlikoff, Laurence, and Lawrence Summers. 1981. The role of intergenerational transfers in aggregate capital accumulation. *Journal of Political Economy* 89 (4): 706–32.

Lewin-VHI, Inc. 1993. The financial impact of the Health Security Act. December. Mimeograph.

McGarry, Kathleen, and Robert Schoeni. 1995. Transfer behavior: Measurement and the redistribution of resources within the family. *Journal of Human Resources* 30: S184–S226.

———. 1997. Transfer behavior within the family: Results from the Asset and Health Dynamics Survey. *Journal of Gerontology* 52B: 82–92.

Mutchler, Jan, and Susan Bullers. 1994. Gender differences in formal care use in later life. *Research on Aging* 16 (3): 235–50.

Soldo, Beth, Douglas Wolf, and Emily Agree. 1990. Family, households, and care arrangements of frail older women: A structural analysis. *Journal of Gerontology* 45 (6): S238–S249.

Stoller, Eleanor Palo, Lorna Earl Forster, and Tamara Sutin Duniho. 1992. Systems of parent care within sibling networks. *Research on Aging* 14 (1): 28–49.

Stone, Robyn, Gail Lee Cafferata, and Judith Sangl. 1987. Caregivers of the frail elderly: A national profile. *Gerontologist* 27 (5): 616–26.

Wolf, Douglas, Vicki Freedman, and Beth Soldo. 1995. The division of family labor: Care for elderly parents. Syracuse, N.Y.: Syracuse University, Center for Policy Research, March. Mimeograph.

Comment   James P. Smith

This paper continues the excellent recent work Kathleen McGarry has been conducting on intergenerational transfers using the newly released data from the Health and Retirement Survey and the survey of Asset and Health Dynamics among the Oldest Old. In her prior work, she demonstrated that the characteristics of children matter (including their incomes) in the direction and magnitude of money transfers across generations. In this paper, she extends that work into much more difficult terrain—the provision of home care for the increasingly frail elderly. This is a more difficult problem in part because parents' health status must be explicitly incorporated into the analysis since the provision of care is often conditioned on some negative health outcome. Bringing health conditions into the model raises a number of analytical issues not the least of which is the endogeneity of health. McGarry largely sidesteps these issues and provides instead an excellent descriptive summary of the primary patterns of exchange in her data. Given that we currently know so little about what the basic facts are about these exchanges between adult children and their impaired parents, this descriptive approach is a very useful and necessary first step. In light of her largely descriptive but important goals, the paper can be judged a success.

But still we want more. There are two analytical models estimated in the paper. The first (summarized in table 5.11) estimates the probability of receiving home care and the type of that care in a sample of parents with at least one ADL or IADL limitation. The second model (table 5.13) estimates the probability of providing home care to parents in a sample of adult children. Let me discuss each in turn.

The first question asked is what determines the provision of home care and the type of such care to elderly parents with at least one functional limitation. The first thing you notice about table 5.11 is that it sure contains a lot of estimated coefficients (there are in fact 129). While it will not win an award for the most coefficients estimated in one table by an economist (I might even be in the running for that award), it may be odds-on favorite if the criterion is the number of statistically insignificant coefficients relative to estimated coefficients. Using conventional statistical standards, I count only 31 statistically significant coefficients among the 129. My strongest suggestion is that a more parsimonious model may be preferable, especially when so many of the variables are attempting to measure the same thing.

While there are plenty of variables in this model, on closer inspection there are really only three concepts being proxied—(1) the health status of parents, (2) their command over resources (e.g., income and wealth), and (3) the nature of the relationship between parents and their adult children. This trichotomy

James P. Smith is senior economist at RAND and holds the RAND Chair in Labor Markets and Demographic Studies.

serves as a useful device for summarizing the principal conclusions of the paper.

The evidence on the first concept is quite easy to summarize. Parents who receive help are much more likely to be sick. On average, they are in poor health and are beset with all sorts of ADL and IADL problems. While it is quite useful to document the nature of this association between parents' need for help and the care they receive, it certainly does not come as a surprise and may even border on a tautology.

Unfortunately, the evidence on the second concept is just as easy to summarize. In sharp contrast to health status, in this case the simplest summary statement is that income appears not to matter much in the provision of care for elderly persons. At first and even second blush, the absence of any role for such a core economic variable as income is disturbing, especially in a paper by an economist at an economics conference. But the absence of any significant effect may simply be a result of the way the analysis has been set up. In order to be included in the sample for this analysis, the parent had to have at least one ADL or IADL limitation. But it is through this conditioning statement that income is most likely to operate. In recent work (Kington and Smith 1997), I have shown that income strongly influences (negatively) the number of functional limitations and does so in a highly nonlinear way. In essence, increases in household income decrease the probability of being included in McGarry's analytical sample.

There is in fact a silent selection mechanism at work in all McGarry's empirical models that makes it difficult to interpret her results. Although she does not model this selection process, it is nothing more than the standard sample selection model where the probability of sample inclusion is estimated and included as a covariate. Since income reduces the probability of sample inclusion, high-income households who remain in the sample must have some unobservable factor that leads the parents to be sicker than expected. This selection-induced correlation between income and parents' health biases all variables in McGarry's analysis. This selection contamination is even more problematic in the analyses in the third and fifth columns of table 5.11. For example, in the third column, a person is included only if he had an ADL and received some sort of care. These remaining observations are clearly sickly, and many of them probably had long histories of illness.

The final concept underlying her model attempts to capture the nature of the relationship between parents and children. These variables are the most theoretically oriented as they are meant to capture some salient motives for exchange that appear in the economic literature. The basic idea is to see whether strategic bequest motives can be isolated where children attempt to manipulate their frail parents' future inheritance by providing some help now. McGarry makes the somewhat strong claim that her results reject the notion of exchange. In the empirical execution of her idea, it becomes quite difficult to interpret her results because there are so many similar empirical proxies competing to measure the same concept. For example, her empirical proxies include the probability of leaving an inheritance, the number of children who received $5,000 or more in the past 10 years, the number of children who received cash assistance in the past year, whether children are mentioned in the will, whether they are the beneficiaries of life insurance, whether they have a deed to the parents' home, whether a trust has been established, and so on. Given this feverous competition, it may not be so surprising that there is not one clear-cut winner.

The paper finishes with an alternative analysis that examines these exchanges from the child's point of view (table 5.13). The issue here is not whether parents receive care but whether a particular child supplies home care. In this analysis, the characteristics of children—other than their sex and number—apparently do not matter all that much. Among the factors that do not matter are children's incomes. The only "exchange" variables that enter significantly into the model are whether the child was named on a deed to a home and whether the child is the beneficiary of a life insurance policy. Once again, any confidence that one is onto something is tempered by the absence of statistical significance for all the other exchange variables.

While this is a useful start on an analysis of home care from the children's point of view, I would like to suggest a somewhat different modeling strategy. The reason for my suggestion is a strong conviction that family effects are dominant for outcomes measuring care for parents. Some families are very close and caring, and, unfortunately, other families are not. Many children in the former families will join in the care of their elderly parents, while none of them may in the latter. Unless these family differences are controlled for (say, through family fixed effects), it will simply be very difficult to isolate substitution possibilities among family members.

Reference

Kingston, Raynard, and James P. Smith. 1997. Socioeconomic status and racial and ethnic differences in functional status associated with chronic disease. *American Journal of Public Health* 87:805–10.

III Measurement, Methodological, and Data Issues

6   Measuring Poverty among the Elderly

Angus Deaton and Christina Paxson

6.1 Introduction

In the United States in 1992, there were four million elderly adults who were officially classified as poor. There were 31 million elderly in the United States in 1992, so that the poverty rate was just under 13 percent. Children were much more likely to be poor than the elderly; 22 percent, or 15 million children, were poor. This paper is about where such numbers come from and what (if anything) they mean. The data used to make the official calculations do not tell us anything about individual poverty. Instead they provide information on the income of *families,* information that is used to construct a set of poverty counts about individuals. The transformation from families to individuals makes many assumptions, about the allocation of resources within the household, about the differential needs of children, adults, and the elderly, and about the extent of economies of scale. Given the data, the effect of these assumptions on the poverty count depends on living arrangements, on how people combine to form families, on whether people are married or cohabit, on whether the elderly live by themselves or with other, younger adults.

In this paper we examine how living arrangements affect poverty measurement among the elderly in the United States, highlighting the importance of living arrangements. In the United States in 1992, 32 percent of those aged 65 or over lived alone, a further 42 percent lived in all-elderly families, and 26

Angus Deaton is the William Church Osborn Professor of Public Affairs and professor of economics and international affairs at Princeton University and a research associate of the National Bureau of Economic Research. Christina Paxson is professor of economics and public affairs at Princeton University and a research associate of the National Bureau of Economic Research.

Thanks are due to seminar participants at the conference, to the discussant, Doug Bernheim, to seminar participants at RAND, and to Bo Honoré. This research was supported by the National Institute on Aging through grants P01-AG05842 and R01-AG11957. The opinions in this paper do not necessarily reflect the views of the NBER or the sponsoring organization.

percent lived in families with at least one nonelderly person. Conclusions about the living standards of the elderly—absolute or relative—are determined not only by the data but also by assumptions about who gets what and how poverty lines vary with household composition. We demonstrate this fact by calculating the sensitivity of poverty counts to key assumptions in their construction, we examine the basis for the assumptions, and we explore whether the empirical evidence has anything useful to contribute.

There are two problems in passing from family resources to individual welfare, one of which is the main topic of this paper. The first issue, on which we shall have little to say, is the intrahousehold allocation of resources. The measurement of individual poverty requires a rule for assigning a welfare level to an individual, based on the consumption or income level of the family or household in which he or she lives. Any rule inevitably contains implicit assumptions about how resources are shared between different household members, for example, by age or sex. The issue is at its most acute in developing countries, where the elderly typically live in extended families. For example, in India where 90 percent of them live with other people, it is impossible to use household survey data to make simple statements about the resources available to elderly people. The issue is of rather less importance in the United States, where a much larger fraction of the elderly live alone or with other elderly adults.

The second problem is the one to which we give most attention here. Even if resources are distributed equitably across household members, the size and age structure of households affects the welfare levels of their members. The same level of income or income per capita does not give the same standard of living to a large family as to a small one, or to an all-adult household compared with one with children. Larger households may be able to take advantage of "scale economies" through shared consumption of public goods in the household, so that members of large households are likely to be better off than those of small households, even controlling for per capita income or total expenditure. Likewise, if children cost less than adults, then households with more children will require lower incomes to achieve a specified standard of living, given total household size. These issues are likely to be of particular importance when comparing poverty rates across age groups and are also likely to play out differently in countries with different living arrangements for elderly individuals. In the United States, where the elderly typically live in small households with few children, the treatment of child costs is unlikely to have large effects on the numbers of old people in poverty, although it can potentially have large effects on the poverty of the old relative to the young. Even when old people live alone, so that we can measure their resources from a household survey, we cannot classify them as poor or nonpoor without a standard of comparison, a standard that cannot be derived without assessing the needs of other nonelderly members of the population. The treatment of scale economies is likely to be an important issue for both absolute and relative poverty rates of the elderly.

Our first task is to examine the sensitivity of poverty measures in the United States to assumptions about child costs and scale economies. We then attempt to estimate the size of scale economies and child costs. We proceed as follows. In section 6.2 we begin by describing how official poverty measures are derived, and we present official poverty counts and rates for members of different age groups. The results are based on data from the 1993 Current Population Survey, which records information on 1992 incomes. We show that poverty measures for different age groups are quite sensitive to the treatment of scale economies and costs of children. In section 6.3 we focus on the measurement of scale economies and child costs, at a theoretical level and using data from the 1990 Consumer Expenditure Survey.

6.2 Poverty and Age

We start with a brief summary of how official poverty counts are derived in the United States. Further information can be obtained from Ruggles (1990) and National Research Council (1995).

In the United States, an individual is said to be poor if he or she lives in a family whose total income falls below a poverty line, where the poverty line depends on the size and age structure of the household. Thus, all individuals within a family are either poor or nonpoor: the implicit assumption is that resources are allocated fairly within households, so that all members have identical welfare levels. Official poverty statistics are based on information from the March Current Population Surveys (CPSs), which are conducted annually and contain information on the demographic characteristics and incomes of households. Income is before tax and includes cash transfer payments from the government but does not include nonmonetary transfers such as food stamps, health benefits, and subsidized housing. Several details deserve mention:

(i) The CPS has a structure that distinguishes between *households* and *families*. Although most households contain only one family, some contain multiple families, and others contain families that live with unrelated individuals. Of the 58,970 households surveyed in the 1993 CPS, 5,763 were not single-family households. For the purposes of measuring poverty, the Census Bureau combines the incomes of families and *related* subfamilies. For example, a married couple living with a son and daughter-in-law would be treated as a single family: their income would be combined and compared to the poverty line for a four-person family to determine whether all household members are in poverty. However, unrelated subfamilies and individuals are not considered part of the main family, and their poverty measures are based on their own incomes. For example, a person who boards with an unrelated family would be in poverty only if his or her personal income fell below the poverty line for a single person. The poverty line would not be adjusted for the fact that such a person, because he or she does not live alone, may benefit from scale economies in consumption.

This definition of families has some odd consequences. For example, unmarried couples who live together are treated as separate families. Each is assigned the poverty line of a single person, and each is defined to be poor if his or her personal income is below the line. This treatment of unmarried couples tends to increase poverty rates over what they would be if unmarried couples were treated the same as married couples, for two reasons. First, the U.S. poverty lines assume large economies of scale, so that the poverty line for a married couple is less than twice (in fact, only 1.29 times) the line for a single adult. Two unmarried adults who live together and are both in poverty can potentially move themselves out of poverty simply by getting married. Second, even with no scale economies built into poverty lines, treating unmarried couples as if they are married will reduce poverty counts. Combining the incomes of unmarried couples imposes a mean-preserving reduction in the spread of income per person, which can be expected to pull some observations out of the tails and thus lower poverty rates. This is exactly the same argument (in reverse) as in Haddad and Kanbur (1990), who show that poverty measures will be understated if it is assumed that resources are allocated equally across family members when in fact they are not. The fact that official U.S. poverty measures depend on legal marital status is worrisome, especially given the increase in the numbers of coresiding unmarried couples over the past several decades.

In what follows, we present poverty measures that are based on the official definition of a family, but we also present measures that are based on the total incomes of all members of a household (whether or not the members are related). For these latter computations we use the poverty line that would be applied if all household members were related. Since we are interested in how household scale economies affect living standards, it makes sense to use the household (i.e., individuals living together in the same quarters) rather than the family (i.e., those related by blood or marriage) as the unit of analysis. The switch from a family to a household basis is also one of the recommendations of the National Academy study on the poverty line.

(ii) The United States has used essentially the same set of poverty lines since the 1960s, adjusting them only for the effects of inflation. The lines depend on the size and age structure of households. They were originally calculated as the cost of the U.S. Department of Agriculture's "low-cost food plan" for households of different sizes and age structures, multiplied by three. The multiplier of three was selected because it was the inverse of the average budget share for food in a 1955 Department of Agriculture survey. Table 6.1 shows a subset of the poverty lines used in 1992 (and applied to the 1993 CPS data, which refer to 1992); to save space we have trimmed off poverty lines for families with more than six members and families with more than four children.

Table 6.1   **U.S. Poverty Lines, 1992**

Size of Family	Related Children under 18 Years				
	None	One	Two	Three	Four
One person					
Under 65 years	7,299				
65 years and over	6,729				
Two persons, with householder					
Under 65 years	9,395	9,670			
65 years and over	8,480	9,634			
Three persons	10,974	11,293	11,304		
Four persons	14,471	14,708	14,228	14,277	
Five persons	17,451	17,705	17,163	16,743	16,487
Six persons	20,072	20,152	19,737	19,339	18,747

Source: These poverty lines are reproduced from U.S. Bureau of the Census, *Poverty in the United States: 1992* (Washington, D.C., 1993), table A, p. vii.

Several features of the table are important for our analysis. First, the poverty lines for one- and two-person families depend on whether the reference person in the family is elderly.[1] The implicit assumption embodied in the table is that older people need less money to achieve a given welfare level, and the poverty line of an elderly person living alone is $570 less than that of a nonelderly person living alone, a "discount" equal to 7.8 percent of the poverty line for the nonelderly person. Note, however, that this adjustment to the poverty line is made only if the reference person is elderly, and families containing elderly who are not the reference person receive no adjustment to their poverty lines. Second, the poverty lines in the table make implicit adjustments for the costs of children and household size. As seems sensible, increases in family size result in less-than-proportional increases in the poverty line, holding the number of children constant. Increases in the number of children, holding family size constant, also affect the poverty line, but in neither a simple nor a reasonable fashion. For example, the poverty line for a three-person family with no children is less than that of a three-person family with one child. In this case the substitution of a child for an adult increases the poverty line by 2.9 percent. The implication is that children cost *more* than adults, which seems odd given that the poverty lines are based on baskets of food. The poverty lines for families with four people are even stranger; the line rises as we go from a four-adult family to a three-adult one-child family, falls as we go to a two-adult two-child family, and then increases for a one-adult three-child family. Overall,

---

1. In the CPS the term "reference person" is synonymous with the term "householder." This person is defined in the CPS documentation as "the person (or one of the persons) in whose name the housing unit is owned or rented (maintained) or, if there is no such person, any adult member, excluding roomers, boarders, or paid employees." If a married couple jointly owns or rents a home, either person may be designated as the reference person.

the poverty lines in table 6.1 contain the implicit assumptions that, given family size, old people are relatively cheap and children are relatively expensive. However, the poverty lines also imply economies of scale, so that the high expense of children may be offset by the fact that children tend to live in larger families. These assumptions about costs of children and old people, and about scale economies, will affect any conclusions about the poverty of the old relative to the young. We will return to these aspects of the table below, but they are useful to keep in mind when comparing official poverty rates across age groups.

Table 6.2 provides estimates for the United States of the numbers and fractions of elderly people, nonelderly adults, and children less than 18 years of age in poverty, using the official poverty lines. The top panel uses family income to measure poverty, and the bottom panel uses household income. Individuals living in "group quarters" were excluded for these and all subsequent calculations. Using official poverty lines, there are 10.9 million more poor children than poor elderly adults. Poverty rates for children are also higher (22.14 percent vs. 12.87 percent), and poverty rates for elderly and nonelderly adults are very close. This is true whether we use the family or the household as the unit of analysis, although as is to be expected, poverty rates using household-level data are slightly lower for all age categories.

Given the arbitrariness and controversy surrounding the choice of poverty lines, it is important to examine the extent to which these results are sensitive

Table 6.2   **U.S. Poverty Rates for Elderly Adults, Nonelderly Adults, and Children**

	All People	Children under 18	Adults 18–64	Adults 65+
		Family-Level Data		
Sample size	154,977	42,869	93,069	19,039
Estimated population (thousands)	253,924	67,062	156,035	30,827
Number poor (thousands)	36,987	14,846	18,174	3,968
Percentage in poverty	14.57	22.14	11.65	12.87
		Household-Level Data		
Number poor (thousands)	33,311	13,800	15,696	3,815
Percentage in poverty	13.12	20.58	10.06	12.38

Source: The data used for this table are from the March 1993 Current Population Survey, which records 1992 income. The sample consists of all individuals who do not live in group quarters. The population weights from the "person" records were used to obtain population estimates. A person was defined to be poor if his or her family income (*top panel*) or household income (*bottom panel*) was below the relevant poverty line for his or her family (*top panel*) or household (*bottom panel*).

to how the lines are set. A useful way to address the question is to graph cumulative distribution functions for income for different groups (children, nonelderly adults, and elderly adults) and see whether the distribution of living standards of some groups first-order stochastically dominate those of other groups. If the distribution of one group stochastically dominates that of another, then the poverty rate for that group will be lower at any poverty line. An immediate difficulty is that there is no single poverty line for the United States. Rather, we have a *set* of poverty lines for families of different sizes and composition. To draw the cumulative distributions we must first "rebase" family income to make it comparable across families with different sizes and numbers of children. Specifically, we choose families with two adults and two children as the "base," with a poverty line of $14,228 from table 6.1. The living standard of person i in family f is then measured as

$$y_{if}^* = y_f(z_b/z_f),$$

where y_f is the income of family f, z_f is its poverty line, and z_b is the poverty line of the base family. We then graph cumulative distribution functions for y_{if}^* for children, nonelderly adults, and elderly adults.

The results of this exercise (which uses the family rather than the household as the unit of analysis) are shown in figure 6.1. The left-hand panel graphs the cumulative distributions for the three groups. Since we are interested in whether the poverty counts are sensitive to choice of poverty line, we graph the distribution functions only up to $20,000, so any conclusions about stochastic dominance are restricted to this range of income. The "base" poverty line of $14,228 is shown as a point of reference. The right-hand panel of the figure graphs two lines: the vertical difference between the cumulative distributions for elderly and nonelderly adults and the vertical difference between the distributions for children and nonelderly adults. The figure shows that the living standards of adults first-order stochastically dominate those of children. The distribution functions for the elderly and nonelderly adults cross at an income

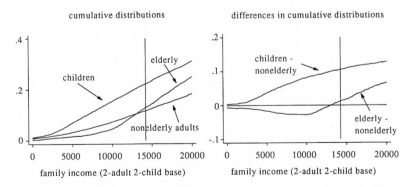

Fig. 6.1   Cumulative distributions of family income by age group

level slightly below the poverty level, indicating that at lower poverty lines the elderly would be less poor than the nonelderly. This may reflect the fact that social security provides an income floor for most elderly citizens.

The key question is how sensitive these results are to treatments of child costs and scale economies different from those implicit in the official poverty lines. One straightforward exercise is to examine how the numbers change if the old-age "discount" to poverty lines is removed, so that one- and two-person families with an elderly reference person receive the same poverty line as do those with younger reference people. The results of these tabulations are shown in table 6.3. When the unit of analysis is the family, the number of elderly in poverty increases by 716 thousand people, from 4 to 4.7 million people, and the rate of poverty among the elderly increases from 12.87 percent to 15.19 percent. There are only tiny increases in poverty among other groups, reflecting the fact that the old-age discount applies to only one- and two-person families with an elderly reference person and most elderly people in two-person families live with other elderly people.

The poverty lines in table 6.1 contain strong implicit assumptions about the costs of children and economies of scale, and it is useful to examine how poverty rates for different age groups change as the assumptions are modified. However, making ad hoc adjustments to the table of poverty lines does not seem especially desirable. The approach we take is to specify the poverty line as a function of the age and size composition of the family and fit this function to the official poverty lines. We can then examine how sensitive poverty measures are to child costs and scale economies by altering the parameters of the function. Specifically, we specify the poverty line for a family with A adults and K children as

Table 6.3		U.S. Poverty Rates with the Old-Age Discount Removed from Poverty Lines		
	All People	Children under 18	Adults 18–64	Adults 65+
		Family-Level Data		
Sample size	154,977	42,869	93,069	19,039
Estimated population (thousands)	253,924	67,062	156,035	30,827
Number poor (thousands)	37,745	14,848	18,213	4,684
Percentage in poverty	14.86	22.14	11.67	15.19
		Household-Level Data		
Number poor (thousands)	34,062	13,800	15,736	4,526
Percentage in poverty	13.41	20.58	10.08	14.68

(1) $$z(A, K) = z_b(A + \alpha K)^\theta,$$

where the term $(A + \alpha K)^\theta$ represents the number of "adult equivalents" in the household and z_b is the per capita poverty line for a base household. In what follows we refer to the term $A + \alpha K$ as the "effective household size." The parameter α measures the cost of children relative to adults, and the parameter θ reflects economies of scale. For example, a value of θ equal to 0.5 implies that doubling effective household size $A + \alpha K$ multiplies the poverty line by the square root of 2, or 1.41.

We take logarithms of equation (1) and fit the resulting equation to the actual data on poverty lines, numbers of adults, and numbers of children. Using the complete list of poverty lines, we obtain the estimates $\alpha = 1.3$ and $\theta = 0.47$. The high value of α reflects the fact that for smaller families the actual poverty lines increase as the numbers of children increase and the majority of families in our sample are small: 77.7 percent of families have fewer than four members, and less than 9 percent have more than four members. When we establish a baseline by recomputing age-specific poverty rates using the poverty lines estimated using equation (1), with $\alpha = 1.3$ and $\theta = 0.47$, we obtain estimates very similar to those using the actual poverty lines: the poverty rate among children is 22.0 percent, among nonelderly adults is 11.5 percent, and among elderly adults is 14.4 percent. That the poverty rate among elderly adults is somewhat higher than the "official" rate of 12.87 percent in table 6.2 is not surprising, given that we have not built an old-age discount into our estimated poverty lines.

We are now in a position to examine how changes in the costs of children, as measured by α, and changes in scale economies, as measured by θ, affect the poverty of the old relative to other age groups. We present these results graphically, by showing cumulative distributions of living standards for people in different age groups, where living standards are measured as

(2) $$y_{if}^* = y_f \frac{z(2,2)}{z(A_f, K_f)} = y_f \frac{(2 + \alpha 2)^\theta}{(A_f + \alpha K_f)^\theta};$$

as before, our "base" family has two adults and two children, so that for families of this type living standards are simply measured as family income.

Before proceeding, it is useful to think about how we might expect changes in α and θ to affect the living standards of individuals relative to those in base households. Taking derivatives of the logarithm of equation (2) with respect to α yields

(3) $$\frac{\partial \ln y_{if}^*}{\partial \alpha} = \theta \left(\frac{2}{2 + \alpha 2} - \frac{K_f}{A_f + \alpha K_f} \right),$$

which is positive for households with smaller ratios of children to effective household size than the base household and negative for others. Increases in the cost of children raise the relative living standards of households with small fractions of members who are children and reduce the relative living standards of those with large fractions. The derivative with respect to θ is

$$
(4) \qquad \frac{\partial \ln y_{if}^*}{\partial \theta} = \ln \left(\frac{2 + \alpha 2}{A_f + \alpha K_f} \right),
$$

which implies that increases in the scale parameter θ will raise the relative living standards of those in families with small numbers of effective members and lower the relative living standards of those in large families. Thus, the living arrangements of the elderly—the size of their families as well as the ratios of children to household size—will determine the effects that changes in child costs and scale economies have on living standards.

Table 6.4 presents evidence on the family sizes and fractions of members who are children for people of different ages. The elderly live in households that are on average smaller than those of children and nonelderly adults. The average household size for an elderly person is 1.94, as opposed to 3.04 for a nonelderly adult and 4.38 for a child. In consequence, poverty measures that assume greater household scale economies will increase the poverty of the old relative to the young, with the primary beneficiaries of scale economies being children. Likewise, the average ratio of children to family size for elderly people is only 0.017, far lower than the average ratios of 0.203 for younger adults and 0.533 for children. Poverty measures that assume smaller costs of children will also increase the poverty of the elderly relative to children and also increase their poverty relative to the younger adults with whom children reside.

Table 6.4   U.S. Average Family and Household Composition

	Children	Nonelderly Adults	Elderly Adults
Family-Level Data			
Number of children	2.39	.86	.08
Number of nonelderly adults	1.95	2.10	.36
Number of elderly adults	.04	.08	1.50
Children + adults	4.38	3.04	1.94
Children/(children + adults)	.533	.203	.017
Household-Level Data			
Number of children	2.42	.90	.09
Number of nonelderly adults	2.02	2.23	.38
Number of elderly adults	.037	.08	1.51
Children + adults	4.81	3.21	1.98
Children/(children + adults)	.524	.208	.018

Note: The table shows averages, across all people in the relevant age category, of family (*top panel*) and household (*bottom panel*) characteristics. For example, children live in families that contain, on average, 2.39 children.

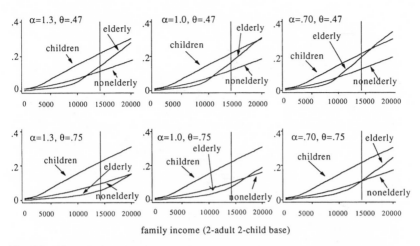

family income (2-adult 2-child base)

Fig. 6.2   Cumulative distributions of income with changes in child costs and scale economies

Figure 6.2 shows the effects of altering α and θ on the cumulative distributions of family income in the United States. The top left-hand graph shows the distributions with $\alpha = 1.3$ and $\theta = 0.47$, the values obtained using the official poverty lines. Consistent with figure 6.1, the distribution of living standards for children is stochastically dominated by that of elderly and nonelderly adults, and the lines for elderly and nonelderly cross near the official poverty line for the base family. As one moves from left to right, α is decreased, from 1.3 to 1.0 to 0.7. As expected, increases in child costs make the elderly less well off relative to children, and at $\alpha = 0.7$ the cumulative distributions for the elderly and for children cross at an income level only slightly above the official poverty line. The three graphs in the bottom panel also let α vary from 1.3 to 0.7, but use a scale parameter θ equal to 0.75 instead of 0.47. Scale economies are less important at higher values of the scale parameter, and as expected the elderly become better off relative to others due to their smaller average family sizes. The information in figure 6.2 is summarized in figure 6.3, which shows the *differences* in the cumulative distributions similar to those shown in figure 6.1.

The effects of changes in α and θ can also be seen in table 6.5, which shows the fraction of individuals with values of y_{if}^* less than the base poverty line of $14,228. Holding θ fixed at 0.47, the poverty rate of the elderly increases from 14.40 to 19.60 and the poverty rate of children declines from 22.02 to 21.61 as the cost of children declines from 1.3 to 0.7. It may seem counterintuitive that when child costs are lowered, the poverty rates of children fall very little and the poverty rates of the elderly rise substantially. It should be kept in mind, however, that we have used a two-adult two-child family as the base and that the incomes of base families are unaltered by changes in α and θ. Since a large

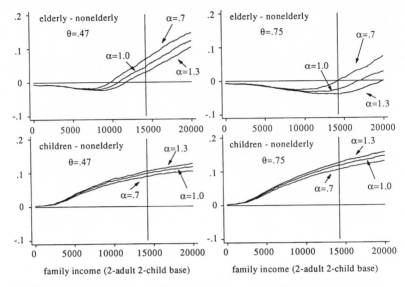

Fig. 6.3   Differences in cumulative distributions with different assumptions about child costs and scale economies

Table 6.5   **U.S. Poverty Rates Using Different Base Household Types**

Child Costs and Scale Economies	Two-Adult Two-Child Base			One-Adult Base		
	Children	Nonelderly Adults	Elderly Adults	Children	Nonelderly Adults	Elderly Adults
$\alpha = 1.3, \theta = 0.47$	22.02	11.46	14.40	23.04	12.28	16.08
$\alpha = 1.0, \theta = 0.47$	21.84	11.97	16.54	21.60	11.81	15.97
$\alpha = 0.7, \theta = 0.47$	21.61	12.66	19.60	19.49	11.11	15.90
$\alpha = 1.3, \theta = 0.75$	22.36	9.75	5.79	35.51	18.21	20.29
$\alpha = 1.0, \theta = 0.75$	22.07	10.29	7.72	31.86	16.89	20.22
$\alpha = 0.7, \theta = 0.75$	21.62	11.03	11.04	27.90	15.48	20.12

fraction of children live in two-adult two-child families, we are effectively guaranteeing that their poverty rates change little as α is increased. The more general point is that the choice of base family has large effects on the measured levels of poverty. This is illustrated by the right-hand panel of table 6.5, which repeats the exercise using a one-adult no-child base. In this case, increases in α reduce poverty rates for all age groups, since there are people in all age groups who live with children, but reduce the poverty rate for children the most.

Table 6.5 also shows the effects of changes in scale economies on relative poverty rates. In general, increases in θ from 0.47 to 0.75 (holding α fixed) increase the poverty of children relative to elderly adults. This is to be expected, given that children live in families that are on average larger than those of other age groups. Again, however, the effect of changes in the scale parameter on absolute poverty rates depends on the definition of the base family. When the base is a two-adult two-child family, the poverty rate of children barely changes, while adult poverty rates decline. Using a one-adult base, increases in the scale parameter result in large poverty increases for all groups, with the largest increase for children.

It is also useful to compare changes in poverty rates as one moves from the case in which both child costs and scale economies are high (i.e., $\alpha = 1.3$ and $\theta = 0.47$) to a possibly more realistic case of lower child costs and scale economies (i.e., $\alpha = 0.70$ and $\theta = 0.75$). These changes in α and θ have offsetting effects, since large families tend to have more children. Using a two-adult two-child base, the poverty rates of children and nonelderly adults are largely unchanged, and that of the elderly declines by less than 4 points. Thus, it is possible that modifying the official poverty lines so that they imply lower child costs *and* lower scale economies will leave aggregate poverty rates for different age groups largely unchanged. This does not imply, however, that the same *people* will be in poverty under the two scenarios.

The conclusion of this section is that the age distribution of poverty is quite sensitive to the treatment of child costs and economies of scale. Official estimates of the numbers and percentages of people in different age groups in poverty hinge on poverty lines that contain strong implicit assumptions about child costs and scale economies. Deviations from the assumptions implicit in official poverty lines result in very different poverty measures for different age groups.

In section 6.3, we examine the empirical evidence on household consumption patterns in a (not very successful) attempt to establish a less arbitrary basis for the costs of children and household economies of scale. As we shall see, there are good reasons to be skeptical of the results. Nevertheless, to the extent that there are results, they are consistent with a value of α around 0.75 and a value of θ of 0.85 or even higher. Such figures generate poverty counts close to those shown in the last row of table 6.5, with $\alpha = 0.70$ and $\theta = 0.75$.

6.3 Calculating Equivalence Scales

6.3.1 Introduction

The official poverty lines in the United States differ for different family sizes as shown in table 6.1. These differentials come from differences in food purchasing patterns in the 1955 survey that Mollie Orshansky used to construct the original poverty line. In consequence, the equivalence scales implicit in the table have some basis in behavior, although, as we have seen, the pattern of child costs and economies of scale is not easy to defend. Several alternatives to the Orshansky scales have been proposed from time to time. For example,

Ruggles (1990) suggests that the scale be proportional to the square root of household size, so that two adults are equivalent to 1.41 single adults, three adults to 1.73 single adults, and so on. As discussed in section 6.2, this rule approximates the Orshansky scale while removing some of its stranger features. Larger families are also typically those with larger numbers of children, and the square root rule should be seen as reflecting not only economies of scale but also that children cost less than adults. It is also possible explicitly to separate adults and children, and the recent report on the poverty line by the National Academy (National Research Council 1995) recommends that scales be calculated according to the formula used above, namely, $(A + \alpha K)^\theta$ for A adults and K children, and recommends values around 0.75 for both α and θ. Alternatively, the Organization for Economic Cooperation and Development (1982) has suggested a scale in which the first adult counts as unity, other adults as 0.7, and children as 0.5, so that economies of scale are not allowed for explicitly but are reflected in the discount for additional adults and a relatively low cost of children.

In this section, we use data from the Consumer Expenditure Survey (CEX) in 1990 to try to tease out information about the relative costs of children and adults, and about the extent of economies of scale. That these data should be relevant for such an exercise seems obvious. The CEX collects information on purchases of goods that are differentially consumed by adults and by children and can be used to infer how these purchases change with the composition of the family. Economies of scale presumably arise because some goods are public and can be shared by several members of the household, and an expenditure survey can tell us how the balance between private and public goods shifts with household size and composition. Even so, attempts to infer equivalence scales from budget data have a long and discouraging history. Although expenditure data are *relevant* to the construction of scales, they are insufficient by themselves to *identify* scales. Additional identifying assumptions are required, and it has been difficult to find such assumptions that are widely acceptable. Worse still, many of the estimates in the literature have been derived under identifying assumptions that are not made explicit, so that it is difficult or impossible to know what the results mean.

We devote subsection 6.3.2 to the theoretical issues: to the identification issue and what it does and does not imply and to the basis for our calculations of child costs and economies of scale. The former rests on familiar ground and calculates the costs of *children* by comparing the behavior of expenditure on *adult goods* across households with different numbers of children. The latter uses a new method, suggested to one of us by Jean Drèze, that uses expenditures on *private goods* to identify the economies of scale to household size that operate through *public goods*.

6.3.2   Identifying Equivalence Scales

We begin by explaining what cannot be done, and the consequences of trying. The theory of equivalence scales parallels that of cost-of-living index numbers, and both begin from a description of household preferences in terms of the cost or expenditure function. If total household expenditure is x, and if this is efficiently spent to maximize the collective utility of a family of A adults and K children, say, then we can write

(5) $$c(u, p, A, K) = x,$$

where u is the collective utility level. By analogy with cost-of-living numbers, the number of single adult equivalents in a family with A adults and K children is (see Deaton and Muellbauer 1980, 205)

(6) $$E(A, K; u, p) = \frac{c(u, p, A, K)}{c(u, p, 1, 0)},$$

an expression that, in general, will depend on prices and on the level of real income of the family. Since the cost function provides a convenient summary of the family's preferences, and since once specified it can be used to yield a set of demand functions, there is an apparently straightforward way of calculating the equivalence scale in equation (6). Write down some suitable cost function (eq. [5]), for example, a translog or almost ideal system, recover the parameters by estimating the associated demand functions, and fill in equation (6). This is what is done, for example, by Slesnick (1993) in his recalculation of poverty in the United States.

Pollak and Wales (1979) have shown that such calculations of equivalence scales ignore the central identification problem that the data do not identify the equivalence scales. In particular, Pollak and Wales point out that all cost functions of the form

(7) $$c(\phi(u, A, K), p, A, K)$$

have the same demand functions irrespective of the function ϕ provided only that it is monotone increasing in u. Relabeling indifference curves in a way that depends on family structure has no effect on demand functions, although it clearly changes how we should measure welfare. As a result, the data do not allow us to calculate equivalence scales without additional assumptions that pin down the function ϕ.

At first blush, it is tempting to associate the identification issue with the fact that parents get utility from children and to try to separate "economic" welfare as represented from the structure of the cost function from the "psychic" welfare that is captured by the function ϕ. But this hope is not only imprecise, it is wrong, as the following example shows. Consider families that contain only adults, and suppose that we model economies of scale by writing

(8) $$c(u, p, A) = A^\theta c(u, p, 1),$$

so that for $\theta \leq 1$ there are economies of scale; we want to estimate θ. To fix ideas, suppose that the cost function for the single-adult household takes the "quasi-homothetic" form in which costs are a linear function of utility:

(9) $c(u, p, A) = A^\theta c(u, p, 1) = A^\theta a(p) + A^\theta b(p)u,$

where $a(p)$ and $b(p)$ are linearly homogeneous functions of the vector of prices p. The demand functions are derived from equation (9) in the usual way; the budget shares take the form

(10) $w_i = \dfrac{p_i q_i}{x} = \alpha_i(p)\dfrac{a(p)A^\theta}{x} + \beta_i(p)\left(1 - \dfrac{a(p)A^\theta}{x}\right),$

where $\alpha_i(p)$ and $\beta_i(p)$ are the elasticities with respect to the ith price of $a(p)$ and $b(p)$, respectively. (That the budget shares for a family of A adults with outlay x are the same as the budget shares for a family with one adult and outlay x/A^θ is a general feature of cost functions of the multiplicative form [8].) According to equations (9) and (10), preferences and the associated behavior are each weighted averages of preferences at subsistence $a(p)$ with associated budget shares $\alpha_i(p)$ and preferences at bliss $b(p)$ with associated budget shares $\beta_i(p)$. Given specifications for $a(p)$ and $b(p)$, the demand functions (10) can be taken to the data, and θ estimated together with the other parameters; see, for example, Lanjouw and Ravallion's (1995) work for Pakistan, where the parameter θ is estimated to be around 0.6.

Economies of scale in equation (8) operate multiplicatively through the cost function, so that in equation (9) costs at subsistence and costs at bliss are subject to the same economies. But because of fixed costs or other effects, the economies of scale might be more or less effective at higher levels of living. One way of generalizing equation (10) to allow this would be to write

(11) $c(u, p, A) = A^\theta a(p) + A^\psi b(p)u,$

where θ and ψ are not necessarily equal. If we now derive the demand functions from these new preferences, either by elementary calculation or by application of the Pollak and Wales (1979) theorem, we once again retrieve equation (10). Hence, as far as their empirical implications are concerned, equations (9) and (11) are indistinguishable. As a corollary, if we take equation (10) to the data and obtain an estimate of θ, it has no particular claim on our attention as a measure of the extent of economies of scale. The scales used in Slesnick's (1993) reworking of the poverty count are obtained by a generalization of the technique outlined above and are subject to the same criticism. Slesnick's and Lanjouw and Ravallion's estimates are identified by assuming that the particular cardinalization of utility that they chose is correct, rather than the infinite number of other cardinalizations that are indistinguishable on the data but that would give different results for the scales. Indeed, since Slesnick's results are perhaps even more bizarre than those in the official scales, it is comforting to know that they can be arbitrarily "corrected" without consequences for the empirical evidence from which they were obtained.

By itself, the empirical evidence on expenditure patterns cannot generate equivalence scales. Instead, we need additional assumptions, typically in the form of prior information that links welfare to behavior. It is to these we now turn.

6.3.3 Alternative Identification Schemes for Child Costs and Economies of Scale

The most famous and venerable of the schemes for linking behavior and welfare is Engel's supposition that families with the same share of food in their budgets are equally well off, irrespective of size and composition. The food share assumption serves as an all-purpose scale identifier, allowing us to measure both child costs and economies of scale. For the former, we start from a two-adult family (say) and calculate for any given level of outlay the additional amount that would be required to bring a two-adult one-child family to the same food share, which by assumption would be at the same level of welfare. We can equally well equate food shares for a large and a small family so as to calculate the relative outlays that make them equally well off and so estimate any economies of scale. If the cost function is multiplicatively separable in family characteristics on the one hand and prices and utility on the other—as is equation (8)—the food share, or any other budget share, does indeed indicate welfare, so the method is consistent with a well-defined theoretical structure. Furthermore, the assumption that the food share indicates welfare solves the identification impasse; for example, it is easy to check that the food share indicates welfare if the cost function is equation (9), but not when the cost function is equation (11). The Engel assumption ties down the function ϕ in equation (7).

Engel's assumption is the *kind* of assumption that we need, but it is not the right one. As first argued by Nicholson (1976) and elaborated by Deaton and Muellbauer (1986), Engel's assumption is quite implausible. The addition of a child with full compensation would normally *increase* the food share, not leave it unchanged, in which case the Engel compensation is too large. A better procedure for measuring child costs uses expenditure on adult goods as an indicator of adult welfare and calculates the compensation that would be required after the addition of the child in order to restore adult expenditures to their previous level. This method was first proposed by Rothbarth (1943) and has been used in the United States by Betson (1990) and (more or less) by Lazear and Michael (1988). The Rothbarth procedure is not without its problems. In particular, it takes no account of possible substitution toward adult goods in the presence of additional children, or of broader rearrangements of consumption patterns that might follow the addition of a child. There is also a shortage of well-measured adult goods in the data. The procedure inevitably uses expenditures on adult clothing and footwear, alcohol, and tobacco, and the last two are much underestimated in the CEX—as in other expenditure surveys around the world—see Gieseman (1987). Even so, the Engel method is clearly wrong, and the transparency of Rothbarth's method and its identification assumptions are in sharp and favorable contrast with the mechanical estimation of equivalence scales from demand systems augmented by demographic variables. We present some results using Rothbarth's method below.

The calculation of economies of scale has a less well trodden history. Although the Engel method provides estimates of scale economies, there is no reason to credit them without some theory of why, in the presence of public goods, the food share should correctly indicate welfare between families with different numbers of people. Indeed, there are good reasons for supposing that the Engel method will give the wrong answer. The argument follows much the same lines as Nicholson's argument about Engel's method for calculating child costs, and we shall adopt a solution that is similar to the Rothbarth method in that case.

Suppose that there exists a pure private good that is not substitutable for public goods, food being the obvious example. Consider what happens when family size increases, for example, by combining two single adults into a family of two adults. Suppose too that compensation is paid, presumably negative compensation since the scale economies in the public good will make the family better off if the two original incomes are simply combined. Because less of the public good is needed than in the two separate single-person families, and because there is no substitution from the private to the public good, the budget share of the private good will increase. But according to Engel, a family with a higher food share must be worse off, and less money should be taken away. In consequence, Engel's method will overstate the amount of money needed for the larger household and thus understate the extent of and discount from economies of scale.

In our own empirical work in this paper, we adopt an approach to economies of scale that parallels Rothbarth's procedure for measuring child costs. We measure child costs by examining adult goods, and we measure economies of scale by examining the behavior of private goods as household size changes. Consider again the example of the previous paragraph in which two people, previously in single-person families, come together to form a two-person family. As before, they no longer need as much heat and light, kitchens, bathrooms, and (possibly) bedrooms so that they have more for private goods, whose share of the budget can be expected to increase. If nothing else happens, we could calculate the extent of the economies of scale, not by restoring the *share* of private goods to its previous value, but by calculating the reduction in total income that would restore the previous *per capita consumption* of private goods. If the reduction is (say) 20 percent of total outlay, we have established that there is a 20 percent discount for two people over one. The major caveat is that public goods are effectively cheaper in larger households; an oriental rug or a painting costs the same but provides pleasure to twice as many people. In consequence, there will be substitution away from private toward public goods, so that a fully compensated two-person family will have lower per capita consumption of private goods than will the two single-person families combined. As a result, the reduction in income that restores the per capita consumption of private goods is less than the utility-preserving reduction and so understates the extent of economies of scale. This effect will be small if private goods are not substitutable for public goods, as, for example, food for housing, or we can calculate the income reduction for a range of private goods and select the one that gives the largest reduction. Although both this method and the Engel (food share) method will understate economies of scale, the latter will do so even in the absence of substitution between private and public goods and will therefore understate by more.

Alternative methods and estimates of economies of scale have been provided by Nelson (1988) and in the National Academy report. The latter starts from the estimates of child costs obtained by the Rothbarth procedure in Betson (1990), who made separate calculations according to the number of adults in the family. His results can therefore be used to give the costs of an additional child relative to an adult in one-adult families, in two-adult families, and so on. If it is supposed that the number of adult equivalents is approximated by the formula $(A + \alpha K)^\theta$, with parameters the same for different household types, then the differences in child costs across different family types reflect economies of scale and can be used to measure them. In particular, in a family with A adults and K children, the cost of an additional child relative to an adult is given by the formula $[(A + \alpha(K + 1))/(A + \alpha K)]^\theta$, which can be fitted to Betson's results to obtain estimates of α and θ. The calculations in the report suggest values of around 0.75 for both α and θ. Unlike the Engel procedure, this method appears to be soundly based, at least if we accept the Rothbarth method of estimating child costs. Even so, it can provide only a summary of the scale economies and yields no insight into the process by which public goods work within the household. Nor does it ensure that we are measuring economies of scale rather than (for example) the possibility that larger households devote less to additional children for some other reason.

Nelson assumes that different goods exhibit different economies of scale, and she uses CEX data on all adult families to estimate a demand system that, following Barten (1964), allows explicitly for the patterns of substitution that come from the changes in effective relative prices that are induced by the differential economies of scale. Although the identification of welfare is left implicit, Nelson's procedures are theoretically consistent with the method adopted below. Her model assumes that economies of scale work so that the fractions of family consumption of each good received by each person can add up to a total different from unity, and that the sum of these fractions is different for different goods, being larger than unity for goods with economies of scale. Because she makes no allowance for fixed costs, economies of scale can only operate this way and must result in substitution effects in line with the price effects that the scaling factors are designed to mimic. She works with five broad groups of goods and finds that all display economies of scale; for housing there are implausibly large economies, with each member of a two-person household receiving twice as much in housing services as would each in a one-person household. Nelson attributes the result to the fact that, in her data, two-person households spend almost the same amount on housing as one-person households, in spite of having incomes that are 50 percent higher. It is also possible that the Barten model should bear some of the blame; high economies of scale act so as to diminish needs and thus consumption, but they also cause an offsetting substitution effect toward the good. When this price effect is substantial, and the data show that two people spend much the same on housing as one person, the model responds by choosing a very large value for the economies of scale. But it is also possible that the model is incorrect, and that economies of scale operate differently, as would be the case if there are fixed costs.

6.3.4   Using Adult Goods to Estimate Child Costs

We used data from the 1990 CEX to examine the behavior of expenditure on adult goods over families with differing numbers of children. Expenditure on adult goods is defined, as is usual, as the sum of expenditures on alcohol, tobacco, and adult clothing and footwear. The 1990 CEX has 20,517 observations in total, and we use all of these in the analysis. The CEX is a rolling panel, in which each household is (in theory) interviewed five times at three-month intervals and asked about consumption in the previous three months. New households are added as other households exit the survey. Because each interview generates an observation, there are only 10,127 different households in the sample. Of these, 3,893 are interviewed once, 3,053 twice, 2,206 three times, and 975 four times. The lower numbers of households with three and four observations are accounted for by the fact that some households miss interviews or drop out of the survey before completing all five interviews: 953 of our households do not complete the full series of interviews or have "gaps" between interviews.

We define total expenditure as the sum of expenditures on food, both away and at home, alcohol, tobacco, clothing, housing, transportation excluding purchases of new cars, entertainment, personal care, medical expenditures, reading materials, and educational expenditures. The Bureau of Labor Statistics computes these semiaggregated expenditure items from the more finely detailed expenditure information collected by the survey and puts them in the "summary expenditure section" of the CEX data tape. It should be noted that "housing" is broadly defined to include utilities, household furnishings, and household equipment. Furthermore, the cost of an owner-occupied house is measured as actual interest payments on mortgages and not as the rental value of the house. This definition of total expenditure is the conditioning variable in our Engel curves, and when we calculate the compensation required to restore adult expenditures to prechild levels, it is the increase in this measure of the total that is used. The validity of the procedure requires that additional children have no effect on total expenditure, so that we are ignoring effects of children on income through changes in labor supply, as well as on saving. To the extent that children *decrease* this definition of total expenditure—which seems the more probable outcome—the costs of children will be *understated* by the amount of the decrease.

In this section and the next, we start with a nonparametric analysis, to explore whether the data are at all consistent with the underlying hypothesis, and then use the results to suggest the more parametric forms that allow the inclusion of a wider range of covariates. For the analysis of adult goods and child costs, the nonparametric analysis adopts the obvious procedure of fitting adult good Engel curves for different family types, comparing households with and without children. The CEX sample will support such an analysis for a limited number of family types; table 6.6 lists the number of families by combinations of adults and children. Given these, it makes sense to fit nonparametric regressions for adult-child combinations of (1,0), (1,1), (1,2), (2,0), (2,1), (2,2), (2,3), (3,1), and (3,2). We do this by calculating the regression function of adult expenditures (in dollars per month) conditional on the logarithm of total annual expenditure using a version of Fan's (1992) local regression smoother. In order to exclude areas of low density at the extremes of rich and poor, we trim the sample to the range of log total outlay shown and then erect a 100-point uniform grid over log outlay. At each point x on this grid, we run a weighted regression with weights given by the quartic kernel:

$$
\begin{aligned}
w_i &= \tfrac{15}{16} \lambda_i (1 - t_i^2)^2, & |t_i| &\leq 1, \\
&= 0, & |t_i| &> 1,
\end{aligned}
$$
(12)

where t_i is the distance of x_i from x in units of the bandwidth h,

$$
t_i = (x - x_i)/h.
$$
(13)

The bandwidth h is chosen by visual inspection of alternative estimates in an attempt to preserve genuine structure while eliminating random fluctuations. The multiplier λ_i is an inflation factor, provided in the CEX, that accounts for the fact that the CEX is not a simple random sample. For each observation i,

Table 6.6   **Number of Households by Composition, CEX 1990**

			Children		
Adults	0	1	2	3	4
1	5,567	554	371	165	48
2	5,452	1,943	2,047	953	258
3	1,195	463	255	126	47
4	406	146	57	52	9
5	94	48	21	13	5

λ_i is equal to the number of households in the U.S. population that the observation represents, so observations that represent more households are given more weight in the regressions.

The results are shown in figure 6.4 for one-adult, two-adult, and three-adult nonpoor families. We restrict our sample to families above the poverty line because families in poverty have very different consumption patterns, as we shall see in subsection 6.3.6. Although the ordering of the curves is not uniformly monotone over the range of total outlay, the ordering is generally in the right direction, and certainly so in the middle of the total expenditure distribution. Holding total expenditure constant, the addition of children reduced expenditure on adult goods. Note also that the slopes of the regression functions are positive, a condition that must be satisfied if we are to calculate the variations in total expenditure that would have effects on adult expenditure equivalent to the addition of children. It is also a condition that is often not satisfied in practice; see, for example, Cramer (1969).

The curves in figure 6.4 are close to one another so that the estimates of child costs that they imply are relatively modest. The mean of log outlay for (1,0) households is 8.06; conditional on this, adult expenditure is predicted to be $252 a month. To have the same predicted adult expenditure, a (1,1) household would need a log outlay of 8.34, and a (1,2) household 8.52. One child costs 28 percent of a single adult, and two children (together) 46 percent of an adult. For a (2,0) family, an additional child is 32 percent of one adult, two children 72 percent, and three children 76 percent. For three-adult families, the first child costs 54 percent of an adult, two children 90 percent of an adult. While these numbers might make sense for India or a similarly poor country, they seem unreasonably small for the United States.

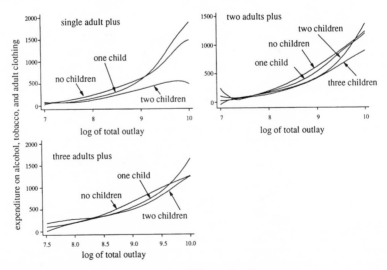

Fig. 6.4   Adult good Engel curves for different family types

Alcohol and tobacco are two items that are notoriously underestimated in household expenditure surveys, including the CEX, so it is wise to reestimate the results using only adult clothing and footwear. But the results are very similar; if anything child costs are estimated to be somewhat lower. This echoes Betson's (1990) findings that the results are not much affected by the choice of the broad or narrow definition of adult expenditures. Another potential source of underestimation is that children consume some of the adult goods. If so, the addition of the child will have a direct positive effect on consumption as well as the negative income effect, so that expenditure on adult goods will be reduced by too little, and child costs underestimated. For alcohol, tobacco, and adult clothing, this is unlikely to be a problem for young children, but it may well be serious for teenagers. However, it is difficult to allow for child age in the nonparametric regressions, so we move to a flexible parametric model.

Our general approach, for the investigation of both child costs and economies of scale, is to allow total expenditure to enter the regression function in a general way, while other variables enter linearly. There is a great deal of information in the data about the shape of the Engel curve, and it is desirable to use it. Because family size and compositional variables are correlated with total expenditure, a failure to model the shape of the Engel curve is likely to compromise the estimates in which we are interested. The model we estimate is written

$$(14) \qquad e_A = f(\ln x) + \beta_1 \ln n + \sum_{k=1}^{K} \gamma_k \frac{n_k}{n} + u,$$

where e_A is expenditure on adult goods, n is household size, x is total outlay, and n_k is the number of people in the kth age-sex category in the household. The right-hand side is motivated by the wish to approximate the "obvious" but nonlinear form

$$(15) \qquad e_A = \phi\left(\frac{x}{(A + \sum a_j k_j)^\theta}\right),$$

which, with an extension to different types of children, is the form with which we began.

We proceed as follows. Equation (14) is first estimated with per capita outlay entered linearly, followed by the Fourier specification

$$(16) \qquad f(t) = \sigma_0 + \sigma_1 t + \sigma_2 t^2 + \sum_{i=1}^{M} (\sigma_{ci} \cos(it) + \sigma_{si} \sin(it)),$$

for which we have generally found that setting M equal to 2 is adequate. The equation is estimated for both narrow (clothing) and broad (clothing, alcohol, and tobacco) definitions of adult goods and is estimated separately for one-adult, two-adult, and three-adult households. Family composition is disaggregated by age and sex, so that we have males and females aged 0–5, 6–11, 12–17, 18–64, and 65 or older. Since the 10 ratios sum to one, we omit that associated with females aged 65 or over, which therefore becomes the reference group.

The regression results are not shown in detail, but a few points are worth noting since they affect the calculations of child costs. The Fourier approximation always improves the fit, but the effects on the other parameter estimates are modest, so we can focus on the more easily interpreted linear form. Clothing and footwear has an expenditure elasticity that is greater than unity, in contrast to the broad aggregate, which is dominated by alcohol and tobacco, the share of which declines with total outlay. The compositional effects work more or less as anticipated. As is required for the model to make any sense, additional prime-age adults increase expenditure on adult goods, although it is adult women who spend most on adult clothing, with little effect for men. Additional children decrease expenditure on adult goods, or at least they do until they are 12 years old, at which point they smoke and drink and, if they are girls, buy adult clothing. We clearly cannot use expenditure on these goods to estimate the costs of older children.

Table 6.7 presents the estimates of child equivalences, calculated separately according to (1) whether we are using all adult expenditure or just clothing, and (2) whether we are using the Fourier approximation or the linear model. The numbers are calculated as follows. In the top panel, we consider the addition of a child to a family containing a single adult female aged 18–64. By equation (14) if $f(\cdot)$ has the linear form $\alpha + \beta \ln x$, adult expenditure in the new larger household will be the same as in the original smaller household if, when the original household has expenditure x, the new one has expenditure x^* given by

$$(17) \qquad \ln \frac{x^*}{x} = \beta^{-1}\left(\beta_1 \ln \frac{1}{2} + \frac{\gamma_{af}}{2} - \frac{\gamma_j}{2}\right),$$

where γ_{af} is the coefficient of the adult female ratio and γ_j is the coefficient of the child ratio in which we are interested. The top panel in the table shows $\ln (x^*/x) - 1$, the proportional additional cost of the child. For the two-adult family, the corresponding formula is

$$(18) \qquad \ln \frac{x^*}{x} = \beta^{-1}\left(\beta_1 \ln \frac{2}{3} + \frac{\gamma_{af}}{6} + \frac{\gamma_{am}}{6} + \frac{\gamma_j}{3}\right),$$

where γ_{am} is the adult male coefficient and the numbers presented in the table are scaled—that is, $2(\ln(x^*/x) - 1)$ in order to present the child cost relative to a single adult rather than a couple. The three-adult household is taken to be an adult male, an adult female, and an elderly female, and the costs are calculated in the corresponding way. When the Fourier approximation to the Engel curve is used, it is no longer possible to derive a closed-form expression for

Table 6.7   **Estimated Child Costs Relative to Single Adults for Various Family Types by Child Age and Sex (percent)**

Family Type	All Adult Expenditures		Adult Clothing and Footwear	
	Linear Form	Flexible Form	Linear Form	Flexible Form
Adult female plus				
Boy 0–5	69	65	90	81
Girl 0–5	70	67	98	91
Boy 6–11	62	69	53	58
Girl 6–11	54	63	72	81
Boy 12–17	68	71	66	66
Girl 12–17	33	45	27	39
Adult couple plus				
Boy 0–5	70	82	53	60
Girl 0–5	72	82	62	68
Boy 6–11	76	83	63	66
Girl 6–11	80	91	76	85
Boy 12–17	36	42	22	24
Girl 12–17	15	19	−5	−6
Three adults plus				
Boy 0–5	60	54	65	58
Girl 0–5	60	57	73	67
Boy 6–11	52	59	28	34
Girl 6–11	43	52	48	57
Boy 12–17	58	61	42	43
Girl 12–17	19	33	−1	13

Notes: The three-adult household is an adult male, an adult female, and a female aged 65 or over. The calculations for the linear form are exact; those for the Fourier flexible form are approximations.

child costs. Instead, we use as an approximation equations (17) and (18) with β replaced by the derivative of the Engel curve with respect to log expenditure evaluated at the mean of log total expenditure. We make no attempt to calculate child costs for children other than the first. While such calculations are straightforward in principle, the differences from the cost of the first child are effectively determined by the choice of functional form (14), rather than by any genuine feature of the data.

In terms of the broad orders of magnitude with which we are concerned, the child cost estimates in table 6.7 are sensitive neither to the choice of functional form for the Engel curve nor to the broad or narrow definition of adult goods. As expected, the estimates for the older children are much too low; "children" between ages 12 and 17 clearly consume these "adult" goods. But the differentiation by age has solved the underestimation problem in the nonparametric results, so that children under age 12 appear to cost around two-thirds to three-quarters of an adult. Comparing the results for single-adult and two-adult families, there is not much evidence of the reduction in child costs that would be expected from economies of scale, although the estimates based on clothing are lower for the smallest children. However, child costs do seem to be lower for the three-adult households. Even so, we could not obtain useful results by following the National Academy procedure and identifying economies of scale by matching the numbers in the table to the ratio of $(A + \alpha K)^\theta$ to A^θ with $K = 1$. To measure economies of scale, we must turn to more direct methods.

6.3.5   Using Private Goods and Economies of Scale

In this subsection we report our attempts to obtain estimates of economies of scale by looking at the relationship between expenditure on private goods, expenditure per head, and family size. The basic idea is illustrated in figure 6.5, which shows the relationship between expenditure per capita on private goods—or on any single private good or group of private goods—and income (or total expenditure) per head. The lower curve is the private good Engel curve for the smaller household with n_1 members, all of whom are assumed to be adults. Consider an increase to n_2 adults with per capita income held constant, for example, when two single adults get married. Since they have the same total resources as before, it is possible for them to keep their consumption pattern unchanged. However, we would not expect this to happen since the larger family thereby ignores the potential economies of scale associated with public goods. Since the nature of public goods is that they do not have to be duplicated for each household member, the larger household need spend less on them, freeing more resources for private goods, so that the Engel curve

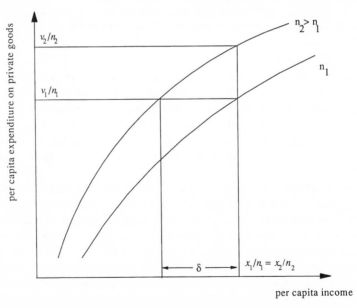

Fig. 6.5   Private good expenditure and the discount to family size

moves upward as shown. The graph shows the amount δ by which per capita income must be reduced so as to restore private expenditures to their previous per capita level. If this amount were deducted from the income of the larger family, that family would still be better off than the smaller family, since a correctly compensated family would presumably take advantage of the relative cheapness of public goods to substitute in their favor and would therefore spend less on private goods. The calculation of δ therefore *understates* the discount from economies of scale. It would be possible to correct for this underestimation by estimating a full demand system that allows for the pricelike effects of economies of scale as in Nelson (1988); the understatement can be minimized by selecting a private good that is a relatively poor substitute for the public goods in the household. For example, people are unlikely to substitute housing and utilities for food just because utility is cheaper through the former the larger is household size.

We therefore began our investigations with food. Although there may be some economies of scale associated with food—bulk buying, reduction of wastage, and saving on items such as cooking oil that are used less than proportionately with scale—the effects seem likely to be modest. There is the further advantage that food is a poor substitute for the most likely public goods. Nevertheless, to our considerable surprise, expenditure on food does not behave as illustrated in figure 6.5. Holding constant per capita outlay, per capita expenditure on food *decreases* with family size, which suggests that the larger the family, the less food each member needs to remain equally well off. Our preliminary investigations for Britain, France, Taiwan, Thailand, and South Africa suggest that this result is true much more broadly than for the United States; the results in Lanjouw and Ravallion (1995) and Ayadi et al. (1995) appear to show the same result in Pakistan and Tunisia, respectively. The detailed evidence would take us too far afield from our main purpose, and a fuller report is contained in Deaton and Paxson (forthcoming). Here we confine ourselves to the main results for the United States, to some possible explanations, and to the search for economies of scale through other potential private goods.

Figure 6.6 shows the locally weighted nonparametric regressions for the food share conditional on the logarithm of per capita expenditure for households with one to four nonelderly adults and zero children. Although the argument in figure 6.5 was presented in terms of per capita food expenditure increasing with family size, the same argument applies to the food share in the budget, which is the ratio of per capita food expenditure to per capita total expenditure, and the latter is being held constant as family size is changed. Although the relationship between the four curves changes with the level of per capita outlay, the one-adult curve is highest through most of the range, and the four-adult curve is the lowest. The curves for two and three adults are close to one another and cross more than once. At the same level of per capita outlay, one-adult households spend more per capita on food than do two- or three-adult households, who in turn spend more than four-adult households. While

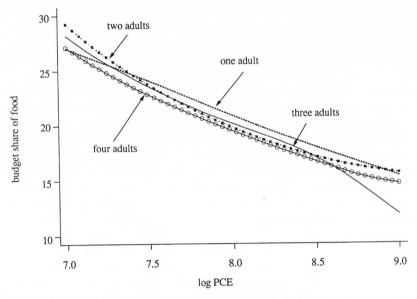

Fig. 6.6   Food Engel curves for nonelderly adult households

it is possible to think of reasons why one-adult families are special—they eat out a great deal, or they buy expensive precooked food, or they waste a great deal of food—it is hard to reconcile the results for the other family types with the presumption that food is a private good and that economies of scale operate through nonfood public goods.

In order to investigate whether the same phenomenon holds for more complex family types and survives the conditioning on a wider range of variables, we once again have to move to a more parametric treatment. In parallel with our earlier discussion of child costs and adult goods, we adopt a flexible functional form for the food budget share of the form

(19) $$w_f = f\left(\ln\frac{x}{n}\right) + \beta_1 \ln n + \sum_{k=1}^{K} \gamma_k \frac{n_k}{n} + \psi\pi + u,$$

where w_f is the food share and π is a dummy indicating whether the family falls below the official poverty line, a dummy that is provided on the CEX tape. Although not shown in equation (19), we also interact household size and the demographic compositional variables with the poverty dummy. This is done, not because poverty itself changes demand patterns—and if it did, the effect would be picked up by a sufficiently flexible function $f(\cdot)$—but because families in poverty, depending on their demographic composition, are eligible for food stamps, housing benefits, and other programs that are likely to change their consumption patterns.

As before, we treat the function $f(\cdot)$ in more than one way: (a) using the linear specification $\alpha + \beta_0 \ln x/n$, (b) using the Fourier flexible form (16), and

(c) following a nonparametric technique of Estes and Honoré (1995). The last works by first sorting the data according to the values of x/n and then fitting equation (19) by ordinary least squares to the first-difference of all the right-hand–side variables excluding x/n. As the sample size increases, and provided that the function $f(\cdot)$ is continuous, the distance between any two successive values decreases at rate n^{-1} so that, in the limit, the influence of x/n is purged from the regression as if it were a (local) fixed effect. The advantage of this procedure—apart from its elegance and simplicity—is that we do not have to specify any functional form. The disadvantage is that we do not obtain an estimate of the slope of the Engel curve, something that is of no importance when our aim is to find the sign of β_1, the coefficient on family size, but that would become necessary if we ever got as far as calculating the compensation as in figure 6.5.

The three sets of results are presented in table 6.8. In the event, getting the shape of the Engel curve right has little effect on the other coefficients, and in

Table 6.8   **Food Share Regressions Using Three Alternative Techniques**

Variable	Linear Form	Fourier Flexible Form	Estes and Honoré Nonparametric Form
ln x/n	−7.25 (39.3)	[a] [a]	[b] [b]
ln n	−0.71 (2.9)	−0.67 (2.7)	−0.95 (4.6)
rm05	−7.28 (7.3)	−7.48 (7.6)	−7.58 (7.8)
rm611	−1.08 (1.0)	−1.27 (1.2)	−0.85 (0.8)
rm1217	2.86 (2.5)	2.78 (2.4)	2.21 (2.1)
rm1864	2.36 (5.2)	2.10 (4.8)	2.13 (5.7)
rm65	3.34 (4.6)	3.29 (4.5)	3.20 (5.5)
rf05	−9.22 (9.1)	−9.41 (9.2)	−9.54 (9.5)
rf611	−2.73 (2.7)	−2.70 (2.8)	−1.32 (1.2)
rf1217	1.14 (1.0)	0.90 (0.8)	0.24 (0.2)
rf1864	−1.22 (2.9)	−1.22 (2.9)	−0.99 (2.7)
π*rm05	11.27 (3.9)	9.62 (3.3)	10.14 (4.6)
π*rm611	6.16 (2.1)	4.77 (1.6)	5.14 (2.3)
π*rm1217	2.87 (1.0)	1.14 (0.4)	−0.80 (0.3)
π*rm1864	−1.73 (1.4)	−1.62 (1.3)	−1.08 (1.3)
π*rm65	−3.90 (2.3)	−3.93 (2.3)	−3.63 (2.7)
π*rf05	6.80 (2.5)	5.27 (2.0)	6.76 (3.1)
π*rf611	6.97 (1.8)	5.31 (1.4)	4.66 (2.0)
π*rf1217	−1.38 (0.5)	−2.15 (0.7)	1.64 (0.7)
π*rf1864	−1.42 (1.4)	−1.31 (1.3)	−1.53 (1.9)
π	1.01 (2.2)	1.61 (2.0)	1.03 (1.7)

Notes: All coefficients multiplied by 100. Numbers in parentheses are absolute values of t-statistics. For the first two columns, the standard errors on which the t-statistics are based have been corrected for random household effects. (Recall that the CEX has a panel element, and a single household may contribute up to four observations.) The Estes and Honoré standard errors have not been corrected for the first-differencing or for household random effects.

[a]Estimated by Fourier flexible form and coefficients not shown.

[b]Estimated as a local fixed effect and eliminated from the regression.

all three specifications, the budget share of food is reduced by between a full point and two-thirds of a point in response to a unit increase in the logarithm of family size. This is not a large effect, but the negative sign is statistically significant, and once again we have the reverse of what would be predicted by our description of economies of scale. The other coefficients in table 6.8 are of some independent interest. Controlling for per capita outlay, children, whether boys or girls, reduce per capita food consumption, and men spend more on food than do women. The poverty dummy has strong positive interactions with the presence of children under the age of 12, presumably through the operation of food stamps and AFDC.

We have no good explanation for the failure of food to behave like a private good. Perhaps there are substantial economies of scale associated with food, or perhaps increases in family size cause more substitution than seems plausible from food toward housing and other public goods. Whatever the story, the conclusion that a negative discount understates the true discount to family size, although hard to challenge, is not very useful. We therefore turn to other goods as potential private goods, although we confess that our confidence in the general methodology is somewhat shaken by the failure of the most promising good to yield useful results.

As for food, we estimate equation (19) for a range of goods from the CEX. We calculate the change in the logarithm of per capita total outlay that keeps per capita expenditure constant in the face of a change in household size with household composition held constant. This is done through the per capita expenditure-constant elasticity, from equation (19):

$$(20) \qquad \frac{d \ln x/n}{d \ln n} = \frac{\beta_1}{w + f'(\ln x/n)},$$

which is evaluated at the sample means.

The results, in table 6.9, are given for a list of commodity groups that sums to total outlay, and they are almost as bewildering as those for food. Of course,

Table 6.9   **Family Size Percentage Discounts for Various Items of Expenditure**

Commodity Group	Discount Using Linear Form	Discount Using Flexible Form
Food	−4.5	−4.4
Alcohol	−82.4	−69.0
Tobacco	−60.6	−88.6
Clothing	5.6	5.9
Transportation	20.3	19.9
Housing and utilities	−10.6	−10.3
Entertainment	9.8	9.8
Personal care	9.1	8.9
Medical expenditures	31.0	36.6
Reading material	−8.6	−7.7
Educational expenditures	17.2	16.7

goods like transportation and housing and utilities are certainly not private goods, and it is no surprise to find that expenditure per capita on housing falls with family size. But commodities like alcohol and tobacco, which might seem to be candidates for private goods, have less spent on them as family size increases. Perhaps these are examples of *negative* public goods, which generate negative externalities for other members of the family, and which therefore become more expensive as family size increases. Transportation and medical expenditures—the latter strongly associated with the elderly in the estimates—are items for which expenditure increases with family size. The former would appear to have a public element, in which case its expenditure would be expected to decrease, while it is hard to see why family size should increase medical expenditures when the age composition of the household is being controlled for. There is perhaps some consolation in the estimates for clothing, personal care, and educational expenditures. If we use these, and ignore the anomalous results elsewhere, we obtain modest economies of scale, with the elasticity of needs to size between 85 and 95 percent. But it is hard to escape the conclusion that expenditure patterns respond to family size in ways that are a good deal more complex than the simple story of public and private goods that we have considered in this paper. Constructing better models of this process remains a challenge for the future.

References

Ayadi, Mohamed, Rafiq Baccouche, Mohamed Goaid, and Mohamed Matoussi. 1995. Spatial variations of prices and household demand analysis in Tunisia. Tunis: University of Tunis III, Faculté des Sciences Economiques et de Gestion de Tunis, January. Processed.

Barten, Anton P. 1964. Family composition, prices, and expenditure patterns. In *Economic analysis for national economic planning,* ed. Peter Hart, Gordon Mills, and John Whitaker. London: Butterworth.

Betson, David M. 1990. Alternative estimates of the cost of children from the 1980–86 Consumer Expenditure Survey. Special Report no. 51. Madison, Wisc.: Institute for Research on Poverty.

Cramer, Jan S. 1969. *Empirical econometrics.* Amsterdam: North-Holland.

Deaton, Angus S., and John Muellbauer. 1980. *Economics and consumer behavior.* New York: Cambridge University Press.

———. 1986. On measuring child costs. *Journal of Political Economy* 94:720–44.

Deaton, Angus S., and Christina H. Paxson. Forthcoming. Economies of scale, household size, and the demand for food. *Journal of Political Economy.*

Estes, Eugena M., and Bo E. Honoré. 1995. Partial regression using one nearest neighbor. Princeton, N.J.: Princeton University. Manuscript in preparation.

Fan, Jianqing. 1992. Design-adaptive nonparametric regression. *Journal of the American Statistical Association* 87:998–1004.

Gieseman, Raymond. 1987. The Consumer Expenditure Survey: Quality control by comparative analysis. *Monthly Labor Review* 110 (3): 8–14.

Haddad, Lawrence, and S. Ravi Kanbur. 1990. How serious is the neglect of intra household inequality? *Economic Journal* 100:866–81.
Lanjouw, Peter, and Martin Ravallion. 1995. Poverty and household size. *Economic Journal* 105:1415–34.
Lazear, Edward P., and Robert T. Michael. 1988. *The allocation of income within the household.* Chicago: University of Chicago Press.
National Research Council. 1995. *Measuring poverty: A new approach.* Washington, D.C.: National Academy Press.
Nelson, Julie A. 1988. Household economies of scale in consumption: Theory and evidence. *Econometrica* 56:1301–14.
Nicholson, J. Leonard. 1976. Appraisal of different methods of estimating equivalence scales and their results. *Review of Income and Wealth* 22:1–18.
Organization for Economic Cooperation and Development. 1982. *The OECD list of social indicators.* Paris: Organization for Economic Cooperation and Development.
Pollak, Robert A., and Terence J. Wales. 1979. Welfare comparisons and equivalence scales. *American Economic Review Papers and Proceedings* 69 (2): 216–21.
Rothbarth, Erwin. 1943. Note on a method of determining equivalent income for families of different composition. In *War time pattern of saving and spending,* ed. Charles Madge. Cambridge: Cambridge University Press.
Ruggles, Patricia. 1990. *Drawing the line.* Washington, D.C.: Urban Institute Press.
Slesnick, Daniel T. 1993. Gaining ground: Poverty in the postwar United States. *Journal of Political Economy* 101:1–38.

Comment   B. Douglas Bernheim

This provocative and ambitious paper wrestles with the difficult problem of measuring poverty consistently across diverse groups of individuals. The paper is divided into two parts. The first part describes current practices regarding the measurement of poverty in the United States, and it examines the sensitivity of official poverty measures to alternative assumptions about the size of appropriate adjustments for differences in household composition. The second part outlines and implements a potentially superior methodology for establishing the size of these adjustments.

Section 6.2 focuses on three specific household composition adjustments that are imbedded in existing poverty thresholds. These adjustments are intended to account for family size, the presence of children, and the presence of elderly households. The paper effectively makes the case that the official methods of making these adjustments are arbitrary, and moreover that the measurement of relative rates of poverty among different population subgroups is quite sensitive to plausible changes in the magnitudes of the adjustments.

The analysis in this part of the paper is, without question, very useful. Still, it should hardly come as a surprise that there is inherent arbitrariness attached to the use of a single summary statistic for income distribution, such as a pov-

B. Douglas Bernheim is the Lewis and Virginia Eaton Professor of Economics at Stanford University and a research associate of the National Bureau of Economic Research.

erty rate (the authors' idea of looking for stochastic dominance relations between income distributions for different population subgroups therefore strikes me as particularly good). One is left at the end of this paper wondering why economists should be engaged in the possibly futile exercise of trying to define meaningful poverty thresholds in the first place. I suspect that we have focused on poverty rates primarily to satisfy the demands of politicians and the press, who generally seem to limit their attention to single numbers. To the extent that economists wish to affect the policy process, it may be necessary to cater to the demand for oversimplification; thus, one justifies the exercise in this paper by arguing that, if politicians insist on using a single number, we should make sure that it is the best number possible. But then the ultimate point of this paper seems to be that the construction of a truly "good" poverty number is impossible.

That said, it should be emphasized that there may well be some conceptually legitimate applications of poverty statistics. Although it may be very difficult, and possibly even meaningless, to compare rates of poverty across population subgroups, it may be justifiable to make comparisons across time for the same subgroup. That is, by comparing poverty rates for the elderly in, say, 1990 and 1965 using some constant-real-dollar poverty threshold, one may be able to learn something important about changes in the lower tail of the income distribution, even if the absolute level of the threshold is inherently arbitrary.

In section 6.3, the authors attempt to develop and implement a methodology for improving two of the household composition adjustments: family size and presence of children. The adjustment for the presence of elderly individuals is conspicuously absent from this list, which is unfortunate; one would expect the measurement of poverty among the elderly (the focus of the paper) to be most sensitive to the elderly adjustment.

This portion of the paper does an extremely thorough job of criticizing itself. The authors have already acknowledged, in some form, most (if not all) of the problems with their approach. My critique differs from the authors' own critique more in emphasis than in substance.

As the authors note, there are two problems associated with moving from family resources to individual measures of welfare. The first problem concerns the intrahousehold allocation of resources. The second problem concerns the effects of household size and age structure on the standard of living. The authors write, somewhat euphemistically, that they "have little to say" about the first problem. Yet is difficult for me to see how one can come up with a coherent resolution to the second problem without resolving the first one.

Consider in particular the authors' method of determining the appropriate poverty line adjustment for children. This involves partitioning consumption into "adult goods" and other goods, on the premise that children do not consume adult goods. But this premise inherently raises the issue of distribution. The underlying hypothesis is simply inconsistent with the view that resources are divided equally within the household. The authors have tried to finesse this problem linguistically, by assuming that resources are distributed "equitably," rather than "equally," among household members. But the meaning of "equitably" in this context is unclear, since equity necessarily involves the comparison of unequal consumption bundles across consumers with presumptively different preferences.

Even if one could articulate a notion of equity that would correspond to equality of standard of living across heterogeneous family members, it is difficult to see why this notion would be held forth as a positive theory of household behavior, rather than as a normative standard. If the authors proceed on the basis of the assumption that intrahousehold allocation is governed by (as yet unspecified) egalitarian principles, while in fact resources are distributed unequally within households, then it is highly unlikely that their methodology will yield appropriate adjustment factors.

Consider the following example. Suppose that all household decisions are made by a completely selfish, dictatorial head. The head consumes all of the household's resources and instructs other family members to beg on the street for sustenance. In that case, it would appear to me that Deaton and Paxson would estimate $\alpha = 0$. However, it seems incorrect to conclude from this finding that policymakers should regard children as costless. Alternatively, imagine that the dictatorial head is not completely selfish but cares less about each member that is added to the family. In that case, Deaton and Paxson would significantly overestimate the true extent of economies to scale.

These examples make it clear that, for most positive theories of household behavior, it is not going to be possible to define a single poverty threshold for the entire household. It makes more sense to define a separate poverty level for each household member, where this threshold is chosen to represent the level of household income at which that member would achieve some measure of subsistence. Thus, in the first example above, there would be some finite poverty threshold for the head, and the formula for this threshold would indeed involve $\alpha = 0$, but the poverty thresholds for other household members would be infinite (since no amount of household income would bring them to subsistence). In the second example, the poverty threshold for the head would rise at a declining rate with the number of household members. However, for any given household composition, younger children would have higher thresholds than older children, and the head would have the lowest threshold of all.

These examples also make the general point that the authors' methodology is likely to produce little more than a measure of the preferences of the household decision maker. To drive this point home, consider the following whimsical suggestion: why not adjust the poverty line for the presence of household pets? This is potentially important in the context of aging, since the elderly are probably significantly more likely to be in pet-less households, and therefore less likely to have to share household resources with pets. How would one calculate the appropriate adjustment? Following Deaton and Paxson's approach, one would divide expenditures into "human goods" and all other goods (including nonhuman goods). This might, of course, prove difficult in practice, since household pets do consume many human goods ("people food" being the leading example). Abstracting from this problem, one could then determine the levels of household income that would equate spending on human goods between households with pets and pet-less households. One would then use this to set an adjustment factor for pets, analogous to α. Thus, the poverty threshold would be higher for households with pets.

I would, however, question the appropriateness of the pet adjustment. First, the ownership of pets is voluntary. The human members of the household would not have acquired a pet unless they thought that they would be better off as a result of owning the pet. Consequently, there is no reason to set a higher poverty threshold for the humans merely because they choose to own a pet. Second, with respect to the welfare of the pet (rather than the welfare of the humans), the division of expenditures between human and nonhuman goods is likely to tell us more about the humans' willingness to spend money on the pet than about the costs of maintaining a pet at subsistence.

These observations are not completely whimsical. Children are, at least to some extent, voluntary choices. Thus, if one were properly defining poverty thresholds for individuals, rather than for households, it is not at all obvious that it would be appropriate to increase the poverty threshold for parents based on number of children. With respect to poverty thresholds for children, the Deaton-Paxson method might measure some aspect of parents' willingness to spend money on children, but it probably does not tell us much about the welfare of children.

Generally, it seems to me that the Deaton-Paxson estimates teach us about preferences, rather than about subsistence standards. Consider again the strategy of differentiating between adult goods and other goods. Even if children do not consume adult goods, their presence may affect (or be correlated with) the preferences of adult household members. For example, adults may prefer to engage in fewer activities involving the consumption of alcohol after having children; alternatively, children may drive their parents to drink. People who have children may simply have different tastes than those without children. If different adult goods have different income expansion paths, then the methodology may simply identify, in a convoluted way, the income elasticities of the adult goods that have been selected for the analysis.

I am also skeptical about the kinds of comparisons that the authors make in their attempt to identify household economies of scale, and I am less surprised by their "puzzling" results concerning food. I agree that food is, almost certainly, a private good. However, the preparation and storage of food are public goods. Economies of scale in preparation and storage may induce smaller families to eat out more often, raising the cost per meal and giving rise to apparent economies of scale in food consumption. Alternatively, the taste for eating at home may change when family size grows, as the social aspects of family meals become better substitutes for the social aspects of eating out.

As I have emphasized, the authors are acutely aware of the limitations of their methodology. The great challenge here is to come up with a better approach. Although I have failed to rise to this challenge, I have two suggestions.

First, it might be possible to design a less arbitrary poverty line if the purpose of the poverty line were more clearly defined. One could, for example, decide to define the poverty line in terms of the adequacy of nutrition. In that case, meaningful poverty thresholds could be constructed as follows. First, set standards of adequacy for nutritional outcomes. Second, collect data on nutritional outcomes, income, and household characteristics. Third, relate nutritional outcomes to income and household characteristics separately for each household position (husband, wife, first male child, first female child, elderly parent, etc.). This would allow one to determine, for each household position, the level of household income necessary to assure nutritional adequacy with some prespecified level of probability.

Second, instead of comparing consumption across different households in cross sections, one might compare consumption for the same household across time, as household composition changes. The life cycle hypothesis, in effect, argues that households should smooth their standards of living through time. Thus, one could examine changes in consumption associated with household additions to determine the amount of resources required to compensate for an addition. One could also examine the manner in which consumption responds to departures from households. This has some advantages, since certain departures (e.g., of grown children) are usually anticipated. Life insurance purchases, which anticipate departures, can also be used to infer household economies of scale.

While this approach has some attractive conceptual features, it also presents some new problems. First, one must subscribe rather unreservedly to the hypothesis of rational intertemporal optimization. Second, the applicability of the method to lower income households may be limited, to the extent that these households are liquidity constrained. The possibility of binding liquidity constraints suggests a somewhat more ad hoc approach: measure the level of income at which the typical household begins to save, and examine how this varies with household composition.

7   The Covariance Structure of Mortality Rates in Hospitals

Douglas Staiger

7.1   Introduction

In 1987 the Health Care Financing Administration (HCFA) began publishing standardized mortality scores for each hospital in the country as an indicator of quality of care (Bowen and Roper 1987). Since then, the use of similar patient mortality measures has become widespread, to the point where some insurance plans base hospital reimbursement on such mortality measures (Minnesota Blues 1991; Perry 1989). At the same time, patient mortality has been widely used in studies of the determinants of quality of care in hospitals (Cutler 1995; Garber, Fuchs, and Silverman 1984; Luft, Hughes, and Hunt 1987; McClellan, McNeil, and Newhouse 1994; Staiger and Gaumer 1995) and in studies of patient choice among hospitals (Luft, Hunt, and Maerki 1987; Luft et al. 1990; Staiger 1993). Despite the widespread use of patient mortality as a proxy for quality of care, there is considerable controversy over the statistical reliability and validity of such measures (Hofer and Hayward 1996; Keeler et al. 1992; Krakauer et al. 1992; Luft and Romano 1993; McNeil, Pedersen, and Gatsonis 1992; Park et al. 1990).

A number of questions are of particular interest to both the research and the policy communities. First, how much useful information is there in such inherently noisy measures of quality; for example, how large is the signal-to-noise ratio? A related question is how persistent are these measures of quality of care: Are hospitals with unexpectedly high mortality rates this year likely to have unexpectedly high mortality rates next year, in five years, in ten years? Is

Douglas Staiger is associate professor of public policy at the John F. Kennedy School of Government, Harvard University, and a faculty research fellow of the National Bureau of Economic Research.

This paper has benefited from discussions with David Cutler, Matthew Eichner, and David Meltzer. Support from the NBER Health and Aging Fellowship is gratefully acknowledged.

the presumption of high persistence, commonly assumed by both the public and by analysts doing fixed-effect models, consistent with the data? A third question is whether there is a correlation in patient mortality for patients with distinct diagnoses admitted to the same hospital? If so, then combining information from different types of patients may prove to be a useful way of summarizing common hospital-level components of quality of care. A final question of interest is what has happened to the cross-sectional distribution of patient mortality over time; for example, has there been convergence or divergence across hospitals? Have there been any noticeable changes in the variation of these measures in recent years as reimbursement and competitive pressures have grown?

This paper uses annual data from 1974–87 for 492 large hospitals to investigate these questions. I analyze data on standardized mortality rates for Medicare admissions in both specific diagnoses and in aggregate. In addition to presenting simple descriptive evidence on the distribution of the mortality measures, I estimate covariance structures using general method of moment (GMM) methods along the lines of MaCurdy (1982) and Abowd and Card (1989). This method provides a simple and powerful description of the basic features of the data.

The empirical work leads to a number of interesting conclusions. First, 75 to 90 percent (depending on the diagnosis) of the variance in mortality is entirely transitory and can be thought of as independent identically distributed (i.i.d.) measurement error. Second, the remaining nontransitory component of mortality is fairly persistent but is in general not well approximated as a permanent fixed effect. Instead, the nontransitory component is fairly well described as an autoregressive (AR(1)) process with a first-order serial correlation of .8–.95 depending on the diagnosis. Third, the combined data are fit fairly well by a simple three-factor model in which mortality consists of (1) i.i.d. error, (2) a fairly transitory diagnosis-specific component, and (3) a very permanent hospital component that is common across diagnoses. Finally, although there are some interesting changes in the cross-sectional distribution of these mortality measures over time (particularly during the 1970s), there is no obvious evidence that these distributions have tended to converge or diverge over time or changed in any interesting ways during the 1980s.

The key difficulty in interpreting these empirical results is the possibility that much of what we observe in these measures may reflect systematic variation in unobserved patient characteristics rather than quality of care. However, to the extent that this variation reflects quality of care, there are a number of useful lessons to be learned. Clearly, the large i.i.d. component in these mortality measures limits the usefulness of historical measures as indicators of current quality. Similarly, to the extent that this i.i.d. component is measurement error, these mortality measures are a poor choice as independent variables to proxy for quality of care. The presence of an important component of mortality that is serially correlated raises questions about the bias of hospital fixed-effect models that have been used to analyze mortality. Finally, the three-factor model is consistent with the notion that quality of care depends on both hospital-level infrastructure (e.g., nursing staff, physical plant), which is relatively unchanging, and diagnosis-specific technology (e.g., surgical techniques, medications), which may be a large source of the variation for some diagnoses but disseminates relatively quickly.

The paper proceeds as follows. Section 7.2 describes the data and estimation approach. Section 7.3 presents simple descriptive evidence on how the mortality rate distribution has evolved over time. Section 7.4 estimates the covariance structure for standardized mortality rates. Section 7.5 concludes.

7.2   Data Sources and Methods

7.2.1   Data

The data are derived from a 25 percent random sample of all short-term general hospitals in the continental United States, developed by Abt Associates. Of these hospitals, only those operating continuously from 1974 to 1987 were included in the analysis. Each observation in the data corresponds to a hospital-year from 1974–87, yielding 14 observations per hospital.

The data set contains information on mortality for acute myocardial infarction (AMI) admissions, congestive heart failure (CHF) admissions, and urgent care admissions (an aggregate group that includes AMI and CHF). These three categories are discussed in more detail below. To be included in the sample, a hospital had to have at least one admission in each diagnosis category in every year. This effectively limits the sample to relatively large, urban hospitals. The final sample includes 492 hospitals, with 14 years of data on each hospital.

I use data on 45-day postadmission mortality for a subsample of Medicare patients, chosen on the basis of 59 conditions necessitating urgent admission (see Gaumer, Poggio, and Coelen 1989). These 59 conditions were selected by clinical panels to include cases for which adverse mortality outcomes might reasonably result as the result of care received. These urgent care conditions accounted for just over 12 percent of all Medicare admissions in 1987. Among the urgent care admissions, AMI and CHF are the most frequent diagnoses and account for roughly one-half of the admissions. Mortality measures are available for AMI and CHF separately, and for urgent care diagnoses as a whole.

The mortality data come from a 20 percent sample of Medicare discharge records (the MEDPAR data) combined with social security death records through 1989. For example, the 45-day mortality rate is based on the fraction of urgent care patients admitted during the calendar year that had a date of death within 45 days of admission. Note that these data include all deaths, not just those in the hospital.

Differences in mortality rates across time and across hospitals may reflect differences in patient mix rather than differences in quality of care. Therefore, I use an expected mortality rate (similar to that used by HCFA in their mortality reporting) for each hospital-year to control for the variation in mortality due to variation in patient mix. The expected mortality rate is based on a reference population of Medicare patients drawn from the MEDPAR data.[1] Mortality rates were computed for the reference population for each of 354 cells defined by diagnosis/procedure (59 groups), gender (2 groups), and age (65–74, 75–84, and over 85). Each study patient was assigned an expected mortality equal to the mean value for the applicable cell. The hospital-year expected mortality rate is the average expected mortality for study patients within each hospital year.

Raw 45-day mortality rates (MR) are transformed into Z-scores by subtracting the expected mortality rate (EMR) and dividing by the estimated standard deviation in mortality. Raw mortality rates display considerable heteroscedasticity, with the variance inversely related to the number of admissions (N). The standard deviation is estimated assuming that mortality is binomially distributed, with the probability of death equal to the expected mortality rate. Thus the mortality Z-score is given by

$$Z = (MR - EMR)/\text{sqrt}[EMR(1 - EMR)/N].$$

This type of Z-score measure is a relatively common method of standardizing across hospitals of different sizes (see, e.g., Luft et al. 1990).

7.2.2   Methods

Modeling and estimating the error structure for a set of variables with panel data is conceptually straightforward. I follow an approach similar to that used by MaCurdy (1982) and Abowd and Card (1989), who use panel data on hours and earnings to decompose the error structure into permanent and transitory components. Since these methods are fairly well known, I will not go into detail on them here.

The basic approach is to choose an error structure for Z_{it} that depends on a $K \times 1$ vector (Θ) of unknown parameters, derive the implied covariance matrix ($\Omega(\Theta)$) for $Z = [Z_{74}, Z_{75}, \ldots, Z_{87}]$, and estimate the unknown parameters by fitting the implied covariance matrix to the actual covariance matrix. For example, if the mortality Z-score is composed of a hospital fixed effect plus i.i.d. noise, then the covariance matrix of Z takes the simple form

$$\Omega_{t,t} = \Theta_0 + \Theta_1$$

$$\Omega_{t,t-k} = \Theta_0 \qquad \text{if } k > 0,$$

---

1. Unfortunately, the reference population changes in 1979. For the years 1974–78, the reference population is all MEDPAR admissions in those years. For the remaining years, the reference population is all MEDPAR admissions during 1979–83. Consequently, expected mortality rates (averaged over the whole sample) take a discrete jump (downward) in 1979. I have rescaled expected mortality rates after 1979 so that, on average, 1978 and 1979 expected mortality rates are equal.

where Θ_1 represents the variance of the i.i.d. measurement error (which only appears in the variances) and Θ_0 represents the variance of the fixed effect (which determines all the off-diagonal covariances).

GMM estimates of Θ minimize an optimally weighted sum of squared deviations between the actual and theoretical covariance matrices. Let M be a $J \times 1$ vector of the nonredundant elements of the sample covariance matrix (so if Z is $N \times L$, the sample covariance matrix $Z'Z/N$ has $L \cdot (L + 1)/2$ distinct elements), and let $m(\Theta)$ be a $J \times 1$ vector of the corresponding theoretical moments. Then Θ_{GMM} minimizes the statistic $Q(\Theta) = N \cdot [M - m(\Theta)]' V^{-1} [M - m(\Theta)]$, where V is the sample covariance matrix of M (fourth moments of Z). The statistic Q evaluated at the GMM estimate is distributed as chi-squared with $J - K$ degrees of freedom and therefore provides a goodness-of-fit test for the model. Furthermore, parameter restrictions are easily tested using the statistic $L = Q_R - Q$, where Q_R and Q are the goodness-of-fit statistics from the restricted and unrestricted models. Under the null corresponding to the restricted model, L is distributed as chi-squared with degrees of freedom equal to the difference in the degrees of freedom of Q_R and Q.

The GMM framework provides a natural method of testing how increasingly restrictive models fit the data. I first test whether the data can be fit well with a stationary covariance structure, that is, a structure in which $\text{Cov}(Z_t, Z_{t-k})$ only depends on k. I then test even more restrictive error structures against the stationary but otherwise unconstrained model.

7.3   Descriptive Evidence

Figures 7.1–7.3 summarize some of the basic facts and trends in 45-day mortality rates for urgent care, AMI, and CHF admissions. Figure 7.1 plots trends in the raw data used to construct the mortality Z-scores from 1974 to 1987. The variables have been scaled to better fit on one graph: the mortality rate and expected mortality rate are given as deaths per 10 admits, while the number of admissions has been logged. Actual mortality rates fell for all three admission categories from 1974 until around 1980 and then flattened out. For example, AMI 45-day mortality rates fell from over 33 percent in 1974 to just over 25 percent in 1980. Expected mortality over this time period was surprisingly flat, suggesting that the decline in observed mortality was due to true improvements in quality of care rather than changing patient mix. At the same time that mortality was trending downward, patient volume was trending upward. For example, CHF admissions roughly tripled between 1974 and 1980.

Figure 7.2 plots trends in the first three moments (mean, variance, skewness) of the mortality Z-score measures. These trends highlight important changes in the distribution of the Z-score over time and provide some evidence on whether hospitals are converging or diverging over time. The trend in the mean of the Z-score parallels the trend in actual mortality, falling until 1980 and then remaining relatively flat for all diagnoses. In contrast, the variance of the Z-score is relatively stable, perhaps trending downward slightly for all diagnoses. The

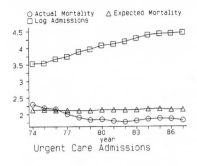

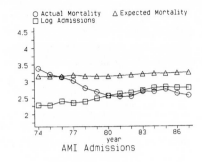

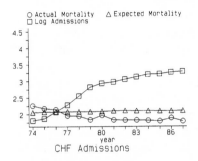

Fig. 7.1 Trends in actual and expected mortality per 10 admissions, and in the log of admissions, 1974–87

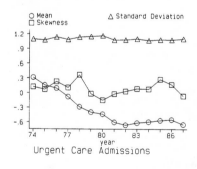

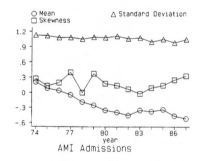

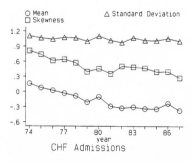

Fig. 7.2 Trends in mortality Z-score moments, 1974–87

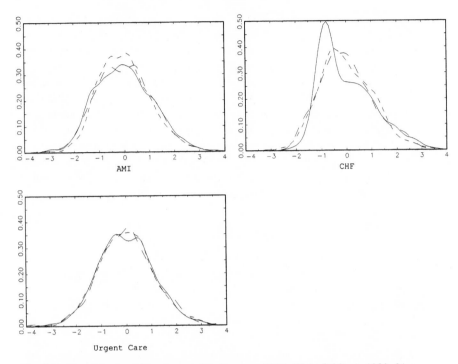

Fig. 7.3   Empirical p.d.f.'s of mortality Z-score: 1974–75 (*solid line*), 1980–81 (*long dashes*), and 1986–87 (*short dashes*)

stability of the variance over time, in spite of a large rise in the number of patients on which these measures are based, may seem surprising. However, recall that the Z-score rescales by an estimate of the standard deviation in mortality and therefore should not be overly sensitive to changes in the number of patients. Finally, the skewness of the Z-score distribution has fallen over time, particularly for CHF between 1974 and 1979.

The trends in the moments of the Z-score raise two issues. First, there is clearly a mean shift in mortality over time, and it will be important to remove year effects from this measure. More important, even after allowing for a mean shift, the distribution of the Z-score does not appear to be stationary. Thus a stationary covariance structure may fit the data poorly, particularly in the early years.

Figure 7.3 plots kernel estimates (using a Gaussian kernel) of the partial distribution functions (p.d.f.'s) as a further way of inspecting changes in the distribution of the Z-scores over time. Each panel plots p.d.f. estimates pooling two years of data for three distinct time periods: 1974–75, 1980–81, and 1986–87. Each year's data were demeaned in order to remove the time effects. The changes in the distributions between 1974–75 and 1980–81 are quite striking. The distribution of AMI mortality is relatively fat tailed and flat topped in 1974–75, while the distribution in later years is generally tighter and seems to exhibit some bimodality. The CHF distribution has a large spike of low-mortality hospitals in 1974–75 with a long tail of higher mortality. By 1980–81 this spike has largely disappeared, and the distribution looks more symmetric.

Overall, a number of interesting facts emerge from figures 7.1–7.3. First, there is no obvious evidence of convergence in the cross-sectional distribution of mortality. Neither is there any striking evidence that this distribution has changed much during the 1980s in response to the changing reimbursement and market conditions facing hospitals. In fact, since some time around 1979–81 the distribution has been remarkably stable in both shape and location. In contrast, over the mid- to late 1970s the mortality distributions changed dramatically: average mortality fell, as did the spread and skewness of the distribution of standardized mortality rates across hospitals.

7.4 Estimates of the Covariance Structure

I now turn to more formal estimates of the covariance structure of the Z-score for mortality in each of the diagnosis categories. The data that provide the basis for these estimates are contained in the sample covariance matrix for each diagnosis category. Since there are 14 years of data, there are $14 \cdot 15/2 = 105$ distinct moments and potential degrees of freedom. I also consider the covariance between AMI mortality and CHF mortality. This matrix is not symmetric (e.g., $\text{Cov}(Z_{AMI,74}, Z_{CHF,75})$ is not equal to $\text{Cov}(Z_{AMI,75}, Z_{CHF,74})$) and therefore provides $14 \cdot 14 = 196$ total degrees of freedom.

Table 7.1 summarizes the results of a series of model specification tests. The first row contains the GMM goodness-of-fit statistic testing whether the data are consistent with a stationary covariance matrix (i.e., a symmetric covariance matrix with constant values along each diagonal). As might be expected from the changes in distributions that were apparent in figure 7.3, only urgent care mortality is fit well by a stationary covariance matrix. The AMI mortality data reject stationarity at the 2 percent level, while CHF and the AMI-CHF covariance overwhelmingly reject stationarity. From direct inspection of the covariance matrices, it is apparent that most of the poor fit is associated with differences between the 1974–78 period and later years.

Despite the poor fit of the unconstrained stationary model, the resulting estimates still provide information about the general covariance pattern found in the data. Figure 7.4 graphs the estimated autocovariances and corresponding 95 percent confidence intervals. These covariograms are the basic data that any stationary model of the error structure is trying to fit. The sharp drop-off in covariance at the first lag for all three diagnoses, combined with the lack of any large contemporaneous correlation between AMI and CHF mortality, suggests significant i.i.d. measurement error in mortality. The magnitude of the decline suggests that as much as 90 percent of the variance in mortality is i.i.d. error. The gradual decline in covariance at higher lags for urgent care and AMI suggests some kind of an AR process—an MA process would be more transitory,

Table 7.1   **Model Specification Tests for Covariance Structure of Mortality Z-Score, 1974–87 (based on GMM goodness-of-fit statistic)**

Model Specification	For Covariance Matrix of			
	Urgent Care	AMI	CHF	AMI′CHF
1. Unconstrained stationary	104.6	120.26	139.00	296.95
covariance (symmetric)	(.156)	(.022)	(.001)	(.000)
	[91]	[91]	[91]	[182]
Tested against model 1				
2. Fixed effect	8.50	16.77	23.48	11.95
+ i.i.d. error	(.290)	(.019)	(.001)	(.102)
+ ARMA(2,2)	[7]	[7]	[7]	[7]
3. Fixed effect	9.29	23.86	26.32	13.60
+ i.i.d. error	(.410)	(.005)	(.002)	(.137)
+ AR(2)	[9]	[9]	[9]	[9]
4. Fixed effect	10.76	27.92	31.04	13.72
+ i.i.d. error	(.377)	(.002)	(.001)	(.186)
+ AR(1)	[10]	[10]	[10]	[10]
5. i.i.d. error	12.68	37.25	32.13	13.92
+ AR(1)	(.315)	(.000)	(.001)	(.237)
	[11]	[11]	[11]	[11]
6. Fixed effect	77.36	85.90	37.06	15.74
+ i.i.d. error	(.000)	(.000)	(.000)	(.203)
	[12]	[12]	[12]	[12]
7. i.i.d. error	147.6	138.8	84.79	41.08
	(.000)	(.000)	(.000)	(.000)
	[13]	[13]	[13]	[13]

Note: Entries in table are GMM goodness-of-fit statistics. Numbers in parentheses are *p*-values; numbers in brackets are degrees of freedom.

while a fixed effect would be more permanent. In contrast, both CHF and the AMI-CHF covariance look small but fairly persistent, as would be expected with a fixed-effect model.

Although stationarity is not generally supported by the data, it is useful to consider still more restrictive models in order to see whether any simple error structure adequately summarizes the covariogram. Rows 2–7 of table 7.1 test increasingly restrictive models of the error structure against the unconstrained stationary model. I begin with a flexible model that includes a fixed effect, i.i.d. error, and an ARMA(2,2) component. The next two rows restrict the ARMA to be AR(2) and then AR(1). Finally, the last three rows remove the fixed effect or the AR(1) or both (leaving just i.i.d. error).

In general, these goodness-of-fit tests suggest that a simple model of i.i.d. error plus an AR(1) does about as well as any other model in fitting each of the covariance structures. Only for AMI mortality is there a clear preference for adding a fixed effect or an ARMA(2,2). A simple fixed-effect model is

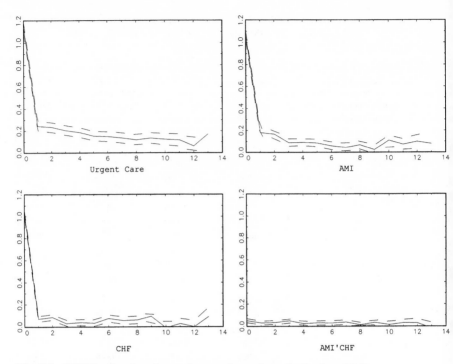

Fig. 7.4   GMM estimates of covariogram (covariance by lag length) for mortality Z-score. Unconstrained stationary covariance and 95 percent confidence interval estimated with data from 1974–87.

soundly rejected for urgent care and AMI. However, for both AMI and CHF, all of the more restrictive models do a poorer job fitting the data than the unconstrained stationary model.

Figure 7.5 illustrates the ability of alternative models to fit the covariogram. These figures graph the estimated covariogram for the unrestricted stationary model (*solid line*), the model with fixed effects, measurement error, and an ARMA(2,2) component (*long dashes*), and a more restrictive model with measurement error and an AR(1) component (*short dashes*). The variance (lag of zero) is estimated equally well by all models and therefore has been left out of these figures to avoid distorting the scale. It is apparent that the more restrictive AR(1) model does a reasonable job fitting the basic features of the data. The more flexible ARMA(2,2) specification is able to pick up some apparent fluctuations in the covariance at short lags while the fixed effect helps to fit the leveling off of the covariogram at longer lags, particularly for AMI mortality.

Table 7.2 provides parameter estimates assuming that mortality is composed of a fixed effect, a stationary AR(1), and stationary i.i.d. error. For example, column (1) estimates that the total variance in urgent care mortality is composed of a large measurement error component (.844) and relatively small

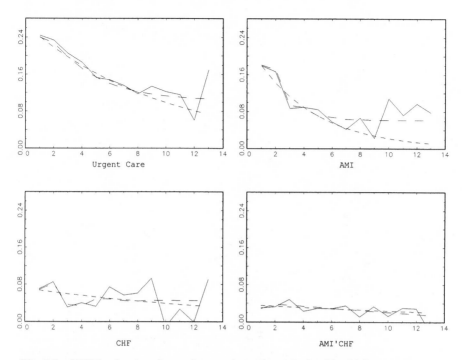

Fig. 7.5   GMM estimates of covariogram (covariance by lag length) for mortality Z-score. Covariance estimated with data from 1974–87: unconstrained (*solid line*), fixed effect + ARMA(2,2) + i.i.d. (*long dashes*), and AR(1) + i.i.d. (*short dashes*).

fixed-effect (.080) and AR(1) (.200) components. The AR(1) is fairly persistent, with a serial correlation of .829. The goodness-of-fit statistic implies that this simple model adequately summarizes the data. Dropping the fixed effect (col. [2]) has little effect on the overall fit of the model but increases the variance and persistence of the AR(1). In other words, the data cannot distinguish between a fixed effect and a somewhat more permanent AR(1). Note that the *t*-tests generally reject the hypothesis that the fixed-effect variance is zero, while chi-squared tests (based on the difference in the goodness-of-fit statistic in models with and without a fixed effect) often do not reject this hypothesis. This is a common feature of GMM models of parameters that are nearly unidentified.

The remainder of the estimates tell a similar story: Measurement error accounts for at least 75 percent of the variance for each diagnosis; the fixed effect accounts for roughly 5 percent of the variance; and a moderately persistent AR(1) accounts for the remainder of the variance, although this component accounts for more of the variance in AMI mortality than in CHF mortality. The covariance between AMI and CHF is quite persistent, making it impossible to

Table 7.2 Variance Decomposition of Error Structure of 45-Day Mortality Z-score, 1974–87

Variance Component	Urgent Care		AMI		CHF		AMI'CHF	
	With Fixed Effect (1)	Without Fixed Effect (2)	With Fixed Effect (3)	Without Fixed Effect (4)	With Fixed Effect (5)	Without Fixed Effect (6)	With Fixed Effect (7)	Without Fixed Effect (8)
Variance of i.i.d. error	0.844 (.021)	0.858 (.017)	0.786 (.029)	0.814 (.021)	0.915 (.041)	0.938 (.017)	0.016 (.011)	0.016 (.010)
Variance of fixed effect	0.080 (.040)	–	0.055 (.016)	–	0.044 (.011)	–	-2.14 (1240)	–
Variance of AR(1)	0.200 (.034)	0.266 (.023)	0.208 (.028)	0.227 (.024)	0.051 (.035)	0.071 (.011)	2.18 (1240)	0.037 (.008)
δ	0.829 (.066)	0.906 (.014)	0.648 (.074)	0.792 (.030)	0.576 (.360)	0.941 (.027)	0.999 (.379)	0.957 (.035)
GMM goodness-of-fit statistic	115.39	117.31	148.18	157.51	170.04	171.13	310.66	310.87
(p-value) [d.f.]	(.155) [101]	(.143) [102]	(.002) [101]	(.000) [102]	(.000) [101]	(.000) [102]	(.000) [192]	(.000) [193]

Notes: Z_{it} = Fixed effect + AR(1) + i.i.d. error. Numbers in parentheses are standard errors of parameter estimates.

identify a fixed effect from a very persistent AR(1). Interestingly, the variance of this persistent effect in the covariance is of roughly the same magnitude as the variance of the fixed effect in the AMI and CHF models. This suggests that AMI and CHF mortality may have a common component that is quite persistent. As a consequence of the failure of stationarity in the data, the goodness-of-fit statistic rejects all the models except urgent care.

The descriptive evidence presented in section 7.3 suggests that the nonstationarity is most evident in the early years of data. Therefore, a simple way to avoid the nonstationarity (and at the same time check on the robustness of the underlying parameter estimates) is to drop the early years from the analysis. Tables 7.3 and 7.4 replicate the results of tables 7.1 and 7.2 using only data for 1979–87. The improvement in the fit of the models is dramatic (see table 7.3). Of course, some of this apparent improvement is due to lower power of these tests with a shorter panel. Still, in striking contrast to table 7.1, stationarity

Table 7.3   **Model Specification Tests for Covariance Structure of Mortality Z-Score, 1979–87 (based on GMM goodness-of-fit statistic)**

	For Covariance Matrix of			
Model Specification	Urgent Care	AMI	CHF	AMI'CHF
1. Unconstrained stationary	31.10	36.30	48.25	67.18
covariance (symmetric)	(.701)	(.455)	(.083)	(.639)
	[36]	[36]	[36]	[72]
Tested against model 1				
2. Fixed effect	3.98	0.55	3.47	3.00
+ i.i.d. error	(.137)	(.758)	(.176)	(.223)
+ ARMA(2,2)	[2]	[2]	[2]	[2]
3. Fixed effect	5.72	5.14	4.11	3.47
+ i.i.d. error	(.221)	(.273)	(.392)	(.482)
+ AR(2)	[4]	[4]	[4]	[4]
4. Fixed effect	7.43	8.10	8.26	3.48
+ i.i.d. error	(.191)	(.151)	(.142)	(.627)
+ AR(1)	[5]	[5]	[5]	[5]
5. i.i.d. error	7.62	8.16	10.08	3.48
+ AR(1)	(.267)	(.227)	(.108)	(.747)
	[6]	[6]	[6]	[6]
6. Fixed effect	32.97	37.38	11.56	3.49
+ i.i.d. error	(.000)	(.000)	(.116)	(.836)
	[7]	[7]	[7]	[7]
7. i.i.d. error	101.6	114.32	54.05	35.05
	(.000)	(.000)	(.000)	(.000)
	[8]	[8]	[8]	[8]

Note: Entries in table are GMM goodness-of-fit statistics. Numbers in parentheses are *p*-values; numbers in brackets are degrees of freedom.

cannot be rejected for any of the covariance matrices. A model of i.i.d. error with an AR(1) cannot be rejected for any of the covariance matrices. For Urgent care and AMI, the fixed-effect model is clearly rejected in favor of the AR(1) model. In contrast, CHF and the AMI-CHF covariance are fit equally well by a fixed-effect model.

Table 7.4 provides parameter estimates of the AR(1) model with and without a fixed effect for the 1979–87 data. Without the fixed effect, these estimates are little changed from those in table 7.2 using the entire panel. The goodness of fit of the models is much improved over table 7.2, as can be seen in the last row of the table. Finally, in contrast to estimates based on the full panel, the fixed-effect component is not particularly well identified.

Overall, the estimates for both the full panel and for the limited 1979–87 data have the same implications. Namely, the mortality data contain significant measurement error, a somewhat transitory serially correlated component, and perhaps a common hospital component that is quite permanent. Table 7.5 investigates whether this simple three-component structure can adequately summarize the joint covariance matrix of the AMI and CHF mortality data. The data that provide the basis for these estimates are contained in the sample covariance matrix for the combined AMI and CHF data (i.e., $Z'Z/N$ where $Z = (Z_{AMI}, Z_{CHF})$). Since there are 14 years of data for each diagnosis group, there are $28 \cdot 29/2 = 406$ distinct moments and potential degrees of freedom. Column (2) of table 7.5 limits the analysis to the 1979–87 data and therefore has $18 \cdot 19/2 = 171$ degrees of freedom.

Data from the full sample once again overwhelmingly reject the stationarity assumption. A simple three-factor model is also soundly rejected against the alternative unconstrained stationary model. The three-factor model assumes that mortality for each diagnosis is composed of (1) a common factor that follows an AR(1) with no measurement error and (2) a diagnosis-specific factor (one for each diagnosis) that consists of i.i.d. measurement error plus an AR(1). Although the model is statistically rejected, it does precisely summarize the key features of the data. There is a very persistent factor that is common to both diagnoses. Added to this is i.i.d. noise for each diagnosis and a relatively transitory AR(1) component with serial correlation of roughly .6 for both diagnoses. Furthermore, the AR(1) component accounts for a much larger share of the variance for AMI mortality than for CHF mortality.

Restricting the sample to 1979–87 dramatically improves the ability of a stationary model to fit the data and improves the fit of the three-factor model as compared to the unconstrained stationary model. Although the goodness-of-fit statistics still reject these models at conventional levels, the rejection is no longer overwhelming. For these data I have estimated the common factor as a fixed effect, since a fixed effect seemed to better fit the AMI-CHF covariance in tables 7.3 and 7.4. The parameter estimates are quite similar to those using the entire panel: there is a persistent common factor, a fairly transitory diagnosis-specific factor, and substantial i.i.d. measurement error.

Table 7.4   Variance Decomposition of Error Structure of 45-Day Mortality Z-score, 1979–87

Variance Component	Urgent Care With Fixed Effect	Urgent Care Without Fixed Effect	AMI With Fixed Effect	AMI Without Fixed Effect	CHF With Fixed Effect	CHF Without Fixed Effect	AMI'CHF With Fixed Effect	AMI'CHF Without Fixed Effect
Variance of i.i.d. error	0.840 (.032)	0.834 (.028)	0.822 (.035)	0.826 (.029)	0.861 (.121)	0.917 (.024)	0.014 (.020)	0.014 (.016)
Variance of fixed effect	−0.224 (1.232)	–	0.016 (.071)	–	0.062 (.017)	–	−0.771 (13652)	–
Variance of AR(1)	0.531 (1.212)	0.313 (.033)	0.234 (.062)	0.246 (.033)	0.086 (.113)	0.090 (.019)	0.822 (13651)	0.051 (.013)
δ	0.945 (.151)	0.893 (.024)	0.778 (.126)	0.802 (.037)	0.397 (.560)	0.939 (.052)	0.999+ (7.105)	0.994 (.057)
GMM goodness-of-fit statistic	38.52 (.581)	38.72 (.616)	44.40 (.330)	44.54 (.369)	56.51 (.054)	58.68 (.045)	70.66 (.681)	70.66 (.710)
(p-value) [d.f.]	[41]	[42]	[41]	[42]	[41]	[42]	[77]	[78]

Notes: Z_{it} = Fixed effect + AR(1) + i.i.d. error. Numbers in parentheses are standard errors of parameter estimates.

Table 7.5   Three-Factor Models for Covariance Structure of AMI and CHF 45-Day Mortality Z-Score

	1974–87 (1)	1979–87 (2)
1. Goodness-of-fit statistic for unconstrained stationary (symmetric) covariance structure	1456.9 (.000) [364]	199.33 (.002) [144]
2. Goodness-of-fit statistic for three-factor model against model 1	726.53 (.000) [34]	38.49 (.008) [20]
3. Parameter estimates		
A. Common factor		
i. Variance of fixed effect	–	0.048 (.007)
ii. Variance of AR(1)	0.056 (0.004)	–
iii. δ_{common}	0.937 (.009)	–
B. AMI factor		
i. Variance of i.i.d. error	0.730 (.015)	0.775 (.030)
ii. Variance of AR(1)	0.187 (.015)	0.207 (.029)
iii. δ_{AMI}	0.571 (.035)	0.679 (.056)
C. CHF factor		
i. Variance of i.i.d. error	0.779 (.017)	0.862 (.051)
ii. Variance of AR (1)	0.071 (.015)	0.074 (.049)
iii. δ_{CHF}	0.578 (.092)	0.518 (.275)

Note: Numbers in parentheses are *p*-values of goodness-of-fit statistics and standard errors of parameter estimates. Numbers in brackets are degrees of freedom.

The ability of this simple three-factor model to fit the data is seen in figure 7.6. This figure graphs the estimated covariogram for the unconstrained stationary model (*solid line*) against the three-factor model (*dashed line*). As in figure 7.5, the variance (lag of zero) has been left out of these figures to avoid distorting the scale. The three-factor model does a reasonable job of fitting the covariograms. The longest lags of CHF are estimated off of relatively few years but suggest that CHF mortality may be more persistent than one would expect from the three-component model.

Overall, this evidence points to two particularly interesting features of the data. First, the covariance structure is reasonably well approximated by a simple three-factor model. A permanent hospital effect accounts for roughly 4 to 5 percent of the variance in mortality. A more transitory diagnosis-specific effect accounts for another 7 percent of the variation in mortality for CHF and nearly 20 percent of the variation in mortality for AMI. This component has a

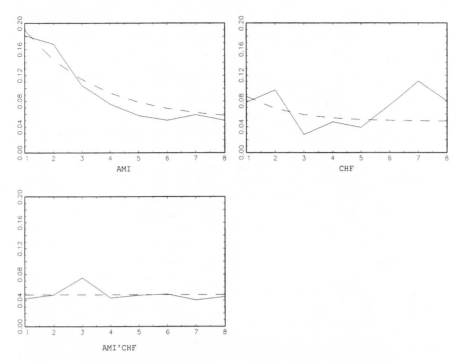

Fig. 7.6   GMM estimates of covariogram (covariance by lag length) jointly estimated for AMI and CHF mortality Z-score. Covariance estimated with data from 1979–87: unconstrained (*solid line*) vs. three-factor model (*dashed line*).

first-order serial correlation in the range of .6, so that diagnosis-specific shocks are mostly dissipated in five years. Finally, the remainder of the variation in mortality appears to be noise. The second interesting feature of the data is the significant nonstationarity in the distribution of mortality between the 1970s and the 1980s.

7.5   Conclusion

The empirical results presented in this paper have a number of implications. For those using these mortality variables as proxies for quality of care, the statistical properties of mortality should raise some concern. The amount of noise in these measures is on the order of 80 to 90 percent of the total variance. In a simple regression using mortality as a right-hand–side proxy for quality, this would lead to an attenuation bias of at least 80 percent, making the estimates of little use. Knowledge of the magnitude of measurement error can allow one to correct for the attenuation bias, so these estimates (or a similar method) might be used to correct for the bias. Even with such a correction, however, such low signal-to-noise ratios severely limit our ability to use such measures to forecast future hospital mortality.

Alternatively, for research that uses mortality as a dependent variable in a panel data setting, these estimates clearly indicate that the empirical model must allow for serially correlated errors. Moreover, the most common approach of adding hospital fixed effects does not appear to be adequate. It remains to be seen whether allowing for a more complicated error structure would significantly affect the conclusions from such studies.

In thinking more generally about the process that determines quality of care in a hospital, the three-factor model may give some insight. An obvious interpretation of the three-factor model is one in which the hospital effect represents general infrastructure such as the nursing staff, physical plant, or skill of the medical staff. These characteristics might be expected to be fairly permanent, and in fact, they represent what one often thinks of when thinking of a top-notch hospital. In contrast, the diagnosis-specific component could be thought of as technological innovations specific to that diagnosis. Casual observation suggests that AMI is a diagnosis that has had more technological innovation over the past 20 years, and this is consistent with the fact that the variance of the diagnosis-specific factor is much larger in AMI than in CHF. On the other hand, such innovations in treatment technology tend to diffuse to other hospitals fairly rapidly, so it is not surprising that this diagnosis-specific component does not persist much beyond five years.

Of course, there are alternative interpretations of the results. For example, the hospital component may reflect permanent differences in the population that each hospital serves, which are not captured by the adjustment for expected mortality. Distinguishing the quality-of-care interpretation from the case-mix interpretation is an important topic of future research.

Finally, the results suggest that there have been important changes in the distribution of patient mortality across hospitals between the 1970s and the 1980s. The reasons for this shift, and the corresponding change in the autocovariance structure of mortality, are unknown. It remains to be seen whether a simple extension of the models considered here can explain this anomaly. One possible explanation is that important technology shocks always begin with flagship hospitals and then diffuse through the remainder of the population. Thus, mortality in "innovative" years might be much more correlated than in average years. This is a topic of future research.

References

Abowd, J., and D. Card. 1989. On the covariance structure of earnings and hours changes. *Econometrica* 57:411–45.

Bowen, O., and W. Roper. 1987. *Medicare hospital mortality information, 1986.* Publication no. 00744. Washington, D.C.: U.S. Department of Health and Human Services, Health Care Financing Administration.

Cutler, D. 1995. The incidence of adverse medical outcomes under prospective payment. *Econometrica* 63:29–50.

Garber, A., V. Fuchs, and J. Silverman. 1984. Case mix, costs and outcomes: Differences between faculty and community services in a university hospital. *New England Journal of Medicine* 310:1231–37.

Gaumer, G., E. Poggio, and C. Coelen. 1989. Effects of state prospective reimbursement programs on hospital mortality. *Medical Care* 27:724–36.

Hofer, T., and R. Hayward. 1996. Identifying poor-quality hospitals: Can hospital mortality rates detect quality problems for medical diagnoses? *Medical Care* 34:737–53.

Keeler, E., L. Rubenstein, K. Kahn, D. Draper, E. Harrison, M. McGinty, W. Rogers, and R. Brook. 1992. Hospital characteristics and quality of care. *JAMA* 268:1709–14.

Krakauer, H., R. C. Bailey, K. Skellan, J. Stewart, A. Hartz, E. Kuhn, and A. Rimm. 1992. Evaluation of the HCFA model for the analysis of mortality following hospitalization. *Health Services Research* 27:317–35.

Luft, H., D. Garnick, D. Mark, D. Peltzman, C. Phibbs, E. Lichtenberg, and S. McPhee. 1990. Does quality influence choice of hospital? *JAMA* 263:2899–906.

Luft, H., S. Hughes, and R. Hunt. 1987. Effects of surgeon volume on quality of care in hospitals. *Medical Care* 25:489–503.

Luft, H., R. Hunt, and S. Maerki. 1987. The volume-outcome relationship: Practice-makes-perfect or selective-referral patterns? *Health Services Research* 22:147–82.

Luft, H., and P. Romano. 1993. Chance, continuity, and change in hospital mortality rates: Coronary artery bypass graft patients in California hospitals, 1983 to 1989. *JAMA* 270:331–37.

MaCurdy, T. 1982. The use of time series processes to model the error structure of earnings in a longitudinal data analysis. *Journal of Econometrics* 18:83–114.

McClellan, M., B. McNeil, and J. Newhouse. 1994. Does more intensive treatment of acute myocardial infarction in the elderly reduce mortality? Analysis using instrumental variables. *JAMA* 272:859–66.

McNeil, B., S. Pedersen, and C. Gatsonis. 1992. Current issues in profiling quality of care. *Inquiry* 29:298–307.

Minnesota Blues payment plan is the first to tie reimbursement to outcomes. 1991. *Outcomes Measurement and Management* 2:1–2.

Park, R. E., R. Brook, J. Kosecoff, J. Keesey, L. Rubenstein, E. Keeler, K. Kahn, W. Rogers, and M. Chassin. 1990. Explaining variations in hospital death rates: Randomness, severity of illness, quality of care. *JAMA* 264:484–90.

Perry, L. 1989. Michigan Blues plan initiates payment bonuses, penalties tied to standards of quality. *Medicine and Health* 19:58.

Staiger, D. 1993. Quality of care and patient volume. Unpublished manuscript.

Staiger, D., and G. Gaumer. 1995. Price regulation and patient mortality in hospitals. August. Unpublished manuscript.

Comment   David Meltzer

In recent years, the need to control health care costs and the recognition that much of health care is of uncertain benefit has increased interest in measuring

David Meltzer is assistant professor in the section of general internal medicine, department of economics, and Harris Graduate School of Public Policy at the University of Chicago and a faculty research fellow of the National Bureau of Economic Research.

the quality of health care. This has been evident at multiple levels of the health care system, with efforts to evaluate the quality of care provided by HMOs operating under prepayment, hospitals operating under diagnosis-related groups, and individual practitioners in a variety of settings. In all these areas, as well as in a number of studies to which the paper alludes, mortality has been used as an indicator of quality. Nevertheless, there has been surprisingly little work examining the statistical properties of these mortality variables. Staiger's paper raises important questions about the use of hospital mortality rates as an indicator of quality.

Staiger uses annual data on mortality after Medicare admission for urgent care, congestive heart failure (CHF), and acute myocardial infarction (AMI) for a sample of about 500 hospitals from 1974 through 1987. He investigates trends in the distribution of these rates using descriptive statistics and generalized method of moments estimators of the covariance structure. There are three major findings. First, that 75 to 90 percent of the variation in mortality is entirely transitory consistent with i.i.d. measurement error, suggesting that mortality is likely to be a poor proxy for quality whether used on the right- or left-hand side of a regression. Second, that mortality rates have a fairly persistent component consistent with a first-order autoregressive (AR(1)) process with an autocorrelation of .8–.95, suggesting that hospital effects may not be well approximated by a fixed-effects model. Third, that the combined AMI/CHF data are well fit by a three-component model with an i.i.d. error, a moderately transitory disease-specific component, and a permanent hospital-specific component, which may provide some insight into the determinants of the quality of care in hospitals.

The result that the vast majority of the variability in adjusted mortality rates is consistent with i.i.d. measurement error is the most striking result of the paper and raises serious questions about the value of mortality rates as a measure of quality. If 75 to 90 percent of the variation in mortality is gone in one year, past variations in hospital mortality provide little information on future mortality. Luft and Hunt (1986) also make this point in the context of work on the volume-outcomes relationship. The variability in annual hospital mortality rates is probably particularly large in Staiger's sample of hospitals because inclusion in the sample requires only a single admission in each diagnosis in each year. One could conceivably restrict the use of such measures to only larger hospitals, but quality may often be of greatest concern in smaller hospitals. Even if a few statistically significant outliers could be identified, little insight would be gained into quality in the majority of hospitals. The crudeness of the Health Care Financing Administration's (HCFA's) severity-of-illness adjustments is also worrisome, particularly if it causes hospitals to select patients for treatment by considering their effect on the hospital's mortality statistics rather than their potential to benefit from treatment.

How, then, should we address the need to assess hospital quality? There are several possibilities. One is to use mortality statistics but improve risk stratification using more detailed clinical data in order to increase the signal-to-noise ratio. It is difficult to know to what extent it may be possible to refine such measures, but a recent study of mortality for CHF suggests that simple clinical measures of severity of illness (blood pressure, respiration rate, EKG changes, and serum sodium on presentation) substantially increase the amount of explained variation in in-hospital mortality compared to age and sex (Chin and Goldman 1996). Another possibility is to measure a broader set of intermediate outcomes (such as postoperative infection or bleeding), which may occur more frequently and therefore exhibit less noise. The issue with that approach is how much weight to put on those outcomes if patients ultimately recover from them. Another strategy is to follow measures of the process of care such as time to thrombolysis or appropriate choice of antibiotics. Like nonfatal adverse outcomes, these have the advantage of occurring more frequently than fatal outcomes and the drawback that they may not necessarily translate into significant outcomes. However, if the connection between process and outcomes is as believed, this approach has the advantage over using outcomes measures that it tells the hospital not only that there is a problem but also what to do about it. This may explain why this approach has been frequently adopted by hospitals in their attempts to improve quality, for example, through the critical pathways approach (Coffey et al. 1992). Interestingly, the Joint Commission on Accreditation of Healthcare Organizations has recently moved toward outcomes-based measures of quality (JCAHO 1995), but the noise inherent in those measures and the potential to game the system by manipulating case mix suggest that monitoring the consequences of those changes will be important.

Despite the large component of variability in these measures, the paper does report a statistically significant persistent component, which may have implications for the use of fixed-effects models with hospital mortality data and provide insights into the behaviors of doctors, hospitals, and the process of technical change. As the paper points out, one needs to be cautious in attributing the persistent component of adjusted mortality rates to quality because there may be persistent differences in the underlying severity of illness across hospitals that are not captured by the crude HCFA severity-of-illness adjustments. One reason that the severity-of-illness adjustments may be misleading is that they are rescaled only once over a 15-year period that contained substantial technical change. Even if patients sorted only on observable differences in severity of illness, technical changes that particularly improved outcomes for sicker or healthier groups would result in persistent deviations of hospitals' outcomes from expected. Future work could address this by using the original Medicare data to perform annual risk adjustment.

Much of the remainder of the paper is devoted to examining whether the error process is stationary, and it finds that stationarity is generally rejected for the full sample, though not for the latter half of the sample. This latter result may simply reflect the low power of the test for the subsample, and it raises the question of what one is to conclude about a process that is intermittently stationary; but the deeper question is why we should be concerned about stationarity. Presumably, it is for prediction; yet the first half of the paper tells us that the vast majority of variation in mortality rates is transient, so knowing that the error structure is stationary is of little consequence in enhancing our ability to predict.

The paper also examines alternative models of the error structure of mortality rates and suggests that it may be inconsistent with the use of hospital fixed effects. This concern is too frequently neglected by researchers using fixed-effects models. Table 7.1 examines increasingly restrictive models from ARMA(2,2) to i.i.d. measurement error and finds that an AR(1) generally does as well as any other model for CHF and urgent care admissions, and that there is only a weak preference for adding an ARMA(2,2) or fixed effect for AMI. Unfortunately, the test statistics reported test only against the unrestricted stationary model. Since the models are generally nested, it would have been useful to test each additional restriction individually. Table 7.2 does report the effect of adding a fixed effect to the AR(1). However, what one really wants to know is whether one can use a fixed-effect model and do without the AR(1), and the paper does not report the more interesting exercise of assuming a fixed effect and adding an AR(1).

The final section of the paper examines the covariance of the CHF/AMI data in order to try to gain some insight into the process underlying these changes in mortality rates over time. It finds that the joint process is rather well fit by a fairly permanent hospital-specific component, a moderately transient disease-specific component, and an i.i.d. term consistent with sampling error. The paper also provides the interesting interpretation that the hospital-specific component might reflect a hospital's infrastructure—such as personnel and physical plant—while the disease-specific component might reflect technical progress in treating individual diseases. Ideally, one would like to measure these factors—technical innovations, knowledge of those innovations by specific providers, volume of experience for both providers and hospitals, and so forth—and test whether they are related to outcomes.

Though significant insights into the determinants of the quality of care seem unlikely to come from examination of the error structure alone, the finding that the majority of variation in hospital mortality rates appears to reflect random variation is of great consequence for the study of quality. It is there that research in this area seems likely to focus in the future.

References

Chin, Marshall, and Lee Goldman. 1996. Correlates of major complications or death in patients admitted to the hospital with congestive heart failure. *Archives of Internal Medicine* 156 (16): 1814–20.

Coffey, R. J., et al. 1992. An introduction to critical paths. *Quality Management in Health Care* 1:45–54.

Joint Commission on Accreditation of Healthcare Organizations (JCAHO). 1995. *JCAHO 1995 accreditation manual.* Oakbrook Terrace, Ill.: Joint Commission on Accreditation of Healthcare Organizations.

Luft, H., and S. Hunt. 1986. Evaluating individual hospital quality through volume statistics. *JAMA* 255 (20): 2780–84.

8 Household Wealth of the Elderly under Alternative Imputation Procedures

Hilary Hoynes, Michael Hurd, and Harish Chand

8.1 Introduction

Although many reach retirement with few resources except housing equity and a claim to social security and Medicare, financial wealth, nonetheless, makes an important contribution to the economic status of many of the elderly. Most of our up-to-date information about the wealth of the elderly is based on the Survey of Income and Program Participation (SIPP), which sometimes adds an asset module to its core survey. As in many surveys of assets, the rate of missing data on individual asset items is high, about 30 to 40 percent among those with the asset. This raises the issue of the reliability of SIPP wealth measures because respondents who refuse or are unable to give a value to an asset item may not be representative of the population. Indeed, in the Health and Retirement Survey (HRS) it is clear that asset data are not missing at random. Through the use of bracketing methods, which we will discuss below, the HRS was able to reduce the rate of missing asset data substantially, and the data that were added in this way increased mean wealth in the HRS by about 40 percent (Smith 1995). Furthermore, because the additional data increased the mean so much, they undoubtedly increased measures of wealth inequality.

Because of the extensive use of bracketing to reduce the rate of nonresponse to asset items and because of its large sample size, the Asset and Health Dynamics among the Oldest Old (AHEAD) survey is likely to produce better

Hilary Hoynes is assistant professor at the University of California, Berkeley, and a faculty research fellow of the National Bureau of Economic Research. Michael Hurd is professor at the State University of New York at Stony Brook, a researcher at RAND, and a research associate of the National Bureau of Economic Research. Harish Chand is a student at the University of California, Berkeley.

The authors thank Li Gan, Dan McFadden, Jim Smith, and seminar participants for helpful suggestions. Financial support from the National Institute on Aging is gratefully acknowledged. Computing support was provided by the Econometrics Laboratory at UC Berkeley.

estimates of the distribution of the wealth of the elderly than other data sets. Even with bracketing, however, imputation of amounts is required, and the imputation method may well influence both the level and distribution of total wealth. In this paper we report the effects of a number of imputation methods on components of wealth and total wealth. In particular we extend the imputation techniques of Chand and Gan (1994) and of Smith (1995). Our methods will preserve covariation among measures of economic status to a greater extent than the previous methods, and this should provide a more accurate description of the wealth holdings and degree of wealth inequality of the elderly.

The paper is organized as follows. Section 8.2 describes the AHEAD data, with particular attention to the use of bracketing to reduce the incidence of missing data. Section 8.3 describes our imputation methodology. Section 8.4 presents the results of the imputation process for selected asset groups. Section 8.5 presents estimates of the distribution of imputed wealth. Section 8.6 concludes.

8.2   The AHEAD Data

Our data come from the survey of the Asset and Health Dynamics among the Oldest Old (AHEAD). This is a biennial panel of individuals born in 1923 or earlier and their spouses. The panel data set began in 1993 with a survey of 8,222 individuals representative of the community-based population except for the oversampling of blacks, Hispanics, and Floridians. The response rate in this first year of the survey was 80.6 percent. The second wave of the panel was fielded in October 1995. The results of this paper are based on the first wave of the panel.

The main goal of AHEAD is to provide panel data from the three broad domains of economic status, health, and family connections so that their co-evolution can be studied. At baseline the survey elicited information about demographics, health, cognition, family structure and connections, health care and costs, housing, job status and history, expectations, income, and assets and insurance (Soldo et al. 1997). We are particularly interested in the data on asset holdings, which we will discuss in detail below.

AHEAD contains considerable detail about income and work history. Among the income components are social security benefits, pensions and annuities, asset income (with disaggregation as to type), earnings, and other transfer income such as supplemental security income. Measured income in AHEAD has been found to aggregate to the levels that are found in Current Population Survey data (Soldo et al. 1997).

Health in AHEAD is measured in a number of ways such as the ability to perform tasks, limitations on activities of daily living and instrumental activities of daily living, disease conditions and severity, and by self-assessment. AHEAD measures cognitive status in a battery of questions that aim to test a number of domains of cognition (Herzog and Wallace 1997).

8.2.1   Estimation Data Set

The AHEAD sample consists of 6,052 households and 8,222 individuals. In a husband-wife household information on income, assets, and insurance were asked only of the financial respondent, that person said to be the most knowledgeable about the household's finances. The husband was the financial respondent in 59 percent of the couple households. A few households did not complete the asset module of the survey, which reduced our sample to 5,973 households. About 38 percent of the households are married couples, 13 percent single men, and 49 percent single women.

Table 8.1 has the mean values of selected categorical variables for the estimation sample. Unless otherwise indicated, all variables correspond to the characteristics of the financial respondent. About a third of the sample has heads between ages 70 and 74. Whites account for 81 percent of the households. Widows and widowers account for almost 50 percent of the observations. About 27 percent of heads are college graduates, and 32 percent have completed high school. We use self-assessed health status for the head and spouse as an overall summary measure of the health of the household. We use a summary measure of cognitive ability to generate an indicator that cognitive performance is in the lowest third of the distribution. We imagine that low cognitive functioning will be reflected in a diminished ability to give informed answers to questions about income and assets.

8.2.2   Wealth Data in AHEAD

The AHEAD data contain information on household debt and 10 types of household assets: checking and savings accounts, CDs, stocks, bonds, individual retirement (IRA) and Keogh accounts, housing, transportation, other real estate, business equity, and other assets.

It is quite common in household surveys that the response to questions about asset value is "don't know" (DK) or "refused" (RF). For example, in the SIPP the rate of missing values among owners is 30 to 40 percent on asset values.[1] These missing values are usually imputed from a model of asset holdings that is fitted over observed values. The HRS and AHEAD use bracketing methods to reduce the rate of missing data. In a typical sequence a respondent would be asked about, for example, stock ownership and, if an owner, the value of stock holdings. A follow-up to a DK or RF about the value of stock holdings is "Would it amount to $25,000 or more?" If the response to that question is yes, the follow-up is "Would it amount to $100,000 or more?" but if the answer is no, the follow-up is "Would it amount to $5,000 or more?" By this sequence, stock holdings were assigned to one of five intervals. Other assets were bracketed in a similar way except that the bracket intervals differed by asset type because of differences in the distributions of each asset in the population.

---

1. See table 8.4, which we will discuss below.

Table 8.1   Means of Covariates in Estimation Sample ($N = 5,973$)

Dummy Variable	Definition	Mean
Age of head	70–74	0.34
	75–79	0.27
	80–84	0.19
	85–89	0.09
	90 or over	0.04
Gender	Female	0.64
Race/ethnicity	Nonwhite	0.14
	Hispanic	0.05
Marital status	Divorced/separated	0.06
	Widowed	0.50
	Never married	0.04
	Married	0.39
Education of head	College graduate	0.27
	High school graduate	0.32
Education of spouse	College graduate	0.11
	High school graduate	0.15
Occupation of head	Professional/managerial	0.13
Occupation of spouse	Professional/managerial	0.05
Occupation of former spouse	Professional/managerial	0.04
Work history of head	Worked 10–20 years	0.52
	Worked 20–30 years	0.18
	Worked 30 or more years	0.23
Work history of spouse	Worked 10–20 years	0.20
	Worked 20–30 years	0.07
	Worked 30 or more years	0.08
Work history of former spouse	Worked 10–20 years	0.45
	Worked 20–30 years	0.01
	Worked 30 or more years	0.03
Cognition/proxy interview	Low cognitive score	0.33
	Missing cognition score	0.03
	Proxy interview	0.07
Health status of head	Excellent	0.11
	Very good	0.23
	Good	0.31
	Fair	0.23
	Poor	0.12
Change in health status (2 yr)	Better	0.13
	Same	0.65
	Worse	0.22
Health status of spouse (0 if no spouse)	Excellent	0.05
	Very good	0.09
	Good	0.12
	Fair	0.09
	Poor	0.05
Change in health status (2 yr)	Better	0.05
	Same	0.27
	Worse	0.08
Income receipt indicator	Veteran's benefits	0.06
	Pension	0.44
	Annuities	0.06

Table 8.1   (continued)

Dummy Variable	Definition	Mean
	IRA	0.09
	Stock	0.16
	Earnings	0.01
	Other	0.10
	Savings account	0.32
	Rental property	0.07
	Investment/trusts	0.01
	Relatives	0.00
High school education of parents	Head's mother	0.47
	Head's father	0.44
	Spouse's mother	0.20
	Spouse's father	0.18
Housing information	Low-income housing	0.04
	Duplex	0.20
	Mobile home	0.03
	Apartment	0.00
	Townhouse	0.01
	Other housing	0.09
Condition of dwelling	Excellent	0.23
	Very good	0.33
	Good	0.29
	Poor	0.11
Safety of neighborhood	Excellent	0.26
	Very good	0.32
	Good	0.28
	Poor	0.09
Likelihood of leaving bequest	≥50 percent	0.24

Source: Authors' calculations from AHEAD. Unless otherwise stated, all calculations are weighted.

The importance of bracketing comes from the highly skewed distribution of many types of assets: knowing that an individual has stock holdings of, say, $5,000 to $25,000 provides much better information about the stock holdings of that individual than could be found from imputing stock holdings because the covariates used in the imputation have rather low explanatory power.

Table 8.2 summarizes the response status of families in AHEAD by type of asset. Some respondents either refuse to say or do not know whether they have a particular asset, resulting in missing data on asset ownership. A general conclusion is that the great majority of respondents can and do say whether they own a particular asset. Missing data on ownership averages only about 0.5 to 3 percent of the sample. The rate of ownership varies greatly by asset type: roughly three-quarters have a checking or savings account, just 5.7 percent own bonds, 19.4 percent own common stock, and the rate of home ownership is around 71 percent. These asset ownership rates are comparable to those found for the elderly in other data sets such as the SIPP.

Table 8.2   Asset Ownership

A. Distribution of Households (percent)

| Type of Asset | Ownership Missing | Ownership Reported | | All |
		Not Owner	Owner	
Checking and savings	2.2	24.4	75.6	100
CDs	2.8	78.7	21.3	100
Stocks	1.9	80.6	19.4	100
Bonds	2.3	94.3	5.7	100
IRA/Keogh	1.2	83.8	16.2	100
Housing	0.5	29.1	70.9	100
Other real estate	1.1	81.0	19.0	100
Business	0.4	95.6	4.4	100
Other assets	1.7	89.8	10.2	100
Debts	1.3	86.0	14.0	100

B. Distribution of Owners (percent)

Type of Asset	Continuous Value	Fully Bracketed[a]	Incomplete Bracket[b]	No Bracket[c]	All
Checking and savings	67.4	22.4	2.3	7.8	100
CDs	60.8	23.3	3.3	12.6	100
Stocks	53.8	31.7	2.6	12.0	100
Bonds	57.2	25.4	3.9	13.5	100
IRA/Keogh	72.6	16.4	1.0	10.0	100
Housing	77.7	19.0	1.2	2.1	100
Other real estate	65.9	22.9	1.5	9.7	100
Business	55.3	32.3	0.9	11.5	100
Other assets	69.2	21.3	0.5	9.1	100
Debts	83.3	10.1	0.5	6.1	100

Source: Authors' calculations from AHEAD. Unless otherwise stated, all calculations are weighted. Households missing data on entire wealth section are dropped.

[a]Asset value is within some bracketed range.

[b]Individuals did not complete bracketing sequence, but partial information is available.

[c]Ownership known, but in response to bracketing questions for value of asset, individual either refused to answer (RF) or did not know (DK).

Respondents who indicated ownership of a particular asset can be divided into four groups depending on their responses to follow-up questions. The bottom panel of table 8.2 shows the distribution of owners of each asset. Beginning from the leftmost column, we have what we call "continuous" values: these come from respondents who stated an actual dollar value for the amount of an asset. Thus, about 67 percent of owners of checking or savings accounts reported a dollar amount. "Fully bracketed" are those respondents who completed the sequence of bracketing questions: 22.4 percent in the case of checking or savings accounts. A few respondents gave some bracketing information but did not complete the sequence. These "incomplete bracket" respondents

Table 8.3   **Missing Data Rates by Type of Asset**

Type of Asset	Percentage of Owners with Missing Data		Overall Missing Data Rates	
	Using Brackets[a]	Not Using Brackets[b]	Using Brackets[c]	Not Using Brackets[d]
Checking and savings	7.8	32.5	8.1	26.8
CDs	12.6	39.2	5.5	11.1
Stocks	12.0	46.3	4.2	10.9
Bonds	13.5	42.8	3.1	4.7
IRA/Keogh	10.0	27.4	2.8	5.6
Housing	2.1	22.3	2.0	16.3
Other real estate	9.7	34.1	2.9	7.6
Business	11.5	44.7	0.9	2.4
Other assets	9.1	30.9	2.6	4.9
Debts	6.1	16.7	2.2	3.6

Source: Authors' calculations from AHEAD. Unless otherwise stated, all calculations are weighted.

[a]Includes observations with no brackets.

[b]Includes observations with incomplete, complete, or no brackets.

[c]Includes observations missing ownership or with no brackets.

[d]Includes observations missing ownership or with incomplete, complete, or no brackets.

(2.3 percent for checking and savings) answered at least the first of the bracketing questions but answered either with a RF or DK on one of the follow-up bracketing questions.[2] The last group, "no bracket," gave no bracketing information at all, answering either RF or DK to the first of the bracket questions. The table shows that there is a great deal of variation in the responses by asset type. Individuals are more likely to give continuous responses to questions about the value of housing and debts and less likely about the value of stocks, bonds, and business assets.

The use of bracketing substantially decreases the rate of missing data. Table 8.3 summarizes the importance of the bracketing questions by comparing the missing data rate in AHEAD with the missing data rate that would result if no bracketing information were used. The first two columns present missing data rates among owners, while the second two columns give overall missing data rates, including missing data on ownership.[3] Without using brackets, as shown in the second column, the rate of missing data among owners would have been

2. E.g., when asked whether the value of the asset was greater or less than $25,000 the respondent said greater. When asked whether the amount was greater or less than $100,000 the respondent answered with DK or RF. This can result in an open or closed interval.

3. For the column labeled "using brackets," missing data among owners consist of those observations without any bracketing information. Ignoring the bracketing questions, the missing data would also include those with incomplete and complete brackets. The overall missing data rates multiply the missing data rate among owners by the ownership rate and add to that the rate of missing data on ownership.

17 to 46 percent. This is reduced to 2 to 14 percent by using bracketing. For example, among owners of common stock, the rate of missing data is reduced from 46 percent to 12 percent because of the bracketing questions. A particularly important example is housing because of its importance in the portfolios of the elderly: the rate of missing data among owners was reduced from 22.3 percent to 2.1 percent by bracketing.

Table 8.3 shows that there is a great deal of variation in the overall missing data rates across asset types, with checking and savings accounts having relatively high missing data rates while housing has relatively low missing data rates. The low rate of missing housing values is especially notable because of the very high ownership rate.[4]

The missing data rates compare favorably to the rates in the SIPP. Table 8.4 shows rates from AHEAD both with and without bracketing information and from the SIPP by age and martial status. The initial rate of nonresponse is about the same, as seen by comparing the SIPP with the AHEAD "not using brackets." For example, for checking accounts among older singles, 38 percent in the SIPP and 34 percent in AHEAD gave an initial nonresponse as to amount. But bracketing in AHEAD reduced this to 7.9 percent. For stock holdings among singles, 66 percent in the SIPP and 52 percent in AHEAD gave an initial nonresponse as to value, but in AHEAD bracketing reduced this to 14 percent. There was a similar reduction in nonresponse among couples in AHEAD from bracketing. We conclude that even though the AHEAD population is quite elderly the use of bracketing reduces item nonresponse to rather low levels.

As shown in table 8.5 the likelihood of asset ownership and of item nonresponse varies with personal characteristics. Those who report owning assets have lower rates of cognitive impairment, are younger, and are more likely to be married. The table shows that the two types of nonresponse correspond to individuals with different characteristics on average. Those who respond DK are more likely to have higher levels of cognitive impairment, are less likely to be married, and are more likely to be over age 80 than those who respond RF.[5] Those who respond with continuous values are younger and have lower levels of cognitive impairment than either kind of nonrespondent. These simple tabulations suggest that the different forms of response display fairly distinct patterns, which will be potentially useful in a model-based imputation procedure. These characteristics also suggest that the option of providing brackets does not crowd out more accurate responses from an able population but rather allows information to be obtained from those unsure about their holdings.

---

4. Of course, knowing an interval for an asset value is not the same as knowing the exact amount, but even continuous reports are not exact amounts. Indeed, a large percentage of continuous reports tend to give a "focal" point answer, suggesting that a substantial amount of rounding occurs even in continuous responses (Chand and Gan 1994).

5. The DK and RF refer to the initial response to a question about asset value.

Table 8.4   **Comparison of Missing Data Rates in SIPP and AHEAD Surveys (percent of owners with missing data)**

A. 1993 SIPP

Type of Asset	All Persons (16+)		Persons Aged 60–69		Persons Aged 70+	
	Married	Single	Married	Single	Married	Single
N	22,491	30,463	2,897	1,152	2,127	2,172
Checking (own)	37.6	30.0	40.3	29.9	47.3	38.1
Checking (joint)	30.8	–	37.6	–	40.4	–
Stocks (own)	35.6	48.4	33.3	60.7	47.1	65.9
Stocks (joint)	42.7	–	50.7	–	50.0	–
IRA	32.4	30.8	35.0	30.1	41.8	31.3
Keogh	46.1	47.3	46.4	27.8	48.6	42.4
Housing	24.2	29.0	28.3	30.0	27.8	35.1

B. AHEAD

Type of Asset	Married		Single	
	Using Brackets[a]	Not Using Brackets[b]	Using Brackets[a]	Not Using Brackets[b]
Checking and savings	7.7	30.8	7.9	33.9
CDs	12.4	38.2	12.8	40.1
Stocks	10.7	41.7	13.6	52.0
Bonds	10.9	33.7	16.8	54.7
IRA/Keogh	9.4	25.9	11.6	31.0
Housing	1.2	14.9	2.9	29.1
Other real estate	8.7	29.4	11.1	40.3
Business	9.7	41.6	15.6	51.7
Other assets	7.8	27.3	10.7	35.4
Debts	6.3	15.4	6.0	17.8

Source: Authors' calculations from AHEAD and SIPP. Unless otherwise stated, all calculations are weighted.

[a]Includes observations with no brackets.

[b]Includes observations with incomplete, complete, or no brackets.

8.3   Wealth Imputation in AHEAD

For those who provide a complete bracket, only an amount within a bracket will need to be imputed. Individuals who do not report whether they own the asset will potentially require ownership, then bracket, and finally amount to be imputed. Because of the relationships between personal characteristics and wealth item nonresponse (table 8.5), the imputations will use covariates. The descriptive tables suggest that the determinants of nonresponse differ between DK and RF. Therefore, whenever possible, we will differentiate between these two sources of nonresponse.

Table 8.5   Personal Characteristics by Asset Ownership Status

Type of Asset and Response	N^a	Low Cognitive Score[b] (%)	Proxy Interview (%)	Married (%)	Over Age 80 (%)
Checking and savings					
Nonowner	1,568	0.58	0.12	0.31	0.38
Missing ownership	133	0.47	0.12	0.33	0.38
DK value	875	0.40	0.07	0.36	0.35
RF value	507	0.29	0.06	0.48	0.31
Gave value	2,890	0.25	0.04	0.44	0.29
Stocks					
Nonowner	4,796	0.41	0.08	0.35	0.34
Missing ownership	113	0.45	0.16	0.41	0.39
DK value	368	0.21	0.03	0.47	0.29
RF value	117	0.18	0.03	0.62	0.26
Gave value	579	0.09	0.01	0.61	0.21
Housing					
Nonowner	1,797	0.51	0.13	0.17	0.45
Missing ownership	30	0.52	0.91	0.79	0.40
DK value	911	0.50	0.05	0.32	0.39
RF value	45	0.47	0.02	0.46	0.30
Gave value	3,190	0.24	0.03	0.53	0.24

Source: Authors' calculations from AHEAD. Unless otherwise stated, all calculations are weighted.

[a]These are unweighted observation counts and do not match the weighted percent distribution of observations that are provided in table 8.2.

[b]Includes also those who do not complete cognition battery.

8.3.1 Imputation of Ownership

As was shown in table 8.2, a small percentage of people did not give information about asset ownership. For these people, we imputed ownership based on logistic estimation. Using the sample of those whose ownership status is known, we estimated $P(O) = L(X'\beta)$, the probability of ownership (O) given observations on the covariates X, which include demographic variables (age, race, marital status), education, work history, profession, cognitive impairment indicators, and reported sources of income, and the logistic function L. Then, for someone whose ownership status is unknown, we imputed ownership based on the estimated probability $P^* = L(X'\beta^*)$ by making a random drawing from a binomial distribution with a probability of success of P^*. Covariates will increase the precision of the imputation because of the variation in ownership by personal characteristics (table 8.5).

8.3.2 Imputation of Brackets

After imputing ownership, we allocate the imputed owners and those with no brackets or incomplete brackets to one of the complete brackets. This was done with ordered logistic estimation. Among those with complete brackets we estimated $P_j(X'\alpha)$, the probability of being in the jth bracket. The covariates, X, include the demographic and other variables used in ownership imputation, supplemented by ownership of other assets and brackets of other assets. Then, for someone with missing bracket information, we imputed a complete bracket based on the fitted probabilities $P_j(X'\alpha^*)$, by making a random assignment according to a drawing on a multinomial random variable with probabilities $P_j(X'\alpha^*)$.

8.3.3 Imputation of Amounts

The final step in the imputation is to assign values to all those who either report a complete bracket or who have been imputed into a bracket. Amounts are imputed through a nearest neighbor approach similar to that in Chand and Gan (1994) and Little, Sande, and Scheuren (1988). For each individual to be imputed, a nearest neighbor is selected from among the continuous reporters who are in the same bracket. The selection is based on a regression of asset amount on individual characteristics. First, we fit over the continuous reporters in bracket j, $S = X'\gamma_j$ where S is the value of the asset for those in bracket j. Then S is predicted over all continuous and bracketed reporters in bracket j using the estimated value of γ_j. For each individual to be imputed from bracket j, the nearest neighbor is that continuous reporter in bracket j whose fitted value is closest to the fitted value of that individual. The value assigned is the actual value of the nearest neighbor, not the fitted value. For this imputation step we use the same covariates as in the imputation to the brackets.

This method is a generalization of the "hotdeck" procedure in which a few characteristics such as education and sex are used to stratify the sample of continuous reporters. Then an imputation for an individual with a missing value is made at random from the cell corresponding to that person's characteristics. If we consider a bracket to be a characteristic, our method is hotdeck with complete stratification by bracket and partial stratification by other characteristics. The advantage of our method is that we can use many more covariates than in a traditional hotdeck, which is limited because of empty cells. Our method has the further advantage of preserving the covariances between the asset value and our covariates within the limits of the functional form $X'\gamma$.

This imputation method contains several differences from that of Chand and Gan (1994), who also use a nearest neighbor approach to impute asset amount. First, whereas the Chand-Gan approach uses the nearest neighbor metric to assign amounts, our method breaks the imputation of bracket and amount into two distinct steps. Second, we impute brackets based on only those observations who provide a complete bracket, while Chand and Gan include observations who provided a continuous amount. We consider this an improvement because in the HRS the distribution of households across brackets is different for the continuous respondents than for the bracketed respondents (Smith 1995). We believe that the respondents who did not complete a bracketing sequence are more like those who were bracketed than those who gave a continuous amount. Third, those who gave no bracketing information at all are imputed to a bracket based on the distribution of those who completed the bracketing and who initially gave the same type of response (DK or RF). This procedure is based on the observation that DK or RF responses have different distributions across asset brackets, with refusers typically falling into the higher brackets. Finally, in contrast to Chand and Gan (1994), greater use of financial information was made in the imputation of asset brackets and amounts. Dummy variables for the ownership of other assets and the brackets of total income and other assets were used as additional covariates to preserve some of the interasset structure of wealth in the imputations.

8.3.4   Implementing Imputation Procedure

Since there are 10 components of wealth, each having either four or five brackets, we use stepwise model selection to choose the explanatory variables (the X) for ownership probability, bracket probability, and asset level within a bracket. We experimented with several significance levels for entering a variable into the statistical model. This is discussed briefly in the appendix, where we give tables with descriptive information on the characteristics of the imputations of two representative assets, stocks and housing, at three different significance levels.

The nearest neighbor approach, in common with all hotdeck procedures, has a stochastic component, which could cause random variation in asset values. For example, in the top bracket, which is open ended, selecting several times the highest observed continuous asset amount would affect the mean of the distribution substantially. To reduce the influence of this stochastic component, the entire imputation procedure was repeated several times. The models without covariates, which exhibit the highest amount of stochastic variation, were repeated nine times, and the models with covariates were repeated four times. In each case, the imputed amount was assigned to be the average across the repetitions.

8.4   Results

8.4.1   Ownership Imputation

Table 8.6 shows the results from imputing ownership. The first column of the table shows the asset ownership rates for those who report ownership. The second column gives the imputed ownership rates for those whose ownership rate is unknown. With the exception of bonds, the rate of ownership is lower where ownership is imputed. With stock ownership, for example, 14.7 percent of those with missing ownership are imputed to own stocks, compared to 19.4 percent among those who report ownership. Note that if covariates were not used in the imputation, the rate of ownership would be, on average, the same in both columns. Lower ownership rates among those with missing data occur

Table 8.6   **Percentage of Households Owning Assets: Actual and Imputed**

Type of Asset	Actual	Imputed[a]
Checking and savings	75.6	73.3
CDs	21.3	15.8
Stocks	19.4	14.7
Bonds	5.7	6.6
IRA/Keogh	16.2	7.4
Housing	70.9	66.3
Other real estate	19.0	12.6
Business	4.4	3.7
Other assets	10.2	6.8
Debts	14.0	19.8

Source: Authors' calculations from AHEAD. All calculations are weighted.

[a]Ownership imputed by using estimates from ownership regression using the sample of those with ownership known. See text for details.

because those who do not report ownership have characteristics that tend to be similar to those of nonowners, such as older age and higher rates of cognitive impairment. This was found earlier in the descriptive analysis in section 8.2. This suggests that ownership nonresponse tends to occur more for reasons of informational uncertainty than for privacy concerns.[6]

8.4.2   Bracket Imputation

Because of the large number of assets to be imputed, we will concentrate the discussion of the results of the imputations on two important and very different assets: stocks and housing wealth. Stocks are illustrative of assets with low ownership and high missing value rates but exhibit a very skewed distribution (large upper tail). Housing is important because it comprises a large proportion of individual wealth holdings.

Table 8.7 shows the effects of bracket imputations for stocks. Each column of the table gives the percentage distribution of observations across the five stock brackets. The first column reports the percentage distribution among those giving continuous responses; the next two columns give the distributions for those with complete brackets and those with imputed brackets.[7] Those completing the bracketing sequence tend to have higher stock values than those providing continuous responses. For example, 18 percent of respondents who gave continuous amounts have from zero to $4,999 in stock equity compared with just 14 percent of those who completed the bracketing sequence. The effect of using covariates in the imputation process can be seen by comparing

6. This makes the AHEAD population different from the HRS population, where nonresponse on assets is typically associated with an unwillingness to reveal large amounts: the imputations increase ownership rates substantially in HRS.

7. Observations requiring imputation of brackets include those missing ownership and those with incomplete brackets.

Table 8.7   Distribution of Owners of Stocks (percent)

| | | Brackets | | |
Range (thousand $)	Continuous	Complete	Imputed[a]	All
0.0–4.9	18	14	11	16
5.0–24.9	24	25	23	25
25.0–99.9	28	37	29	29
100.0–499.9	25	19	30	23
500+	4	6	6	5
All	100	100	100	100

Source: Authors' calculations from AHEAD. Unless otherwise stated, all calculations are weighted. Columns may not sum to 100 percent because of rounding.
[a]Includes observations with no brackets and incomplete brackets.

Table 8.8   Distribution of Owners of Housing (percent)

| | | Brackets | | |
Range (thousand $)	Continuous	Complete	Imputed[a]	All
0.0–49.9	26	42	46	30
50.0–99.9	39	35	33	38
100.0–199.9	25	16	15	23
200.0+	10	7	6	9
All	100	100	100	100

Source: Authors' calculations from AHEAD. Unless otherwise stated, all calculations are weighted. Columns may not sum to 100 percent because of rounding.
[a]Includes observations with no brackets and incomplete brackets.

the distribution of the complete brackets with the imputed brackets: since the imputation is based on the sample of complete brackets, if no covariates were used, on average they would be the same. We see that the covariates shift the distribution to higher values, implying that those who give incomplete responses have greater socioeconomic status: we estimate that 14 percent of those who completed the bracketing sequence have stock holdings between zero and $4,999 compared with just 11 percent of those with imputed brackets.

Table 8.8 shows the results of imputing housing brackets. This table shows that, in contrast to results for stocks (and most other assets), those with incomplete responses on housing have personal characteristics that make them more likely to have low housing values. Continuous reports are systematically greater than the bracket reports, and the covariates used to impute brackets reduce the bracketed distribution even further. The differences are large: 35 percent of the continuous reports have housing equity of $100,000 or more, whereas just 21 percent of the imputed bracket cases are in that range.

Table 8.9   **Average Stock Wealth within Brackets (thousand dollars)**

Range (thousand $)	Continuous	Brackets
0.0–4.9	1.2	1.2
5.0–24.9	13.5	13.9
25.0–99.9	49.3	50.0
100.0–499.9	185.6	190.7
500+	862.3	751.0

Source: Authors' calculations from AHEAD. Unless otherwise stated, all calculations are weighted.

Table 8.10   **Average Stock Holdings by Type of Observation**

Type of Observation	Number of Observations	Average Value (thousand $)
Continuous	579	97.9
Complete bracket	359	90.2
Incomplete bracket	126	148.8
No bracket	16	163.6

8.4.3 Imputing Amounts

Table 8.9 shows the imputations of amounts of stock holdings within each bracket. The first column gives the average value for stock wealth among all households providing continuous responses in the given range. The second column gives the average imputed value within a bracket. Although the differences are not large, the average amount within the bracketed range tends to be higher than the average continuous amount. For example, within the $100,000–$499,999 range, the average over continuous reporters is about $185,600, which is what the average imputed amount would be if no covariates were used. Among those with brackets, the covariates increase the average amount to about $190,700. This implies that imputed individuals have covariates that are associated with higher stock holdings than those of continuous reporters.

However, this table does not show differences across the subgroups of imputed observations. Those requiring imputation of values within brackets include those who have incomplete brackets, those with complete brackets, and those with no brackets. These groups appear to be very different. On average, those with no brackets have covariates associated with higher levels of stocks relative to those with continuous values, while those with complete brackets have lower values. This can be seen from average stock values for these groups in table 8.10. The figures in that table reflect differences in the distribution of observations across brackets as well as differences in average values within brackets.

Table 8.11 shows the results of imputing the value of housing wealth within

Table 8.11   **Average Housing Wealth within Brackets (thousand dollars)**

Range (thousand $)	Continuous	Brackets
0.0–49.9	26.7	26.2
50.0–99.9	64.3	66.2
100.0–199.9	121.4	122.6
200.0+	332.8	291.8

Source: Authors' calculations from AHEAD. Unless otherwise stated, all calculations are weighted.

Table 8.12   **Average Housing Wealth by Type of Observation**

Type of Observation	Number of Observations	Average Value (thousand $)
Continuous	3,190	95.8
Complete bracket	816	75.4
Incomplete bracket	140	68.6
No bracket	23	68.8

Table 8.13   **Mean Asset Values by Nonresponse Status, by Type of Asset**

		Nonresponse Status	
Type of Asset	Continuous Amount Reported	Bracket Reported	Bracket Imputed
Checking and savings	21.9	22.2	22.6
CDs	42.4	33.6	44.5
Stocks	97.9	90.2	150.4
Bonds	62.4	88.6	116.7
IRA	48.3	63.5	61.4
Housing	95.8	75.4	68.6
Other real estate	117.0	158.7	126.1
Business	101.7	225.9	348.3
Other assets	28.4	29.6	32.0
Debt	6.0	4.7	13.8

Source: Authors' calculations from AHEAD. Unless otherwise stated, all calculations are weighted.

brackets. No pattern emerges here: the averages are about the same, indicating that there is little systematic difference in the covariates that explain housing value between the continuous respondents and the bracketed respondents.

Adding in the differences in the distribution across brackets changes these results substantially as shown in table 8.12. Respondents who provide brackets have lower housing wealth than respondents who give continuous amounts, in contrast to holdings of stocks.

Differences between stock and housing wealth illustrate one of the important findings from this study: there are differences in the character of nonresponse across asset types and nonresponse categories. This is shown in table 8.13, which has a summary description of the results of the bracket imputation. The average amounts for three different types of responses are shown. Because those who provide continuous amounts tend to fall into lower brackets than those who provide brackets, those who provide continuous amounts generally have the lowest average wealth components. The notable exception is housing wealth, where those who provide a continuous amount have the highest average housing value. However, the effect of covariates in imputing brackets varies considerably. Some assets have bracket imputation resulting in higher average amounts such as for stocks, bonds, and business, while other assets such as housing, real estate, and IRAs display the opposite tendency.

8.5   The Distribution of Wealth and the Importance of Bracketing and Imputation

The results presented in the previous section show that imputed wealth differs significantly by type of nonresponse. This suggests more generally that the use of brackets to reduce missing data may lead to significant changes in the estimates of the distribution of household wealth. Our imputation methodology stresses not only the importance of bracketing but also the importance of using covariates at each stage of estimation. To explore the importance of these issues, tables 8.14–8.16 show how the distributions of nonhousing, housing, and total wealth differ under progressively more complicated imputation methods. The different methods vary along two main dimensions: how the bracketing information is used and whether covariates are used in the imputation procedure.

In all three tables, we show the distribution of wealth under seven imputation procedures. The imputation method becomes increasingly complex with each successive row in the table. The following summarizes the methods:

1. Assign ownership by the probability of ownership among that population where ownership is known. Impute amounts from unconditional draws from the continuous amounts. No covariates or bracketing information is used. This is known as unconditional hotdeck.

2. Same as method 1 except impute amounts to those in the complete brackets from the continuous amounts within brackets.

3. Same as method 2 except impute incomplete brackets from pool of completed brackets.

4. Same as method 3 except impute incomplete brackets from pool of completed brackets who provided the same response (DK or RF) to the initial question about amount.

5. Same as method 4 except impute ownership using covariates.

6. Same as method 5 except impute brackets using covariates.

7. Same as method 6 except use covariates to find nearest neighbor for imputation of amount.

Table 8.14   **Effects of Imputation on Distribution of Nonhousing Wealth (thousand dollars)**

Imputation Method[a]		Nonhousing Wealth		
	Mean	10th Percentile	Median	90th Percentile
1. Unconditional hotdeck	94.7	0.0	24.0	251.5
2. Bracketed hotdeck	97.7	0.0	21.0	255.6
3. Imputing brackets without covariates	97.1	0.0	21.0	258.0
4. Imputing brackets without covariates, stratify by DK/RF	99.9	0.0	21.2	262.0
5. Adding covariates to ownership imputation	99.5	0.0	21.0	264.8
6. Adding covariates to bracket imputation	101.7	0.0	20.0	261.0
7. Adding covariates to level imputation	100.8	0.0	20.0	260.0

Source: Authors' calculations from AHEAD. All calculations are weighted.

[a]Imputation methods described in text. Each successive method nests the method before it. For example, the stratification by don't know (DK) vs. refused (RF) in method 4 is also used in methods 5–7.

Table 8.14 shows the effects of the different methods on estimated values for nonhousing wealth.[8] Going from method 1 to method 2 increases the mean of nonhousing wealth by about 3 percent, which is caused by the brackets. That is, simply knowing what bracket someone falls into increases the estimate of mean wealth. At the same time, the median is reduced, implying that the entire distribution is affected by the brackets. Further, because the 90th percentile increases only marginally, some of the influence on the mean must be coming from the very wealthy. Method 4 shows that differentiating between DK and RF is important, shifting up the distribution at all points. Methods 5 through 7, which vary primarily by the extent of the use of covariates, affect estimates of the distribution of wealth only minimally.

Table 8.15 shows the effects of the different methods on housing wealth averaged over both owners and nonowners. Here the bracketing and covariates all reduce the mean and median. The changes accumulate to be fairly large on the mean: the entry for method 7 is about 5 percent less than for method 1.

Table 8.16 has similar results for total wealth.

We found that the value of stock holdings differed if the response was DK rather than RF, which we attribute to differences in personal characteristics such as cognition. Thus we would expect that individuals answering DK about

8. Nonhousing wealth includes all categories of wealth except housing (checking, CDs, stocks, bonds, IRAs, other real estate, business, and other assets).

Table 8.15   **Effects of Imputation on Distribution of Housing Wealth (thousand dollars)**

	Housing Wealth				
Imputation Method[a]	Mean if Greater Than Zero	Mean	10th Percentile	Median	90th Percentile
1. Unconditional hotdeck	95.8	67.9	0.0	45.0	150.0
2. Bracketed hotdeck	92.8	65.7	0.0	40.0	150.0
3. Imputing brackets without covariates	92.9	65.6	0.0	40.0	150.0
4. Imputing brackets without covariates, stratify by DK/RF	93.4	65.3	0.0	40.0	150.0
5. Adding covariates to ownership imputation	92.5	65.3	0.0	40.0	150.0
6. Adding covariates to bracket imputation	93.0	65.3	0.0	40.0	150.0
7. Adding covariates to amount imputation	91.2	64.4	0.0	40.0	150.0

Source: Authors' calculations from AHEAD. All calculations are weighted.

[a]Imputation methods described in text. Each successive method nests the method before it. For example, the stratification by don't know (DK) vs. refused (RF) in method 4 is also used in methods 5–7.

Table 8.16   **Effects of Imputation on Distribution of Total Wealth (thousand dollars)**

	Total Wealth			
Imputation Method[a]	Mean	10th Percentile	Median	90th Percentile
1. Unconditional hotdeck	162.6	0.6	88.5	375.0
2. Conditional hotdeck	163.3	0.5	80.0	378.0
3. Imputing brackets without covariates	162.7	0.5	80.0	379.0
4. Imputing brackets without covariates, stratify by DK/RF	165.2	0.5	80.0	384.5
5. Adding covariates to ownership imputation	164.8	0.5	80.0	387.0
6. Adding covariates to bracket imputation	167.1	0.5	79.0	382.5
7. Adding covariates to level imputation	165.2	0.5	77.2	380.0

Source: Authors' calculations from AHEAD. All calculations are weighted.

[a]Imputation methods described in text. Each successive method nests the method before it. For example, the stratification by don't know (DK) vs. refused (RF) in method 4 is also used in methods 5–7.

Table 8.17   Effects of Imputation on Distribution of Wealth by Response Type
                    (thousand dollars)

Imputation Method[a]	Response	Nonhousing Wealth		Housing Wealth		Total Wealth	
		Mean	Median	Mean	Median	Mean	Median
1. Unconditional hotdeck	DK	109.1	33.0	189.2	108.0	200.3	115.0
	RF	98.8	41.0	168.9	115.0	182.7	123.5
	Both	133.2	58.0	218.2	142.0	230.4	158.2
2. Bracketed hotdeck	DK	109.0	27.0	183.5	93.0	186.0	93.0
	RF	126.1	42.0	196.4	108.2	200.7	111.0
	Both	156.2	49.5	239.7	125.0	247.2	129.0
4. Imputing brackets without covariates, stratify by DK/RF	DK	110.6	27.0	184.6	92.0	187.2	91.0
	RF	132.6	43.0	202.7	110.0	233.8	107.2
	Both	182.6	59.5	267.8	139.0	285.2	140.0
6. Adding covariates to bracket imputation	DK	114.3	25.5	188.3	92.5	182.7	91.5
	RF	139.1	35.0	209.1	100.0	203.9	101.0
	Both	184.5	49.0	271.6	130.5	262.3	130.0
7. Adding covariates to level imputation	DK	110.9	25.3	183.3	90.6	183.3	90.6
	RF	135.8	35.0	205.3	100.0	205.3	100.0
	Both	193.1	45.2	275.7	128.2	275.7	128.2

Source: Authors' calculations from AHEAD. All calculations are weighted.

[a]Imputation methods described in text. Each successive method nests the method before it. For example, the stratification by don't know (DK) vs. refused (RF) in method 4 is also used in methods 6 and 7.

one type of asset would have differences in overall wealth from individuals who answer RF. Table 8.17 compares the distribution of wealth across selected imputation methods for the various types of nonresponse. For each method, households who require any imputation are divided into three categories: those who answered DK to at least one asset question, those who answered RF to at least one asset question, and those who answered DK to at least one and RF to at least one asset question. In the unconditional hotdeck method, the mean is lower for RF observations than for DK or both.[9] However, all other methods produce greater total wealth among the RF than among the DK. The main difference comes from using brackets, method 2. The implication is that the RF tend to be in higher brackets.

9. Observations with both an RF and a DK may have larger mean asset values since they, by definition, correspond to individuals who hold at least two assets.

Table 8.18   **Imputation Results by Nonresponse Type**

	Mean Amount (thousand $)		
Type of Asset	Amount Reported	DK	RF
Checking and savings	21.9	19.8	26.2
CDs	42.4	34.7	42.2
Stocks	97.9	81.5	183.9
Bonds	62.4	85.2	123.6
IRA	48.3	75.1	48.2
Housing	95.8	74.2	76.2
Other real estate	117.0	138.6	210.0
Business	101.7	226.8	340.4
Other assets	28.4	25.4	50.5
Debt	6.0	8.1	2.8

Source: Author's calculations. All calculations are weighted. Results are from the preferred imputation method (method 7).

As shown in table 8.18, the importance of differentiating across DK and RF responses holds in almost all asset types, with the exception of IRAs. Imputed wealth for those who refuse to answer the question about asset value is consistently higher than for those who respond that they do not know.

We summarize our results in table 8.19, which shows mean and median wealth by various personal characteristics. At the median the divorced or separated have the lowest wealth. Wealth declines sharply with age and with worse health. A low cognition score is associated with substantially lower wealth.

8.6   Conclusion

We have studied the effects of a number of imputation methods on aggregate measures of wealth such as the median, mean, and percentiles. There are many conclusions that emerge from this study. First, using bracketing in survey design can dramatically reduce the rate of missing data and increase the quality of asset data. Second, using covariates in the imputation process affects the distributions of individual asset holdings substantially. The net effects are minimal, however, in that aggregate wealth is not significantly affected by the introduction of covariates. An implication is that imputation based on covariates may provide an important gain in assigning assets at the individual level even though the effect on the population may not be large. Third, missing data can be the result of the respondent's not knowing (DK) or refusing to answer (RF). We find that these two groups are very different; DK respondents typically have characteristics like those with lower asset levels and RF respondents have characteristics like those with high asset levels. Differentiating between these two groups in the imputation process has important effects on the distribution of wealth.

Table 8.19   Mean and Median Wealth by Demographic Characteristics

Characteristic	N	Nonhousing Wealth		Total Wealth	
		Mean	Median	Mean	Median
Marital status					
Married	2,324	161.8	50.0	250.1	132.0
Divorced/separated	399	58.8	7.0	104.4	28.0
Widowed	3,015	58.1	10.3	107.5	52.5
Never married	235	84.7	12.1	124.8	50.8
Age					
70–74	1,975	133.6	32.5	208.4	98.5
75–79	1,567	101.2	18.3	171.1	80.0
80–84	1,217	69.1	12.7	120.0	60.8
85+	892	54.4	7.5	94.7	35.8
Health					
Excellent/very good	2,004	151.0	42.0	237.4	113.0
Good	1,842	96.1	24.7	159.5	87.0
Fair/poor	2,121	54.0	7.0	96.8	40.4
Not married					
Male	735	96.1	18.0	154.7	61.0
Female	2,914	51.0	8.9	96.8	47.0
Cognition					
Normal	3,655	129.6	40.2	207.8	110.0
Low or missing	2,318	49.4	4.6	89.1	32.7

Source: Author's calculations. All calculations are weighted. Results are from the preferred imputation method (method 7).

Our analysis uses a single cross section from the AHEAD data for all imputations. Because of the unique combination of sample size, measures of health, economic status, and family connections in the AHEAD data, many researchers will use similar cross-sectional samples of the data. We hope that our imputations will be helpful in this context. AHEAD is, however, a panel data set, and future work should extend this imputation procedure to utilize the panel nature of the data.

Appendix

Appendix tables 8A.1A and 8A.1B provide details of the imputation procedure for housing and stocks. Stocks represent an asset with high rates of missing values and a skewed distribution. Housing has lower missing value rates and a more uniform distribution. The format of the two tables is identical. Column (1) gives the number of "donors" (continuous responses that are used to match to the missing data), and column (2) gives the number of observations missing

Table 8A.1A   Characteristics of Imputation Matches for Stocks

F-Value for Entry	Range (thousand $)	No. of Donor Observations (1)	No. of Imputed Observations (2)	No. of Covariates Entered (3)	Percentage of Observations with		
					No Match (4)	Unique Match (5)	Multiple Matches (6)
0.15	0.0–4.9	107	60	21	51.7	25.0	23.3
	5.0–24.9	137	122	18	53.3	27.1	19.7
	25.0–99.9	158	179	13	58.1	29.1	12.9
	100.0–499.9	154	109	13	48.6	33.0	18.4
	500+	24	31	12	32.3	5.6	41.9
	All	580	501	–	52.5	28.7	18.8
0.25	0.0–4.9	107	59	43	93.2	6.8	0.0
	5.0–24.9	137	120	51	100.0	0.0	0.0
	25.0–99.9	158	166	35	95.2	4.8	0.0
	100.0–499.9	154	111	34	97.3	2.7	0.0
	500+	24	45	12	31.1	22.2	46.7
	All	580	501	–	90.8	5.0	4.2
0.50	0.0–4.9	107	63	101	100.0	0.0	0.0
	5.0–24.9	137	119	46	99.2	0.8	0.0
	25.0–99.9	158	172	60	100.0	0.0	0.0
	100.0–499.9	154	116	61	100.0	0.0	0.0
	500+	24	35	12	31.4	22.9	45.7
	All	580	505	–	95.0	1.8	3.2

Source: Authors' calculations from AHEAD. Unless otherwise stated, all calculations are weighted.

Table 8A.1B   **Characteristics of Imputation Matches for Housing**

F-Value for Entry	Range (thousand $)	No. of Donor Observations (1)	No. of Imputed Observations (2)	No. of Covariates Entered (3)	Percentage of Observations with		
					No Match (4)	Unique Match (5)	Multiple Matches (6)
0.15	0.0–49.9	925	435	30	68.5	21.2	10.3
	50.0–99.9	1,227	331	26	49.2	21.8	29.0
	100.0–199.9	748	146	19	19.2	19.9	61.0
	200+	294	67	26	73.1	20.9	6.0
	All	3,194	979	–	55.0	21.1	23.9
0.25	0.0–49.9	925	432	44	87.5	10.7	1.9
	50.0–99.9	1,227	337	43	92.6	7.1	0.3
	100.0–199.9	748	144	36	88.2	11.8	0.0
	200+	294	63	40	98.4	1.6	0.0
	All	3,194	976	–	90.1	9.0	0.9
0.50	0.0–49.9	925	439	64	96.6	3.4	0.0
	50.0–99.9	1,227	338	68	100.0	0.0	0.0
	100.0–199.9	748	140	51	98.6	1.4	0.0
	200+	294	61	59	100.0	0.0	0.0
	All	3,194	978	–	98.3	1.7	0.0

Source: Authors' calculations from AHEAD. Unless otherwise stated, all calculations are weighted.

asset values, for each bracketed range.[10] Column (3) gives the number of covariates used in estimating the regression for the particular bracket given the F-value criterion in the stepwise regression. Columns (4) through (6) give the percentage distribution of the imputed observations by the type of match. A multiple exact match represents the case where two or more donor observations have the same fitted value as the observation requiring imputation. No match corresponds to the case where no donor observation has the same fitted value as the observation requiring imputation, while the unique and multiple match cases correspond to the cases where one or more than one donor has the same fitted value.[11] As expected, changing the significance level from 0.15 to the lowest significance level (0.50) dramatically increases the number of covariates selected into the model, usually more than doubling the number. As a result, the probability that an exact match of fitted values will be found is greatly decreased. Among stocks, at a significance level of 0.15, about 25 percent have a unique exact match while 23 percent have multiple exact matches. Lowering the significance level drastically reduces the probability that an exact match will be found. In order to avoid the potential of overfitting the imputation model, an F-value of 0.15 was used for ordinary least squares regressions and 0.05 for logistic regressions, unless noted otherwise.[12] While the character of the matches varies across the F-significance levels, the distribution of wealth does not change dramatically.[13]

References

Chand, Harish, and Li Gan. 1994. Wealth imputation in the AHEAD. Berkeley: University of California. Mimeograph.

Herzog, A. Regula, and Robert Wallace. 1997. Measure of cognitive functioning in the AHEAD study. *Journal of Gerontology* 52B:37–48.

Little, Roderick J., I. G. Sande, and Fritz Scheuren. 1988. Missing-data adjustments in large surveys. *Journal of Business and Economic Statistics* 6 (3): 117–31.

Smith, James P. 1995. Racial and ethnic differences in wealth. *Journal of Human Resources* 30:S158–S183.

10. Note that, due to randomness in the (previous stages of) assignment of ownership and brackets, the number of observations across brackets is not constant across significance levels.

11. Because the regression consists of categorical variables, an exact match is possible.

12. Since the logistic regressions are used to form probabilities for Bernoulli draws rather than for nearest neighbor fits, a more conservative F-value is warranted to preserve the empirical distribution.

13. In a previous version of this paper, we did not use stepwise regression to limit the number of regressors in the imputation models. As a consequence, estimation of brackets with small samples resulted in perfect fitting of the model. In the case of the highest (open) bracket for stocks, this resulted in a very large value for stocks ($6 million) being imputed to more than one observation, leading to a large increase in mean wealth. We feel that using the stepwise regression procedure generates more robust imputation results.

————. 1997. Wealth inequality among older Americans. *Journal of Gerontology* 52B:74–81.
Soldo, Beth, Michael Hurd, Willard Rodgers, and Robert Wallace. 1997. Asset and health dynamics among the oldest old: An overview of the AHEAD study. *Journal of Gerontology* 52B:1–20.

Comment   James P. Smith

Hoynes, Hurd, and Chand (hereafter HHC) have written an excellent paper using the recently released data from the survey on Asset and Health Dynamics among the Oldest Old (AHEAD). Their paper makes two important contributions, one methodological and the other substantive. The methodological contribution presents a new method of imputing missing asset data in social science surveys.

HHC deal with the implications of an important recent survey innovation—follow-up bracket questions—that was used extensively in both the Health and Retirement Survey (HRS) and AHEAD. When respondents did not answer a question on the value of an asset, instead of simply going on to the next question as most surveys do, both HRS and AHEAD asked a series of follow-up questions to determine whether the unknown asset value lay above or below certain selected amounts. I can only agree with HHC's bottom line conclusion on the importance of follow-up brackets for the imputation of missing values. As HHC show, the value of these follow-up brackets is that they substantially reduce item nonresponse to asset questions. Using an illustration from their paper, nonresponses to questions about the value of housing are reduced by almost 80 percent by the use of follow-up bracket questions.

The second reason why brackets matter so much is that they substantially reduce the estimation error in predicting the missing asset amount. It is one thing to try to assign a missing business value when all one knows are the characteristics of the owner. It is a much less daunting problem when one also knows that the value of the business lies between $50,000 and $100,000. HHC's basic results on the value of follow-up brackets are quite consistent with those I obtained with both the HRS (Smith 1995) and AHEAD (Smith 1997). Follow-up brackets are an important survey innovation that I predict will be adopted extensively in other surveys. While I agree with the major points in HHC's paper, I do have two quarrels with how they estimate their imputations. The first deals with missing values on asset ownership and the second with the sensitivity of their estimates to outliers.

James P. Smith is senior economist at RAND and holds the RAND Chair in Labor Markets and Demographic Studies.

Missing Value on Owners

The first step in their imputation procedure involved assigning missing values for cases in which respondents were uncertain or refused to say whether they had the asset. Since it affects only roughly 2 percent of the sample, imputations for this subsample of uncertain owners will not be very important in the overall scheme of things. However, it does caution us against too mechanistic an approach in our missing value algorithms. To assign a missing value, HHC estimate a logistic function for the probability of ownership using the full sample of nonmissing value respondents. Covariates in their logistic model included a rather standard and noncontroversial list of demographic and other characteristics. Imputed missing asset ownership was assigned based on a prediction from this model with a random draw from the residual distribution.

Their predictions actually imply a somewhat lower rate of asset ownership among nonresponses than was observed in the full sample, implying that, on average, characteristics of nonresponses on asset ownership are tilted toward those attributes reducing the odds of ownership. Since asset ownership is relatively rare in this age group, HHC end up assigning very low rates of ownership to these missing values. I would like to caution against this conclusion, largely because it relies on too mechanistic an approach to the entire imputation exercise. Before estimating missing values, we must first step back and ask what the nature of the process leading to nonresponse is. The approach HHC follow assumes that the forces producing nonresponses to ownership questions are basically identical (after stratifying by characteristics in the imputation algorithm) to the factors that distinguish owners and nonowners of asset in the full sample. This assumption is unlikely to be true.

There are actually two distinct reasons why respondents have missing values on whether they even own an asset. These nonresponses filter from those respondents who either said they did not know or those respondents who refused to reply. Given the relative simplicity of the question (do you know whether you have an asset?), the don't know responses in part include the cognitively impaired or those who are simply confused about the meaning of the question. This category also includes respondents who have already decided that they do not want to participate in this survey but are too polite to terminate the interview. The quickest way to get through the survey is to answer "I do not know." Supporting evidence for this view is that more than half of wave 1 respondents in the companion HRS who said that they did not know whether they had an asset had attrited from the HRS by wave 2. On average, these attriters were high wealth holders, implying that many of these respondents who said that they did not know whether they had an asset were likely to have it. Similarly, refusals represent those respondents generally quite sensitive to income or wealth questions. In most cases, such respondents probably do have the asset in question. A nonresponse is an excellent way of telling the interviewer that their wealth holdings are not his or her business. The upshot of these arguments

Table 8C.1   Distribution of Open-Ended Cases (Stocks) among
                  Continuous Reporters

Asset Value ($)	Number of Cases
500,000	11
600,000	6
700,000	1
750,000	2
800,000	2
3,000,000	1
5,000,000	1

is that ownership rates among nonresponses to asset questions are likely to be much higher than observed for the full AHEAD sample and considerably higher than HHC predict.

Missing Data on Amounts

My second quarrel with the HHC imputations is far more critical since it can significantly affect the mean imputations of missing values. HHC impute missing values by first assigning those with missing bracket information a bracket category using ordered logistic regressions. Within-bracket imputations of exact amounts were then assigned based on a regression over those respondents with continuous amount data within the bracket. Using what they label "the nearest neighbor approach," HHC impute each individual from a continuous reporter whose fitted value is closest to the fitted value for the missing amount individual. The value assigned is the actual value of the nearest neighbor, not the fitted value.

Based on their methodology, imputation had a large impact on estimated missing values. For stocks, their estimates imply that imputed values for bracketed respondents were more than two and one-half times the amount for continuous reporters. Virtually all of this difference stems from amounts imputed in the open-ended interval for stocks (more than $500,000). In this range, mean values among continuous reporters were $871,000, compared to $2,613,000 among those whose values were imputed. Virtually all of this difference stems from the use of covariates in the imputation algorithm. Roughly similar results were obtained for other forms of nonhousing wealth. In summary, HHC's results imply that imputed values with brackets had a reasonably large impact on estimates of nonhousing wealth, particularly among those at the very top of the wealth distribution. This impact largely flowed from the use of personal covariate information in the upper open-ended brackets.

How much confidence should we place on these results? I would like to urge considerable caution due to their sensitivity to a few outlier observations. The reasons for my caution are illustrated in table 8C.1, which illustrates a typical distribution of continuous reporter cases in the open-ended interval—in this case for stocks. There were only 24 continuous reported cases with values in this open-ended interval, only two of which had values that exceeded $1,000,000. The mean across these 24 continuous reported cases was $871,000. Yet, HHC assign a mean of $2,614,000 to the 21 bracket cases for stocks. The only way that this could happen is that virtually all of the missing value cases were matched to those continuous reporter cases at the top of the open-ended interval. For example, if 11 of the 21 cases were matched to the $800,000 case and the remainder divided between the $3 and $5 million cases, we will still be below their estimated mean of $2,614,000. It is clear then that in the open-ended interval HHC are matching most missing value respondents with the highest value cases. Instead of the "nearest neighbor approach," their algorithm might be more aptly titled the "richest neighbor approach."

References

Smith, James P. 1995. Racial and ethnic differences in wealth. *Journal of Human Resources* 30:S158–S183.
————. 1997. Wealth inequality among older Americans. *Journal of Gerontology* 52B (May): 74–81.

9   Subjective Survival Curves and Life Cycle Behavior

Michael Hurd, Daniel McFadden, and Li Gan

9.1   Introduction

Many economic models are based on forward-looking behavior on the part of economic agents. Although it is often said that "expectations" about future events are important in these models, more precisely it is the probability distributions of future events that enter the models. For example, consumption and savings decisions of an individual are thought to depend on what he or she thinks about future interest rates, the likelihood of dying, and the risk of substantial future medical expenditures. According to our theories, decision makers have probability distributions about these and other events, and they use them to make decisions about saving. This implies that data on these distributions should be used in estimation.

In a few microeconomic models, we have data on probability distributions that may plausibly be assumed to approximate those required by the models. Life cycle models of consumption in which mortality risk helps determine saving are the leading example, so we will put our discussion in the context of such models.

Suppose that instantaneous utility, or felicity, is given by

$$u(c_t) = \frac{c_t^{1-\gamma}}{1 - \gamma},$$

that the real interest rate r is constant, and that lifetime utility is time separable. Then, in a common formulation, the first-order conditions imply

Michael Hurd is professor of economics at the State University of New York at Stony Brook, a researcher at RAND, and a research associate of the National Bureau of Economic Research. Daniel McFadden is professor of economics at the University of California, Berkeley, and a research fellow of the National Bureau of Economic Research. Li Gan is a graduate student at the University of California, Berkeley.

$$\frac{1}{c_t} \cdot \frac{dc_t}{dt} = \frac{-h_t + r - \rho}{\gamma},$$

where ρ is the subjective time rate of discount and h_t is mortality risk at time t. Thus, the rate of change of consumption depends on mortality risk h_t and will be negative if h_t is large. Furthermore, from variations in h_t, the risk aversion parameter γ is econometrically identified. Notice that if there is unobserved heterogeneity in h_t, the coefficient on h_t will tend toward zero, and γ will be estimated to be large. That is, the consumption decisions of individuals will appear not to be responsive to variations in mortality risk.

There have been two approaches to the problem of obtaining mortality risk data to be used in estimation based on the first-order condition above. In the first, an individual is assumed to believe his mortality risk is the same as that contained in a life table, adjusted for age, and possibly sex and race. Under this assumption, if the individual chooses consumption based on his beliefs about mortality risk, the analyst can use data from life tables to explain saving behavior (Hurd 1989b).

The assumption that individuals have reasonable knowledge of the population mortality risk is considerably stronger than in typical demand analysis, which has only the reasonable requirement that individuals know their incomes and that they observe prices. Furthermore, in demand analysis, consumers have observed past variation in prices, and they have had the experience of choosing consumption through repeated trials. It is much less obvious how they would learn about the level of mortality risk in the population. Even if individuals do know about population average mortality risk, the average mortality risk of a cohort may not be well approximated by the life tables because of changing risk. For example, members of a younger cohort may forecast mortality improvements, so the life tables overstate their mortality risk.

A second approach to finding data on survival probabilities is especially pertinent for studies of life cycle behavior. It is based on the well-known variation in mortality rates by economic status (Kitagawa and Hauser 1973; Shorrocks 1975; Hurd and Wise 1989; Jianakoplos, Menchik, and Irvine 1989; Feinstein 1992). If the subjective probability distributions of individuals of differing economic status vary in the same way as the observed mortality rates, using standard life tables in the model estimation will cause the parameters to be misestimated. A further consequence will be that a forecast of the distribution of economic status will be incorrect: for example, poorer individuals who believe their mortality risk is higher than average will dissave faster than what is predicted by the model, causing future poverty rates to be underestimated by the model. Thus, the model will not be able to uncover a possible explanation of the high poverty rates of the oldest old: the poorest at retirement dissaved fastest because of their subjective probability distributions of mortality risk. Variation in mortality risk according to observable characteristics can, in principle, be accounted for by estimating the variation in mortality outcomes in panel data that have been linked to the national death index as in Lillard and Weiss (1997). Although this method is undoubtedly an improvement over using unconditional life tables, it often depends on functional form assumptions for identification. To see this, suppose that life table survival probabilities have been adjusted with covariates such as wealth in a model of life cycle wealth change in panel data. A typical estimating equation would be

$$w_{t+1} = f(w_t, \{q_t\}),$$

where w_t is wealth at time t and $\{q_t\}$ is the path of survival rates. If $\{q_t\}$ depends on wealth, then identification depends to a certain extent on functional form assumptions. This would be true of any covariate that is used to adjust $\{q_t\}$ and that also appears elsewhere in the utility maximization problem. An additional implication is that utility cannot be allowed to depend on age because it is the main determinant of $\{q_t\}$.

Even if adjustments can be made to life tables by using observed covariates, individuals are likely to have subjective probability distributions that are related to unobservable as well as observable variables. It is these subjective probability distributions that should enter life cycle models of saving, so that any models that rely on observed probability distributions have intrinsic limitations.

The importance of accounting for individual-level evaluation of mortality risk is shown in the following example. It has been observed that there is a great deal of heterogeneity both in the results of saving (wealth) and in observed saving rates. From this point of view, the life cycle model of saving is inadequate: for example, it cannot say why apparently similar individuals reach retirement with very different wealth levels (Hurd and Wise 1989), and why they save at different rates following retirement. It could be that most of the variation in saving behavior is due to taste differences across individuals or to forces we do not understand. An alternative explanation is that there is a great deal of variation at the individual level in mortality risk, but we do not usually observe this variable.

9.2 Data

Our data come from the survey of the Asset and Health Dynamics among the Oldest Old (AHEAD). This is a biennial panel of individuals born in 1923 or earlier and their spouses. At baseline in 1993, it surveyed 8,222 individuals representative of the community-based population, except for oversamples of blacks, Hispanics, and Floridians. The main goal of AHEAD is to provide panel data from the three broad domains of economic status, health, and family connections (Soldo et al. 1997). This is reflected in the questionnaire sections and average interview timings as follows:

A. Demographics (3.3 minutes)
B. Health (7.3)
C. Cognition (4.5)
D. Family (8.2)
E. Health care and costs (11.9)
F. Housing (3.8)
G. Job status and history (4.0)
H. Expectations (3.3)
 J. Income (5.7)
K. Assets (3.2)
R. Insurance (3.2)

Our main interest in this paper is in the data from the expectations section and its relationship to personal characteristics, particularly cognition. The survey has eight measures of subjective probabilities. In this paper we will give some descriptive statistics on them, but our main attention will be on the subjective probability of survival. We will show that it has informational content, but that it cannot be used without modification as a right-hand variable in a model of decision making because of cognition and observation error. We will propose and estimate a model of cognition error and then apply the model to life tables and to data from AHEAD to produce usable subjective probabilities of survival.

Subjects were asked the following series of questions about the likelihood of future events:

[Using any] number from 0 to 100 where "0" means that you think there is absolutely no chance and "100" means that you think the event is absolutely sure to happen . . . What do you think are the chances that:
  1. You will have to give major financial help to family members during the next 10 years?
  2. You will receive major financial help from family members during the next 10 years?
  3. You will leave a financial inheritance?
  If the response was in the range [1, 100] a follow-up question was asked:
    a. You will leave an inheritance of at least $10,000?
  If the response was in the range [31, 100], a further follow-up question was asked:
    b. You will leave an inheritance of at least $100,000?
  4. You will move to a nursing home over the next five years?
  5. You will move during the next five years?
  6. Medical expenses will use up all your savings sometime during the next five years?
  7. Your income will keep up with inflation during the next five years?
  In the following question asked of respondents (R) of age less than 90, A is 80 for R of age less than 70, 85 for R aged 70–74, 90 for R aged 75–79, 95 for R aged 80–84, and 100 for R aged 85–89:
  8. You will live to be at least A?

The expectations questions were not asked in proxy interviews in AHEAD; we have 7,393 responses to these questions. We treat responses to these questions as if they are subjective probabilities of the events, up to possible reporting error.

The remaining variables employed in the analysis of subjective survival probabilities are quite standard, except for measures of cognitive ability. AHEAD measures cognitive status in a battery of questions that aim to test a number of domains of cognition (Herzog and Wallace 1997): learning and memory are assessed by immediate and delayed recall from a list of 10 words that were read to the subject; reasoning, orientation, and attention are assessed from serial 7s (in which the subject is asked to subtract 7 from 100, and then to continue subtracting 7 from each successive difference for a total of five subtractions), counting backward by 1, and the naming of public figures, dates, and objects. We aggregate these responses into an indicator for cognitive disability that is one if the number of correct answers to all the cognitive questions falls below a threshold level. This identifies, approximately, the lowest quartile in cognitive function.

Subjective probabilities. Subjective survival probabilities measured in the Health and Retirement Survey (HRS) provide a benchmark for AHEAD responses. The HRS subjects were aged 51–61. Average survival probabilities to age 75 were 0.65, which is very close to a weighted average from a 1990 life table of 0.68 (Hurd and McGarry 1995). The survival probabilities vary with risk factors in the same way as mortality outcomes in the population. For example, those with higher socioeconomic status (measured by education, income, or wealth) give higher survival probabilities; smokers give lower probabilities, moderate drinkers give higher probabilities than either teetotalers or heavy drinkers, and those whose parents survived to old age give higher survival probabilities. These subjective survival probabilities correlate with actual mortality experience of subgroups of the HRS population.

In the HRS subjects were asked about their probability of working past age 62 or 65. These probabilities vary with financial and job characteristics in the same way as actual retirement outcomes. For example, those with defined benefit pension plans that offer early retirement give low probabilities of working past 62, those with employer-paid retiree health insurance give low probabilities, and those on jobs where it is usual to retire early give low probabilities (Hurd and McGarry 1993). We take these results to be good evidence that the HRS respondents understood questions about subjective probabilities and gave appropriate responses. However, the AHEAD population is older and has higher levels of cognitive impairment, so it may be that its responses are less appropriate.

Table 9.1 shows the average and median survival probabilities from AHEAD and from 1992 life tables for the target ages used in the AHEAD survival question (e.g., 85 for subjects aged 70–74, 90 for subjects aged 75–79, with minor

Table 9.1   Survival Probabilities

	Target Age			
	85	90	95	100
Means				
AHEAD	0.51	0.38	0.31	0.29
Life table	0.50	0.33	0.16	0.05
Medians				
AHEAD	0.50	0.40	0.20	0.10
Life table	0.55	0.37	0.18	0.06

Source: Hoynes, Hurd, and Chand (1995).

spillover from timing of birthdays and interviews). As in the HRS, the AHEAD respondents at the younger ages (70–79) have average subjective survival probabilities that are close to averages from life tables, but at older ages the averages are substantially higher. Besides the obvious explanation that cognitive function declines with age, there are several other explanations. First, at baseline the AHEAD was a community-based survey: those in nursing homes and other institutional care facilities were excluded. Thus AHEAD represents a healthier population than is represented by life tables, with the implication that if the populations were the same the difference in survival probabilities would be reduced. Second, the questions about subjective probabilities were asked only in self-interviews, not in proxy interviews. Subjects who are interviewed by proxy have worse health, and because the frequency of proxy interviews increased with age the population of self-interviews has better health than the complete AHEAD population. Third, even among self-interviews the frequency of nonresponse to the questions about subjective probabilities increases with age, and nonrespondents have worse health than respondents.

We have not attempted any analysis of the magnitude of the bias that results from these levels of sample selection, but they could be substantial: the overall rates of nonresponse to the question about survival probabilities are 12.2, 15.2, 19.5, and 19.3 percent in our four age groups. We have no way to assess the bias resulting from the exclusion of the institutionalized population. Even with these kinds of adjustments, however, it is unlikely that in the older two age groups the means would be reduced to the levels of the life tables.

As shown in table 9.1, the medians from AHEAD and from the life tables are much closer than the means. Apparently, a few AHEAD respondents gave very high probabilities of survival, increasing the mean substantially. This is verified in figures 9.1 through 9.4, which show the distributions. The figures are noteworthy because even at advanced ages a number of respondents give survival probabilities of 1.0. Particularly in the oldest age group, even a fairly small number of such responses will increase the mean because the life table means are so small. The figures show a leftward shift with age in the distribution as is expected. But in all the age groups a large fraction of respondents give what we call focal-point responses: 0.0, 0.5, or 1.0. The prevalence of

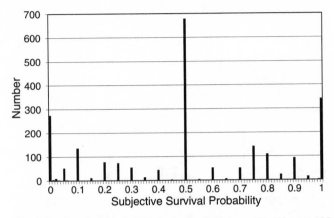

Fig. 9.1   Survival probabilities to age 85 among 70–74-year-olds

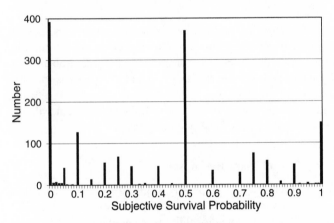

Fig. 9.2   Survival probabilities to age 90 among 75–79-year-olds

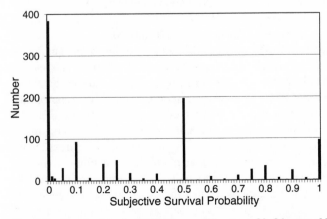

Fig. 9.3   Survival probabilities to age 95 among 80–84-year-olds

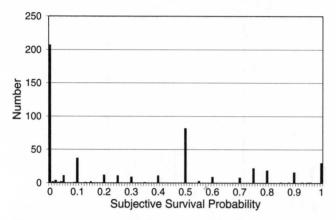

Fig. 9.4   Survival probabilities to age 100 among 85–89-year-olds

focal-point responses shows that the measure of subjective probabilities in AHEAD cannot represent the true probabilities, both because the distribution of true probabilities should be continuous and because the true probabilities cannot be literally either zero or one. A major focus of this paper is to learn about the determinants of the likelihood that a respondent will give a focal-point response and to specify and estimate a model of cognition that will account for the observed tendency for focal-point responses.

9.3   Determinants of Focal-Point Responses

In this section, we investigate the propensity to give a focal response (0.0, 0.5 or 1.0) on one or more of the eight measures of subjective probabilities. Our view is that the stated subjective probabilities, including focal responses, have informational content, but it may not be accurate to take them at face value. To investigate the question of informational content, we use as a standard of comparison the view that they are simply independent random responses to a request to name a number between 0 and 100.

Figure 9.5 shows the distribution of respondents according to the number of responses of zero to the probability questions. About 11 percent of the respondents to the subjective questions gave no zero responses, and the remainder gave a modal number of three. Of course, a response of zero can be appropriate depending on the event because some of the events have almost no stochastic element for some respondents. For example, the probability of receiving major financial help could be zero for someone with no family connections. Similarly, moving is controlled by the respondent, and the probability of moving could be close to zero. However, 59 respondents answered zero to seven of the subjective probability questions. In that the events are mostly controlled

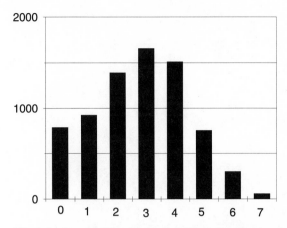

Fig. 9.5   Focal subjective probabilities: distribution by number of zeros

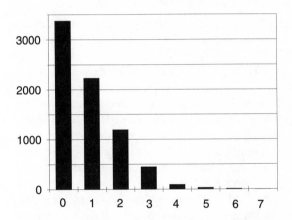

Fig. 9.6   Focal subjective probabilities: distribution by number of 0.5s

stochastic processes, with a mixture of level of control, it is hard to see how a well-informed assessment of the true probabilities could so often be zero. More likely these respondents did not understand the nature of the question or were uncooperative.

Figure 9.6 gives a similar distribution with respect to responses of 0.5. The distribution is quite different from the distribution of zeros: 51 percent gave none, and the distribution declines sharply. Thus, although there is overall a fairly high propensity to give a 0.5, it is mainly concentrated among a few respondents and to a few events. The distribution of 1.0s has a similar shape (fig. 9.7) except that the left-hand part of the distribution is heavier. For example, just 3.2 percent of the respondents gave responses of 1.0 on three or

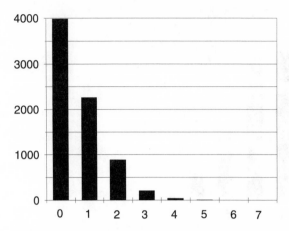

Fig. 9.7   Focal subjective probabilities: distribution by number of 1.0s

more of the subjective probabilities, whereas 7.2 percent gave responses of 0.5 on three or more. The conclusion is that the focal point of zero attracts the most responses, followed by 0.5.

The distributions of focal-point responses indicate that some individuals often give focal-point responses to the subjective probability questions, suggesting that there is an individual-level propensity to give a focal-point response that may be independent of the event that is queried. To examine this we study the probability of giving a focal-point response to the question about the likelihood of survival as a function of the number of focal-point answers given to the other questions about subjective probabilities. For example, we specify that $P(S = 0) = f(n_0)$, where $S = 0$ means the survival probability is reported to be zero and n_0 is the number of zeros on the other subjective probabilities. If the likelihood of giving a focal-point response to the survival question is independent of whether focal-point responses were given to the other subjective probability questions, we should find no relationship between n_0 and $P(S = 0)$.

Figure 9.8 shows the unconditional probability as a function of n_0. About 16 percent of the respondents report a survival probability of zero. Among those who have no zero responses on the other subjective probabilities, just 1 percent gave a zero probability of survival. The likelihood of giving a zero for the survival probability increases in the number of zeros on the other subjective probabilities, so that among those who have zeros on all six of the other subjective probabilities, 30.4 percent gave a zero on the survival probability. One possible explanation for this result is that there are individual characteristics that make the probability of all these events truly low, approaching zero. However, the nature of the questions is that some of the events are desirable and would be positively correlated with socioeconomic status and other character-

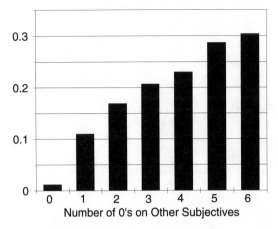

Fig. 9.8 Focal subjective responses: proportion with survival response zero

istics, and some are undesirable and would be negatively correlated. For example, a rough judgment would put them into the following classification:

Positive events
Your income will keep up with inflation during the next five years?
You will live to be at least A? (where A is the target age)
You will leave a financial inheritance?

Negative events
You will move to a nursing home in the next five years?
Medical expenses will use up all your savings sometime during the next five years?
You will have to give major financial help to family members during the next 10 years?

Neutral events
You will receive major financial help from family members during the next 10 years?
You will move during the next five years?

Someone with a small probability of using all his savings on medical expenses is likely to be in good health and to have adequate resources. Such a person is likely to have good survival chances and to leave an inheritance and, therefore, should give high probabilities to the questions about them. Indeed the raw correlation coefficient between the probability of medical expenses and the probability of survival is .13 and between medical expenses and leaving a financial inheritance is .18.

Figure 9.9 has similar results where the focal point of the survival probability is 0.5. The average frequency of giving 0.5 is about 0.21, but among those who give no 0.5s on the other subjective probability questions the frequency

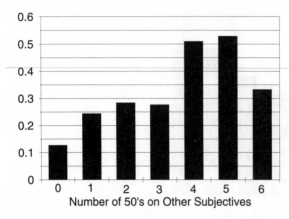

Fig. 9.9   **Focal subjective responses: proportion with survival response 0.5**

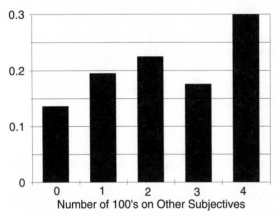

Fig. 9.10   **Focal subjective responses: proportion with survival response 1.0**

is just 0.13. It increases to 0.51 among the subjects who answered 0.5 to four other subjective probability questions. Figure 9.10 shows that the unconditional frequency of giving 1.0 as the survival probability is about 0.17. Except for the fourth entry, which is based on 19 observations, there is a monotonic increase in the frequency as the number of 1.0s given on the other subjective probability questions increases, reaching 0.3.

We interpret these results to be good evidence of an individual-level propensity to give focal-point responses. Although it seems unlikely that the patterns could be due to covariates or personal characteristics that are related to the probabilities of actual outcomes, we investigate this by a regression (logits) of the probability of giving a focal-point answer on the number of other focal-point answers (as above) and on a number of personal characteristics. That is, we estimate

Table 9.2   **Determinants of the Probability of Giving a Focal-Point Response (linear probability model for survival probabilities)**

Variable	Focal of 0.0		Focal of 0.5		Focal of 1.0	
	Coefficient	S.E.	Coefficient	S.E.	Coefficient	S.E.
Intercept	−0.026	0.025	0.215	0.024	0.159	0.020
$n = 1$	0.154	0.019	0.115	0.013	0.133	0.011
$n = 2$	0.246	0.017	0.170	0.017	0.245	0.017
$n = 3$	0.292	0.016	0.192	0.027	0.346	0.040
$n = 4$	0.308	0.016	0.258	0.051	0.381	0.075
$n = 5$	0.369	0.018	0.602	0.089		
$n = 6$	0.411	0.025	0.271	0.147		
$n = 7$	0.459	0.040	0.852	0.415		
Age						
70–74	0.019	0.020	0.026	0.020	−0.011	0.016
75–79	0.111	0.020	−0.027	0.021	−0.076	0.017
80–84	0.170	0.021	−0.063	0.022	−0.093	0.018
85–89	0.112	0.022	−0.120	0.024	−0.155	0.020
Male	−0.014	0.011	0.000	0.011	−0.001	0.010
Health						
Excellent	−0.074	0.019	−0.006	0.019	0.102	0.016
Very good	−0.058	0.014	0.000	0.015	0.040	0.012
Fair	0.073	0.014	−0.033	0.015	−0.025	0.013
Poor	0.122	0.017	−0.089	0.020	−0.032	0.017
Health change						
Better	−0.010	0.015	−0.007	0.016	0.005	0.013
Worse	0.031	0.013	−0.024	0.015	−0.024	0.013
Wealth						
Quartile 2	0.043	0.015	0.036	0.017	−0.021	0.014
Quartile 3	0.057	0.015	0.043	0.017	−0.042	0.014
Quartile 4	0.011	0.016	0.028	0.017	−0.076	0.014
Cognitive impairment	−0.026	0.011	−0.035	0.013	0.024	0.010

Source: Authors' calculations from AHEAD.

Notes: n is the number of focal points with the same value on other subjective probabilities. The reference is $n = 0$, age 65–69, female, good health, lowest wealth quartile, no cognitive impairment. S.E. = standard error.

$$P(S = 0) = f(n_0) + X\beta,$$

where X is a vector of personal characteristics. Table 9.2 shows the results of the linear regressions. The first two columns have the coefficients and standard errors from the regression of a variable that takes the value one if the subjective survival probability is zero and takes the value zero otherwise. The important regressors are categorical variables (the ns) that represent the number of zeros on the other seven subjective probabilities, age intervals, self-assessed health categories, health change, wealth quartiles, and a categorical variable that may indicate cognitive impairment.

The table shows the same pattern by n as figure 9.8: those with the fewest

Table 9.3   **Logit Probability of a Focal-Point Response (survival probabilities, base case except variable indicated)**

	Focal	
Variable	At Zero	At One
$n = 0$	0.003	0.143
$n = 1$	0.057	0.357
$n = 2$	0.103	0.509
$n = 3$	0.130	0.632
$n = 4$	0.140	0.642
$n = 5$	0.160	
$n = 6$	0.207	
$n = 7$	0.240	
Age		
65–69	0.140	0.143
70–74	0.162	0.133
75–79	0.272	0.081
80–84	0.351	0.067
85–89	0.280	0.025
Female	0.140	0.143
Male	0.130	0.140
Health		
Excellent	0.083	0.264
Very good	0.096	0.193
Good	0.140	0.143
Fair	0.206	0.110
Poor	0.267	0.096
Health change		
Better	0.134	0.148
Same	0.140	0.143
Worse	0.173	0.107
Wealth		
Quartile 1	0.140	0.143
Quartile 2	0.184	0.115
Quartile 3	0.196	0.098
Quartile 4	0.148	0.073
No cognitive impairment	0.14	0.143
Cognitive impairment	0.125	0.175

Source: Authors' calculations from AHEAD.

Note: n is the number of focal points with the same value on other subjective probabilities. The base case is $n = 0$, age 65–69, female, good health, health same, lowest wealth quartile, no cognitive impairment.

responses of zero on the other subjective probabilities have the lowest probability of having a zero subjective survival probability: for example, if someone gave zeros on all seven of the other subjective probabilities, the likelihood of giving a zero on the survival probability is 0.459 greater than if he had no zeros on the other subjective probabilities. The other covariates show reasonable patterns. The probability of giving a zero increases with age and increases both at lower levels of self-assessed health and with worsening health.

The next two columns have similar results where the left-hand variable takes the value one if the response to subjective survival is 0.5, and zero otherwise. Again the probability is strongly increasing in n, verifying the results of figure 9.9. Unlike the case when the left-hand variables indicates a zero response, we have no particular prior beliefs about the pattern with age: the likelihood of responding with a 0.5 could increase with age because of increasing cognition difficulties, but it could decrease with age because the true probability of survival (as measured by life tables) falls rapidly toward zero. Indeed, the empirical outcome is that the probability of giving a focal response of 0.5 decreases in age and in poor health status and worsening health. The last two columns have the results for a focal response of 1.0. Again the probability is increasing in n. The age pattern is as expected: the older respondents are less likely. The variation by health level and health change is consistent with our other results. Our cognitive impairment indicator shows, when viewed across the three probabilities, that having an impairment increases the likelihood of giving a focal response of 1.0 compared with a focal response of zero or 0.5. To the extent that cognitive impairment is an additional indicator of underlying health status the effect should be the opposite. That is, cognitive impairment increases the likelihood of making an objectively incorrect assessment of the probability of survival.

Table 9.3 shows fitted probabilities from logistic estimation of the same relationships. The pattern as n varies is the same as in table 9.2, but the magnitude of the variation is attenuated. Now it is quite close to the variation shown in figures 9.8 through 9.10. For example, the probability of a focal response of zero varies by about 0.21 as n varies from 0 to 6; in figure 9.8 the (unconditional) variation is 0.27. The table shows that the probabilities of focal responses vary substantially with the other covariates: as health varies from excellent to poor the likelihood of a focal response of zero increases by 0.184 whereas the likelihood of a focal response of 1.0 falls by 0.168. Having a cognitive impairment increases the likelihood of a focal response of 1.0 compared with the likelihood of a response of zero by about 0.05, which is not realistic.

9.4   A Model for Personal Survival Curves

Each individual faces a survival curve, $q(t \mid a,z,\varepsilon)$, giving the probability that remaining life will exceed t years. This curve will depend on the current age a of the individual and may depend on observed and unobserved covariates, denoted by z and ε, respectively. A rational individual who engages in life cycle planning will utilize subjective beliefs about this survival curve. For example, a life cycle optimizer who has a time-separable felicity function $u(c_a)$ of consumption at age a, a discount rate ρ, and no bequest motive and faces no uncertainty other than date of death will seek to maximize

$$\int_a^{+\infty} u(c_{a+t}) \cdot e^{-\rho t} \cdot q(t \mid a, z, \varepsilon)\, dt.$$

The survival curve q is now interpreted as the subjective belief of the individual at age a. Suppose that the covariates (z, ε) influencing these beliefs are time invariant, and that the beliefs are intertemporally consistent, so that $q(t+\tau \mid a,z,\varepsilon) = q(t \mid a,z,\varepsilon) \cdot q(\tau \mid a+t,z,\varepsilon)$. Then the optimization does not involve strategic consideration of possible changes in beliefs. The optimization is carried out subject to a given initial wealth W_a and a condition that future wealth be nonnegative. The equation of motion of wealth is

$$\nabla_t W_{a+t} = rW_{a+t} + y_{a+t} - c_{a+t},$$

where y_{a+t} is annuity income and r is the interest rate. When wealth is positive over an interval $[a,a+t)$, the optimal consumption stream satisfies

$$u'(c_a) = u'(c_{a+t}) \cdot e^{(r-\rho)t} \cdot q(t \mid a, z, \varepsilon).$$

The individual will display decreasing consumption, implying decreasing wealth, if $r - \rho - h(t \mid a,z,\varepsilon) < 0$, where $h(t \mid a,z,\varepsilon) \equiv -\nabla_t \log q(t \mid a,z,\varepsilon)$ is the mortality hazard rate. More generally, the larger $q(t \mid a,z,\varepsilon)$, the lower consumption and the larger net saving. Rising mortality hazard should then eventually lead among survivors to declining consumption and negative saving.

A standard formulation of the life cycle savings model assumes that all individuals of the same age have a *common* survival curve that coincides with national life tables, and that the individuals know this curve, so there is no variation in subjective beliefs about survival. Then a parameterization of $u(c)$ such as the constant relative risk aversion function $u(c) = c^{1-\gamma}/(1 - \gamma)$ allows the model above to be estimated from panel data. A qualitative characterization of the estimation results of Hurd (1990) and others is that there is less dissaving than might be expected with commonly assumed levels of risk aversion and no bequest motive, and substantially more variability in saving rates than a model with homogeneous preferences and survival curves would suggest. Explanations that have been offered for the relatively low rates of dissaving include strong bequest motives, high risk aversion toward the end of life, and unanticipated taste changes, due say to health, that reduce the marginal utility of consumption. Another possible explanation, which also explains some of the high variability in saving rates, is that survival curves are heterogeneous, and selection progressively removes individuals with low survival probabilities and high rates of dissaving, so that average wealth holdings of survivors do not decline rapidly with age. Heterogeneity in the degree of risk aversion and in bequest motives would also contribute to variability in saving behavior.

In this section, we start from the assumption that there is a personal survival curve known to the individual, with the econometrician observing some but not all of the covariates that personalize this curve. We will assume that questions about survival probabilities to specified ages provide information, not necessarily exact, on the personal survival curve. We use this information, plus covariates, to fit an estimated personal survival curve for each individual in the AHEAD sample. In following sections, we investigate the link between this survival curve and saving behavior.

Two critical assumptions will provide the foundation for our model of personal survival curves. First, assume the personal survival curve of an individual can be represented by a *Cox proportional hazards* survival curve at elapsed time t from initial age a,

$$q(t \mid a, v, z, \varepsilon) = \exp(-(\Lambda_v(t + a) - \Lambda_v(a))e^{z\beta - \sigma\varepsilon}),$$

where a is starting age, t is elapsed time, $\Lambda_v(a)$ is an *integrated baseline hazard* function at age a for an individual born in year v, measured starting from age zero, z are covariates, β are parameters, ε is a disturbance idiosyncratic to the individual that is normalized to have zero mean and unit variance, and σ is a scale parameter. The second critical assumption regards the perceptual and reporting errors that may enter stated subjective survival probabilities. We allow for the possibility that individuals may be systematically optimistic or pessimistic by introducing *time scale distortion,* or *accelerated failure time,* in which individuals view their personal clocks as running faster or slower than the chronological clock. We also consider the possibility of focal responses in reporting subjective probabilities. The details of these assumptions are given later.

9.4.1   The Algebra of Heterogeneous Personal Survival Curves

Selection determines the relationship between the personal survival curve $q(t \mid a, v, z, \varepsilon)$, the expected survival curve $Q(t \mid a, v, z)$ of individuals of age a with observed covariates z, and the population mean survival curve $Q(t \mid a, v)$. Let $f(\varepsilon \mid 0)$ denote the density at birth of the unobserved factor ε, and let $g(z \mid 0)$ denote the density at birth of the observed covariates z. Then

$$Q(a \mid 0, v, z) = \int q(a \mid 0, v, z, \varepsilon) f(\varepsilon \mid 0) \, d\varepsilon,$$

$$Q(a \mid 0, v) = \int Q(a \mid 0, v, z) g(z \mid 0) \, dz,$$

the density of ε among survivors of vintage v at age a, given z, is

$$f(\varepsilon \mid a, v, z) = f(\varepsilon \mid 0) \cdot q(a \mid 0, v, z, \varepsilon) / Q(a \mid 0, v, z),$$

and the density of z among survivors of vintage v at age a is

$$g(z \mid a, v) = g(z \mid 0) \cdot Q(a \mid 0, v, z) / Q(a \mid 0, v).$$

Therefore,

$$Q(t \mid a, v, z)$$

$$= \int q(a + t \mid a, v, z, \varepsilon) \cdot f(\varepsilon \mid a, v, z) \, d\varepsilon$$

$$= \int q(a + t \mid 0, v, z, \varepsilon) \cdot f(\varepsilon \mid 0) \, d\varepsilon / Q(a \mid 0, v, z)$$

$$= Q(t + a \mid 0, v, z) / Q(a \mid 0, v, z),$$

and

$$Q(t \mid a, v)$$

$$= \int Q(t \mid a, v, z) g(z \mid a, v) \, dz$$

$$= \iint q(a + t \mid 0, v, z, \varepsilon) \cdot f(\varepsilon \mid 0) \cdot g(z \mid 0) \, d\varepsilon \, dz / Q(t \mid 0, v)$$

$$= Q(t + a \mid 0, v) / Q(a \mid 0, v).$$

Let $s = e^{-\sigma \varepsilon}$, and let $k(s)$ be the density of s induced by the density $f(\varepsilon \mid 0)$; that is, $k(s) = f(-\log(s)/\sigma \mid 0)/s\sigma$. Let $\psi(r) = \int_0^{+\infty} e^{-rs} \cdot k(s) \, ds$ be the Laplace transform of k. Then

$$Q(a \mid 0, v, z) = \int_{-\infty}^{+\infty} f(\varepsilon \mid 0) \cdot \exp(-\Lambda_v(a)e^{z\beta - \sigma\varepsilon}) \, d\varepsilon$$

$$= \int_0^{+\infty} k(s) \cdot \exp(-\Lambda_v(a)e^{z\beta}s) \, ds = \psi(\Lambda_v(a)e^{z\beta}).$$

The density of s given a, z then satisfies

$$k(s \mid a, v, z) = k(s) \cdot \exp(-\Lambda_v(a)e^{z\beta}s)/\psi(\Lambda_v(a)e^{z\beta}).$$

The moment-generating function $m(r)$ for the density $k(s \mid a, v, qz)$ is

$$m(r) = \mathbf{E}\{e^{rs} \mid a, v, z\} = \psi(\Lambda_v(a)e^{z\beta} - r)/\psi(\Lambda_v(a)e^{z\beta}).$$

From this, $\mathbf{E}\{s \mid a, z\} = -\psi'(\Lambda_v(a)e^{z\beta})/\psi(\Lambda_v(a)e^{z\beta})$ and one has the moments

$$\mathbf{E}\{\log q(t \mid a, v, z, \varepsilon) \mid a, v, z\} = [\Lambda_v(t + a) - \Lambda_v(a)] \cdot e^{z\beta} \cdot \frac{\psi'(\Lambda_v(a)e^{z\beta})}{\psi(\Lambda_v(a)e^{z\beta})},$$

$$\mathbf{V}\{\log q(t \mid a, v, z, \varepsilon) \mid a, v, z\} = [\Lambda_v(t + a) - \Lambda_v(a)]^2 \cdot e^{2z\beta} \cdot \mathbf{M}(z),$$

with

$$\mathbf{M}(z) \equiv \frac{\psi''(\Lambda_v(a)e^{z\beta})}{\psi(\Lambda_v(a)e^{z\beta})} - \left(\frac{\psi'(\Lambda_v(a)e^{z\beta})}{\psi(\Lambda_v(a)e^{z\beta})}\right).$$

Similarly, let $\tau = e^{z\beta - \sigma\varepsilon}$, and let $j(\tau)$ be its density induced by the joint density $f(\varepsilon \mid 0) \cdot g(z \mid 0)$ of ε and z; that is,

$$j(\tau) = \frac{1}{\sigma\tau}\int f\left(\frac{z\beta - \log(\tau)}{\sigma}\bigg|0\right) \cdot g(z|0)\,dz.$$

Let $\vartheta(r)$ denote the Laplace transform of j. Then

$$Q(a|0, v) = \int_{-\infty}^{+\infty}\int_{-\infty}^{+\infty} f(\varepsilon|0)g(z|0) \cdot \exp(-\Lambda_v(a)e^{z\beta - \sigma\varepsilon})\,d\varepsilon\,dz$$

$$= \int_0^{+\infty} j(\tau) \cdot \exp(-\Lambda_v(a)\tau)\,d\tau = \vartheta(\Lambda_v(a))$$

and

$$Q(t|a, v) = Q(t + a|0, v)/Q(a|0, v) = \vartheta(\Lambda_v(a + t))/\vartheta(\Lambda_v(a)).$$

Summarizing, selection thins the left tail of $f(\varepsilon \mid a,v,z)$ relative to the right tail, as individuals with unfavorable draws of ε die out. As a result, $Q(t \mid a,v,z)$ declines less rapidly with t than does $q(t \mid a,v,z,\varepsilon)$ for any fixed ε. Similarly, selection thins the regions of z that elevate mortality risk, so that $Q(t \mid a,v)$ declines less rapidly with t than does $Q(t \mid a,v,z)$ for any fixed z. Further, selection induces a correlation of ε and z, so that combinations of z that elevate mortality risk are among survivors positively associated with ε. A completely consistent analysis of personal mortality risk that combines individual data and life table data for persons of different ages has to handle these selection effects. We do this by parameterizing $j(\tau)$.

A fundamental identification question is what can be learned about $\Lambda_v(a)$ in the presence of the unknown function ϑ. For any increasing function $\rho(r)$ such that $\vartheta(\rho(r))$ continues to have the properties of a Laplace transform, one clearly cannot distinguish the model with ϑ and $\Lambda_v(a)$ from the model with ϑ^* and $\Lambda_v^*(a)$ that satisfies $\vartheta^*(r) = \vartheta(\rho(r))$ and $\Lambda_v^*(a) = \rho^{-1}(\Lambda_v(a))$. Consequently, any econometric specification that attempts to estimate $\Lambda_v(a)$ nonparametrically in combination with a parameterization of ϑ that allows monotonically varying alternatives must fail.

With this limitation in mind, we consider the parametric assumption that τ has the gamma density $j(\tau) = \omega^\omega\tau^{\omega-1}e^{-\omega\tau}/\Gamma(\omega)$ with mean one and variance $1/\omega$. The Laplace transform of this density is $\vartheta(r) = (1 + r/\omega)^{-\omega}$. Consider a quadratic spline approximation to $\Lambda_v(a)$:

$$\Lambda_v(a) = \alpha_0 a + \sum_{i=1}^{I}\alpha_{i0}\mathbf{1}(a > A_i)(a - A_i)^2 + \sum_{j=1}^{J}\alpha_{0j}(v - V_j)$$

$$+ \sum_{i=1}^{I}\sum_{j=1}^{J}\alpha_{ij}\mathbf{1}(a > A_i)\mathbf{1}(v > V_j)(a - A_i)^2(v - V_j),$$

where the αs are parameters, the A_i are ages at five-year intervals defined so there are life table sample points below the lowest and above the highest A_i, and the V_j are vintages at 20-year intervals defined so there are life tables for vintages below the lowest and above the highest V_j. This form then yields a piecewise linear drift in hazard rates with vintage and with age. The estimation task is then to use life tables for different ages and vintages to determine the relationship

$$
Q(a|0,v) = \begin{cases} [1 + \Lambda_v(a)/\omega]^{-\omega} & \text{if } \omega > 0, \\ \exp(-\Lambda_v(a)) & \text{if } \omega = 0. \end{cases}
$$

Recognizing that this model corresponds to a Box-Cox transformation,

$$
\frac{Q(a|0,v)^{-\omega} - 1}{\omega} = \Lambda_v(a) + \xi,
$$

a computationally efficient way to carry out the estimation is by pseudomaximum likelihood, treating the disturbance ξ as normal. The results of this estimation are that the likelihood is maximized over the interval $\omega \geq 0$ consistent with the Laplace transform at the boundary value $\omega = 0$, corresponding to an absence of unobserved heterogeneity. In light of the previous discussion of identification, this provides no real evidence for or against the presence of heterogeneity in mortality hazard, but rather indicates that the spline approximation to the integrated hazard is sufficiently flexible to capture the effects of heterogeneity, so that the additional parameter ω is not needed to characterize the life tables. In the subsequent analysis, we use the fitted baseline integrated hazard function obtained from the regression of log $Q(a \mid 0,v)$ on $\Lambda_v(a)$. Keep in mind that this characterization then includes the average effect of population heterogeneity.

9.4.2   Subjective Survival Probabilities

If an individual knows that he or she has a personal survival curve given by the Cox proportional hazards form, with known covariates z and ε, and with the baseline integrated hazard $\Lambda_v(a)$, and is fully rational, then this curve will enter life cycle savings decisions and may also provide the basis for reported subjective survival probabilities. Alternatively, individuals may not be fully rational and instead may be systematically optimistic or pessimistic about survival. We will parameterize this by allowing individuals to distort the scale of chronological time. An individual of age a who contemplates survival for an interval t is assumed to convert this to an equivalent value

$$
T_a(t) = (t + 1)^{\alpha_1 + \alpha_2 \cdot a} - 1,
$$

where α_1 and α_2 are parameters. This equivalent value will replace the chronological interval t in the subjective survival curve. If $\alpha_1 = 1$ and $\alpha_2 = 0$, there is no systematic bias about survival. If $\alpha_1 + \alpha_2 \cdot a < 1$, then individuals are systematically optimistic, underestimating mortality risk over a time interval t. If $\alpha_2 < 0$, then individuals become more optimistic as they age. This specification is a parametric specialization of what is termed an accelerated failure time model.

Time scale distortion may appear in individuals' beliefs if they are not fully rational and may influence behavior. Thus, a systematically optimistic individual will be reluctant to dissave, since wealth will have to be spread over a long anticipated remaining life. However, time scale distortion may be more superficial, affecting responses to survey questions on mortality without altering beliefs. Context and framing effects appear in survey responses much less personal than survival and seem to be related to the persona individuals choose to project as well as to psychometric illusions. It is not difficult to imagine that these effects could distort reported survival probabilities. Analysis of subsequent waves of the AHEAD panel should reveal the extent to which systematic distortion in stated survival probabilities infects behavior.

Suppose the subjective probability p^* of surviving for elapsed time τ is known for an individual. Then $p^* = \exp(-(\Lambda_v(a + T_a(\tau)) - \Lambda_v(a))e^{z\beta - \sigma\varepsilon})$ determines

$$\sigma\varepsilon = -\log(-\log p^*) + z\beta + \log(\Lambda_v(a + T_a(\tau)) - \Lambda_v(a)).$$

Substituting this in the survival curve,

$$q(t\,|\,a, p^*) = (p^*)^{\left[\frac{\Lambda_v(a + T_a(t)) - \Lambda_v(a)}{\Lambda_v(a + T_a(\tau)) - \Lambda_v(a)}\right]}.$$

In subsequent analysis, we shall assume that the density at birth of the unobserved factor $s = e^{-\sigma\varepsilon}$ is gamma with mean one and variance $1/\kappa$, so that the subjective probability p^* of survival over elapsed time τ satisfies

$$V \equiv \mathbf{E}\{\log p^*\,|\,a, z\} = -[\Lambda_v(a + T_a(\tau)) - \Lambda_v(a)] \cdot e^{z\beta} \cdot \kappa/[\kappa + \Lambda_v(a)e^{z\beta}],$$

$$\lambda^2 \equiv \mathbf{V}\{\log p^*\,|\,a, z\} = [\Lambda_v(a + T_a(\tau)) - \Lambda_v(a)]^2 \cdot e^{2z\beta} \cdot \kappa/[\kappa + \Lambda_v(a)e^{z\beta}]^2.$$

Note that this distributional assumption on s is distinct from, although consistent with, the earlier assumption that the entire proportional hazard term in the Cox survival function at birth had a gamma distribution. In particular, if the integrated hazard function were free of the effects of heterogeneity, then one would expect the parameter κ in the formula above to be larger than the parameter ω in the formula for the life table probabilities. However, lack of identification makes this consistency check impossible.

If the subjective probability p^* were observed without error, then the nonlinear regression equation

$$-\log p^* = V - \lambda\xi$$

$$\equiv [\Lambda_v(a + T_a(\tau)) - \Lambda_v(a)] \cdot e^{\beta_0 + z_1\beta_1} \cdot \kappa/[\kappa + \Lambda_v(a)e^{z\beta}] - \lambda\xi,$$

which has $\mathbf{E}\xi = 0$ and $\mathbf{E}\xi^2 = 1$ by construction, could be used to estimate the parameters α, β, and κ. Note that positive ξ is associated with larger survival probabilities.

9.4.3   Reporting Errors

We anticipate that stated subjective probabilities p will deviate from true (latent) subjective probabilities p^* due to two types of reporting errors, in addition to systematic time distortion, which may be a reporting effect. First, we observe concentrations of responses at the focal points 0, 1/2, and 1 that appear to be the result of gross classification behavior by respondents. Second, there may be reporting noise in nonfocal responses. We now describe a model that includes these reporting errors. The model allows for the possibility of correlated unobserved factors that influence both the latent survival probability and the propensity to give focal responses. Small p^* is associated with V large positive, and hence with ε large negative. There is a latent selection model

$$w^* = z\gamma + \rho\xi + \sqrt{1 - \rho^2}\,v$$

that determines whether the individual gives a continuous nonfocal response or a focal response; ρ is a parameter that permits unobserved factors to influence both "frailty" and the propensity to give a focal response. If $w^* > 0$, then the individual reports a continuous response p that satisfies

$$v \equiv -\log p = V - \lambda\xi + \delta\eta$$

$$\equiv [\Lambda_v(a + T_a(\tau)) - \Lambda_v(a)] \cdot e^{z\beta} \cdot \kappa/[\kappa + \Lambda_v(a)e^{z\beta}] - \lambda\xi + \delta\eta,$$

where η is a disturbance arising from reporting noise that is assumed to have mean zero and variance one and δ is a scale parameter. If $w^* \leq 0$, then the individual reports a focal response determined by threshold parameters ψ_0 and ψ_1, with $\psi_0 \leq \psi_1$ and

$$p = \begin{cases} 0 & \text{if } v^* > -\psi_0, \\ 1/2 & \text{if } -\psi_0 \geq v^* \geq -\psi_1, \\ 1 & \text{if } v^* < -\psi_1. \end{cases}$$

For further analysis, the disturbances ξ, v, and η are assumed to be independent standard normal. Note that this specification for ξ is an approximation that cannot be exact because of the effects of selection. However, since the true ξ matches the first two moments of the standard normal, we expect this approximation to have no effect on the consistency of parameters estimated by nonlinear least squares and do not believe it will have any significant economic effect on the final estimated survival curves.

9.4.4   Selection of Focal versus Nonfocal Response

The marginal probability of a focal response, given z, is

$$P(w^* \leq 0 | z) = \Phi(-z\gamma).$$

Then, defining d_+ to be an indicator for a nonfocal response, the marginal log likelihood for selection between focal versus nonfocal responses is

$$l_s = d_+ \cdot \log \Phi(z\gamma) + (1 - d_+) \cdot \log \Phi(-z\gamma).$$

The Likelihood of a Nonfocal Response

Given ε, a nonfocal response $v = -\log p$ is observed if $v > -(z\gamma + \rho\xi)/\sqrt{1 - \rho^2}$ and $\eta = (v - V - \lambda\xi)/\delta$. Unconditioning ξ, the density of a nonfocal response v is then

$$\int_{-\infty}^{+\infty} \phi(\xi) \cdot \Phi\left(\frac{z\gamma + \rho\xi}{\sqrt{1 - \rho^2}}\right) \cdot \frac{1}{\delta} \cdot \phi\left(\frac{v - V - \lambda\xi}{\delta}\right) d\xi$$

$$= \frac{1}{\sqrt{\lambda^2 + \delta^2}} \cdot \phi\left(\frac{v - V}{\sqrt{\lambda^2 + \delta^2}}\right) \cdot \Phi\left(\frac{z\gamma\sqrt{\lambda^2 + \delta^2} - \rho\lambda(v - V)}{\sqrt{(1 - \rho^2)\lambda^2 + \rho^2\delta^2}}\right).$$

Then, the log density of p, conditioned on a, τ, z, and a nonfocal response, is

$$l_N = -\log\left(p \cdot \Phi(z\gamma) \cdot \sqrt{\lambda^2 + \delta^2}\right) - \log(-\log p)$$

$$- \frac{1}{2}\left[\frac{v - V}{\sqrt{\lambda^2 + \delta^2}}\right]^2 + \log \Phi\left(\frac{z\gamma\sqrt{\lambda^2 + \delta^2} - \rho\lambda V}{\sqrt{(1 - \rho^2)\lambda^2 + \rho^2\delta^2}}\right).$$

When $\rho = 0$, this log density simplifies to

$$l_N = -\log\sqrt{\lambda^2 + \delta^2} - \log p - \log(-\log p) - \frac{1}{2}\left[\frac{v - V}{\sqrt{\lambda^2 + \delta^2}}\right]^2.$$

In this case, consistent asymptotically normal estimates of the parameters are obtained by computing nonlinear least squares estimates for the regression

$$-\log p = [(\Lambda_v(a + T_a(\tau)) - \Lambda_v(a)] \cdot e^{z\beta} \cdot \kappa/[\kappa + \Lambda_v(a)e^{z\beta}] + \zeta,$$

ignoring heteroscedasticity, then retrieving estimated residuals $\hat{\zeta}$ and fitted values $\hat{V}$, and finally applying ordinary least squares to the regression

$$\hat{\zeta}^2 = \hat{V}^2/\kappa + \delta^2 + \varphi,$$

where φ is a mean zero disturbance. The consistency of this procedure does not require that the disturbances ζ be normal.

If $\rho \neq 0$ and ξ, v are standard normal, a Heckman-type consistent estimator of β, γ, α, and κ can be obtained by considering

$$\mathbf{E}_N(-\log p) = V - \lambda \cdot \mathbf{E}\{\xi | w^* > 0\}$$

$$= [\Lambda_v(a + T_a(\tau)) - \Lambda_v(a)] \cdot e^{z\beta} \cdot \kappa/[\kappa + \Lambda_v(a)e^{z\beta}]$$

$$- \rho\lambda \cdot \phi(z\gamma)/\Phi(z\gamma),$$

where $\mathbf{E}_N$ denotes an expectation conditioned on nonfocal response. Recalling that $\lambda^2 = V^2/\kappa$, the regression can be rewritten

$$-\log p = V \cdot [1 - (\rho/\sqrt{\kappa}) \cdot \phi(z\gamma)/\Phi(z\gamma)] + \zeta.$$

The inverse Mills ratio term in this regression comes from

$$(v | w^*) \sim N(V - \rho\lambda(w^* - z\gamma), \delta^2 + (1 - \rho^2)\lambda^2),$$

and $\mathbf{E}\{w^* - z\gamma | w^* > 0) = \phi(z\gamma)/\Phi(z\gamma)$. Calculation of the variance yields

$$\mathbf{V}(v | w^* > 0) = \delta^2 + V^2/\kappa + V^2(\rho^2/\kappa) \cdot \frac{\phi(z\gamma)}{\Phi(z\gamma)} \cdot \left[z\gamma - \frac{\phi(z\gamma)}{\Phi(z\gamma)} \right].$$

A consistent test of $\rho = 0$ can be carried out using the T-statistic on the term $\rho/\sqrt{\kappa}$ in the second term of the regression; a White robust estimator for the standard errors is used in calculating this statistic since the equation is heteroscedastic.

The Likelihood of a Focal Response

We next obtain the conditional log likelihood of an observed focal point p, given a focal response. Define the expressions

$$b_0 = \sqrt{\kappa}(1 + \psi_0/V), \qquad A_0 = \Phi(b_0),$$

$$b_1 = \sqrt{\kappa}(1 + \psi_1/V), \qquad A_1 = \Phi(b_1),$$

$$A_3 = 1 - A_1, \qquad A_4 = A_1 - A_0.$$

The probability of the event $w^* \leq 0$ and $V > -\psi_0$, or a response $p = 0$, conditioned on the event of a focal response, is

$$P_0 = \int_{-\infty}^{b_0} \phi(\varepsilon) \cdot \Phi\left(\frac{-z\gamma - \rho\xi}{\sqrt{1 - \rho^2}} \right) d\varepsilon / \Phi(-z\gamma)$$

$$= A_0 \cdot \int_0^1 \Phi\left(\frac{-z\gamma - \rho\Phi^{-1}(t A_0)}{\sqrt{1 - \rho^2}} \right) / \Phi(-z\gamma) dt.$$

When $\rho = 0$, this probability reduces to $P_0 = A_0$. The second form of the integral, obtained by the transformation of variables $t = \Phi(\varepsilon)/A_0$, is convenient for numerical integration.

Similarly, the probability of the event $w^* \leq 0$ and $V < -\psi_1$, or focal response $p = 1$, conditioned on the event of a focal response, is

$$P_1 = \int_{b_1}^{+\infty} \phi(\varepsilon) \cdot \Phi\left(\frac{-z\gamma - \rho\varepsilon}{\sqrt{1 - \rho^2}}\right) d\varepsilon / \Phi(-z\gamma)$$

$$= A_3 \cdot \int_0^1 \Phi\left(\frac{-z\gamma - \rho\Phi^{-1}(A_1 + A_3 t)}{\sqrt{1 - \rho^2}}\right) / \Phi(-z\gamma) \, dt,$$

which reduces to $P_1 = A_3$ when $\rho = 0$.

Finally, the probability of the event $w^* \leq 0$ and $-\psi_0 \geq V \geq -\psi_1$, or focal response $p = 1/2$, conditioned on the event of a focal response, is

$$P_{1/2} = \int_{b_0}^{b_1} \phi(\varepsilon) \cdot \Phi\left(\frac{-z\gamma - \rho\varepsilon}{\sqrt{1 - \rho^2}}\right) d\varepsilon / \Phi(-z\gamma)$$

$$= A_4 \cdot \int_0^1 \Phi\left(\frac{-z\gamma - \rho\Phi^{-1}(A_0 + A_4 t)}{\sqrt{1 - \rho^2}}\right) / \Phi(-z\gamma) \, dt,$$

which reduces to $P_{1/2} = A_4$ when $\rho = 0$.

Let d_0, $d_{1/2}$, and d_1 be indicators for the events that observed p takes on the focal point values 0, 1/2, and 1, respectively. Then the conditional log likelihood of the observed focal point, given a focal response, is

$$I_f = d_0 \cdot \log P_0 + d_1 \cdot \log P_1 + d_{1/2} \cdot \log P_{1/2}.$$

When $\rho = 0$, this is an ordered probit model.

9.4.5 Prediction of Personal Survival Curves

The final step of the analysis, once the parameters of the model are estimated, is to estimate a subjective personal survival curve for each sample person. It is convenient to work with the log of the survival curve. Recall that

$$\log q(t \mid a, v, z, p) = \frac{\Lambda_v(a + T_a(t)) - \Lambda_v(a)}{\Lambda_v(a + T_a(\tau)) - \Lambda_v(a)} \cdot \log p^*.$$

To forecast this quantity, we replace $\log p^*$ by its expectation, given z and given the stated subjective probability p. For the alternative that time distortion is interpreted as pure reporting error, $T_a(t)$ in this formula would be replaced by t. Consider the case $\rho = 0$. First consider nonfocal respondents. The conditional distribution of $-\log p^*$ given v is normal with mean $(\delta^2 V + \lambda^2 v)/(\lambda^2 + \delta^2)$ and variance $\lambda^2 \delta^2/(\lambda^2 + \delta^2)$. Then the predicted personal survival curve is given by

$$-\log \hat{q}(t \mid a, v, z, p) = \frac{\Lambda_v(a + T_a(t)) - \Lambda_v(a)}{\Lambda_v(a + T_a(\tau)) - \Lambda_v(a)} \cdot \frac{\delta^2 V + \lambda^2 v}{\lambda^2 + \delta^2}.$$

It is of interest to single out two extreme cases. If $\delta = 0$, there is no reporting noise in nonfocal responses, and they identify the individual ξ effects. Then

$$\log \hat{q}(t \,|\, a, v, z, p) = \frac{\Lambda_v(a + T_a(t)) - \Lambda_v(a)}{\Lambda_v(a + T_a(\tau)) - \Lambda_v(a)} \cdot \log p.$$

Alternatively, if $\lambda = 0$, corresponding to $\kappa = +\infty$, and the disturbance in the regression that maximizes I_N is due to pure reporting noise, then

$$-\log \hat{q}(t \,|\, a, v, z, p) = [\Lambda_v(a + T_a(\tau)) - \Lambda_v(a)] \cdot e^{z\beta}.$$

Finally, consider focal respondents in the case $\rho = 0$. These individuals have

$$\mathbf{E}\{\xi \,|\, p, z\} = \frac{1}{P_p} \int_{b'(p)}^{b''(p)} \xi \phi(\xi) d\xi = -\frac{\phi(b''(p)) - \phi(b'(p))}{\Phi(b''(p)) - \Phi(b'(p))},$$

where $b'(p)$ and $b''(p)$ are the bounds giving the focal response p, so that $(b'(p), b''(p))$ is $(-\infty, b_0)$ for $p = 0$, (b_0, b_1) for $p = 1/2$, and $(b_1, +\infty)$ for $p = 1$. Then, for focal responses, the estimated personal survival curve is

$$-\log \hat{q}(t \,|\, a, v, z, p) = \frac{\Lambda_v(a + T_a(t)) - \Lambda_v(a)}{\Lambda_v(a + T_a(\tau)) - \Lambda_v(a)}$$

$$\cdot V\left[1 + \frac{1}{\sqrt{\kappa}} \cdot \frac{\phi(b''(p)) - \phi(b'(p))}{\Phi(b''(p)) - \Phi(b'(p))}\right].$$

In the case of pure reporting noise, $\kappa = +\infty$, this formula reduces to the same estimated proportional hazards model that applied to the nonfocal respondents. Thus, in the case of pure reporting noise and $\rho = 0$, the stated survival probabilities are used only to calibrate the proportional hazards model in observable covariates.

Finally, consider prediction of personal survival curves when $\rho \neq 0$. First consider nonfocal respondents. The joint density of $-\log p^*$, v, and w^* is

$$\begin{bmatrix} -\log p^* \\ v \\ w^* \end{bmatrix} \sim N\left(\begin{bmatrix} V \\ V \\ z\gamma \end{bmatrix}, \begin{bmatrix} \lambda^2 & \lambda^2 & -\rho\lambda \\ \lambda^2 & \delta^2 + \lambda^2 & -\rho\lambda \\ -\rho\lambda & -\rho\lambda & 1 \end{bmatrix}\right).$$

Then

$$(-\log p^* \,|\, v, w^*)$$

$$\sim N\left(\frac{\delta^2 V + \lambda^2(1 - \rho^2)v}{\delta^2 + \lambda^2(1 - \rho^2)} - \frac{\rho\lambda\delta^2(w^* - z\gamma)}{\delta^2 + \lambda^2(1 - \rho^2)}, \frac{\lambda^2\delta^2(1 - \rho^2)}{\delta^2 + \lambda^2(1 - \rho^2)}\right).$$

Then the predicted survival curve is given by

$$-\log \hat{q}(t \,|\, a, v, z, p)$$

$$= \frac{\Lambda_v(a + T_a(t)) - \Lambda_v(a)}{\Lambda_v(a + T_a(\tau)) - \Lambda_v(a)} \cdot \left(\frac{\delta^2 V + \lambda^2(1 - \rho^2)v}{\lambda^2(1 - \rho^2) + \delta^2} + \frac{\rho\lambda\delta^2\phi(-z\gamma)/\Phi(-z\gamma)}{\delta^2 + \lambda^2(1 - \rho^2)}\right).$$

For focal respondents, $-\log p^* = V - \lambda\xi$, so that

$$E\{\xi | w^* \leq 0, b'(p) \leq -\log p^* \leq b''(p)\}$$

$$= \Phi(-z\gamma) \cdot \int_{b'(p)}^{b''(p)} \xi \cdot \phi(\xi) \cdot \Phi\left(\frac{z\gamma - \rho\xi}{\sqrt{1 - \rho^2}}\right) d\xi / P_p \equiv \frac{V}{\sqrt{\kappa}} \cdot e_p$$

with

$$e_p = \frac{1}{P_p \cdot \Phi(z\gamma)} \cdot$$

$$\left\{ \phi(b''(p)) \cdot \Phi\left(\frac{-z\gamma - \rho b''(p)}{\sqrt{1 - \rho^2}}\right) - \phi(b'(p)) \cdot \Phi\left(\frac{-z\gamma - \rho b'(p)}{\sqrt{1 - \rho^2}}\right) \right.$$

$$\left. -\rho \cdot \phi\left(-z\gamma\sqrt{1 - \rho^2}\right) \cdot \left[\Phi\left(\frac{b''(p) + z\gamma\rho}{\sqrt{1 - \rho^2}}\right) - \Phi\left(\frac{b'(p) + z\gamma\rho}{\sqrt{1 - \rho^2}}\right) \right] \right\}.$$

The numerical integration formulas introduced for this case are required for evaluation of the denominator in this expression. Then

$$-\log \hat{q}(t | a, v, z, p) = \frac{\Lambda_v(a + T_a(t)) - \Lambda_v(a)}{\Lambda_v(a + T_a(\tau)) - \Lambda_v(a)} \cdot V \cdot \left(1 - \frac{e_p}{\sqrt{\kappa}}\right).$$

9.5   Estimation Results

This section gives estimates of the model developed in section 9.4. Table 9.4 describes the covariates used in this analysis and gives their descriptive statistics. The estimates for the binomial probit model for focal response are given in table 9.5. Effects that increase the propensity for a focal response have positive coefficients. We find that cognitive disability, fair or poor health, unmarried status, and missing data on other subjective probability questions are all associated with significantly higher propensities to give a focal response, and high wealth and education are associated with a significantly lower propensity. Thus, focal responses appear to be associated with a lack of aptitude for, or interest in, the survey.

Table 9.6 reports the results of estimating the regression model

$$-\log p = [\Lambda_v(a + T_a(\tau)) - \Lambda_v(a)] \cdot e^{z\beta} \cdot \kappa/[\kappa + \Lambda_v(a)e^{z\beta}] + \zeta$$

on the subsample of individuals who do *not* report a focal response of 0, 1/2, or 1. The integrated hazard function Λ_v is the quadratic spline approximation to life tables, quadratic in age with linear drift, as discussed earlier, with separate curves for males and females. A negative coefficient in this table is associ-

Table 9.4   **Definitions of Explanatory Variables**

Mnemonic	Description	Sample Mean	Sample Standard Deviation	Sample Maximum	Sample Minimum
MALE	Sex of respondent (male = 1, female = 0)	0.3717	0.4833	0.0000	1.0000
COGN	Indicator for cognitive disability	0.2860	0.4519	0.0000	1.0000
BLACKS	Race of respondent (black = 1, nonblack = 0)	0.1062	0.3081	0.0000	1.0000
HEXCEL	Indicator for self-reported excellent health	0.1210	0.3262	0.0000	1.0000
HVGOOD	Indicator for self-reported very good health	0.2510	0.4336	0.0000	1.0000
HGOOD	Indicator for self-reported good health (omitted category)	0.3128	0.4636	0.0000	1.0000
HFAIR	Indicator for self-reported fair health	0.2147	0.4106	0.0000	1.0000
HPOOR	Indicator for self-reported poor health	0.1005	0.3007	0.0000	1.0000
HBETTER	Indicator for improvement in health, last two years	0.1357	0.3425	0.0000	1.0000
HSAME	Indicator for no change in health, last two years (omitted category)	0.6757	0.4681	0.0000	1.0000
HWORSE	Indicator for decline in health, last two years	0.1886	0.3912	0.0000	1.0000
COLLEGE	Indicator for college graduate	0.3018	0.4591	0.0000	1.0000
PAPAGE	Father's (expected) age at death PAPAGE1 = PAPAGE*MALE, PAPAGE0 = PAPAGE*(1 − MALE)	74.0691	15.9661	18.0000	109.0000
MOMAGE	Mother's (expected) age at death MOMAGE1 = MOMAGE*MALE, MOMAGE0 = MOMAGE*(1 − MALE)	72.0878	14.8299	20.0000	107.1111

		Mean	SD	Min	Max
SMNOW	Indicator for smoker now	0.1088	0.3114	0.0000	1.0000
SMOLD	Indicator for previous smoker	0.4379	0.4962	0.0000	1.0000
MARRIED	Indicator for married	0.5731	0.4947	0.0000	1.0000
NURSE	Subjective probability of nursing home admission	13.0966	22.5391	0.0000	100.0000
MEDX	Subjective probability of major medical expenditures	26.0126	31.7783	0.0000	100.0000
INFLAT	Subjective probability of income lagging inflation	35.2017	34.7054	0.0000	100.0000
NURSMIS	Missing nursing home response	0.0656	0.2477	0.0000	1.0000
MEDXMIS	Missing medical expenditure response	0.0932	0.2907	0.0000	1.0000
INFLAMIS	Missing inflation response	0.0961	0.2948	0.0000	1.0000
WQUART2	Indicator for 25–50 percent wealth quartile	0.2281	0.4196	0.0000	1.0000
WQUART3	Indicator for 50–75 percent wealth quartile	0.2769	0.4475	0.0000	1.0000
WQUART4	Indicator for 75–100 percent wealth quartile	0.3315	0.4708	0.0000	1.0000
AGE1	Age/70	1.0780	0.0871	0.5429	1.2857
AGE2	$(AGE1)^2$	1.1697	0.1861	0.2947	1.6531
AGE3	$(AGE1)^3$	1.2771	0.3026	0.1600	2.1254

Note: Sample size = 6,139.

Table 9.5   Binomial Probit Model for Focal Response

Variable	Coefficient	Standard Error	T-Statistic
Constant	4.5812	6.1242	0.748
MALE	−0.2286	0.2288	−0.999
COGN	0.0241	0.0112	2.147
BLACKS	−0.0838	0.0550	−1.523
HEXCEL	0.0218	0.0558	0.391
HVGOOD	−0.0470	0.0437	−1.077
HFAIR	0.0945	0.0468	2.017
HPOOR	0.2172	0.0643	3.377
HBETTER	0.0139	0.0490	0.283
HWORSE	0.0543	0.0467	1.161
COLLEGE	−0.1238	0.0379	−3.261
PAPAGE1	−0.0011	0.0017	−0.632
PAPAGE0	−0.0014	0.0013	−1.088
MOMAGE1	0.0010	0.0018	0.531
MOMAGE0	−0.0015	0.0014	−1.092
SMNOW	−0.0014	0.0561	−0.025
SMOLD	0.0253	0.0371	0.682
MARRIED	−0.0921	0.0400	−2.305
NURSE	−0.0001	0.0008	−0.150
MEDX	−0.0006	0.0006	−1.038
INFLAT	−0.0002	0.0005	−0.308
NURSMIS	−0.0424	0.0730	−0.581
MEDXMIS	0.1798	0.0659	2.730
INFLAMIS	0.1518	0.0637	2.384
WQUART2	−0.0196	0.0502	−0.391
WQUART3	−0.0443	0.0512	−0.866
WQUART4	−0.1807	0.0569	−3.178
AGE1	−11.9112	18.5949	−0.641
AGE2	11.3407	18.6604	0.608
AGE3	−3.38169	6.18114	−0.547
Focal response (%)	59.6		
N	6,144		
Log likelihood	−4,095.87		

Notes: Dependent variable: focal = 1, nonfocal = 0. Estimation method is maximum likelihood estimation.

ated with lower mortality hazard and a higher subjective probability of survival. We estimate this model both with and without a correction term for selection, which involves an inverse Mills ratio. Overall, we find a strong relationship between personal survival probabilities and covariates, generally in the expected direction. We find that males are more optimistic than females. Blacks are more optimistic than nonblacks. Married individuals are slightly more optimistic than nonmarried ones. This may reflect both the objective fact that married individuals live longer and in many cases the impact on optimism of the death of a spouse. We do not find a significant relationship between optimism about survival and either an index of cognition or an index of education. There is a strongly significant relationship between self-rated health status and survival expectations: those with better than good health (the omitted category) have sharply higher subjective probabilities, and those in worse than good health have sharply lower subjective probabilities. Changes in health status also influence optimism in the expected directions. Improvements in health status make respondents significantly more optimistic; declines in health status go the other way, but they are not statistically significant.

Conventional wisdom is that individuals weigh the longevity of the same-sex parent heavily in forming their own survival expectations. We include the age of death of father and mother or, if surviving, the expected age of death conditioned on the age attained, calculated from standard life tables. These variables are interacted with the sex of the respondent; then PAPAGE1 and MOMAGE0 are the same-sex parental longevity variables. In all cases, greater parental longevity is associated with greater optimism. However, the only statistically significant effect is that female optimism is higher when father's longevity is higher. These results then do not support the conventional wisdom on the effects of parental longevity.

If the individual has been a smoker in the past, or is a smoker now, then the subjective survival probability is lower. However, the effects are not statistically significant. These results go in the direction of clinical evidence, but do not appear to be strong enough to account rationally for the effect of smoking. This suggests that denial of mortality risk, or an attitude of imperviousness to danger, may be part of smoking behavior. It is also possible that self-rated health status captures some of the effects of smoking.

Subjects gave subjective probabilities of moving to a nursing home within five years, of incurring medical costs within five years that would wipe out their savings, and of seeing inflation within five years that would erode their income. For the inflation variable, we find that a higher subjective probability of the event is associated with greater optimism about survival. This suggests that we are seeing in respondents' behavior a rather carefully articulated calculation of the probability of being at risk for these events as a result of survival, rather than heterogeneity in generalized optimism. For medical expenditure and nursing home variables, decreased optimism about mortality is associated with increased pessimism about the likelihood of nursing home admission or, less significantly, major medical costs. This is consistent with the conventional wisdom that individuals systematically overestimate the probability that their last days will be spent in a nursing home or extended hospital stay. There were a significant number of subjects with missing responses on these subjective probability questions; these events are flagged with dummy variables. If responses are missing at random, then the dummy variable coefficient should equal the coefficient for the variable in the case of nonmissing responses times the average level of the variable. For the nursing home question, the estimated coefficient is 0.3456, compared with the value 0.0576 that would be expected

Table 9.6   Regression Model for Nonfocal Responses

Variable	Model without Heckman Correction			Model with Heckman Correction		
	Coefficient	S.E.	T-Statistic	Coefficient	S.E.	T-Statistic
CONSTANT	3.5436	0.4186	8.465	3.3485	0.5776	5.797
MALE	-1.5323	0.5001	-3.064	-1.5705	0.5322	-2.951
COGN	0.0070	0.0201	0.348	0.0031	0.0224	0.140
BLACKS	-0.2376	0.1069	-2.222	-0.2210	0.1159	-1.907
HEXCEL	-0.6387	0.1253	-5.096	-0.6431	0.1292	-4.976
HVGOOD	-0.4884	0.0950	-5.142	-0.4809	0.0954	-5.039
HFAIR	0.2677	0.0913	2.932	0.2464	0.0993	2.480
HPOOR	0.3418	0.1336	2.559	0.2888	0.1616	1.787
HBETTER	-0.3107	0.0990	-3.138	-0.3110	0.0998	-3.116
HWORSE	0.0790	0.0838	0.942	0.0667	0.0907	0.735
COLLEGE	0.0471	0.0673	0.700	0.0720	0.0851	0.846
PAPAGE1	-0.0009	0.0028	-0.323	-0.0007	0.0029	-0.232
PAPAGE0	-0.0117	0.0031	-3.735	-0.0114	0.0034	-3.396
MOMAGE1	-0.0049	0.0029	-1.676	-0.0049	0.0029	-1.668
MOMAGE0	-0.0036	0.0028	-1.282	-0.0033	0.0029	-1.136
SMNOW	0.0602	0.1003	0.600	0.0564	0.1080	0.522
SMOLD	0.0233	0.0684	0.340	0.0212	0.0682	0.311
MARRIED	-0.0889	0.0718	-1.239	-0.0788	0.0760	-1.037

	Coef.	S.E.	t-ratio	Coef.	S.E.	t-ratio
NURSE	0.0044	0.0016	2.711	0.0044	0.0018	2.444
MEDX	0.0010	0.0011	0.921	0.0012	0.0013	0.938
INFLAT	−0.0078	0.0014	−5.571	−0.0077	0.0014	−5.343
NURSMIS	0.3456	0.1536	2.250	0.3429	0.1593	2.153
MEDXMIS	−0.0305	0.1368	−0.223	−0.0552	0.1550	−0.356
INFLAMIS	−0.4753	0.1454	−3.268	−0.4956	0.1789	−2.770
WQUART2	0.2046	0.1002	2.043	0.2090	0.1099	1.902
WQUART3	0.1024	0.0987	1.037	0.1119	0.1050	1.066
WQUART4	0.0875	0.1024	0.854	0.1208	0.1310	0.922
α_1, male	1.3137	0.1755	7.487	1.3691	0.2004	6.832
α_2, male	−0.0068	0.0021	−3.203	−0.0075	0.0024	−3.111
α_1, female	1.2742	0.0692	18.426	1.2829	0.0842	15.232
α_2, female	−0.0071	0.0012	−5.990	−0.0072	0.0014	−5.235
$1/\kappa$	0.1771	0.0418	4.240	0.2023	0.1053	1.922
σ	0.9568	0.0266	35.993	0.9569	0.0266	35.993
Inverse mills ratio				−0.1680	0.4162	−0.404
Sample size	2,591			2,591		
Multiple correlation	.1370			.1370		

Notes: Dependent variable is $-\log p$. Estimation method is nonlinear least squares. S.E. = standard error.

if the variable were missing at random. Thus, missing data here is associated with significantly more pessimism. For the inflation question, the estimated coefficient is -0.4753, compared with the expected value -0.2746. Thus, missing data on inflation is associated with significantly more optimism. This suggests that missing responses to these questions may be associated with an unwillingness to articulate pessimistic beliefs.

The wealth of individuals is identified by quartile, with the lowest quartile as the omitted category. We find a clear, although not consistently statistically significant, pattern that moving from the second to the third to the top quartile increases optimism about survival. This pattern agrees with the observation at the aggregate level that increased wealth is associated with increased longevity, and with the life cycle model implication that individuals with higher subjective survival probabilities should, other things equal, hold more assets. On the other hand, the lowest quartile, whose coefficient is implicitly zero, is more optimistic than the second quartile. This is inconsistent both with the observed negative correlation of mortality risk with wealth and with the prediction of the life cycle model that optimism will be positively correlated with wealth accumulation. One interpretation of the weak statistical relationship between wealth and stated survival probability is that a simple correlation of wealth and longevity in the population reflects in part the contribution of covariates such as health status and behavioral choices such as smoking that are accounted for in the model. Further, individuals in the lowest wealth quartile may be there in part because of beliefs that "fate" will provide not only long life but also the resources needed to live.

The parameter κ in this model determines the spread of unobserved heterogeneity at birth in the population. The estimated value $\kappa = 5.6460$ implies that 90 percent of the values of s from the density $k(s)$ describing unobserved heterogeneity lie in the interval $(0.421, 1.870)$. If this factor indeed measures heterogeneity in unobserved relative mortality risk, rather than a reporting effect, and this factor is known to the consumer, then it has a potentially large economic effect on behavior.

Consider the time-scaling function $T_a(t) = (1 + t)^{\alpha_1 + \alpha_2 \cdot a} - 1$. For males, the estimated parameters $\alpha_1 = 1.3137$ and $\alpha_2 = -0.0068$ imply that individuals over age 46 are systematically optimistic about survival, and that optimism increases with age. The degree of optimism is substantial. For example, a 70-year-old male has $T_a(t) = (1 + t)^{0.8377} - 1$, and a time interval of 15 years is scaled to an equivalent of 9.2 years in the standard life table. An 80-year-old male has $T_a(t) = (1 + t)^{0.7697} - 1$, and an interval of 15 years is scaled to an equivalent of 7.4 years in the standard life table. For females, the estimated parameters $\alpha_1 = 1.2742$ and $\alpha_2 = -0.0071$ imply that individuals over age 39 are optimistic; a 70-year-old scales a 15-year interval to 7.6 years, and a 80-year-old scales a 15-year interval to 5.6 years. If these are genuine beliefs about mortality hazard, then it is not surprising that individuals hold on to their wealth to cover their expected remaining life.

Table 9.7   **Ordered Probit Model for Focal Points**

Variable	Coefficient	Standard Error	T-Statistic
Low threshold	−1.394	0.023	−60.530
High threshold	−0.439	0.021	−20.824
$\sqrt{\kappa}$	1.407	0.051	27.475
Log likelihood	−3,486.25		
	3,553		

Note: Dependent variable: 0, 50, 100 for responses of 0, ½, 1, respectively.

When the model is estimated with a correction term for selection between nonfocal and focal responses, we find no statistical evidence for a common unobserved effect that causes the subjective survival probability to fall and the propensity for a focal response to rise. Further, the coefficients on covariates in the model are relatively unaffected, and the patterns of significant effects are unchanged. We have chosen to maintain the hypothesis $\rho = 0$ for subsequent estimation and prediction tasks.

An estimate of δ^2 and a second estimate of κ are obtained by regressing squared residuals from the model in table 9.6 (without the correction for selection) on a constant and the square of the fitted value of the equation, $\hat{V}^2$. The estimate of δ^2 is 0.5401 (S.E. = 0.0476) and the estimate of $1/\kappa$ is 0.2385 (S.E. = 0.0261), implying an estimate $\kappa = 4.1921$. Then the heteroscedasticity in this regression equation appears to be consistent with the theoretical model, yielding an estimate of κ that is not far from the previous estimate.

Estimates for the ordered probit model for observed focal points among those giving focal responses are given in table 9.7. In this estimation, the probability of the observed focal point is given by $\Phi(b''(p)) - \Phi(b'(p))$, where

$$(b'(p),b''(p)) = \begin{cases} (-\infty, b_0) & \text{if } p = 0, \\ (b_0, b_1) & \text{if } p = 1/2, \\ (b_1, +\infty) & \text{if } p = 1, \end{cases}$$

and letting $\hat{V}$ denote the predicted value of V from the regression on nonfocal responses,

$$b_0 = \sqrt{\kappa}(1 + \psi_0/V) \approx \sqrt{\kappa}(1 + \psi_0/\hat{V}),$$

$$b_1 = \sqrt{\kappa}(1 + \psi_1/V) \approx \sqrt{\kappa}(1 + \psi_1/\hat{V}).$$

The parameters ψ_0, ψ_1, and $\sqrt{\kappa}$ are estimated, using $\hat{V}$ as the covariate. This implies an estimate of 1.9796 for κ, compared with the regression model estimate of 5.6460. This difference is statistically significant (under the maintained hypothesis $\rho = 0$), using a standard error for $\sqrt{\kappa}$ that is not corrected for the use of an estimated variable. This result may then be a statistical artifact,

Table 9.8   Fitted Survival Probabilities

Age Group	Target Age	Life Table	Nonfocal Respondents Predicted	Nonfocal Respondents Stated	Focal Respondents Predicted	Focal Respondents Stated	All Respondents Predicted	All Respondents Stated
Female								
70–74	85	0.588	0.532	0.500	0.481	0.516	0.503	0.509
75–79	90	0.425	0.454	0.440	0.363	0.353	0.400	0.388
80–84	95	0.224	0.364	0.369	0.295	0.267	0.319	0.303
Male								
70–74	85	0.397	0.481	0.473	0.492	0.538	0.487	0.509
75–79	90	0.250	0.391	0.371	0.382	0.392	0.386	0.382
80–84	95	0.113	0.352	0.350	0.336	0.320	0.342	0.332

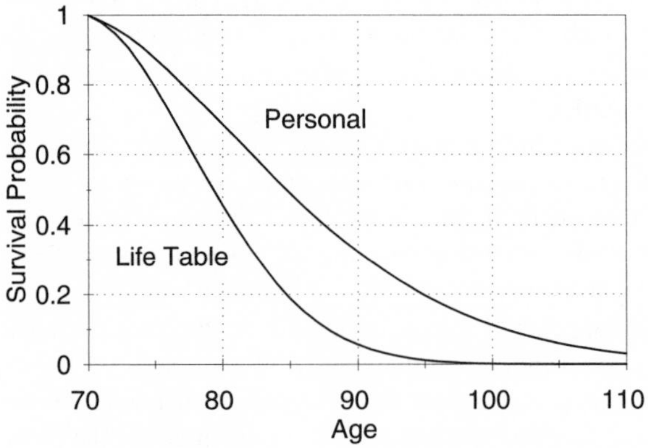

Fig. 9.11   Survival curves: males aged 70

or may indicate a specification problem in the model for focal-point choice or the impact of $\rho \neq 0$.

Personal survival curves are predicted from the models estimated under the maintained hypothesis $\rho = 0$. We produce estimates for the general case in which there is both unobserved heterogeneity in latent personal survival curves (e.g., $\kappa < +\infty$) and reporting error in nonfocal responses ($\delta > 0$). The value of λ^2, obtained from the formula $\lambda^2 = V^2/\kappa$ using estimates from the model in table 9.6 without correction for selection, is approximately 0.7713, which with the estimate $\delta^2 = 0.5401$ implies that the general case predictor places about 59 percent weight on the stated survival probability and 41 percent weight on the fitted proportional hazards model. Thus, this model indicates substantial, but imperfect, information in the stated probabilities. Table 9.8 summarizes these results. In figures 9.11 through 9.14, we plot average predicted personal survival curves for age 70 and age 80 females and males in the sample. For

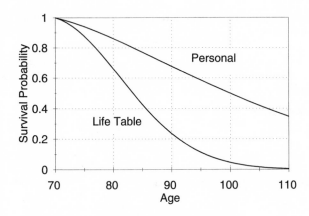

Fig. 9.12   Survival curves: females aged 70

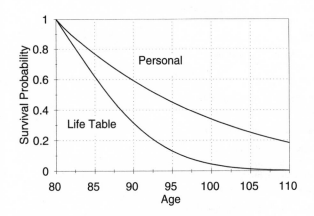

Fig. 9.13   Survival curves: males aged 80

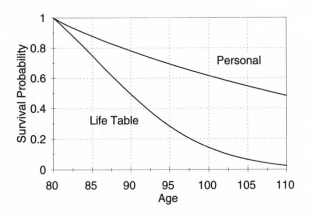

Fig. 9.14   Survival curves: females aged 80

Table 9.9   **Subjective Relative Risks (for a 70-year-old with a 0.54 probability of living to age 85)**

Risk Factor	Relative Risk (%)
Cognitive disability	1.87
Self-reported health (relative to good health)	
Excellent	−24.73
Very good	−21.50
Fair	25.25
Poor	48.60
Change in self-reported health (relative to no change)	
Better	−11.49
Worse	9.66
College education (relative to none)	−3.42
Father's age at death (20 years longer than average)	
For son	−2.94
For daughter	−12.20
Mother's age at death (20 years longer than average)	
For son	−4.75
For daughter	−4.65
Smoker now (relative to never smoked)	3.45
Previous smoker (relative to never smoked)	1.91
Married (relative to not currently married)	−9.70
Subjective probabilities of events	
Nursing home admission	13.29
Major medical expenditure	1.09
Inflation exceeding income growth	−18.16
Wealth quartile (relative to lowest quartile)	
Second quartile	9.28
Third quartile	−1.78
Fourth quartile	−3.94

comparison, we plot the standard life table survival curves in each case. The predicted personal survival curves become progressively more optimistic as duration increases. Since the effects of selection should lead an average personal survival function to decline more steeply than the life table curve, this illustrates the increasing optimism with duration that is present in personal beliefs.

To summarize the estimation results for the effects of covariates, table 9.9 gives the *perceived* relative risks associated with various risk factors. The computation is done for an individual aged 70 who has a perceived probability of 0.54 of living to age 85. The perceived relative risk is calculated from the formula

$$\text{RR} \equiv \log\frac{q(t\,|\,a,v,z+\Delta z,\varepsilon)}{q(t\,|\,a,v,z,\varepsilon)} = q(t\,|\,a,v,z,\varepsilon) \cdot (e^{\Delta z\beta} - 1),$$

where z, ε correspond to a base case, here specified so that $q(t\,|\,a,v,z,\varepsilon) = 0.54$, and Δz is the change in covariates from the base case. The table shows, first, strong relative risks associated with self-reported health status, compared to the baseline of good health, and also with changes in health status. Other economically significant relative subjective risk factors are father's age of death (for women), marital status, subjective probability of nursing home admission or inflation, and low but not bottom wealth quartile.

9.6 Subjective Mortality Risk and Saving Behavior

Subjective measures of mortality risk appear to be useful in forecasting the survival probabilities of individuals. Cumulative experience with mortality in the AHEAD panel will determine whether the heterogeneity in perceived risk has a real counterpart. The primary *economic* interest in these stated beliefs is whether they influence, or at least vary with, economic behavior. There are a number of areas where these beliefs might matter, ranging from willingness to go to a doctor, and discretionary adjustments in exposure to risk factors such as smoking, to estate planning and saving behavior.

In this paper, we take a preliminary, and simplistic, look at the relationship between stated saving behavior and beliefs about survival. It is well known that saving is positively related to income and wealth, with substantial variability. The life cycle model predicts that under most circumstances, saving rate should be positively correlated with objective probabilities of survival for various intervals, or with life expectancy, since remaining wealth needs to be spread over a longer remaining lifetime. The AHEAD wave 1 survey collects qualitative information on whether each respondent is (a) a net saver, (b) a zero saver, or (c) a net dissaver. Saving is defined to exclude contributions to trusts; this is appropriate for assets intended as bequests but is arguably inappropriate for trusts that are revocable or that are established to shelter unintended bequests. (Continuous responses on saving are highly erratic, with many cases of missing or implausible data, and have not been used.) The survey questions are ambiguous on whether saving is net of current interest, dividends, and real capital gains. Thus, an individual who consumes asset income while keeping real principal intact may report dissaving, even though there is none from a life cycle point of view.

We use a simple ordered probit to ask whether, in addition to the usual income and wealth effects, saving varies systematically with the predicted subjective survival probability that takes into account individual stated perceptions of mortality risk. We are particularly interested in the nuance of this hypothesis that says individuals respond behaviorally to perceptions rather than to life table survival probabilities. The estimates are given in tables 9.10

Table 9.10 Survival Probability and Saving for Individuals (ordered probit)

Variable	Model 1			Model 2			Model 3			Model 4			Model 5		
	Coeff.	S.E.	T-Stat.	Coeff.	S.E.	T-Stat.	Coeff.	S.E.	T-Stat.	Coeff.	S.E.	T-Stat.	Coeff.	S.E.	T-Stat.
WQUART2	−0.0297	0.0451	−0.6586	−0.0247	0.0451	−0.5472	−0.0253	0.0452	−0.5593	−0.0176	0.0452	−0.3902	−0.0243	0.0451	−0.5392
WQUART3	0.2820	0.0561	5.0291	0.2866	0.0561	5.1085	0.2886	0.0561	5.1427	0.2894	0.0561	5.1558	0.2882	0.0561	5.1359
WQUART4	0.6402	0.0562	11.4002	0.6475	0.0562	11.5155	0.6431	0.0563	11.4313	0.6417	0.0563	11.4047	0.6458	0.0562	11.4823
AIQUART2	−0.1331	0.0474	−2.8057	−0.1375	0.0475	−2.8979	−0.1338	0.0475	−2.8169	−0.1312	0.0475	−2.7616	−0.1350	0.0475	−2.8424
AIQUART3	−0.0915	0.0533	−1.7184	−0.0926	0.0533	−1.7371	−0.0937	0.0533	−1.7572	−0.0910	0.0533	−1.7060	−0.0918	0.0533	−1.7220
AIQUART4	0.1957	0.0576	3.3965	0.2008	0.0577	3.4830	0.1936	0.0577	3.3537	0.1942	0.0577	3.3642	0.1991	0.0577	3.4523
WHI&AILO	−0.0671	0.0661	−1.0155	−0.0640	0.0661	−0.9676	−0.0694	0.0662	−1.0484	−0.0670	0.0662	−1.0118	−0.0675	0.0661	−1.0203
LIFESP				−0.2106	0.0747	−2.8182	−0.1085	0.0814	−1.3331	−0.0979	0.0816	−1.1992	−0.1133	0.0822	−1.3789
SUBJSP − LIFESP							0.7142	0.0550	3.1668						
SUBJSP/LIFESP										0.2167	0.0594	3.6502			
RPTSP − SUBJSP										−0.2434	0.1303	−1.8681	0.0243	0.0086	2.8348
CONSTANT	0.6746	0.0439	15.3559	0.7584	0.0531	14.2871	0.7148	0.0549	13.0310	0.7037	0.0552	12.7542	0.6836	0.0592	11.5399
THRESHOLD1	1.5594	0.0231	67.4741	1.5607	0.0231	67.4664	1.5626	0.0232	67.4476	1.5632	0.0232	67.4449	1.5621	0.0232	67.4574
Log likelihood	−5,797.8			−5,493.8			−5,488.8			−5,487.1			−5,489.7		
N	5,725			5,725			5,725			5,725			5,725		
Dependent variable															
Share of −1	0.1906			0.1906			1.1906			0.1906			0.1906		
Share of +1	0.2721			0.2721			0.2721			0.2721			0.2721		

Notes: Dependent variable is negative (−1), zero, or positive (+1) saving. S.E. = standard error.

AIQUART2, AIQUART3, and AIQUART4 are indicators for quartiles of the distribution of annuity income.

WHI&AILO is an indicator for above-median wealth and below-median annuity income.

LIFESP is the life table survival probability, 12.5 years ahead, for the individual.

SUBJSP is the predicted subjective survival probability, 12.5 years ahead, for the individual.

RPTSP is the reported subjective survival probability, 12.5 years ahead, for the individual.

THRESHOLD1 is the threshold parameter for the +1 saving category; the threshold for the −1 category is normalized to zero.

through 9.12. Table 9.10 gives results for all individuals in the sample, with single-person households and each person in two-person households treated as individual observations. The explanatory variables are household annuity income; household wealth; the life table probability for the individual of surviving 12.5 years beyond current age; the predicted subjective survival probability for the individual in 12.5 years, computed using his or her covariates and stated survival probabilities, under the maintained hypothesis that $\rho = 0$, as outlined in section 9.4 and used in the construction of table 9.9; and the "raw" stated subjective survival probability (to an age that is 10 to 15 years ahead, depending on current age). Income and wealth are classified by quartile to reduce the effects of measurement error and spurious correlation. This model takes no account of the interdependence of saving decisions of different family members. We find that the probability of saving rises significantly with increased income or wealth. One would expect less savings when wealth is high and annuity income is low; the coefficient has the expected sign but is insignificant. Higher life table survival probabilities are associated with *less* saving, contrary to the predictions of the life cycle model (model 2). However, in models that contain both the life table survival probability and the predicted survival probability based on the individual's subjective response, it is the latter variable that has explanatory power, with the expected sign. In particular, when the subjective survival probability is entered as a deviation from the life table survival probability, or as a ratio to this probability, then only the difference or ratio is statistically significant (models 3 and 5). Thus, these results suggest strongly that saving behavior is responding to subjective beliefs about personal mortality risk, rather than to life table hazards. The relationship is economically as well as statistically significant. The proportion of individuals selecting positive saving will vary by 22.0 percent as the subjective probability of survival varies from its upper limit of one to its lower limit of zero (model 3). The regressions establish that the "raw" subjective response has no added explanatory power, once the fitted survival probability is included in the model (model 4). This provides at least weak evidence that focal responses are a reporting bias rather than a true belief that drives behavior, and it supports our approach of estimating latent beliefs for focal respondents. An important research implication is that the subjective survival curves appear to have some power to explain saving behavior. A possible policy implication is that the upward bias in subjective survival probabilities, increasing with age, will retard dissaving. This could lead to what appears to be large bequest or precautionary saving motives and may provide a partial explanation for the stylized fact that people accumulate too little and then save too much to be consistent with the most simplistic life cycle model.

An analysis that pools individuals whether they are single or members of a couple overlooks the interdependence of decisions within a household. More critically, it fails to account for the rather different joint survival calculations facing a couple compared with those facing a single person, or for the possibility that preferences of singles and couples are different. Table 9.11 looks only at single-person households. Saving of these individuals increases significantly as a function of income or wealth, with significantly less saving from individuals with high wealth and low annuity income. Saving by males is higher than that of females, other things equal. This effect may be due to the problems faced by widows in reconciling consumption habits with reduced income following the death of the spouse. We find no significant effect of either life table or subjective survival probabilities, although the coefficient on the subjective survival probability is positive, as predicted by the life cycle model. The economic effect of subjective mortality risk, yielding a 19.0 percent swing in the probability of positive saving when the subjective probability varies from the extreme of one to the extreme of zero, goes in the direction consistent with the life cycle model and is not strikingly different from this percentage for all pooled individuals.

Table 9.12 examines the saving behavior of couples, where each couple is treated as a single decision-making unit. Again, income and wealth are significantly positively correlated with saving. To analyze the effects of mortality hazards, it is necessary to take account of the probabilities that both members will survive *and* that at least one will survive. For survival for a specific future time interval, one has

$$\text{Prob(Both survive)} = \text{Prob(Husband survives)} \cdot \text{Prob(Wife survives)},$$

$$\text{Prob(Exactly one survives)} = \text{Prob(Husband survives)} \cdot \text{Prob(Wife dies)}$$

$$+ \text{Prob(Husband dies)} \cdot \text{Prob(Wife survives)},$$

$$\text{Prob(One or more survives)} = 1 - \text{Prob(Husband dies)} \cdot \text{Prob(Wife dies)}.$$

Saving behavior may depend on one or more of these joint probabilities. In reality, the saving calculation may be even more complex, as the order of death is likely to influence the annuity income stream. Of course, treatment of the life cycle mortality risk as a dynamic stochastic programming exercise also complicates the analysis.

In table 9.12, model 2 shows that saving increases with the subjective probability that at least one member of the household will survive 12.5 more years; this effect is significant, and the life table probability of this event is insignificant. The economic impact is substantial: as the subjective probability of at least one survivor varies from the extreme of zero to one, the probability of positive saving varies by 30.6 percent. In model 3, the survival probabilities of the male and female are entered separately. Again, the life table probabilities are insignificant, while the subjective probabilities are jointly significant at the 95 percent level. (The coefficients are not individually significant due to their high correlation.) Model 4 distinguishes the events that both members survive for 12.5 years, that the male only survives, and that the female only survives.

Table 9.11   Survival Probability and Saving for Singles (ordered probit)

Variable	Model 1 Coeff.	S.E.	T-Stat.	Model 2 Coeff.	S.E.	T-Stat.	Model 3 Coeff.	S.E.	T-Stat.	Model 4 Coeff.	S.E.	T-Stat.	Model 5 Coeff.	S.E.	T-Stat.
WQUART2	-0.0519	0.0588	-0.8833	-0.0503	0.0588	-0.8557	-0.0444	0.0589	-0.7541	-0.0430	0.0590	-0.7297	-0.0495	0.0588	-0.8421
WQUART3	0.3530	0.0903	3.9083	0.3553	0.0903	3.9328	0.3604	0.0904	3.9860	0.3606	0.0904	3.9882	0.3559	0.0903	3.9392
WQUART4	0.7132	0.0954	7.4734	0.7167	0.0955	7.5064	0.7169	0.0955	7.5075	0.7156	0.0955	7.4921	0.7168	0.0955	7.5070
AIQUART2	-0.0505	0.0573	-0.8811	-0.0501	0.0573	-0.8732	-0.0484	0.0574	-0.8436	-0.0476	0.0574	-0.8297	-0.0495	0.0574	-0.8629
AIQUART3	-0.0571	0.0743	-0.7674	-0.0527	0.0744	-0.7078	-0.0553	0.0745	-0.7430	-0.0548	0.0745	-0.7364	-0.0520	0.0744	-0.6983
AIQUART4	0.2293	0.0993	2.3101	0.2373	0.0995	2.3860	0.2308	0.0996	2.3179	0.2310	0.0996	2.3199	0.2375	0.0995	2.3874
WHI&AILO	-0.2499	0.1002	-2.4947	-0.2483	0.1002	-2.4785	-0.2532	0.1003	-2.5257	-0.2516	0.1003	-2.5091	-0.2497	0.1002	-2.4914
MALE	0.1343	0.0558	2.4066	0.1087	0.0593	1.8340	0.1031	0.0594	1.7370	0.1036	0.0594	1.7441	0.1065	0.0594	1.7918
LIFESP				-0.1694	0.1316	-1.2865	-0.0926	0.1405	-0.6590	-0.0659	0.1443	-0.4569	-0.1402	0.1435	-0.9771
SUBJSP − LIFESP							0.1268	0.0812	1.5618	0.1651	0.0940	1.7563			
SUBJSP/LIFESP													0.0064	0.0126	0.5115
RPTSP − SUBJSP										-0.1874	0.2318	-0.8083			
CONSTANT	0.7152	0.0531	13.4805	0.7819	0.0742	10.5328	0.7503	0.0769	9.7502	0.7364	0.0788	9.3423	0.7168	0.0845	8.4855
THRESHOLD1	1.7980	0.0368	48.8895	1.7988	0.0368	48.8815	1.8001	0.0368	48.8677	1.8004	0.0368	48.8666	1.7990	0.0368	48.8799
Log likelihood	-2,315.1			-2,314.3			-2,313.1			-2,312.8			-2,314.2		
N	2,562			2,562			2,562			2,562			2,562		
Dependent variable															
Share of −1	0.2014			0.2014			0.2014			0.2014			0.2014		
Share of +1	0.1862			0.1862			0.1862			0.1862			0.1862		

Notes: Dependent variable is negative (−1), zero, or positive (+1) saving. S.E. = standard error.

AIQUART2, AIQUART3, and AIQUART4 are indicators for quartiles of the distribution of annuity income.

WHI&AILO is an indicator for above-median wealth and below-median annuity income.

LIFESP is the life table survival probability, 12.5 years ahead, for the individual.

SUBJSP is the predicted subjective survival probability, 12.5 years ahead, for the individual.

RPTSP is the reported subjective survival probability, 12.5 years ahead, for the individual.

THRESHOLD1 is the threshold parameter for the +1 saving category; the threshold for the −1 category is normalized to zero.

Table 9.12 Survival Probability and Saving for Couples (ordered probit)

Variable	Model 1			Model 2			Model 3			Model 4		
	Coeff.	S.E.	T-Stat.	Coeff.	S.E.	T-Stat.	Coeff.	S.E.	T-Stat.	Coeff.	S.E.	T-Stat.
WQUART2	0.0019	0.1069	0.0174	0.0016	0.1072	0.0154	0.0043	0.1074	0.0396	0.0080	0.1081	0.0745
WQUART3	0.2906	0.1123	2.5877	0.2854	0.1128	2.5306	0.2849	0.1129	2.5248	0.2906	0.1134	2.5629
WQUART4	0.6202	0.1109	5.5945	0.6125	0.1117	5.4846	0.6101	0.1118	5.4577	0.6145	0.1123	5.4723
AIQUART2	−0.3379	0.1387	−2.4369	−0.3468	0.1393	−2.4897	−0.3434	0.1395	−2.4619	−0.3421	0.1396	−2.4515
AIQUART3	−0.2359	0.1338	−1.7633	−0.2332	0.1341	−1.7389	−0.2493	0.1345	−1.8536	−0.2515	0.1346	−1.8681
AIQUART4	0.0579	0.1349	0.4292	0.0573	0.1349	0.4247	0.0479	0.1351	0.3544	0.0462	0.1352	0.3416
WHI&AILO	0.0395	0.1532	0.2576	0.0442	0.1533	0.2882	0.0329	0.1534	0.2146	0.0270	0.1537	0.1757
LIFESP12				−0.0275	0.1436	−0.1912						
SUBJSP12 − LIFESP12				0.2890	0.1262	2.2908						
LIFESPM							−0.3049	0.2176	−1.4012			
LIFESPF							0.0767	0.1215	0.6309			
SUBJSPM − LIFESPM							0.1929	0.1116	1.7287			
SUBJSPF − LIFESPF							0.2107	0.1232	1.7101			
LIFESPB										−0.1703	0.2920	−0.5832
LIFESPM1										−0.4324	0.3987	−1.0844
LIFESPF1										−0.0574	0.3086	−0.1859
SUBJSPB − LIFESPB										0.4215	0.1550	2.7197
SUBJSPM1 − LIFESPM1										0.1062	0.1808	0.5874
SUBJSPF1 − LIFESPF1										0.1146	0.1983	0.5778
CONSTANT	0.6938	0.1339	5.1796	0.7101	0.1608	4.4156	0.7592	0.1563	4.8563	0.8071	0.1897	4.2544
THRESHOLD1	1.3619	0.0430	31.6871	1.3657	0.0431	31.6783	1.3684	0.0432	31.6741	1.3687	0.0432	31.6739

Log likelihood	−1,483.1	−1,479.8	−1,477.4	−1,477.2
N	1,498	1,498	1,498	1,498
Dependent variable				
Share of −1	0.1816	0.1816	0.1816	0.1816
Share of +1	0.3498	0.3498	0.3498	0.3498

Notes: Dependent variable is negative (−1), *zero*, or positive (+1) saving. S.E. = standard error.

AIQUART2, AIQUART3, and AIQUART4 are indicators for quartiles of the distribution of annuity income.

WHI&AILO is an indicator for above-median wealth and below-median annuity income.

LIFESP12 is the life table survival probability, 12.5 years ahead, for one or both members of the couple.

SUBJSP12 is the predicted subjective survival probability, 12.5 years ahead, for one or both members of the couple.

LIFESPM is the life table survival probability, 12.5 years ahead, for the male.

SUBJSPM is the predicted subjective survival probability, 12.5 years ahead, for the male.

LIFESPF is the life table survival probability, 12.5 years ahead, for the female.

SUBJSPF is the predicted subjective survival probability, 12.5 years ahead, for the female.

LIFESPB is the life table survival probability, 12.5 years ahead, for both members of the couple.

SUBJSPB is the predicted subjective survival probability, 12.5 years ahead, for both members of the couple.

LIFESPM1 is the life table survival probability, 12.5 years ahead, of the male only.

SUBJSPM1 is the predicted subjective survival probability, 12.5 years ahead, of the male only.

LIFESPF1 is the life table survival probability, 12.5 years ahead, of the female only.

SUBJSPF1 is the predicted subjective survival probability, 12.5 years ahead, of the female only.

THRESHOLD1 is the threshold parameter for the +1 saving category; the threshold for the −1 category is normalized to zero.

Saving is found to rise significantly with the subjective joint survival probability, and to increase insignificantly with the probabilities of the remaining two events. These results suggest that saving behavior of couples fails to give the life cycle planning of a surviving spouse as much weight as the planning in the event of joint survival. A possible explanation is that saving decisions may be dominated by males who are unwarrantedly optimistic about their own survival and thus underestimate the probability of the event that their widows will have substantial life cycle requirements.

Several cautions should be kept in mind in assessing the results in tables 9.10 through 9.12. As noted, the definition of positive or negative saving is somewhat ambiguous and may be misinterpreted by some subjects. We have not accounted for factors that may influence bequest motives, such as the number and economic status of relatives. We have not taken into account the possibility of reverse causality, where poor health that lowers the personal survival probability is associated with medical expenditures that require dissaving. There are substantial questions about the accuracy of reported saving and wealth data in elderly populations. Selection is potentially a severe problem, as the sample selects individuals who do not have sufficient impairments to require proxy respondents, and who as a consequence may have higher survival probabilities and fewer current medical expenditures that drain savings. More definitive tests of whether there is informational value added in personal probabilities, beyond that contained in life tables, will rely on changes in wealth over time. As further waves of AHEAD become available, these tests will become possible.

9.7 Conclusions

This paper has examined the characteristics of survival probabilities stated by AHEAD respondents, particularly their relationship to standard life tables and their relationship to stated saving behavior. We find that stated probabilities are distorted by focal points. The evidence from the model is that there is in addition reporting error in nonfocal responses, but that this error is small relative to variation in individual heterogeneity. We conclude that nonfocal responses can be used with relatively minor adjustments to predict personal survival curves. More substantial adjustments are required to predict survival curves for focal respondents. With or without adjustment, subjective survival probabilities show expected variations with known relative risks and increasing optimism with increasing age. Future waves of the AHEAD survey will reveal the actual information content of these probabilities for survival. However, it is clear that in aggregate it will be necessary to adjust personal survival probabilities down as age rises in order to track aggregate survival statistics.

Our preliminary analysis of the relationship between personal survival probabilities and saving suggests that there is a significant positive correlation, and that consumers are responding to subjective beliefs about mortality rather than to life table probabilities. This tie, combined with the optimistic bias about survival that increases with age, gives one explanation for the fact that saving rates do not fall as rapidly with age as a classical life cycle model would suggest. Thus, this phenomenon may be in part due to a bias in perception, rather than to strong precautionary or bequest motives.

References

Feinstein, J. 1992. The relationship between socioeconomic status and health: A review of the literature. *Milbank Quarterly* 71 (2): 279–322.

Herzog, Regula, and Robert Wallace. 1997. Measures of cognitive functioning in the AHEAD study. *Journal of Gerontology* 52B (May): 37–47.

Hoynes, Hilary, Michael Hurd, and Harish Chand. 1995. Wealth, subjective survival probabilities, and social security wealth. Paper presented at the NBER Conference on the Economics of Aging, May.

Hurd, M. 1987a. Dissaving after retirement: Testing the pure life cycle hypothesis: Comment. In *Issues in pension economics,* ed. Z. Bodie, J. Shoven, and D. Wise, 275–79. Chicago: University of Chicago Press.

———. 1987b. Savings of the elderly and desired bequests. *American Economic Review* 77 (3): 298–312.

———. 1989a. The annuity value of social security. In *The political economy of social security,* B. Gustafsson and A. Klevmarken, 67–82. Amsterdam: North-Holland.

———. 1989b. Mortality risk and bequests. *Econometrica* 57 (4): 779–813.

———. 1990. Research on the elderly: Economic status, retirement, and consumption and saving. *Journal of Economic Literature* 28 (2): 565–637.

Hurd, M., and K. McGarry. 1993. The relationship between job characteristics and retirement. Paper presented at the HRS Early Results Workshop, Ann Arbor, September, and NBER Working Paper no. 4558. Cambridge, Mass.: National Bureau of Economic Research.

———. 1995. Evaluation of the subjective probabilities of survival in the health and retirement study. *Journal of Human Resources* 30: S268–S292.

Hurd, Michael, and David Wise. 1989. The wealth and poverty of widows: Assets before and after the husband's death. In *The economics of aging,* ed. D. Wise, 177–99. Chicago: University of Chicago Press.

Jianakoplos, N., P. Menchik, and O. Irvine. 1989. Using panel data to assess the bias in cross-sectional inferences of life-cycle changes in the level and composition of household wealth. In *The measurement of saving, investment, and wealth,* ed. R. Lipsey and H. Tice, 553–640. Chicago: University of Chicago Press.

Kitagawa, Evelyn M., and Philip M. Hauser. 1973. *Differential mortality in the United States: A study in socioeconomic epidemiology.* Cambridge, Mass.: Harvard University Press.

Lillard, Lee, and Yoram Weiss. 1997. Uncertain health and survival: Effects on end-of-life consumption. *Journal of Business and Economic Statistics* 15 (2): 254–68.

Shorrocks, A. 1975. The age-wealth relationship: A cross-section and cohort analysis. *Review of Economics and Statistics* 57 (2): 155–63.

Soldo, Beth, Michael Hurd, Willard Rodgers, and Robert Wallace. 1997. Asset and health dynamics among the oldest-old: An overview of the survey. *Journal of Gerontology* 52B (May): 1–20.

Comment   Axel Börsch-Supan

When I saw the title of this paper I was reminded of a menu in a three-star restaurant, headed by three chefs, so I was very curious and forward looking. And, alas, the first course did what an hors d'oeuvre is supposed to: generate appetite. First, it showed the general importance of the subject. Almost all our behavioral models use expectations. This is particularly stark in life-cycle–based models. As inputs, we need the paths of expected income streams and expected major fixed expenditures; and we need expected lifetime.

The conventional way is to employ population averages for these expectations, sometimes stratified or taken as predictions from regressions, for example, earnings regressions. In terms of expected life span, this amounts to using (un)conditional life tables. The use of population averages can be motivated by learning. The authors of this paper stress learning from one's own experience, relevant for, say, repeated purchases of consumer goods, and they are therefore skeptical about using life tables as approximations for expected life span—a singular event for anybody. However, one can also learn from other peoples' experiences, even from other peoples' life spans. Manski has provided a formal proof of the conditions that generate consistent expectations by learning from others: the authors are certainly aware of this literature, but I think it is relevant also for this paper.

The authors take a different route and propose a—at least for economists—rather unconventional way to infer peoples' expectations. They exploit what people answer when they are asked about their expectations. Economists have been rather skeptical about this method. First, subjects may just be reluctant to reveal their expectations, specifically about their own life expectancy, partly because of superstition, partly because of "Verdrängung." Second, cognitive dissonance between own beliefs and own actions may lead to biased answers vis-à-vis individual behavior: people may act according to population averages although they do not concede the truth to themselves (and the interviewer). Everybody feels like an above average car driver, for example. Finally, people may give strategic answers when they are asked to reveal their beliefs. I actually think that this problem is of least importance, but it creates the most fun for economists.

The authors try to disprove this skepticism by correlating the survey responses to life table and epidemiological data. Preliminary evaluation of Health and Retirement Survey (HRS) responses shows an astounding coincidence with such life tables. Even more important, the covariance with risk factors such as smoking and drinking corresponds precisely with the epidemiological evidence.

Whether these HRS results also obtain in the data from the survey of Asset

Axel Börsch-Supan is professor of economics at the University of Mannheim and a research associate of the National Bureau of Economic Research.

and Health Dynamics among the Oldest Old (AHEAD) is a nontrivial question because the AHEAD sample is much older. Indeed, as table 9.1 shows, the younger ages' subjective survival probabilities are in line with life tables, while the older ages' are far too optimistic. This reflects a common problem in empirical analysis: if we find coincidence with the life table data, the subjective probabilities have little added information; if we do not, we do not know how reliable the new information is. At the least, we need more data and more waves in order to believe in the stability of the results of table 9.1. Better, we need to perform more experiments to find out what typical response patterns are. I will come back to this point later.

The authors are careful to address two statistical problems that may hinder a direct interpretation of the answers to questions about subjective probabilities. First, sample selectivity goes in the same direction as exaggerated optimism because people who have private information about an above average life expectancy will survive longer. The second statistical issue is the frequency of focal-point responses, that is, survival probabilities of exactly zero, 0.5, and 1.0. Incidentally, such responses are also frequent in the HRS but do not bias the averages there! The authors provide some insight in the correlation among focal-point answers and a selection of covariates. However, they do not analyze the relation between the number of focal-point answers and the respondent's characteristics, say, in a count data model. Because there may be an unobserved trait generating focal-point answers, the analysis in table 9.2 may be biased because it takes the number of other focal-point answers as exogenous.

It is very important for the analysis later in the paper to know whether focal-point answers are to be treated as round-off errors or as an expression of cognitive dissonance. To strengthen the econometrician's belief in the informational content of the beliefs of those being econtomeasured, the data collectors in AHEAD should do more testing and retesting, for example, by asking the same question in different sections of the questionnaire and by asking questions once in a positive and once in a negative formulation. It is important to verify that the focal points switch accordingly and that the subjective probabilities are consistent. Of course, this cannot be done in the entire AHEAD sample. Psychometricians have done a lot of work in experiments on those issues, and economists are beginning to realize that one can learn a lot from these experiments. This literature is—inappropriately—completely absent in this paper. The statistical problems of sample selectivity and focal points require econometric treatment. The main point of this paper is to show that the raw data need some smoothing before they can fruitfully be used in economic analyses.

This brings me to the second hors d'oeuvre. A second hors d'oeuvre is usually a very light one, a sorbet or—fashionable in these days in my region—a glass of vinegar made from Trockenbeerenauslese. The one here is anything but light. It is a structural model of how to relate the observed subjective probabilities to covariates, where the subjective probabilities are interpreted as points on each individual's own survival curve. The task is to fit these personalized survival curves taking account of observed heterogeneity—using the covariates provided in the data—as well as unobserved heterogeneity creating selectivity.

The methodology is fairly involved. The statistical model has two components. The first component models the selection process that describes true beliefs, while the second component links true beliefs to those measured with error and/or as focal-point answers. The selection model starts with unobserved heterogeneity that is fixed at the time of birth. People have different traits that make them once and for all more or less resilient. Modeled as gamma distributed, this heterogeneity generates a likelihood of observing a nonfocal-point answer not subject to measurement error. I am not sure the authors convinced me that predisposition is what fixes the survival probability of an entire life. I would rather have it modeled as a random walk in which shocks hit individuals, say, drawn from a Poisson distribution with covariates such as smoking, and thereby select individuals out of the sample once a certain threshold is passed.

The second component models the transformation of an exact continuous probability response to one that is measured with error or truncated to a focal point. The authors' model is very general and permits a rather flexible correlation pattern between measurement errors and classification errors into focal points, although they do not estimate the model in its full generality.

The model arrives at three pieces to estimate: a binomial probit model that separates focal-point from nonfocal-point responses, a nonlinear regression model of (potentially mismeasured) nonfocal-point responses, and an ordered probit model describing the three focal points.

The regression model is derived from three assumptions: a Cox proportional separation of baseline and individual hazard, a Weibull baseline modified by the survival selection process, and the result of the parametric unobserved heterogeneity fixing resiliency at birth. Taking logarithms yields the nonlinear regression equation, the main empirical result of the paper, table 9.6.

The results in this table show some reasonable covariation, for example, with health. Also the wealth pattern conforms to our priors: the wealthier have higher subjective survival rates. But table 9.6 also contains a host of surprises. Males and blacks have higher survival probabilities, in contradiction to the evidence. The ages of mother and father do not matter even though we know that they are powerful predictors of life expectancy that appear to be widely used as such.

The authors are aware of this. However, they change their interpretation by now talking about "optimism about survival" rather than "survival" as such. The careful reader recognizes that this is less than consistent with the first part of the paper in which responses in the HRS were proudly taken at face value.

The credibility of this second part of the paper would improve if the authors would give the reader some idea of how well this procedure works. Since the main problem is determining the extent of informational content of the subjective probabilities—that is, finding a balance between believing in the subjective survival probabilities as they are stated and massaging them using prior structural assumptions—any kind of validation would be helpful. One way would be to use a hold-out sample for the purpose of validation. Another way, of course, is to be patient and see whether the subjects in the panel will display actual mortality in accordance to their beliefs.

Just as an aside, I would like to raise a flag when I see wealth included in this regression—I will come back to this identification problem during the main course of this feast.

Indeed, the main course promises to be gorgeous: "Subjective Mortality Risk and Saving Behavior." Unfortunately, it comes on a small plate. For all I can get from this glimpse at the stated main purpose of the paper, my taste buds are a little irritated.

The idea behind this main part is straightforward. The authors plug the predicted subjective survival probabilities into the maximand of the life cycle problem, derive the implied saving-to-wealth ratio, and investigate its correlation to the observed saving-to-wealth ratio by a simple regression. If more waves of data had been available, the authors could have fed them directly into the first-order conditions that were spelled out in the first part of the paper and could have compared the predicted with the observed saving paths.

This sounds very reasonable. I have two problems. Unfortunately, the paper is not specific about what subsample is really used for this exercise—focal-point and/or nonfocal-point respondents?—and does not describe what is used as a predictor for the smoothed subjective survival probability.

My second problem relates to the identification problem mentioned above and the authors' criticism of identifying functional form restrictions by other authors at the beginning of the paper. The personalized survival curve is a function of wealth, but wealth is accumulated according to a trajectory determined by expectations about life span. The authors successfully endogenized mortality and described wealth at the same time. Hence, their approach cannot relieve us from identification by functional form. This third and somewhat rudimentary part of the paper should therefore spell out what exactly can be identified, either by functional form or by suitable instruments.

The results in table 9.10 are disappointing. No R^2 is reported, but it appears to be very low. The two factors are insignificant. However, it is important to stress that the set of savings data in this first AHEAD wave is a pure substitute to what an economist wants. The poor performance visible in table 9.10 is likely to reflect this more than anything else.

Thus, after these two mouth-watering hors d'oeuvres, I am particularly hungry and forward looking to a full main course and a selection of desserts once the authors have reliable data that permit them to test the link to their carefully processed subjective survival probabilities.

10   Cause-Specific Mortality among Medicare Enrollees

Jayanta Bhattacharya, Alan M. Garber,
and Thomas E. MaCurdy

10.1   Introduction

Attempts to forecast health expenditures, to determine costs of specific ill-nesses, and to assess the long-term impact of programs designed to prevent or relieve specific diseases all require accurate estimates of mortality rates. Many such efforts build on information about the cause and timing of death for people who have certain diseases. However, the empirical basis for making accurate projections of cause-specific mortality, particularly for well-defined demographic and clinical subgroups, is often weak.

The standard life table framework offers a simple and powerful method for drawing inferences about the distribution of survival. Yet seldom have the data proved capable of supporting detailed studies of mortality by cause for well-defined populations. Standard U.S. life tables, based on birth records and death certificate data, with cause of death data, are published every several years by the National Center for Health Statistics (1991). Life tables compiled by age, race, and sex are published annually (National Center for Health Statistics 1994). Although these sources offer useful information about mortality trends by demographic group, they provide little information about the survival distribution pertinent to people with specific health conditions and risk profiles. Thus it is difficult to obtain, for example, a life table applicable to 70-year-

This research was supported in part by grants R29-AG07651 and P01-AG05842 from the National Institute on Aging. Jayanta Bhattacharya was supported in part by training grant T32-HS00028 from the Agency for Health Care Policy and Research.

Jayanta Bhattacharya is a graduate student in economics and a medical student at Stanford University. Alan M. Garber is a Senior Health Services Research and Development Senior Research Associate of the Department of Veterans Affairs; associate professor of medicine, economics, and health research and policy at Stanford University; and a research associate and director of the Health Care Program at the National Bureau of Economic Research. Thomas E. MaCurdy is professor of economics at Stanford University and a research associate of the National Bureau of Economic Research.

old men who are discharged from a hospital with a diagnosis of myocardial infarction. Small clinical studies and registries often provide information of this kind, but they usually are limited either by the selection criteria used to define the study population or by small sample sizes. They are not sufficiently comprehensive to cover a wide range of conditions, or to analyze a nationally representative sample.

In this paper, we describe the first steps toward developing such life tables. We lay out an approach to estimating survival patterns among the elderly that is based on longitudinal analysis of data from Medicare eligibility and claims files. These files offer a nationally representative sample of the elderly. Information about the cause of death, derived from hospital discharge files, allows us to link additional information about the terminal hospitalization and gives us the opportunity to obtain confirmatory data that are not routinely available from death certificate information. For our statistical modeling, we develop a flexible functional form to relate annual mortality rates to a set of individual characteristics.

The longitudinal analysis described below, which focuses on cause of death, can be a building block for studies that address a number of additional issues. For example, it can be extended to estimate future Medicare expenditures for the care of individuals who carry specific diagnoses (i.e., the longitudinal costs of incident cases of specific diseases). It can provide information about the expected pattern of expenditures for persons with a given set of characteristics, including not only age and gender, but also race, comorbidities, and prior hospital utilization. Similarly, such analyses can be used to identify populations who should be targeted for either preventive interventions or the identification and treatment of diseases. Finally, it can inform efforts to determine whether otherwise identical patients who receive different treatments have different outcomes.

10.2   Data Source

We obtained from the Health Care Financing Administration (HCFA) a 5 percent random sample of all Medicare enrollees, recorded in the Health Insurance Skeleton Eligibility Write-Off (HISKEW), for the years 1986–90 inclusive. This 5 percent sample consists of 1,518,108 people. The HISKEW file includes a unique identifier for each enrollee, in addition to basic demographic information such as age, sex, and race, and the date of death for each enrollee who died during the period of study. We also obtained the MEDPAR files, which contain information on every hospital admission during the study period, for every patient included in the 5 percent sample. MEDPAR includes dates of admission and discharge, discharge diagnoses, and discharge status, including whether the patient died in a hospital.

Using the unique identifier from the HISKEW file, we link each patient's demographic information to a complete hospitalization record over the five-year period. This allows us to confirm the mortality information in the demographic file and to ascertain whether people who died during the study period died in a hospital. Furthermore, for those who died in a hospital, we are able to observe their primary discharge diagnosis, which we assign as the main cause of death.

Diagnoses are coded using the standard ICD-9-CM coding scheme. We perform two separate analyses of causes of death using broad and more specific diagnostic information. The analysis using the broad diagnostic classification, which employs the standard list of ICD-9 major diagnostic categories, permits a comprehensive picture of the main causes of death. There are 17 mutually exclusive ICD-9 code major categories ranging from code I, "infectious diseases," to code XVII, "injuries and poisonings." Codes that have a very small or zero sample size, reflecting the age composition of Medicare enrollees, are excluded from the analysis. In particular we exclude patients with the following causes of death: code XI, "complications of pregnancy, childbirth, and the puerperium"; code XIV, "congenital abnormalities"; and code XV, "conditions originating in the perinatal period." With these categories excluded, there remain 14 mutually exclusive broad causes of death. There are also two supplementary codes for special purpose categories, as described below.

The analysis using finer level diagnostic information allows us to determine the relative contributions of certain diseases, which are of broad policy interest, to total mortality rates. These categories include "heart attacks" (codes 410.XX and 411.XX, where XX denotes all subcodes), "strokes" (codes 430.XX through 438.XX), "congestive heart disease" (code 428.0), "lung cancer" (codes 162.XX), "breast cancer" (codes 174.XX), and "prostate cancer" (codes 233.4, 222.2, 236.5, 239.5, and 185.XX).

Most of the diagnostic labels in the broad scheme are self-explanatory. "E- and V-codes," however, are special purpose categories that supplement the standard diagnostic classifications. Essentially, V-codes apply to patients who are seeking care for a past diagnosis, such as a patient receiving chemotherapy for an already diagnosed cancer. E-codes allow the classification of environmental conditions which are the main cause of accidents or poisonings. The vast majority of Medicare patients classified in this category are admitted for V-codes, rather than E-codes.

We use information on all Medicare enrollees in the HISKEW file between the ages of 65 and 100 inclusive. We exclude enrollees younger than 65 years of age; they constitute a distinct population who are eligible because of a disability or because they require renal dialysis. For the analysis of cause of death, we use the sample of patients who died between 1986 and 1990 inclusive, whether or not they died in a hospital. For those patients who experienced a hospital stay and who died outside the hospital within one week of their discharge, we attribute the cause of death to the primary discharge diagnosis. For all other patients who died outside the hospital, we designate the cause of death as unknown. Of the 1,518,108 people in the 1986 HISKEW file, 397,383 people died during the sample period.

10.3 Empirical Approach

To develop a statistical framework describing the incidence and causes of death, we separate the modeling tasks into two steps: the first introduces a distribution characterizing age-specific mortality in the elderly population; the second models health circumstances near the time of death.

10.3.1 Formulating a Model for Mortality Rates

A duration analysis provides a natural framework for characterizing age-specific survival probabilities. We describe here how such an analysis summarizes subsequent survival for an individual drawn from a population at age 65 of a given demographic makeup. A duration distribution describing the likelihood that an individual lives τ years beyond age 65 takes the form

$$(1) \qquad f(\tau \mid X) = S(\tau - 1 \mid X) H(\tau, X),$$

$$(2) \qquad S(\tau - 1 \mid X) = \prod_{t=1}^{\tau-1} [1 - H(t, X)].$$

where the covariates X include factors other than duration that influence the lengths of survival times. The hazard rate $H(t, X)$ determines the fraction of the population who, having lived until age $65 + t - 1$, will die at age $65 + t$; the function $f(\tau \mid X)$ specifies the likelihood that an individual with attributes X will die exactly at age τ, and the quantity $S(\tau - 1 \mid X)$, the survivor function, depicts the probability that an individual will live until at least age $65 + \tau - 1$, given survival to age 65. The covariates X in the subsequent analysis include race and sex, the observed demographic characteristics. We break the sample into cells based on these observed characteristics and estimate separate survivor functions for each cell.

We estimate the hazard rate at age t, $H(t, X)$, by calculating the fraction of people in a given cell, alive at age t, who do not survive to $t + 1$. We subsequently calculate the survival distribution using equation (2).

10.3.2 Modeling Causes of Death

A second aspect of our empirical analysis characterizes the health conditions present at the time of death. For those who die, we designate one of 15 diagnoses as the cause of death, with a 16th category termed "other" for no diagnosis assigned at time of death (sometimes this is termed "natural causes"). Define

$$(3) \qquad \Pr(\text{alive} \rightarrow i) \equiv \Pr(\text{alive} \rightarrow i \mid \tau, X) \qquad i = 1, \ldots, 16,$$

as the probability that an individual who dies at τ and is a member of demographic group X has diagnosis i assigned as the cause of death. Formally, the quantity Pr (alive $\rightarrow i$) represents the probability that an individual dies from disease i conditional on dying at age τ and on the covariates X. There are 16 potential causes of death corresponding to the 16 diagnosis categories.

To offer a flexible specification, we parameterize these quantities using a multinomial logit specification, of the form

$$(4) \qquad \text{Pr}(\text{alive} \rightarrow i) = \frac{e^{g_i(\tau, X, \alpha_i)}}{\displaystyle\sum_{j=1,...,16} e^{g_j(\tau, X, \alpha_j)}}, \qquad i = 1,...,16,$$

where the function $g_i(\tau, X, \alpha_i)$ determines how the likelihood of various sources of death changes with age and α_i, $i = 1, \ldots, 16$, is a set of parameters to be estimated that determines the shape of g. We normalize the model by setting $g_{16}(\tau, X, \alpha_{16})$ to zero.

In equation (4), the function $g_i(\tau, X, \alpha_i)$ not only captures how the diagnoses and rate of death vary with age, but the presence of X in g_i also allows these relationships to differ across demographic groups. Spline models are an attractive approach for modeling duration effects, since they fit the data with a flexible and smooth function of duration. Implicit in conventional spline models, which fit polynomial functions to a series of intervals over duration, is a trade-off between smoothness and goodness of fit. Fit can be improved by increasing the number of polynomial functions, but nondifferentiability at the boundaries requires a sacrifice in smoothness. Limiting the number of intervals or the order of the polynomial functions yields a smoother curve but diminishes the capabilities of detecting complicated forms of duration dependence.

To develop a flexible empirical specification for $g_i(t, X, \alpha_i)$, we apply a parameterization introduced in Garber and MaCurdy (1993) called overlap polynomials:

$$(5) \qquad g_i(t, X, \alpha_i) = \sum_{j=1}^{J} \left[\Phi_{ij}(t) - \Phi_{i,j-1}(t) \right] \left[p_x(t, \alpha_{ij}) \right].$$

The quantity $\Phi_{ij}(t)$ denotes the cumulative distribution function (cdf) of a normal random variable possessing mean μ_{ij} and variance σ_{ij}^2, while $p_x(t, \alpha_{ij})$ is a polynomial in t, parameterized by α_{ij}. We estimate equation (4) separately for every race-sex cell and thus allow g_i to vary flexibly with demographic covariates.

The presence of the cdf's in equation (5) permits us to incorporate spline features in g_i so that the polynomial $p_x(t, \alpha_{ij})$ represents g_i over only a specified range of t. For example, suppose we wish to set $g_i = p_x(t, \alpha_{i1})$ for values of t between zero and t^* and to set $g_i = p_x(t, \alpha_{i2})$ for values of t between t^* and some upper bound $\bar{t}$. To create a specification of g that satisfies the property, assign $J = 2$ in equation (5), fix the three means determining the cdf's as $\mu_{i0} =$

0, $\mu_{i1} = t^*$, and $\mu_{i2} = \bar{t}$, and pick very small values for the three standard deviations σ_{i0}, σ_{i1}, and σ_{i2}. These choices for the μs and the σs imply that the quantity $\Phi_{i1}(t) - \Phi_{i0}(t)$ equals one over the range $(0, t^*)$ and is zero elsewhere, and the quantity $\Phi_{i2}(t) - \Phi_{i1}(t)$ equals one over the range $(t^*, \bar{t})$ and is zero elsewhere. Since the differences in the cdf's serve as weights for the polynomials, g_i possesses the desired property. Further, $g_i(t, X_2, \alpha_i)$ is nth-order differentiable in t for any value of n without imposing any continuity restrictions at the knot t^*, as one would have to specify if one were to use standard splines. With the values of the μ_{ij} and the σ_{ij} set in advance of estimation, $g_i(t, X_2, \alpha_i)$ is strictly linear in the parameters α and in known functions of t and X_2. We control where each spline or polynomial begins and ends by adjusting the values of the μs. We also control how quickly each spline cuts in and out by adjusting the values of the σs, with higher values providing for a more gradual and smoother transition from one polynomial to the next.

10.4   Empirical Results

10.4.1   Estimation Results for Survival Rates

As noted above, we estimate distinct survival models for each age-race cell in the sample. In particular, we estimate survivor functions for the entire population of Medicare-eligible elderly and for four demographic groups: white males, black males, white females, and black females. Our formulation for X allows for distinct hazard rates within each cell.

Table 10.1 presents survival estimates (percentage still alive at given ages) for individuals who have survived until age 65. These figures reflect well-known racial and gender differences in age-specific mortality rates; for example, blacks have higher mortality rates than whites, except at far-advanced ages, and mortality rates for men exceed those for women. The qualitative similarity with findings from other sources of demographic information help to validate the use of the long-term survivor functions that are estimated by taking advantage of the longitudinal aspect of this administrative data set that spans only five years.

In fact, the estimates that we obtain are quantitatively similar to those found

Table 10.1   Survival Rates for Elderly

Demographic Group	Percentage of 65-Year-Olds Living until at Least Age					
	70	75	80	85	90	95
Entire population	89.75	76.08	59.28	40.77	23.00	9.86
White men	86.05	68.90	49.15	30.47	15.40	6.54
White women	91.93	80.89	66.17	48.26	28.87	13.80
Black men	80.59	60.42	41.06	24.16	13.14	6.71
Black women	88.39	74.22	57.36	41.58	26.14	14.09

in standard life tables for all ages and demographic groups. For example, for white males, the standard 1987 life table, compiled by the National Center for Health Statistics (1988), reports that the probability of mortality within five years given for a person who reaches age 70 is 20.4 percent. Using the HCFA administrative database, we estimate the corresponding probability to be 20.0 percent. Similarly, the 1987 life table predicts that an unspecified individual 65 years old will have a five-year mortality of 10.6 percent while our estimate is 10.3 percent. For the demographic categories generally, our results closely match the life tables derived from the U.S. vital statistics system.

Such agreement is not surprising given that the date of death reported in the HCFA statistical files is likely to correlate well with death certificate data, from which life tables are constructed. While others have noted this correlation (Kestenbaum 1992), this is the first report of life tables calculated from these data.

10.4.2 Implications of the Findings for Survival

Accurate life tables are integral tools for health care policymakers interested in predicting the consequences of changing survival patterns. Construction of these tables, however, can be cumbersome. Death certificate information must be compiled, coded, and analyzed. The preceding results suggest that mortality rates, and the components of the life tables, can be estimated from the HCFA statistical database without requiring the use of death certificate data.

One limitation of life tables is that they are usually constructed only for a limited range of demographic subgroups, such as age categories by race and sex. This level of detail may be sufficient for many situations, but particularly when interest centers on the prognosis associated with certain diseases and treatments, more narrowly defined subgroups are needed. For example, one may be interested in the prognosis associated with the presence of a diagnosis of coronary heart disease. With our approach, it is easy to calculate the survivor function associated with such patients at a specific age.

In other words, the estimation of survivor functions for clinically important groups of people can serve as an effective tool in developing better information about prognosis. Even a well-conducted prospective observational study or a randomized clinical trial, the usual source of disease-specific prognostic information, may not provide comparable information. Randomized trials, for example, often lack generalizability: it is difficult to extrapolate from the results of the trial to infer results in classes of patients who were not included. By using a nationally representative sample, with no subgroup exclusions, our method avoids this pitfall.

10.4.3 Diagnosis Probabilities: Estimation Results and Implications

To estimate the probabilities Pr(alive $\rightarrow i$) defined by equation (4), we apply standard maximum likelihood procedures in a multinomial logit framework to compute values for the parameters α appearing in equation (4). We use the sample of 397,383 patients who died during the study period.

In this analysis we use a specification of $g(t, X_2, \alpha)$ that sets $J = 4$ in equation (5), with $\mu_0 = 0$, $\sigma_0 = 4$, $\mu_1 = 70$, $\sigma_1 = 4$, $\mu_2 = 80$, $\sigma_2 = 4$, $\mu_3 = 90$, $\sigma_3 = 4$, $\mu_4 = 150$, and $\sigma_4 = 4$. Thus, the polynomial $p_X(t, \alpha_{i1})$ determines g_i from age 65 to age 70. After age 70, g_i switches to the polynomial $p_X(t, \alpha_{i2})$, which determines its value until approximately age 80, and so on. For every interval, we specify p_X to be quadratic in age. Given this specification, we estimate α by maximum likelihood.

We first perform the analysis using the 15 broad diagnostic categories mentioned in section 10.2, with the 16th category consisting of patients who were not assigned a cause of death because they died outside of the hospital more than a week after final discharge. Table 10.2 presents the smoothed probability of dying from condition i, given that death occurred in the age interval, for the entire population at various ages. For presentation purposes, we integrate the smoothed probabilities over age ranges in the table. Tables 10.3 and 10.4 present these same probabilities for white females, black females, white males, and black males. As table 10.2 shows, the most common causes of death are circulatory diseases (including myocardial infarction, congestive heart failure, stroke, and many other conditions), lung disease, and cancer. About three-

Table 10.2   Diagnosis Associated with Deaths: Entire Population

Diagnosis	Percentage of Deceased Who Died with Diagnosis in Age Group						
	65–69	70–74	75–79	80–84	85–89	90–94	95+
Infectious diseases	2.02	2.31	2.53	2.83	2.97	2.90	2.49
Neoplasms (cancer)	15.90	14.52	11.51	8.46	5.84	3.97	2.36
Immune and metabolic disease[a]	3.27	3.60	3.53	4.00	4.26	4.11	4.08
Blood diseases[b]	0.74	0.73	0.70	0.64	0.73	0.59	0.61
Mental disorders	0.71	0.71	0.78	0.84	0.73	0.54	0.45
Nervous system disease[c]	0.98	0.92	0.95	0.79	0.66	0.46	0.41
Circulatory diseases	20.98	23.13	24.05	24.15	22.73	19.53	15.28
Respiratory diseases	9.98	11.05	11.80	12.20	12.70	12.78	12.67
Digestive diseases	5.43	5.67	5.72	5.94	6.18	5.90	5.73
Genitourinary diseases	2.06	2.71	3.33	3.81	4.14	4.03	3.51
Skin diseases	0.58	0.70	0.88	1.04	1.25	1.32	1.35
Musculoskeletal disease[d]	0.86	0.87	0.76	0.75	0.66	0.53	0.55
Ill-defined conditions[e]	2.41	2.51	2.54	2.50	2.49	2.37	0.23
Injury and poisoning[f]	2.45	2.86	3.48	4.25	5.35	5.86	5.96
E & V codes	1.55	1.14	0.78	0.53	0.30	0.25	0.15
Other	30.09	26.57	26.64	27.26	29.00	34.86	42.12

[a]Category includes endocrine, nutritional, immune system, and metabolic disease.
[b]Category includes diseases of blood and blood-forming organs.
[c]Category includes diseases of the nervous system and sense organs.
[d]Category includes diseases of the skin and subcutaneous tissue.
[e]Category includes diseases of the musculoskeletal system and connective tissue.
[f]Category includes symptoms, signs, and ill-defined conditions.

Table 10.3 **Diagnosis Associated with Deaths: Women by Race**

Diagnosis	Percentage of Deceased Who Died with Diagnosis in Age Group						
	65–69	70–74	75–79	80–84	85–89	90–94	95+
	White Women						
Infectious diseases	2.30	2.53	2.58	2.74	2.86	2.68	2.10
Neoplasms (cancer)	17.90	15.37	11.21	7.43	4.90	3.46	2.05
Immune and metabolic diseases	3.94	3.76	3.73	3.83	4.03	3.89	3.60
Blood diseases	0.87	0.83	0.74	0.59	0.67	0.54	0.53
Mental disorders	0.83	0.70	0.75	0.79	0.65	0.48	0.35
Nervous system diseases	1.17	1.10	0.95	0.78	0.63	0.39	0.42
Circulatory diseases	21.41	23.46	25.05	25.03	23.38	19.64	15.10
Respiratory diseases	10.37	10.40	10.38	10.67	11.17	11.46	11.25
Digestive diseases	5.86	6.15	6.22	6.52	6.52	6.15	5.98
Genitourinary diseases	1.96	2.40	2.87	3.38	3.54	3.62	2.82
Skin diseases	0.64	0.75	0.97	1.06	1.23	1.25	1.27
Musculoskeletal diseases	1.13	1.14	0.88	0.88	0.70	0.55	0.45
Ill-defined conditions	2.56	2.40	2.62	2.39	2.30	2.29	1.94
Injury and poisoning	2.88	3.33	4.13	4.95	6.07	6.40	6.29
E & V codes	1.71	1.27	0.84	0.56	0.32	0.27	0.14
Other	24.48	24.41	26.07	28.40	31.05	36.92	45.72
	Black Women						
Infectious diseases	3.20	3.41	4.17	4.47	5.64	6.43	6.32
Neoplasms (cancer)	14.97	13.29	10.26	7.63	5.71	4.04	3.42
Immune and metabolic diseases	5.65	6.08	6.02	7.13	6.95	8.38	11.89
Blood diseases	0.76	0.71	0.74	0.86	0.94	0.73	0.43
Mental disorders	0.58	0.75	0.82	0.68	0.46	0.39	0.44
Nervous system diseases	0.90	0.99	0.97	0.71	1.09	1.24	0.57
Circulatory diseases	23.07	23.31	23.15	23.58	23.09	20.26	18.44
Respiratory diseases	6.30	7.40	7.61	7.61	10.23	10.94	11.99
Digestive diseases	4.75	4.95	5.31	5.79	6.41	5.96	4.87
Genitourinary diseases	2.92	3.86	4.41	5.69	6.87	6.42	4.37
Skin diseases	0.92	1.65	1.81	2.23	2.80	4.09	2.63
Musculoskeletal diseases	0.80	0.68	0.58	0.36	0.51	0.15	0.67
Ill-defined conditions	2.70	2.45	2.42	3.26	3.22	2.65	3.95
Injury and poisoning	2.42	2.09	2.39	2.44	3.12	2.78	3.69
E & V codes	1.57	1.12	0.81	0.33	0.15	0.21	4.68
Other	28.48	27.25	28.53	27.22	22.82	25.34	21.63

fourths of all deaths in this population occur during or soon after hospitalization. Note that black men are somewhat less likely to die of circulatory diseases than white men and, below the age of 85, are less likely to die in the hospital (table 10.4). Black women, on the other hand, are somewhat *more* likely to die in the hospital than white women, above the age of 79 (table 10.3).

By estimating the same model on the same set of patients with the finer

Table 10.4   Diagnosis Associated with Deaths: Men by Race

	Percentage of Deceased Who Died with Diagnosis in Age Group						
Diagnosis	65–69	70–74	75–79	80–84	85–89	90–94	95+
White Men							
Infectious diseases	1.70	2.01	2.23	2.64	2.70	2.77	2.42
Neoplasms (cancer)	14.98	14.19	11.96	9.74	7.33	5.05	3.11
Immune and metabolic diseases	2.44	3.09	2.94	3.61	3.93	3.65	3.53
Blood diseases	0.64	0.67	0.69	0.68	0.86	0.75	0.84
Mental disorders	0.65	0.70	0.81	0.93	0.95	0.69	0.78
Nervous system diseases	0.87	0.80	0.93	0.85	0.69	0.52	0.41
Circulatory diseases	21.12	23.71	24.16	24.08	22.11	19.44	15.89
Respiratory diseases	10.11	11.86	13.60	14.58	15.77	16.37	16.81
Digestive diseases	5.32	5.46	5.49	5.43	5.60	5.29	5.22
Genitourinary diseases	1.94	2.74	3.61	4.21	4.80	4.40	5.35
Skin diseases	0.49	0.53	0.65	0.76	0.96	0.98	1.21
Musculoskeletal diseases	0.73	0.68	0.66	0.63	0.63	0.52	0.79
Ill-defined conditions	2.27	2.56	2.48	2.55	2.68	2.47	2.81
Injury and poisoning	2.24	2.64	3.08	3.78	4.59	5.34	5.88
E & V codes	1.50	1.14	0.77	0.56	0.33	0.25	0.20
Other	32.99	27.22	25.96	24.98	26.08	31.50	34.78
Black Men							
Infectious diseases	2.60	2.94	3.79	4.64	4.38	3.96	5.60
Neoplasms (cancer)	13.90	13.46	11.97	10.68	9.23	6.37	3.92
Immune and metabolic diseases	4.23	4.89	5.13	6.97	7.41	7.17	7.02
Blood diseases	0.88	0.75	0.67	0.84	0.56	0.40	0.45
Mental disorders	0.74	0.93	0.64	0.87	0.80	1.29	0.01
Nervous system diseases	0.81	0.88	1.37	1.11	0.72	0.55	1.01
Circulatory diseases	17.44	19.22	18.91	18.88	19.25	16.47	13.88
Respiratory diseases	9.42	10.64	10.89	12.87	13.17	13.48	17.17
Digestive diseases	3.94	4.91	3.99	4.72	5.92	6.38	5.01
Genitourinary diseases	2.80	3.94	4.73	5.06	6.55	7.80	6.60
Skin diseases	0.52	0.95	1.11	1.85	2.11	2.00	3.85
Musculoskeletal diseases	0.34	0.51	0.38	0.50	0.35	0.35	0.62
Ill-defined conditions	2.55	2.79	2.65	2.63	3.22	2.71	3.35
Injury and poisoning	2.11	2.46	2.62	2.50	2.93	2.85	3.78
E & V codes	1.15	0.72	0.65	0.60	0.20	13.81	3.15
Other	36.57	29.99	30.49	25.28	23.19	14.42	24.60

diagnostic classification scheme, as described in section 10.2, we obtain the results shown in tables 10.5–10.7. In this scheme, the cause of death is classified by the principal diagnosis (hence these figures exclude individuals who had one of these conditions if the condition was only considered a contributory cause of death or an incidental diagnosis); the "other" category includes patients who were not assigned a diagnosis and patients who do not fall into any of the other diagnostic categories. Table 10.5 presents the smoothed probability

Table 10.5   Selected Diagnosis Associated with Deaths: Entire Population

Diagnosis	Percentage of Deceased Who Died with Diagnosis in Age Group						
	65–69	70–74	75–79	80–84	85–89	90–94	95+
Heart attack	5.75	6.36	6.25	4.65	3.98	2.62	1.37
Strokes	4.30	5.48	6.08	6.88	6.69	5.63	4.87
Congestive heart failure	4.51	5.50	6.35	7.26	6.82	5.91	5.53
Lung cancer	3.44	3.16	2.07	1.00	0.58	0.28	0.17
Breast cancer	0.23	0.20	0.24	0.11	0.14	0.19	0.10
Prostate cancer	0.43	0.57	0.58	0.51	0.40	0.42	0.04
Other	81.34	78.73	78.42	79.59	81.39	84.95	87.92

Table 10.6   Selected Diagnosis Associated with Deaths: Women by Race

Diagnosis	Percentage of Deceased Who Died with Diagnosis in Age Group						
	65–69	70–74	75–79	80–84	85–89	90–94	95+
White Women							
Heart attack	5.77	6.22	6.21	5.46	4.22	2.88	1.64
Strokes	4.53	5.67	6.75	7.31	7.36	6.17	4.92
Congestive heart failure	4.51	5.31	6.28	6.98	7.02	6.84	5.74
Lung cancer	3.08	2.59	1.48	0.65	0.30	0.12	0.07
Breast cancer	0.69	0.50	0.37	0.26	0.18	0.18	0.10
Other	81.42	79.71	78.90	79.35	80.91	83.82	87.53
Black Women							
Heart attack	3.99	3.85	3.32	2.90	2.86	1.73	1.86
Strokes	6.58	6.94	7.71	8.41	7.96	7.34	6.26
Congestive heart failure	5.06	5.69	5.32	6.14	6.11	6.09	4.33
Lung cancer	1.94	1.71	0.93	0.50	0.38	0.35	0.14
Breast cancer	0.59	0.48	0.57	0.17	0.16	0.12	0.33
Other	81.83	81.32	82.15	81.89	82.53	84.36	87.08

Table 10.7   Selected Diagnosis Associated with Deaths: Men by Race

Diagnosis	Percentage of Deceased Who Died with Diagnosis in Age Group						
	65–69	70–74	75–79	80–84	85–89	90–94	95+
White Men							
Heart attack	5.82	6.08	6.06	5.41	4.57	3.23	1.91
Strokes	3.60	4.42	5.21	5.90	6.00	5.53	4.23
Congestive heart failure	4.72	5.68	6.23	6.71	6.72	6.36	6.58
Lung cancer	4.17	3.67	2.64	1.71	1.01	0.52	0.34
Prostate cancer	0.70	0.88	1.05	1.07	1.09	0.79	0.42
Other	80.99	79.27	78.81	79.19	80.60	83.56	86.53
Black Men							
Heart attack	2.61	2.49	2.83	2.20	3.27	1.93	0.34
Strokes	5.35	6.27	5.64	6.76	5.97	5.52	5.53
Congestive heart failure	4.10	4.63	4.69	4.77	4.71	4.67	5.18
Lung cancer	3.62	3.02	2.99	1.86	1.05	0.67	0.02
Prostate cancer	1.26	1.68	1.67	1.62	1.90	2.21	1.10
Other	83.05	81.91	82.18	82.78	83.11	85.00	87.83

of dying from the conditions included in the scheme: acute myocardial infarction (heart attack), stroke, congestive heart failure, lung cancer, breast cancer, and prostate cancer. The first three diagnoses usually reflect diseases of the blood vessels; congestive heart failure is often a consequence of myocardial infarction, which is usually due to obstruction of the coronary arteries, and stroke is usually a consequence of obstruction in the arteries supplying blood to the brain or of blood clots that form in other arteries. These six diagnoses account for about 20 percent of all deaths among the elderly, according to these results. None shows a clear age trend except lung cancer, which accounts for a declining fraction of all deaths at greater ages.

Information on what diseases are most likely to be causes of death is clearly an important intermediate product in locating sources of cost growth in medical care. Since the overlap polynomial method allows flexible identification of those diseases that have the largest impact on mortality, one can cull detailed data—stratified by age, sex, and other clinical information—on the most important causes of death. Combining this information with cost data allows one to think about such questions as: Is a disproportionately large share of medical resources devoted to the oldest old, who may benefit little from the types of care they receive? Is there a cutoff age below which health care interventions are cost-effective? And what is the most appropriate method by which to determine priorities for the allocation of resources to research on the prevention and treatment of various diseases?

10.5   Conclusions

The Medicare claims files offer an important set of building blocks for studies that focus on mortality, health care utilization, expenditures, and health outcomes among the elderly. The preliminary work presented here demonstrates how the eligibility and hospital insurance claims files can be used to estimate survival curves by demographic group and by other characteristics, such as a diagnosis of one or more chronic diseases. The claims files further offer a basis for analyses of cause-specific death rates; although claims files are not considered as accurate as detailed audits of cause of death that are often performed as part of clinical research studies, they may well be more accurate than the death certificate data that usually serve as the major source of cause-of-death information in population-based studies. Furthermore, the longitudinal features of the claims files make it possible to explore supporting information for cause-of-death codes, by searching prior hospitalizations for discharge diagnoses of the cause of death and of related conditions (e.g., revealing a prior hospitalization for congestive heart failure or myocardial infarction in a person with a death diagnosis of cardiac arrhythmia, which is often associated with one of the other diagnoses).

Insofar as national data sources can be found to compare to the estimates of our models, the results are comparable. For example, our survival figures are comparable to the life table figures supplied as part of the series of vital statistics of the United States. Our data on cause of death are largely consistent with results of studies that look at both causes of death and morbidity in the elderly (see, e.g., Johnson, Mullooly, and Greenlick 1990), although the national vital statistics system may be more successful in assigning a specific cause to each death, when compared with our procedures (Sutherland, Persky, and Brody 1990).

The data used here will soon be expanded in three ways: new data files will provide us with a larger percentage of enrollees, we will soon have more years of the files, and we will merge Part B (outpatient) data. The expanded data capabilities will enable us to estimate the survival models for a larger number of years per observation, and to pursue more finely detailed diagnostic categories (for analysis of both antecedent conditions and of cause of death).

With these data, we plan to attach Medicare expenditure and cost data for both inpatient and outpatient care, adapting our methods to estimate lifetime profiles of Medicare expenditures for individuals falling into various demographic and clinical categories. The framework can also be extended to analyze the mortality and utilization associated with use of specific procedures. We can compare, for example, the profile of expenditures and mortality for individuals with admissions for coronary heart disease who either do or do not undergo surgical treatment; the claims files offer a great deal of information about clinical characteristics of the patients, which when combined with geographic information has been used for instrumental variables analysis of the effects of alternative treatment strategies on health outcomes and costs.

Finally, this work can be extended to model the effects of preventive interventions on subsequent utilization and expenditures. For example, interventions that prevent or delay the development of prostate cancer will change the pattern of expenditures in ways that the longitudinal approach developed here can help predict.

References

Garber, Alan M., and Thomas E. MaCurdy. 1993. Nursing home discharges and exhaustion of Medicare benefits. *Journal of the American Statistical Association* 88:727–36.

Johnson, Richard E., John P. Mullooly, and Merwyn R. Greenlick. 1990. Morbidity and medical care utilization of old and very old persons. *Health Services Research* 25:639–65.

Kestenbaum, B. 1992. A description of the extreme aged population based on improved Medicare enrollment data. *Demography* 29:565–80.

National Center for Health Statistics. 1991. *Vital statistics of the United States, 1988.* Vol. 2, *Mortality, part A.* Washington, D.C.: Public Health Service.

———. 1994. *Vital statistics of the United States, 1990.* Vol. 2, Sec. 6, *Life tables.* Washington, D.C.: Public Health Service.

Sutherland, John E., Victoria W. Persky, and Jacob A. Brody. 1990. Proportionate mortality trends: 1950 through 1986. *Journal of the American Medical Association* 264:3178–84.

Comment   Angus Deaton

This paper is the first report on an interesting and important research project. Using Medicare eligibility and claims files, it is possible to replicate life tables for the elderly, and more important, to extend them by conditioning on a richer set of covariates than just sex and race. As the authors emphasize in their introduction, such information could be useful for a wide range of economic and health purposes, from assessing the likely costs of demographic change and alternative delivery systems, to helping target medical innovations toward groups that can benefit the most. The current paper is a very preliminary one; it establishes that standard life tables can be more or less replicated—though it would have been useful to see the correspondence more fully and formally demonstrated—and it extends the life tables by breaking up death by various causes. This is certainly a useful first cut, though for the reasons I shall discuss, cause of death is perhaps not the most interesting or useful of the covariates that will be examined in the subsequent research.

The data consist of 397,383 Medicare enrollees aged 65 or over who died in calendar years 1986 through 1990. These deaths came from 1,518,000 people at risk, themselves a 5 percent sample of the population. The first set of calculations in the paper are of hazard rates by age, race, and sex, calculations that are obtained essentially by cross-tabulation, and that can be compared against standard mortality tables by age. The authors then disaggregate these mortality rates by cause of death. The decomposition by sex and race is retained, but some of the cause-specific age cells are now too small to support accurate estimation of the hazards, so the authors smooth by age using (nonstandard) splines. As the project advances into more complex calculations, the spline technology is likely to be more useful than in this paper, where a more straightforward alternative would have been to increase the sample size from the 5 percent used here. I am also a little skeptical that this particular spline technology is the most appropriate for the task. Since the estimation is done by generalized logit, a simpler—and presumably more efficient—solution would have been to use locally weighted logits, so that the calculation, if not fully disaggregated by age, would use mortality information from neighboring ages, with information weighted more heavily the more relevant it is.

Turning to the substance, there is surely cause for concern in pooling the

Angus Deaton is the William Church Osborn Professor of Public Affairs and professor of economics and international affairs at Princeton University and a research associate of the National Bureau of Economic Research.

information for the five years and all ages, with no allowance made for possible cohort effects. Although the pooling is perhaps natural over a five-year period, there is no reason to suppose that mortality or cause-specific mortality for a 70-year-old black male should be the same in 1990 as it was (say) in 1970. Patterns and standards of living change, as does the health delivery system, and there is no reason to suppose that there will not be time or cohort effects in mortality, as well as the age effects that are modeled here. The separate identification of age, year, and cohort effects is not straightforward, but it is surely an issue that will have to be faced in this work before it can be used with any confidence to forecast health expenditure patterns or mortality rates.

The other substantive issue that is insufficiently acknowledged in the current paper is measurement error. Even when recording is perfect, there are difficult conceptual issues in classifying causes of death. A great deal more attention is paid to cause of death for young patients than for older ones, the immediate cause of death is often not the same as the fundamental cause of death, and some diagnoses are wide enough to be little more than a confirmation that the patient is dead. It is also unfortunate that so many of the deaths in the analysis are diagnosed as "other" or "natural causes," especially when this is one of the few categories where there are systematic patterns with age. While I think that cause of death poses the greatest difficulty for this paper, it is not the only variable for which there are problems. Age reporting is notoriously inaccurate for the very old, and it would have been useful if the paper had been clearer about the source of the age information used in the analysis; for example, self-reported age at hospital admission may be different from that in the social security records.

Of course, measurement error is no reason to abandon the data or the exercise. But the specific difficulties over cause of death seem to require a good deal of further investigation. In particular, I would welcome some demonstration that these reported diagnoses are at all useful for any of the original aims of the paper. For example, is there enough information in the data to allow any link with costs? Do age/sex/race decompositions of cause of death tell us anything about which groups to target in future health care reforms? Is it reasonable to suppose that cause-of-death diagnosis will be invariant under changes in the health delivery system? The paper would have been strengthened by the discussion of any of these important issues.

Contributors

Nancy Dean Beaulieu
Department of Health Policy and
  Management
Harvard School of Public Health
677 Huntington Avenue
Boston, MA 02115

B. Douglas Bernheim
Department of Economics
Stanford University
Stanford, CA 94305

Jayanta Bhattacharya
Department of Economics
Stanford University
Stanford, CA 94305

Axel H. Börsch-Supan
Department of Economics
University of Mannheim
D-68131 Mannheim
Germany

Harish Chand
Department of Economics
University of California, Berkeley
609 Evans Hall
Berkeley, CA 94720

David M. Cutler
Department of Economics
Harvard University
Cambridge, MA 02138

Angus Deaton
221 Bendheim Hall
Princeton University
Princeton, NJ 08544

Matthew J. Eichner
Columbia Graduate School of Business
Columbia University
Uris Hall
3022 Broadway
New York, NY 10027

Li Gan
Department of Economics
University of California, Berkeley
Berkeley, CA 94720

Alan M. Garber
Stanford University
204 Junipero Serra Boulevard
Stanford, CA 94305

Jonathan Gruber
Department of Economics
Massachusetts Institute of Technology
Room E52-355
Cambridge, MA 02139

Hilary Hoynes
Department of Economics
University of California, Berkeley
549 Evans Hall #3880
Berkeley, CA 94720

Michael Hurd
RAND Corporation
1700 Main Street
Santa Monica, CA 90407

Thomas E. MaCurdy
Department of Economics
Stanford University
Stanford, CA 94305

Brigitte C. Madrian
Graduate School of Business
University of Chicago
1101 East 58th Street
Chicago, IL 60637

Mark B. McClellan
Department of Economics
Stanford University
Stanford, CA 94305

Daniel L. McFadden
Department of Economics
University of California, Berkeley
549 Evans Hall #3880
Berkeley, CA 94707

Kathleen McGarry
Department of Economics
University of California, Los Angeles
405 Hilgard Avenue
Los Angeles, CA 90095

David Meltzer
Section of General Internal Medicine
University of Chicago
5841 South Maryland, W-700
Chicago, IL 60637

Christina Paxson
219 Bendheim Hall
Princeton University
Princeton, NJ 08544

James M. Poterba
Department of Economics
Massachusetts Institute of Technology
Room E52–350
Cambridge, MA 02139

John B. Shoven
Dean's Office of Humanities and
    Sciences
Building One
Stanford University
Stanford, CA 94305

James P. Smith
RAND Corporation
1700 Main Street
Santa Monica, CA 90407

Douglas Staiger
Kennedy School of Government
Harvard University
Cambridge, MA 02138

James H. Stock
Kennedy School of Government
Harvard University
Cambridge, MA 02138

Steven F. Venti
Department of Economics
6106 Rockefeller Center
Dartmouth College
Hanover, NH 03755

David A. Wise
Kennedy School of Government
Harvard University
Cambridge, MA 02138

Author Index

Subject Index

Activities of daily living (ADLs): information from AHEAD survey, 12, 134–38; kinds of help and people administering care for, 138–54; as predictor of paid care, 143t, 149–50t, 152, 154. *See also* Instrumental activities of daily living (IADLs)

Acute myocardial infarction (AMI): AR and ARMA processes to estimate mortality resulting from, 212–21, 226; cost of, 4; distribution across demographic groups (1984–91), 63–66; growth in Medicare spending for (1984–91), 61–64; i.i.d. error in measurement of mortality resulting from, 206, 212–13, 216–20; innovation in technologies to treat, 3–4, 52, 222; invasive cardiac procedures, 57; treatment groups, 55–58

ADLs. *See* Activities of daily living (ADLs)

AHEAD. *See* Asset and Health Dynamics among the Oldest Old (AHEAD)

AMI. *See* Acute myocardial infarction (AMI)

Angioplasty (PTCA): growth rates in different metropolitan statistical areas (1984–91), 67–68; growth rates in relation to major teaching centers, 69–70; Medicare reimbursement for, 57–58; rates for patients grouped by hospital, 72–75; as substitute for bypass surgery, 66–70, 79–80

Asset and Health Dynamics among the Oldest Old (AHEAD): bracketing, 11–12, 229–31, 233–37; panel data, 8, 230–40, 261–66; recommendation for data collection for, 307; subjective probability measures in, 13, 261–66

Asset ownership: bracket imputation of, 241–45, 250–57; imputation method to assess, 240–41, 254–57. *See also* Wealth of elderly

Bracketing methods: critique of use of, 254–57; in HRS and AHEAD survey data, 229–31, 233–37, 254; importance of, 245–50, 254; using AHEAD data to impute wealth of elderly, 237–45. *See also* Imputation method

Bypass surgery. *See* Coronary artery bypass graft (CABG)

CABG. *See* Coronary artery bypass graft (CABG)

Cardiac catheterization rates, 71–72, 80

Care: determinants of quality in hospitals, 222, 224–26; mortality as indicator of, 224

Care of elderly: care from children, 150t, 153–54; from child's perspective, 154–61; costs of long-term, 7; kinds of care and people administering, 138–54; paid and unpaid, 150–54. *See also* Activities of daily living (ADLs); Home care; Home health care; Instrumental activities of daily living (IADLs)

CEX. *See* Consumer Expenditure Survey (CEX)

CHF. *See* Congestive heart failure (CHF)

Children: as caregivers to elderly, 140–54, 162; decisions related to care of elderly, 154–61; Engel's measurement of costs